A Book Of

LABOUR LAWS

For
MPM Semester - II

SHARAD D. GEET
M.A. (Eco.), M.Com., LL.B., D.C.L.
NASHIK.

Mrs. ASMITA A. DESHPANDE
B.Com., M.B.A.,
PUNE.

LABOUR LAWS : MPM (Semester - II)　　　**ISBN 978-93-83750-79-5**
First Edition　:　January 2014
©　　　　　:　**Authors**

The text of this publication, or any part thereof, should not be reproduced or transmitted in any form or stored in any computer storage system or device for distribution including photocopy, recording, taping or information retrieval system or reproduced on any disc, tape, perforated media or other information storage device etc., without the written permission of Authors with whom the rights are reserved. Breach of this condition is liable for legal action.

Every effort has been made to avoid errors or omissions in this publication. In spite of this, errors may have crept in. Any mistake, error or discrepancy so noted and shall be brought to our notice shall be taken care of in the next edition. It is notified that neither the publisher nor the authors or seller shall be responsible for any damage or loss of action to any one, of any kind, in any manner, therefrom.

Published By :　　　　　　　　　　　　　　　　　　　**Printed By :**
NIRALI PRAKASHAN　　　　　　　　　　　　　　　Repro Knowledgecast Limited,
Abhyudaya Pragati, 1312, Shivaji Nagar,　　　　　　　　Thane
Off J.M. Road, PUNE – 411005
Tel - (020) 25512336/37/39, Fax - (020) 25511379
Email : niralipune@pragationline.com

DISTRIBUTION CENTRES
PUNE

Nirali Prakashan　　　　　　　　　　　　　　*Nirali Prakashan*
119, Budhwar Peth, Jogeshwari Mandir Lane　　S. No. 28/27, Dhyari,
Pune 411002, Maharashtra　　　　　　　　　　Near Pari Company, Pune 411041
Tel : (020) 2445 2044, 66022708, Fax : (020) 2445 1538　　Tel : (020) 24690204, Fax : (020) 24690316
Email : niralilocal@pragationline.com　　　　　Email : bookorder@pragationline.com

MUMBAI
Nirali Prakashan
385, S.V.P. Road, Rasdhara Co-op. Hsg. Society Ltd.,
Girgaum, Mumbai 400004, Maharashtra
Tel : (022) 2385 6339 / 2386 9976, Fax : (022) 2386 9976
Email : niralimumbai@pragationline.com

DISTRIBUTION BRANCHES

NAGPUR　　　　　　　　　　　　　　　　　　**JALGAON**
Pratibha Book Distributors　　　　　　　　　*Nirali Prakashan*
Above Maratha Mandir, Shop No. 3, First Floor,　34, V. V. Golani Market, Navi Peth, Jalgaon 425001,
Rani Jhanshi Square, Sitabuldi, Nagpur 440012,　Maharashtra, Tel : (0257) 222 0395
Maharashtra, Tel : (0712) 254 7129　　　　　　Mob : 94234 91860

BENGALURU　　　　　　　　　　　　　　　　**KOLHAPUR**
Pragati Book House　　　　　　　　　　　　　*Nirali Prakashan*
House No. 1, Sanjeevappa Lane, Avenue Road Cross,　New Mahadvar Road,
Opp. Rice Church, Bengaluru – 560002.　　　　Kedar Plaza, 1st Floor Opp. IDBI Bank
Tel : (080) 64513344, 64513355,　　　　　　　Kolhapur 416 012, Maharashtra. Mob : 9855046155
Mob : 9880582331, 9845021552
Email:bharatsavla@yahoo.com

CHENNAI
Pragati Books
9/1, Montieth Road, Behind Taas Mahal, Egmore,
Chennai 600008 Tamil Nadu, Tel : (044) 6518 3535,
Mob : 94440 01782 / 98450 21552 / 98805 82331, Email : bharatsavla@yahoo.com

RETAIL OUTLETS
PUNE

Pragati Book Centre　　　　　　　　　　　　　*Pragati Book Centre*
157, Budhwar Peth, Opp. Ratan Talkies,　　　　676/B, Budhwar Peth, Opp. Jogeshwari Mandir,
Pune 411002, Maharashtra　　　　　　　　　　Pune 411002, Maharashtra
Tel : (020) 2445 8887 / 6602 2707, Fax : (020) 2445 8887　Tel : (020) 6601 7784 / 6602 0855

Pragati Book Centre　　　　　　　　　　　　　*PBC Book Sellers & Stationers*
Amber Chamber, 28/A, Budhwar Peth,　　　　　152, Budhwar Peth, Pune 411002, Maharashtra
Appa Balwant Chowk, Pune : 411002, Maharashtra,　Tel : (020) 2445 2254 / 6609 2463
Tel : (020) 20240335 / 66281669
Email : pbcpune@pragationline.com

MUMBAI
Pragati Book Corner
Indira Niwas, 111 - A, Bhavani Shankar Road, Dadar (W), Mumbai 400028, Maharashtra
Tel : (022) 2422 3526 / 6662 5254, Email : pbcmumbai@pragationline.com

Preface ...

We are pleased to present to the M.P.M. students of Pune University this text book of **'Labour Laws'**. This book is written according to the syllabus of 'Labour Laws' prescribed by the University of Pune for M.P.M. Part-I, Semester - II effective from June 2013.

Our book on 'Labour Laws' for M.P.M. Part - I, Semester - I has been well received by the student and teacher community alike. We hope that they will receive this book also with the same enthusiasm.

We are sure that this book will be of immense use to the students from the view point of their examination and will help them to enhance the knowledge of the Acts prescribed for their examination.

In spite of sincere efforts, printing errors might have crept in the book at some places. We hope that we will be excused for the same.

We would like to express our gratitude to Shri. Dineshbhai Furia, Shri. Jignesh Furia, Mrs. Nirja Sharma, Mr. Girish Redkar, Mr. Parag Ghamandi, Mr. Malik Shaikh, Mr. Prasad Chintakindi and the entire staff of Nirali Prakashan, Pune without whose untiring efforts, wholehearted co-operation and sincerity, this edition of the book would never have come out in time.

We shall consider our labour amply rewarded if this book is appreciated by those for whom it is meant.

Pune
January, 2014

Prof. Sharad D. Geet
Mrs. Asmita A. Deshpande

Syllabus ...

1. The Employees Provident Fund and Miscellaneous Provisions Act, 1952
(Number of Sessions 8 + 2)

Sec. 1 - Short Title, Extent, Application and Commencement, Sec. 2 - Defines, Sec. 3 - Power to apply Act to an Establishment which has a common PF with another Establishment.

Sec. 4 - Power to add to Schedule-I, Sec. 5 - Employees PF Scheme, Sec. 6 - Contributions and matters which may be provided for in the Scheme, Sec. 7 - Modification of the Scheme, Sec. 8 - Mode of recovery of moneys' due from employers, Sec. 9 - Fund to be recognized under Act 11 of 1922, Sec. 10 - Protection against Attachment, Sec. 11 - Priority of Payment of Contributions over Other Debts, Sec. 12 - Employer not to reduce Wages, etc., Sec. 13 - Inspectors, Sec. 14 - Penalties, Sec. 15 - Special Provision relating to existing PF, Sec. 16 - Act not to apply to certain establishments, Sec. 17 - Power to Exempt, Sec. 19 - Delegation of Powers, Sec. 20 - Power of Central Government to give Directions, Schedule I, II, III, IV.

2. The Employees State Insurance Act, 1948   (Number of Sessions 6 + 2)
3. Industrial Disputes Act 1947   (Number of Sessions 7 + 2)
4. The Maternity Benefit Act, 1961 (Social Security Legislation)
(Number of Sessions 8 + 2)

Sec. 1 - Short Title Extent and Commencement,

Sec. 2 - Application of the Act, Sec. 3 - Definitions, Sec. 4 - Employment of or Work by, Woman prohibited during certain period, Sec. 5 - Right to Payment of Maternity Benefit, Sec. 6 - Notice of Claim for Maternity Benefit and Payment thereof, Sec. 7 - Payment of Maternity Benefit in case of Death of Woman. Sec. 8 - Payment of Medical Bonus, Sec. 9 - Leave for Miscarriage, etc. Sec. 10 - Leave for Illness arising out of Pregnancy, Delivery, Premature Birth of Child, Miscarriage, Medical Transmission of Pregnancy, Tubectomy Operations. Sec. 11 - Nursing Breaks, Sec. 12 - Dismissal during Absence or Pregnancy, Sec. 14 - Appointment of Inspectors, Sec. 16 - Power of Duties of Inspectors, Sec. 17 - Power of Inspectors to Direct Payments to be made, Sec. 18 - Forfeiture of Maternity Benefit, Sec. 19 - Abstract of Act and rules there under to be exhibited, Sec. 20 - Registers and etc., Sec. 21 - Penalty for Contravention of Act by Employer, Sec. 22 - Penalty for Obstructing Inspector, Sec. 23 - Cognizance of Offences, Sec. 24 - Protection for Action taken in Good Faith, Sec. 25 - Power of Central Government to be given Directions, Sec. 26 - Power to Exempt Establishments. Sec. 27 - Effect of Laws and Agreement Inconsistent with this Act. Sec. 28 - Power to make rules.

5. The Payment of Gratuity Act, 1972

***

Contents ...

1. The Employees' Provident Funds and Miscellaneous Provisions Act, 1952

   1.1 – 1.46

2. The Employees' State Insurance Act, 1948 2.1 – 2.80

3. The Industrial Disputes Act, 1947 3.1 – 3.108

4. The Maternity Benefit Act, 1961 4.1 – 4.30

5. The Payment of Gratuity Act, 1972 5.1 – 5.50

Publisher's Note

In spite of the best efforts, care and caution, errors might have crept in for which the students, readers, and the like will please bear with us. The publication is being sold on the condition and understanding that the information given in this book is merely for guidance and reference. It must not be taken as having authority of, or binding in any way on the author, publisher, sellers etc. who do not owe any responsibility for any damage or loss to any person, who may or may not be a purchaser of this publication on account of any action taken on the basis of this publication. However, if any discrepancies, omissions, errors and the like are noticed, kindly bring the same to our notice, so that we can take necessary steps to correct them in the next edition.

***

Chapter **1**...

The Employees' Provident Funds And Miscellaneous Provisions Act, 1952

Contents ...

1.1 The Object and Application of the Act [Sections 1, 2-A, 3 and 4]
1.2 Definitions of the Terms, Concepts, Words used in the Act [Section 2]
1.3 Employees' Provident Fund Scheme (EPF Scheme) [Sections 5 and 6]
1.4 Employees' Pension Scheme [Section 6-A]
1.5 Employees' Deposit-Linked Insurance Scheme [Sections 6-C and 7]
1.6 Administration of the Schemes [Sections 5-A, 5-AA, 5-B, 5-C, 5-D, 5-DD, 5-E]
1.7 Provisions of the Act relating to 'Determination of Moneys (Amounts) due from Employers (Section 7-A) Review of Orders Passed under Section 7-A (Section 7B), Determination of Escaped Amount (Section 7-C), Employees Provident Fund Appellate Tribunals (Section 7-D) etc.
1.8 Mode of Recovery of Moneys Due from Employers [Sections 8, 9, 10, 11, 12]
1.9 Appointments and Powers of the Inspectors Appointed under this Act [Section 13]
1.10 Penalties and Offences [Section 14]
1.11 Other Miscellaneous Provisions of the Act [Sections 15, 16, 17, 18, 19, 20, 21 and 22]
• Questions for Discussion

In India, there is a network of laws which provides for social security for the working class. In the publication of the I.L.O., "Approaches to Social Security (1949)", the meaning of social security is given.

It is stated in the "Approach to Social Security" that, *"social security is the security that society furnishes through appropriate organisation against certain risks to which its members are exposed. These risks are essentially contingencies of life which the individual of small means cannot effectively provide by his own ability, or foresight alone or even in private combination with his fellows"*.

There are mainly three important types of insecurity which confront the working class i.e. (1) Income Insecurity, (2) Occupational Insecurity, and (3) Natural Insecurity. Natural insecurity is due to natural factors such as old age (for which provisions of pension, provident fund, gratuity can be made), death of bread winner, sickness, etc.

In view of the poverty of masses, no doubt there is a great need of social security in India. From this point of view, various Acts such as the The Workmen's Compensation Act, The Employees State Insurance Act, The Maternity Benefit Act, The Payment of Gratuity Act etc. have been passed and made applicable according to the demand of the circumstances. The EPF Act of 1952 is one such Act.

There was much discussion regarding the compulsory institution of contributory provident funds in industrial undertakings at several times at tripartite meetings in which the representatives of the Central and State Governments, the representatives of employers and workers participated.

As a result, a large measure of agreement was reached that there should be such a legislation. In 1948, a non-official bill on the subject of provident fund was introduced in the Central Legislature. But it was withdrawn on the assurance given by the Government that it would introduce the comprehensive bill on the subject of provident fund. Thereafter, the comprehensive bill was presented and passed in March, 1952.

The main object of the EPF Act of 1952 is to provide for the institution of provident funds and pension and deposit-linked insurance schemes to provide social security for employees employed in factories and other establishments. As a social security measure, the schemes of provident funds are meant to induce the employees to save a certain portion of their present incomes or earnings for a rainy day.

The EPFAMP Act and Employees' Provident Fund Schemes were made applicable in 1952. Initially, this Act was made applicable to six major industries viz. (1) Cement, (2) Cigarette, (3) Electrical and General Engineering Products, (4) Iron and Steel, (5) Paper and, (6) Textiles, employing Fifty or more persons. Thus, making a modest beginning from six major industries by amending the Act from time to time, the number of industries and classes of establishment has increased up to 174 to which this Act has been made applicable. By amending the Act in 1956, the scope of the Act was extended to cover non-factory establishments such as plantations, mines other than coal mines, commercial establishments etc. As a result, the number of subscribers to the Fund increased from about 12 lakhs at the end of March, 1953 to 166.15 lakhs at the end of March, 1992 and today, it is more than 175 lakhs. There are more than 3 lakh establishments under the E.P.F. Schemes.

It should be noted that originally, factories and establishments employing fifty or more persons were covered under this Act. But the minimum limit of coverage was reduced to twenty or more with effect from 31st December, 1960 by making an amendment in the Act. Further, the membership of the Employees' Provident Fund Scheme was initially restricted to employees whose monthly wages did not exceed Three hundred. Because of fall in the value of money due to inflation, this pay-limit has been increased from time to time. It was Two Thousand Five Hundred up to 31st October, 1990 and from 1st November 1990; it was increased up to Three Thousand and Five Hundred. It is further raised to Six Thousand and Five Hundred with effect from 1-6-2001.

This Act has been amended fifteen times since 1952. The latest amendment to the Act was made in 1998. The provisions of the Act are stated below.

1.1 The Object and Application of the Act [Sections 1, 2-A, 3 and 4]

As already made clear, the main objective of the EPFAMP Act of 1952 is to provide for the institution of provident funds, pension fund and deposit-linked insurance fund for the employees in factories and other establishments to which the Act has been made applicable. Thus, this Act is enacted to provide a kind of social security to the industrial workers.

Of course, the social security provided to the industrial workers under this Act differs from the security provided to them under the Workmen's Compensation Act or the Employees' State Insurance Act. This Act basically provides retirement benefits such as provident fund, superannuation pension, family pension, deposit-linked insurance, etc.

There are 23 Sections and 4 Schedules included in the Act. Section 1 relates to the short title, extent and application of the Act. The provisions of Section 1 are as follows:

1.1.1 Short Title or Caption

This Act may be called "The Employees' Provident Funds and Miscellaneous Provisions Act, 1952 [Section 1 (1)].

1.1.2 Extent

This Act extends to the whole of India except to the State of Jammu and Kashmir [Section 1 (2)].

1.1.3 Application of the Act to Establishments

Subject to the provisions contained in Section 16, it applies –

(a) to every establishment which is a factory engaged in any industry specified in Schedule I and in which twenty or more persons are employed, and

(b) to any other establishment employing twenty or more persons or class of such establishments which the Central Government may, by notification the Official Gazette, specify in this behalf [Section 1 (3)].

1.1.4 Power of the Central Government to apply this Act to Establishments

According to the proviso of Section 1 (2), the power is given to the Central Government to apply this Act to any establishment subject to certain conditions. It is stated in the proviso that, *"The Central Government may, after giving not less than two months' notice of its intention so to do, by notification in the Official Gazette, apply the provisions of this Act to any establishment employing such number of persons less than twenty as may be specified in the notification"*.

It is further stated in Section 1 (4) of this Act that, "notwithstanding anything contained in sub-section (3) of this section (1) of Section 16, where it appears to the Central Provident Fund Commissioner, whether on an application made to him in this behalf or otherwise, that the employer and the majority of employees in relation to any establishment have agreed that the provisions of this Act should be made applicable to the establishment, he may, by notification in the Official Gazette, apply the provisions of this Act to that establishment on and from the date of such agreement or from any subsequent date specified in such agreement".

The provisions of Section 16 are given in this chapter under the heading, "Act not to apply to certain establishments".

1.1.5 Continuance of Application of the Act [Section 1 (5)]

Section 1 (5) provides that, "An establishment to which the Act applies shall continue to be governed by this Act notwithstanding that the number of persons employed at any time falls below twenty".

1.1.6 Power of the Central Government to apply this Act to an Establishment which has a common Provident Fund with another Establishment [Section 3]

Section 3 provides that, "Where immediately before this Act becomes applicable to an establishment there is in existence a Provident Fund which is common to the employees employed in that establishment and employees in any other establishment, the Central Government may, by notification in the Official Gazette, direct that the provisions of this Act shall also apply to such other establishment".

1.1.7 Power is given to the Central Government to add to the Schedule I under Section 4 of the Act

In Section 4 (1), it is stated that, "The Central Government may, by notification in the Official Gazette, add to Schedule I any other industry in respect of the employees whereof it is of opinion that a Provident Fund Scheme should be framed under this Act, and thereupon the industry so added shall be deemed to be an industry specified in Schedule I for the purposes of this Act". While Section 4 (2) makes it clear that all notifications under sub-section (1) shall be laid before Parliament, as soon as, after they are issued".

1.1.8 Establishment to include all Departments and Branches [Section 2-A]

In order to remove the doubts relating to different departments and branches of an establishment, the provision has been made in Section 2-A. It is stated in Section 2-A that, "For the removal of doubts, it is hereby declared that where an establishment consists of different departments or has branches, whether situate in the same place or in different places, all such departments or branches shall be treated as parts of the same establishment".

1.2 Definitions of the Terms, Concepts, Words used in the Act [Section 2]

In the Act, various terms, concept, words, etc. are used and their definitions are given in Section 2 of the Act. Unless the context otherwise requires, their definitions and meanings are given as follows.

1. **Appropriate Government [Section 2 (a)]:**
   "Appropriate Government" means –
   (i) in relation to an establishment belonging to, or under the control of, the Central Government or in relation to an establishment connected with a railway company, a major port, a mine or an oilfield or a controlled industry, or in relation to an establishment having departments or branches in more than one State, the Central Government; and

(ii) in relation to any other establishment, the State Government;

2. **Authorised Officer [Section 2 (aa)]:**

"Authorised Officer" means the Central Provident Fund Commissioner, Additional Central Provident Fund Commissioner, Deputy Provident Fund Commissioner, Regional Provident Fund Commissioner or such other officer as may be authorised by the Central Government, by notification in the Official Gazette.

3. **Basic Wages [Section 2 (b)]:**

"Basic Wages" means all emoluments which are earned by an employee while on duty or on leave or on holidays with wages in either case in accordance with the terms of the contract of employment and which are paid or payable in cash to him, but does not include –

(i) the cash value of any food concession;
(ii) any dearness allowance (that is to say, all cash payments by whatever name called paid to an employee on account of a rise in the cost of living), house-rent allowance, overtime allowance, bonus, commission or any other similar allowance payable to the employee in respect of his employment or of work done in such employment;
(iii) any presents made by the employer;

This definition of 'Basic Wages' is inclusive as well as exclusive. It is stated in the definition that Basic Wage includes all emoluments which are earned by an employee while on duty or on leave or on holidays with wages in either case in accordance with the terms of the contract of employment and which are paid or payable in cash to him. Thus, it is inclusive. But what is not included in the basic wages is also mentioned.

4. **Contribution [Section 2 (c)]:**

"Contribution" means a contribution payable in respect of a member under a Scheme or the contribution payable in respect of an employee to whom the Insurance Schemes applies.

5. **Controlled Industry [Section 2 (d)]:**

"Controlled Industry" means any industry the control of which by the Union has been declared by a Central Act to be expedient in the public interest;

The Industries (Development and Regulation) Act, 1951 was passed and brought into force on 8th May, 1952. The First Schedule appended to that Act includes certain industries which have been taken under the control of the Union in the public interest. Such industries are called controlled industries.

6. **Employer [Section 2 (e)]:**

Employer means –

(1) in relation to an establishment which is a factory, the owner or occupier of the factory, including the agent of such owner occupier, the legal representative of a decreased owner or occupier and, where a person has been named as a manager of the factory under clause (f) of sub-section (1) of Section 7 of the Factories Act, 1948 (63 of 1948), the person

so named [Section 2 (e) (i)] and (2) in relation to any other establishment, the person who, or the authority which, has the ultimate control over the affairs of the establishment, and where the said affairs are entrusted to a manager, managing director or managing agent, such manager, managing director or managing agent [Section 2 (e) (ii)].

7. Employee [Section 2 (f)]:

"Employee", means any person who is employed for wages in any kind of work, manual or otherwise, in or in connection with the work of an establishment, and who gets his wages directly or indirectly from the employer, and includes any person –

(i) employed by or through a contractor or in connection with the work of the establishment;

(ii) engaged as an apprentice, not being an apprentice engaged under the Apprentices Act, 1961 (52 of 1961), or under the standing orders of the establishment".

8. Exempted Employee [Section 2 (ff)]:

"Exempted Employee" means an employee to whom a Scheme or the Insurance Scheme, as the case may be, would, but for the exemption granted under Section 17, have applied.

9. Exempted Establishment [Section 2 (fff)]:

"Exempted Establishment" means, an establishment in respect of which an exemption has been granted under Section 17 from the operation of all or any of the provisions of any Scheme or the Insurance Scheme, as the cast may be whether such exemption has been granted to the establishment as such or to any person or class of persons employed therein.

10. Factory [Section 2 (g)]:

"Factory" means any premises, including the precincts thereof, in any part of which a manufacturing process is being carried on or is ordinarily so carried on, whether with the aid of power or without the aid of power.

11. Fund [Section 2 (h)]:

"Fund" means the Provident Fund established under a Scheme.

12. Industry [Section 2 (i)]:

"Industry" means any industry specified in Schedule I, and includes any other industry added to the Schedule by notification under Section 4;

13. Insurance Fund [Section 2 (i-a)]:

"Insurance Fund" means the Deposit-Linked Insurance Fund established under sub-section (2) of Section 6-C;

14. Insurance Scheme [Section 2 (i-b)]:

"Insurance Scheme" means the Employees' Deposit-Linked Insurance Scheme framed under sub-section (1) of Section 6-C;

15. Manufacture or Manufacturing Process [Section 2 (i-c)]:

"Manufacture" or "Manufacturing process" means any process for making, altering, repairing, ornamenting, finishing, packing, oiling, washing, cleaning, breaking up, demolishing or otherwise treating or adapting any article or substance with a view to its use, sale, transport, delivery or disposal".

16. Member [Section 2 (r)]:
"Member" means a member of the Fund.

17. Occupier of a Factory [Section 2 (k)]:
"Occupier of a factory" means the person who has ultimate control over the affairs of the factory, and, where the said affairs are entrusted to a managing agent, such agent shall be deemed to be the occupier of the factory.

18. Pension Fund [Section 2 (kA)]:
"Pension Fund" means the Employees' Pension Fund established under sub-section (2) of Section 6-A.

19. Pension Scheme [Section 2 (kB)]:
"Pension Scheme" means the Employees' Pension Scheme framed under sub-section (1) of Section 6-A.

20. Prescribed [Section 2 (ka)]:
"Prescribed" means prescribed by rules made under this Act.

21. Recovery Officer [Section 2 (kb)]:
"Recovery Officer" means any officer of the Central Government, State Government or the Board of Trustees constituted under Section 5-A, who may be authorised by the Central Government, by notification in the Official Gazette, to exercise the powers of a Recovery under this Act.

22. Scheme [Section 2 (*l*):
"Scheme" means the Employees' Provident Fund Scheme framed under Section 5.

23. Superannuation [Section 2 (*ll*):
"Superannuation", in relation to an employee, who is the manager of the Pension Scheme, means the attainment, by the said employee, of the age of fifty-eight years.

24. Tribunal [Section 2 (m)]:
"Tribunal" means in the Employees' Provident Fund Appellate Tribunal constituted under Section 7-D.

1.3 Employees' Provident Fund Scheme [EPF Scheme] [Sections 5 and 6]

The Employees' Provident Fund Scheme is framed according to the provisions of Section 5 of the Act. We find important provisions relating to this scheme mainly in the 5th and 6th Sections of the Act. From these provisions, we come to know the features of the EPF Scheme, e.g. framing of the scheme, contents, effects, contributions, etc. These aspects of the EPF Scheme are studied below.

1.3.1 Framing of the Scheme

The Central Government may, by notification in the Official Gazette frame a Scheme to be called the Employees' Provident Fund Scheme for the establishment of Provident Funds under this Act for employees or for any class of employees and specify the establishment or class of establishments to which the said Scheme shall apply and there shall be established, as soon as may be after the framing of the Scheme, a Fund in accordance with the provisions of this Act and the Scheme [Section 5 (1)].

1.3.2 Establishment of Fund [Section 5 (1)]

Provisions of Section 5 (1) are stated above. We come to know from these provisions that as soon as may be after the framing of the FPF Scheme, there shall be established Employees' Provident Fund in accordance with the provisions of the Act and the EPF Scheme.

1.3.3 Administration of the Fund Scheme

It is stated in Section 5 (1-A) that the Fund shall vest in, and be administered by the Central Board constituted under Section 5-A of the Act.

1.3.4 Contents of the Scheme [Section 5 (1-B)]

A scheme framed under sub-section (1) of Section 5 may provide all or any of the matters specified in Schedule II of the Act. Schedule II is reproduced below for your information.

SCHEDULE II

MATTERS FOR WHICH PROVISION MAY BE MADE IN A SCHEME

1. The employees or class of employees who shall join the Fund, and the conditions under which employees may be exempted from joining the Fund or from making any contribution.

2. The time and manner in which contribution shall be made to the Fund by employers and by, or on behalf of, employees, whether employed by him directly or by or through a contractor, the contributions which an employee may, if he so desires, make under, Section 6, and the manner in which such contributions may be recovered.

2-A The manner in which employee's contributions may be recovered by contractors for employees employed by or through such contractors.

3. The payment by the employer of such sums of money as may be necessary to meet the cost of administering the Fund and the rate at which and the manner in which the payment shall be made.

4. The constitution of any committee for assisting any Board of Trustees.

5. The opening of regional and other offices of any Board of Trustees.

6. The manner in which accounts shall be kept, the investment of moneys belonging to the Fund in accordance with any directions issued or conditions specified by the Central Government, the preparation of the budget, the audit of accounts and the submission of reports to the Central Government or to any specified State Government.

7. The conditions under which withdrawal from the Fund may be permitted and any deduction or forfeiture may be made and the maximum amount of such deduction or forfeiture.
8. The fixation by the Central Government in consultation with the Boards of Trustees concerned of the rate of interest payable to members.
9. The form in which an employee shall furnish particulars about himself and his family whenever required.
10. The nomination of a person to receive the amount standing to the credit of a member after his death and the cancellation or variation of such nomination.
11. The registers and records to be maintained with respect to employees and the returns to be furnished by employers or contractors.
12. The form or design of any identity card, token or disc for the purpose of identifying any employee, and for the issue, custody and replacement thereof.
13. The fees to be levied for any of the purposes specified in this Schedule.
14. The contraventions or default which shall be punishable under Sub-section (2) of Section 14.
15. The further powers if any, which may be exercised by Inspectors.
16. The manner in which accumulations in any existing Provident Fund shall be transferred to the Fund under Section 15, and the mode of valuation of any assets which may be transferred by the employers in this behalf.
17. The conditions under which a member may be permitted to pay premium on life insurance, from the Fund.
18. Any other matter which is to be provided for in the Scheme or which may be necessary or proper for the purpose of implementing the Scheme.

1.3.5 Effects [Section 5 (2)]

According to the provisions of Section 5 (2), "A scheme framed under sub-section (1) of Section 5 may provide that any of its provisions shall take effect either prospectively or retrospectively on such date as may be specified in this behalf in the Scheme".

1.3.6 Applicability of the EPF Scheme

The EPF Scheme applies to all factories and all other such establishments to which this Act applies or is applied under Section 1 (3), 1 (4) and Section 3 of the Act. However, the applicability of the EDP Scheme is subject to the provisions in the Act in Section 16 (exempting certain establishments from its purview) and Section 17 giving power to the appropriate Government to exempt certain establishments.

1.3.7 Contributions

We have already seen that the main objective of this Act is to provide for the institution of the provident funds for employees, as the social security in the factories and also other establishments to which the Act applies or is made applicable. The responsibility is placed upon the concerned employers to put the Employees' Provident Fund, Pension Schemes etc.

into operation and to make contributions of both their shares as well as their employees' share to the funds, and to deduct from the wages of the employees their share as per the provisions of the Act. In Section 6, we find the provisions relating to the statutory contributions and matters which may be provident for in the schemes. The provisions of Section 6 are given below.

"The contribution which shall be paid by the employer to the Fund shall be ten per cent of the basic wages, dearness allowance and retaining allowance, if any, for the time being payable to each of the employees, whether employed by him directly or through a contractor and the employee's contribution shall be equal to the contribution payable by the employer in respect of him and may, if any employee so desires, be an amount exceeding ten percent of his basic wages, dearness allowance and retaining allowance (if any), subject to the condition that the employer shall not be under an obligation to pay any contribution over and above his contribution payable under this Section".

It is provided that, "In its application to any establishment or class of establishments which the Central Government, after making such enquiry as it deems fit, may, by notification in the Official Gazette specify, this section shall be subject to the modification that for the words ten per cent, at both the places where they occur the words "twelve per cent" shall be substituted [Proviso 1 to Section 6].

It is provided further that where the amount of any contribution payable under this Act involves a fraction of a rupee, the Scheme may provide for the rounding off of such fraction to the nearest rupee, half of a rupee or quarter of a rupee [Proviso 2 to Section 6].

For the purposes of this Section dearness allowance shall be deemed to include also the cash value of any food concession allowed to the employee [Explanation 1].

For the purposes of this section "retaining allowance" means an allowance payable for the time being to an employee of any factory or other establishment during any period in which the establishment is not working, for retaining his service. [Explanation 2].

The statutory rate of contribution both for members of the Provident Fund and the employer originally was six and a quarter percent. It was increased up to Eight and One-third percent and later on to Ten percent. Today, it is Ten percent. The meaning of 'dearness allowance' and 'retaining allowance' is given in explanation 1 and 2 respectively.

1.4 Employees' Pension Scheme [Section 6-A]
1.4.1 Framing of the Employees' Pension Scheme [Section 6-A]

Under Section 6-A (1) of this Act, the provisions have been made to frame the Employees' Pension Scheme by stating the purposes of providing the scheme. The provisions of Section 6-A (1) are given below.

"The Central Government may, by notification in the Official Gazette frame a Scheme to be called the Employees' Pension Scheme for the purpose of providing for –
  (a) superannuation pension, retiring pension or permanent total disablement pension to the employees of any establishment or class of establishments to which this Act applies; and
  (b) widow or widower's pension, children pension or orphan pension payable to the beneficiaries of such employees".

The President of India promulgated the Labour Provident Fund Laws (Amendment) Ordinance of 1971 on 13th February, 1971 and later on, it was replaced by the Labour Provident Fund Laws (Amendment) Act, 1972. In the Act, there was a provision for the creation of an Employees' Family Pension Fund, and Family Pension Scheme. The Employees' Provident Fund Act of 1952 was renamed as the Employees' Provident Fund and Family Pension Act, 1952 by amending the Act. Thereafter, the word 'Family' was omitted by Act No. 25 of 1996 dated 16-8-1996 with effect from 16th November, 1995. At present, it is known as 'The Employees' Provident Funds and Miscellaneous Provisions Act, 1952'.

1.4.2 Pension Fund [Section 6-A (2)]

"Notwithstanding anything contained in Section 6, there shall be established a Pension Fund as soon as may be after framing of the Pension Scheme".

1.4.3 Contribution to Pension Fund [Section 6-A]

Before 1996, the employees' Family Pension Scheme was in operation. But Section 6-A was amended and Section 6-B was omitted by Act No. 25 of 1996 dated 16-8-1996 w.e.f. 16.11.1995. Section 6 (3) expressly provides for the cessation of the Family Pension Scheme which runs as follows:

"On the establishment of the Pension Fund, the Family Pension Scheme hereinafter referred to as the ceased scheme shall cease to operate and all assets of the ceased scheme shall vest in and shall stand transferred to, and all liabilities under the ceased scheme shall be enforceable against, the Pension Fund and the beneficiaries under the ceased scheme shall be entitled to draw the benefits, not less than the benefits they were entitled to under the ceased scheme, from the Pension Fund" [Section 6-A (3)].

Section 6-A (2) throws light on the contribution and certain related aspects. It is stated in Section 6-A (2) that, Notwithstanding anything contained in section 6, there shall be established, as soon as may be after framing of the Pension Scheme, a Pension Fund into which there shall be paid, from time to time, in respect of every employee who is a member of the Pension Scheme,

(a) such sums from the employer's contribution under section 6, not exceeding eight and one-third per cent, of the basic wages, dearness allowance and retaining allowance, if any, of the concerned employees, as may be specified in the Pension Scheme;

(b) such sums as are payable by the employers of exempted establishments under sub-section (6) of Section 17;

(c) the net assets of the Employees' Family Pension Fund as on the date of the establishment of the Pension Fund;

(d) such sums as the Central Government may, after due appropriation by Parliament by law in this behalf, specify.

1.4.4 Administration of the Pension Fund

"The Pension Fund shall vest in and be administered by the Central Board in such a manner as may be specified in the Pension Scheme [Section 6-A (4)]. Schedule III is given below.

1.4.5 Contents of the Pension Scheme

In Section 6-A (5), it is stated that, "subject to the provisions of this Act, the Pension Scheme may provide for all or any of the matters specified in Schedule III".

SCHEDULE III
MATTERS FOR WHICH PROVISION MAY BE MADE IN THE PENSION SCHEME

1. The employees or class of employees to whom the Pension Scheme shall apply.
2. The time within which the employees who are not members of the Pension Scheme under section 6A as it stood before the commencement of the Employees' Provident Funds and Miscellaneous Provisions (Amendment Act, 1996 (hereinafter, in this Schedule, referred to as the amending Act) shall opt for the Pension Scheme.
3. The portion of employers' contribution to the Provident Fund which shall be credited to the Pension Fund and the manner in which it is credited.
4. The minimum qualifying service for being eligible for pension and the manner in which the employees may be granted the benefits of their past service under section 6A, as it stood before the commencement of the Amending Act.
5. The regulation of the manner in which and the period of service for which no contribution is received.
6. The manner in which employees' interest will be protected against default in payment of contribution by the employer.
7. The manner in which the accounts of the Pension Fund shall be kept and investment of moneys belonging to Pension Fund to be made subject to such pattern of investment as may be determined by the Central Government.
8. The form in which an employee shall furnish particulars about himself and the members of his family whenever required.
9. The forms, registers and records to be maintained in respect of employees, required for the administration of the Pension Scheme.
10. The scale of pension and pensioner benefits and the conditions relating to grant of such benefits to the employees.
11. The manner in which the exempted establishments have to pay contribution towards the Pension Scheme and the submission of returns relating thereto.
12. The mode of disbursement of pension and arrangements to be entered into with such disbursing agencies as may be specified for the purpose.
13. The manner in which the expenses for administering the Pension Scheme will be met from the income of the Pension Fund.
14. Any other matter which is to be provided for in the Pension Scheme or which may be necessary or proper for the purpose of implementation of the Pension Scheme.

1.4.6 Effects of the provisions of the Pension Scheme

"The Pension Scheme may provide that all or any of its provisions shall take effect either prospectively or retrospectively on such date as may be specified in that behalf in that Scheme" [Section 6-A (6)].

1.4.7 Provisions relating to Placing of the Pension Scheme before the Parliament

"A Pension Fund Scheme, framed under sub-section (1) shall be laid, as soon as may be after it is made, before each House of Parliament, while it is in session, for a total period of thirty days which may be comprised in one session or in two or more successive sessions, and if, before the expiry of the session immediately following the session or the successive sessions aforesaid, both Houses agree in making any modification in the Scheme or both Houses agree that the scheme should not be made, the scheme shall thereafter have effect only in such modified form or be of no effect, as the case may be; so, however, that any such modification or annulment shall be without prejudice to the validity of anything previously done under that scheme" [Section 6-A (7)].

1.5 Employees' Deposit-Linked Insurance Scheme [Section 6-C and 7]

The Employees' Deposit-Linked Insurance Scheme was introduced in 1976 by inserting a new Section 6-C in the Act w.e.f. 1-8-1976 and for that purpose, this Act was amended. The provisions relating to the framing of the scheme, Establishment of the Fund contribution, administration of the scheme, etc. have been made in Section 6-C. Now, let us consider these provisions as given in this Act.

1.5.1 Framing of the Employees' Deposit-Linked Insurance Scheme and its Purpose

"The Central Government may, by notification in the Official Gazette, frame a scheme to be called the Employees' Deposit-Linked Insurance Scheme for the purpose of providing life insurance benefits to the employees of any establishment or class of establishments to which this Act applies [Section 6-C (1)].

1.5.2 Establishment of Deposit-Linked Insurance Fund

There shall be established, as soon as may be after the framing of the Insurance Scheme, a Deposit-Linked Insurance Fund into which shall be paid by the employer from time to time in respect of every such employee in relation to whom he is the employer, such amount, not being more than one per cent of the aggregate of the basic wages, dearness allowance and retaining allowance (if any) for the time being payable in relation to such employee, as the Central Government may, by notification in the Official Gazette, specify [Section 6-C (1)].

"For the purposes of this sub-section, the expressions 'dearness allowance' and 'retaining allowance' have the same meanings as in Section 6 [Explanation to Section 6-C (1)].

1.5.3 Provisions relating to the Contribution to the Fund

Provisions relating to the contribution to the Deposit-Linked Insurance Fund are made in Section 6-C (2) and 6-C (4) (a) which are as follows:

(1) The employer shall pay into the Deposit-Linked Insurance Fund from time to time in respect of every such employee in relation to whom he is the employer, such an amount, not being more than one percent of the aggregate of the basic wages, dearness allowance and retaining allowance (if any) for the time being payable in relation to such employee, as the Central Government may, by notification in the Official Gazette, specify.

For the purposes, of this Section 6-C (2), the expressions 'dearness allowance' and 'retaining allowance' have the same meaning as given in Section 6 [Section 6-C (2)] and explanation to Section 6-C (2). Besides this, the employer has to make further contribution to the said Fund according to the provisions of Section 6-C (4) (a)] which are given below.

"The employer shall pay into the Insurance Fund such further sums of money, not exceeding one-fourth of the contribution which he is required to make under sub-section (2) of Section 6-C, as the Central Government may, from time to time, determine to meet all the expenses in connection with the administration of the Insurance Scheme other than the expenses towards the cost of any benefits provided by or under that Scheme".

1.5.4 Administration of the Insurance Fund

"The Insurance Fund shall vest in the Central Board and be administered by it in such a manner as may be specified in the Insurance Scheme" [Section 6-C (5)].

1.5.5 Effect

The Insurance Scheme may provide that any of its provisions shall take effect either retrospectively on such a date as may be specified in this behalf in that Scheme [Section 6-C (7)].

1.5.6 Contents

"The Insurance Scheme may provide for all or any of the matters specified in Schedule IV". (Section 6-C [6]). The Schedule IV referred to in Section 6-C [6] making clear the matters to be provided for in the Employees' Deposit-Linked Insurance Scheme is reproduced below.

SCHEDULE IV
MATTERS TO BE PROVIDED FOR IN THE EMPLOYEES DEPOSIT-LINKED INSURANCE SCHEME

1. The employees or class of employees who shall be covered by the Insurance Scheme.
2. The manner in which the accounts of the Insurance Fund shall be kept and the investment of moneys belonging to the Insurance Fund subject to such pattern of investment as may be determined, by order, by the Central Government.
3. The form in which an employee shall furnish particulars about himself and the members of his family whenever required.
4. The nomination of a person to receive the insurance amount due to the employee after his death and the cancellation or variation of such nomination.
5. The registers and records to be maintained in respect of employees; the form or design of any identity card, token or disc for the purpose of identifying any employee or his nominee or member of his family entitled to receive the insurance amount.

6. The scales of insurance benefits and conditions relating to the grant of such benefits to the employees.

7. This item is omitted w.e.f. 1-8-1988.

8. The manner in which the amount due to the nominee or the member of the family of the employee under the scheme is to be paid including a provision that the amount shall not be paid otherwise than in the form of a deposit in a savings bank account, in the name of such nominee or member of family in any corresponding new bank specified in the First Schedule to the Banking Companies (Acquisition and Transfer of Undertakings) Act, 1970, (5 of 1970).

9. Any other matter which is to be provided for in the Employees' Deposit-Linked Insurance Scheme or which may be necessary or proper for the purpose of implementing that Scheme.

1.5.7 Laying of the Schemes before Parliament

Every scheme framed under Section 5, Section 6-A and Section 6-C shall be laid, as soon as may be after it is framed, before each House of Parliament, while it is in session, for a total period of thirty days which may be comprised in one session or in two or more successive sessions, and if, before the expiry of the session immediately following the session or the successive sessions aforesaid, both Houses agree in making any modification in the scheme, or both Houses agree that the scheme should not be framed, the scheme shall thereafter have effect only in such modified form or be of no effect, as the case may be; so, however, that any such modification or annulment shall be without prejudice to the validity of anything previously done under that scheme" [Section 6-D].

1.5.8 Modification of Scheme

The Central Government may, by notification in the Official Gazette, add to amend or vary, either prospectively or retrospectively, the Scheme, the Pension Scheme, or the Insurance Scheme as the case may be [Section 7 (1)].

It is also stated in Section 7 (2) that, "Every notification issued under sub-section (1) of Section 7 shall be laid, as soon as may be after it is issued, before each House of Parliament while it is in session, for a total period of thirty days, which may be comprised in one session or in two or more successive sessions, and if, before the expiry of the session immediately following the sessions or the successive sessions aforesaid, both Houses agree in making any modification in the notification, or both Houses agree that the notification should not be issued, the notification shall thereafter have effect only in such modified form or be of no effect, as the case may be; so, however, that any such modification or annulment shall be without prejudice to the validity of anything previously done under that notification".

1.6 Administration of the Schemes [Sections 5-A, 5-AA, 5-B, 5-C, 5-D, 5-DD and 5-E]

We find provisions relating to the administration of the Schemes under this Act in Sections 5-A, 5-AA, 5-B, 5-C, 5-D, 5-DD and 5-E of this Act. These provisions are as under:

1.6.1 Central Board [Section 5-A]

In Section 5-A, provisions have been made in respect of the constitution, members of the Central Board, Constitution of Board of Trustees, etc.

[A] Constitution of the Central Board [Section 5-A (1)]

"The Central Government may, by notification in the Official Gazette, constitute with effect from such date as may be specified therein, a Board of Trustees for the territories to which this Act extends (hereinafter in this Act referred to as the Central Board).

[B] Members of the Central Board [Section 5-A (1)]

It is mentioned in Section 5-A (1) that the Central Board consists of the following persons as members –

(1) Chairman and a Vice-Chairman to be appointed by the Central Government;

(2) The Central Provident Fund Commissioner, Ex-officio;

(3) Not more than five persons appointed by the Central Government from amongst its officials;

(4) Not more than fifteen persons representing Governments of such States as the Central Government may specify in this behalf appointed by the Central Government;

(5) Ten persons representing employers of the establishment to which the Scheme applies, appointed by the Central Government after consultation with such organisations of employers as may be recognised by the Central Government in this behalf; and

(6) Ten persons representing employees in the establishments to which the Scheme applies, appointed by the Central Government after consultation with such organisations of employees as may be recognised by the Central Government in this behalf.

It is further made clear in Section 5-A (2) that, "The terms and conditions subject to which a member of the Central Board may be appointed and the time, place and procedure of the meetings of the Central Board shall be such as may be provided for in the Scheme".

[C] Functions and Duties of the Central Board

The following functions and duties have been entrusted to the Central Board under this Act.

(1) The Central Board shall, subject to the provisions of Section 6-A and Section 6-C, administer the fund vested in it in such manner as may be specified in the Scheme [Section 5-A (3)].

(2) The Central Board shall perform such other functions as it may be required to perform by or under any provisions of the Scheme, the Pension Scheme and the Insurance Scheme [Section 5-A (4)].

(3) The Central Board shall maintain proper accounts of its income and expenditure in such form and in such manner as the Central Government may, after consultation with the Comptroller and Auditor-General of India, specify in the Scheme [Section 5-A (5)].

(4) It shall be the duty of the Central Board to submit also to the Central Government an annual report of its work and activities and the Central Government shall cause a copy of the annual report, the audited accounts together with the report of the Comptroller and Auditor-General of India and the comments of the Central Board thereon to be laid before each House of Parliament [Section 5-A (9)].

[D] Provisions relating to the audited accounts

(1) The accounts of the Central Board shall be audited annually by the Comptroller and Auditor-General of India and any expenditure incurred by him in connection with such audit shall be payable by the Central Board to the Comptroller and Auditor-General of India [Section 5-A (6)].

(2) The Comptroller and Auditor-General of India and any person appointed by him in connection with the audit of the accounts of the Central Board shall have the same rights and privileges and authority in connection with such audit as the Comptroller and Auditor-General has, in connection with the audit of Government Accounts and, in particular, shall have the right to demand the production of books, accounts, connected vouchers, documents and papers and inspect any of the offices of the Central Board [Section 5-A (7)].

(3) The accounts of the Central Board as certified by the Comptroller and Auditor-General of India or any other person appointed by him in this behalf together with the audit report thereon shall be forwarded to the Central Board which shall forward the same to the Central Government along with its comments on the report of the Comptroller and Auditor-General [Section 5-A (8)].

1.6.2 Provisions of the Act relating to the Executive Committee [Section 5-AA]

In Section 5-AA of this Act, provisions have been made relating to the constitution of 'Executive Committee' its members and their terms and conditions, etc. Section 5 A-A is reproduced below.

(1) The Central Government may, by notification in the Official Gazette, constitute, with effect from such date as may be specified therein, an Executive Committee to assist the Central Board in the performance of its functions [Section 5-AA (1)].

(2) The Executive Committee shall consist of the following persons as members, namely:

(a) a Chairman appointed by the Central Government from amongst the members of the Central Board;

(b) two persons appointed by the Central Government from amongst the persons referred to in clause (b) of sub-section (1) of Section 5-A;
(c) three persons appointed by the Central Government from amongst the persons referred to in clause (c) of sub-section (1) of Section 5-A;
(d) three persons representing the employers elected by the Central Board from amongst the persons referred to in clause (d) of sub-section (1) of Section 5-A;
(e) three persons representing the employees elected by the Central Board from amongst the persons referred to in clause (e) of Sub-section (1) of Section 5-A;
(f) the Central Provident Fund Commissioner, ex-officio [Section 5-AA (2)].

(3) The terms and conditions subject to which a member of the Central Board may be appointed or elected to the Executive Committee and the time, place and procedure of the meetings of the Executive Committee shall be such as may be provided for in the Scheme [Section 5-AA (3)].

This Section 5-AA has been introduced by amending this Act in 1988 w.e.f. 1-8-1988 in order to assist the Central Board of Trustees in the discharge of its functions and duties and accordingly, the provision has been made to set up an Executive Committee.

1.6.3 Provisions of Section 5-B relating to the Constitution, Powers and Duties of State Board

(1) The Central Government may, after consultation with the Government of any State, by notification in the Official Gazette, constitute for that State a Board of Trustees (hereinafter in this Act referred to as the State Board), in such a manner as may be provided for in the Scheme [Section 5-B (1)].
(2) A State Board shall exercise such powers and perform such duties as the Central Government may assign to it from time to time [Section 5-B (2)].
(3) The terms and conditions subject to which a member of a State Board may be appointed and the time, place and procedure of the meetings of a State Board shall be such as may be provided for in the Scheme [Section 5-B (3)].

1.6.4 Board of Trustees to be Body Corporate

Every Board of Trustees constituted under Section 5-A or Section 5-B shall be a body corporate under the name specified in the notification constituting it, having perpetual succession and a common seal and shall by the said name sue and be sued [Section 5-C].

1.6.5 Appointment of Officers

Provisions relating to the appointment of officers by the Central Government and other related matters are found in Section 5-D which is as follows:
(1) The Central Government shall appoint a Central Provident Fund Commissioner who shall be the Chief Executive Officer of the Central Board and shall be subject to the general control and superintendence of that Board. [Section 5-D (1)].

(2) The Central Government may also appoint a Financial Adviser and Chief Accounts Officer to assist the Central Provident Fund Commissioner in the discharge of his duties [Section 5-D (2)].

(3) The Central Board may appoint, subject to the maximum scale of pay, as may be specified in the scheme, as many Additional Central Provident Fund Commissioners, Deputy Provident Fund Commissioners, Regional Provident Fund Commissioners, Assistant Provident Fund Commissioners and such other officers and employees as it may consider necessary for the efficient administration of the Scheme, the Pension Scheme and the Insurance Scheme [Section 5-D (3)].

(4) No appointment to the post of the Central Provident Fund Commissioner or an Additional Central Provident Fund Commissioner or a Financial Adviser and Chief Accounts Officer or any other post under the Central Board carrying a scale of pay equivalent to the scale of pay of any Group 'A' or Group 'B' post under the Central Government shall be made except after consultation with the Union Public Service Commission [Section 5-D (4)].

It is provided that no such consultation shall be necessary in regard to any such appointment

    (a) for a period not exceeding one year; or

    (b) if the person to be appointed is at the time of his appointment

        (i) a member of the Indian Administrative Service, or

        (ii) in the service of the Central Government or a State Government or the Central Board in a Group 'A' or Group 'B' post [Proviso to Section 5-D (4)].

(5) A State Board may, with the approval of the State Government concerned, appoint such staff as it may consider necessary [Section 5-D (5)].

(6) The method of recruitment, salary and allowances, discipline and other conditions of service of the Central Provident Fund Commissioner, and the Financial Adviser and Chief Accounts Officer shall be such as may be specified by the Central Government and such salary and allowances shall be paid out of the Fund [Section 5-D (6)].

(7) (a) The method of recruitment, salary and allowances, discipline and other conditions of service of the Additional Central Provident Fund Commissioner, Provident Fund Commissioner, Regional Provident Fund Commissioner, Assistant Provident Fund Commissioner and other officers and employees of the Central Board shall be such as may be specified by the Central Board in accordance with the rules and orders applicable to the officers and employees of the Central Government drawing corresponding scales of pay [Section 5-D (7) (a)].

It is provided that where the Central Board is of the opinion that it is necessary to make a departure from the said rules or orders in respect of any of the matters aforesaid, it shall obtain the prior approval of the Central Government [Proviso to Section 5-D (7) (a)].

(b) In determining the corresponding scales of pay of officers and employees under clause (a), the Central Board shall have regard to the educational qualifications, method of recruitment, duties and responsibilities of such officers and employees under the Central Government and in case of any doubt, the Central Board shall refer the matter to the Central Government whose decision thereon shall be final [Section 5-D (7) (b)].

(8) The method of recruitment, salary and allowances, discipline and other conditions of service of officers and employees of a State Board shall be such as may be specified by that Board, with the approval of the State Government concerned [Section 5-D (8)].

1.6.6 Acts and proceedings of the Central Board or its Executive Committee or the State Board not to be invalidated on certain grounds

"No act done or proceeding taken by the Central Board or the Executive Committee constituted under Section 5-AA or the State Board shall be questioned, on the ground merely of the existence of any vacancy in, or any defect in the constitution of, the Central Board or the Executive Committee or the State Board, as the case may be [Section 5-DD].

1.6.7 Delegation

The Central Board may, delegate to the Executive Committee or to the Chairman of the Board or to any of its officers and a State Board may delegate to its Chairman or to any of its officers, subject to such conditions and limitations, if any, as it may specify, such of its powers and functions under this Act as it may deem necessary for the efficient administration of the Scheme, the Pension Scheme and the Insurance Scheme [Section 5-E].

1.7 Provisions of the Act Relating to 'Determination of Moneys (Amounts) Due from the Employers' [Section 7-A], Review of Orders Passed under Section 7-A [Section 7(B), Determination of Escaped Amount [Section 7-C], Employees' Provident Funds Appellate Tribunals [Section 7-D], etc.

The provision of setting up independent machinery for recovery of the outstanding dues of provident fund as well as other dues has been made under this Act. It has also made the provisions for setting up Tribunals for hearing of appeals filed against the orders of the provident fund authorities in the matter of applicability of the provisions of this Act, assessment or dues, levy of damages etc. All these provisions are given as follows.

1.7.1 Power of the Commissioners to determine of moneys due from employers [Section 7-A (1)]

"The Central Provident Fund Commissioner, any Additional Central Provident Fund Commissioner, any Deputy Provident Fund Commissioner, any Regional Provident Fund Commissioner or any Assistant Provident Fund Commissioner may, by order –

(a) in a case where a dispute arises regarding the applicability of this Act to an establishment, decide such dispute; and

(b) determine the amount due from any employer under any provision of this Act, the Scheme or the Pension Scheme or the Insurance Scheme, as the case may be, and for any of the aforesaid purposes may conduct such inquiry as he may deem necessary".

1.7.2 Powers of the Inquiry Officer under the C.P. Code

"The Officer conducting the inquiry under sub-section (1) of Section 7-A shall, for the purposes of such inquiry, have the same powers as are vested in a Court under the Code of Civil Procedure, 1908 (5 of 1908), for trying a suit in respect of the following matters, namely –

(a) enforcing the attendance of any person or examining him on oath;

(b) requiring the discovery and production of documents;

(c) receiving evidence on affidavit;

(d) issuing commissions for the examination of witnesses;

and any such inquiry shall be deemed to be a judicial proceeding within the hearing of Sections 193 and 228, and for the purpose of Section 196, of the Indian Penal Code (45 of 1860) [Section 7-A (2)].

1.7.3 Employer be given Reasonable Opportunity to be Heard [Section 7-A (3)]

No order shall be made under sub-section (1) of Section 7A, unless the employer concerned is given a reasonable opportunity of representing his case.

1.7.4 Power of the Inquiry Officer where the Employer, Employee or any other Person fails to produce necessary Documents [Section 7-A (3-A)]

"Where the employer, employee or any other person required to attend the inquiry under sub-section (1) of Section 7-A fails to attend such inquiry without assigning any valid reason or fails to produce any document or to file any report or return which called upon to do so, the officer conducting the inquiry may decide the applicability of the Act or determine the amount due from any employer as the case may be, on the basis of the evidence adduced coring such inquiry and other documents available on record".

1.7.5 Provisions of Section 7-A (4) and (5) relating to setting aside an order or application

"Where an order under Sub-section (1) of Section 7-A is passed against an employer *ex parte*, he may, within three months from the date of communication of such order, apply to the officer for setting aside such order and if he satisfies the officer that the show cause notice was not duly served or that he was prevented by any sufficient cause from appearing when the inquiry was held, the officer shall make an order setting aside his earlier order and shall appoint a date for proceeding with the inquiry. [Section 7-A (4)].

It is provided that no such order shall be set aside merely on the ground that there has been an irregularity in the service of the show-cause notice if the officer is satisfied that the employer had notice of the date of hearing and had sufficient time to appear before the officer [Proviso to Section 7-A (4)].

"Where an appeal has been preferred under this Act against an order passed *ex-parte* and such appeal has been disposed of otherwise than on the ground that the appellant has withdrawn the appeal, no application shall lie under this sub-section for setting aside the ex-parte order" [Explanation to Section 7-A (4)].

"No order passed under this Section shall be set aside on any application under sub-section (4) of Section 7-A unless notice thereof has been served on the opposite party [Section 7-A (5)].

1.7.6 Review of Orders Passed under Section 7-A

(1) Any person aggrieved by an order made under sub-section (1) of section 7A, but from which no appeal has been preferred under this Act, and who, from the discovery of new and important matter or evidence which, after the exercise of due diligence was not within his knowledge or could not be produced by him at the time when the order was made, or on account of some mistake or error apparent on the face of the record or for any other sufficient reason, desires to obtain a review of such order may apply for a review of that order to the officer who passed the order [Section 7-B (1)].

It is also provided that "such officer may also on his own motion review his order if he is satisfied that it is necessary so to do on any such ground" [Proviso to Section 7-B (1)].

(2) Every application for review under sub-section (1) of Section 7-B shall be filed in such form and manner and within such time as may be specified in the Scheme [Section 7-B (2)].

(3) Where it appears to the officer receiving an application for review that there is no sufficient ground for a review, he shall reject the application [Section 7-B (3)].

(4) Where the officer is of the opinion that the application for review should be granted, he shall grant the same [Section 7-B (4)].

Provided that,

(a) no such application shall be granted without previous notice to all the parties before him to enable them to appear and be heard in support of the order in respect of which a review is applied for, and

(b) no such application shall be granted on the ground of discovery of new matter or evidence which the applicant alleges was not within his knowledge or could not be produced by him when the order was made without proof of such allegation [Provisio to Section 7-B (4)].

(5) No appeal shall lie against the order of the officer rejecting an application for review, but an appeal under this Act shall lie against an order passed under review as if the order passed under review were the original order passed by him under section 7-A [Section 7-B (5)].

1.7.7 Determination of Escaped Amount

"Where an order determining the amount due from an employer under section 7-A or section 7-B has been passed and if the officer who passed the order –

(a) has reason to believe that by reason of the omission or failure on the part of the employer to make any document or report available, or to disclose, fully and truly, all material facts necessary for determining the correct amount due from the employer, any amount so due from such employer for any period has escaped his notice;

(b) has, in consequence of information in his possession, reason to believe that any amount to be determined under section 7-A or section 7-B has escaped from his determination for any period notwithstanding that has been no omission or failure as mentioned in clause (a) on the part of the employer, he may, within a period of five years from the date of communication of the order passed under section 7-A or section 7-B, re-open the case and pass appropriate orders re-determining the amount due from the employer in accordance with the provisions of this Act" [Section 7 (C)].

It is provided that "no order re-determining the amount due from the employer shall be passed under this section unless the employer is given a reasonable opportunity of representing his case" [Proviso to Section 7].

1.7.8 Employees' Provident Funds Appellate Tribunal

(1) The Central Government may, by notification in the Official Gazette, constitute one or more Appellate Tribunals to be known as Employees' Provident Funds Appellate Tribunal to exercise the powers and discharge the functions conferred on such Tribunal by this Act and every such Tribunal shall have jurisdiction in respect of establishments situated in such area as may be specified in the notification constituting the Tribunal [Section 7-D (1)].

(2) A Tribunal shall consist of one person only to be appointed by the Central Government [Section 7-D (2)].

(3) A person shall not be qualified for appointment as a Presiding Officer of a Tribunal (hereinafter referred to as the Presiding Officer) unless he is, or has been or is qualified to be,
  (i) a Judge of a High Court; or
  (ii) a District Judge [Section 7-D (3)].

1.7.9 Term of Office

The Presiding Officer of a Tribunal shall hold office for a term of five years from the date on which he enters upon his office or until he attains the age of sixty-two years, whichever is earlier [Section 7-E].

1.7.10 Resignation

(1) "The Presiding Officer may, by notice in writing under his hand addressed to the Central Government, resign his office [Section 7-F (1)].

It is provided that the Presiding Officer shall, unless he is permitted by the Central Government to relinquish his office sooner, continue to hold office until the expiry of three months from the date of receipt of such notice or until a person duly appointed as his successor enters upon his office or until the expiry of his term of office, whichever is the earliest [Proviso to Section 7-7 (1)].

(2) The Presiding Officer shall not be removed from his office except by an order made by the President on the ground of proved misbehaviour or incapacity after an inquiry made by a Judge of the High Court in which such Presiding Officer had been informed of the charges against him and given a reasonable opportunity of being heard in respect of those charges [Section 7-F (2)].

(3) The Central Government may, by rules, regulate the procedure for the investigation of misbehaviour or incapacity of the Presiding Officer. [Section 7-F (3)].

1.7.11 Salary and Allowances and other Terms and Conditions of Service of Presiding Officer

The salary and allowances payable to, and the other terms and conditions of service (including pension, gratuity and other retirement benefits) of the Presiding Officer shall be such as may be prescribed [Section 7 (G)].

It is provided that neither the salary and allowances nor the other terms and conditions of service of the Presiding Officer shall be varied to his disadvantage after his appointment [Proviso to Section 7 (G)].

1.7.12 Staff of Tribunal

(1) "The Central Government shall determine the nature and categories of the officers and other employees required to assist a Tribunal in the discharge of its functions and provide the Tribunal with such officers and other employees as it may think fit" [Section 7 (H) (1)].

(2) "The officers and other employees of a Tribunal shall discharge their functions under the general superintendence of the Presiding Officer" [Section 7 (H) (2)].

(3) The salaries and allowances and other conditions of service of the officers and other employees of a Tribunal shall be such as may be prescribed. [Section 7(H) (3)].

1.7.13 Appeals to Tribunal

(1) "Any person aggrieved by a notification issued by the Central Government, or an order passed by the Central Government or any authority, under the proviso to sub-section (3), or sub-section (4), of section 1, or section 3, or sub-section (1) of section 7-A, or section 7-B except an order rejecting an application for review referred to in sub-section (4) thereof, or section 7-C, or section 11B may prefer an appeal to a Tribunal against such notification or order". [Section 7-I (1)].

(2) "Every appeal under sub-section (1) Section 7 (I) shall be filed in such form and manner, within such time and be accompanied by such fees, as may be prescribed" [Section 7-I (2)].

1.7.14 Procedure of Tribunals

(1) "A Tribunal shall have power to regulate its own procedure in all matters arising out of the exercise of its powers or of the discharge of its functions including the places at which the Tribunal shall have its sittings [Section 7-J (1)].

(2) "A Tribunal shall, for the purpose of discharging its functions, have all the powers which are vested in the officers referred to in section 7-A and any proceeding before the Tribunal shall be deemed to be a judicial proceeding within the meaning of sections 193 and 228, and for the purpose of section 196, of the Indian Penal Code, (45 of 1860) and the Tribunal shall be deemed to be a Civil Court for all the purposes of section 195 and Chapter XXVI of the Code of Criminal Procedure, 1973 (2 of 1974) [Section 7-J (2)].

1.7.15 Right of Appellant to take assistance of Legal Practitioner and of Government etc., to appoint Presenting Officers

(1) "A person preferring an appeal to a Tribunal under this Act may either appear in person or take the assistance of a legal practitioner of his choice to present his case before the Tribunal" [Section 7-K (1)].

(2) "The Central Government or a State Government of any other authority under this, Act may authorise one or more legal practitioners or any of its officers to act as presenting officers and every person so authorised may present the case with respect to any appeal before a Tribunal" [Section 7-K (2)].

1.7.16 Orders of Tribunal

(1) "A Tribunal may, after giving the parties to the appeal, an opportunity of being heard, pass such orders thereon as it thinks fit, confirming, modifying or annulling

the order appealed against or may refer the case back to the authority which passed such order with such directions as the Tribunal may think fit, for a fresh adjudication or order, as the case may be, after taking additional evidence, if necessary" [Section 7-L (1)].

(2) A Tribunal may, at any time within five years from the date of its order, with a view to rectifying any mistake apparent from the record, amend any order passed by it under sub-section (1) of Section 7-L and shall make such amendment in the order if the mistake is brought to its notice by the parties to the appeal [Section 7-L (2)].

It is provided that "an amendment which has the effect of enhancing the amount due from, or otherwise increasing the liability of, the employer shall not be made under this sub-section, unless the Tribunal has given notice to him of its intention to do so and has allowed him a reasonable opportunity of being heard" [Proviso to Section 7-L (2)].

(3) "A Tribunal shall send a copy of every order passed under this section to the parties to the appeal" [Section 7-L (3)].

(4) Any order made by a Tribunal finally disposing of an appeal shall not be questioned in any Court of law [Section 7-L (4)].

1.7.17 Filling up of Vacancies

"If, for any reason, a vacancy occurs in the office of the Presiding Officer, the Central Government shall appoint another person in accordance with the provisions of this Act, to fill the vacancy and the proceedings may be continued before a Tribunal from the stage at which the vacancy is filled" [Section 7-M].

1.7.18 Finality of Orders constituting a Tribunal

"No order of the Central Government appointing any person as the Presiding Officer shall be called in question in any manner, and no act or proceeding before a Tribunal shall be called in question in any manner on the ground merely of any defect in the constitution of such Tribunal" [Section 7-N].

1.7.19 Deposit of Amount due, on Filing Appeal

No appeal by the employer shall be entertained by a Tribunal unless he has deposited with it seventy-five per cent of the amount due from him as determined by an officer referred to in Section 7-A" [Section 7-O].

It is provided that the Tribunal may, for reasons to be recorded in writing, waive or reduce the amount to be deposited under this section" [Proviso to Section 7-O].

1.7.20 Transfer of certain Applications to Tribunals

"All applications which are pending before the Central Government under Section 19-A, before its repeal, shall stand transferred to a Tribunal exercising jurisdiction in respect of establishment in relation to which such applications had been made as if such applications were appeals preferred to the Tribunal".

1.7.21 Interest Payable by the Employer

"The employer shall be liable to pay simple interest at the rate of twelve per cent per annum or at such higher rate as may be specified in the Scheme on any amount due from him under this Act from the date on which the amount has become so due till the date of its actual payment" [Section 7-Q].

It is provided that higher rate of interest specified in the Scheme shall not exceed the lending rate of interest charged by any scheduled bank [Proviso to Section 7-Q].

1.8 Mode of Recovery of Moneys Due from Employers [Sections 8, 9, 10, 11 and 12]

We find provisions relating to the mode of recovery of moneys due from employers, recovery of moneys by employers and contractors, issue of certificate to the Recovery Officer, etc. in Sections 8 and from 8-A to 8-G. These provisions are as under:

1.8.1 Mode of Recovery of Moneys Due from Employers [Section 8]

Any amount due –

(a) from the employer in relation to an establishment to which any Scheme or the Insurance Scheme applies in respect of any contribution payable to the Fund or, as the case may be, the Insurance Fund, damages recoverable under Section 14-B, accumulations required to be transferred under sub-section (2) of section 15 or under sub-section (5) of section 17 or any charges payable by him under any other provision of this Act or of any provision of the Scheme or the Insurance Scheme or

(b) from the employer in relation to any exempted establishment in respect of any damages recoverable under section 14-B or any charges payable by him to the appropriate Government under any provision of this Act or under any of the conditions specified under section 17 or in respect of the contribution payable by him towards the Pension Scheme or the Insurance Scheme under the said section 17, may, if the amount is in arrear, be recovered in the manner specified in Sections 8 B to 8 G [Section 8].

1.8.2 Recovery of Moneys by Employers and Contractors [Section 8-A]

(1) "The amount of contribution (that is to say the employer's contribution as well as the employee's contribution in pursuance of any Scheme and the employer's contribution in pursuance of the Insurance Scheme) and any charges for meeting the cost of administering the Fund paid or payable by an employer in respect of an employee employed by or through a contractor may be recovered by such employer from the contractor, either by deduction from any amount payable to the contractor under any contract or as a debt payable by the contractor [Section 8-A (1)]."

(2) "A contractor from whom the amounts mentioned in sub-section (1) may be recovered in respect of any employee employed by or through him, may recover from such employee the employee's contribution under any Scheme by deduction from the basic wages, dearness allowance and retaining allowance (if any) payable to such employee" [Section 8-A (2)]."

(3) "Notwithstanding any contract to the contrary, no contractor shall be entitled to deduct the employer's contribution or the charges referred to in sub-section (1) from the basic wages, dearness allowance and retaining allowance (if any) payable to an employee employed by or through him or otherwise to recover such contribution or charges from such employee" [Section 8-A (3)]."

"In this section, the expressions, 'dearness allowance' and 'retaining allowance' shall have the same meanings as in Section 6" [Explanation to Section 8-A (3)].

1.8.3 Issue of Certificate to the Recovery Officer [Section 8-B]

(1) "Where any amount is in arrears under Section 8, the authorised officer may issue, to the Recovery Officer, a certificate under his signature specifying the amount of arrears and the Recovery Officer, on receipt of such certificate, shall proceed to recover the amount specified therein from the establishment or, as the case may be, the employer by one or more of the modes mentioned below –

(a) attachment and sale of the movable or immovable property of the establishment or as the case may be, the employer;
(b) arrest of the employer and his detention in prison;
(c) appointing a receiver for the management of the movable or immovable properties of the establishment or, as the case may be, the employer". [Section 8-B (1)].

It is provided that the attachment and sale of any property under this section shall first be effected against the properties of the establishment and where such attachment and sale is insufficient for recovering the whole of the amount of arrears specified in the certificate, the Recovery Officer may take such proceedings against the property of the employer for recovery of the whole or any part of such arrears" [Proviso to Section 8-B (1)].

(2) "The authorised officer may issue a certificate under sub-section (1), notwithstanding that proceedings for recovery of the arrears by any other mode have been taken" [Section 8-B (2)].

1.8.4 Recovery Officer to whom Certificate is to be Forwarded [Section 8-C]

(1) The authorised officer may forward the certificate referred to in Section 8-B to the Recovery Officer within whose jurisdiction the employer –

(a) carries on his business or profession or within whose jurisdiction the principal place of his establishment is situate; or
(b) resides or any movable or immovable property of the establishment or the employer is situate. (Section 8-C [1]).

(2) Where an establishment or the employer has property within the jurisdiction of more than one Recovery Officers and the Recovery Officer to whom a certificate is sent by the authorised officer –

(a) is not able to recover the entire amount by the sale of the property, movable or immovable, within his jurisdiction; or

(b) is of the opinion that, for the purpose of expediting or securing the recovery of the whole or any part of the amount, it is necessary so to do, he may send the certificate or, where only a part of the amount is to be recovered, a copy of the certificate certified in the prescribed manner and specifying the amount to be recovered to the Recovery Officer within whose jurisdiction the establishment or the employer has property or the employer resides, and thereupon that Recovery Officer shall also proceed to recover the amount due under this section as if the certificate or the copy thereof had been the certificate sent to him by the authorised officer [Section 8-C (2)].

1.8.5 Validity of Certificate and Amendment thereof [Section 8-D]

(1) "When the authorised officer issues a certificate to a Recovery Officer under Section 8-B, it shall not be open to the employer to dispute before the Recovery Officer the correctness of the amount, and no objection to the certificate on any other ground shall also be entertained by the Recovery Officer" [Section 8-D (1)].

(2) "Notwithstanding the issue of a certificate to a Recovery Officer, the authorised officer shall have power to withdraw the certificate or correct any clerical or arithmetical mistake in the certificate by sending an intimation to the Recovery Officer" [Section 8-D (2)].

(3) The authorised officer shall intimate to the Recovery Officer any orders withdrawing or cancelling a certificate or any correction made by him under sub-section (2) or any amendment made under sub-section (4) of Section 8-E" [Section 8-D (3)].

1.8.6 Stay of Proceedings under Certificate and Amendment or Withdrawal thereof [Section 8-E]

(1) "Notwithstanding that a certificate has been issued to the Recovery Officer for the recovery of any amount, the authorised officer may grant time for the payment of the amount, and thereupon the Recovery Officer shall stay the proceedings until the expiry of the time so granted" [Section 8-E (1)].

(2) "Where a certificate for the recovery of amount has been issued, the authorised officer shall keep the Recovery Officer informed of any amount paid or time granted for payment, subsequent to the issue of such certificate". [Section 8-E (2)].

(3) "Where the order giving rise to a demand of amount for which a certificate for recovery has been issued has been modified in appeal or other proceeding under this Act, and, as a consequence thereof, the demand is reduced but the order is the subject-matter of a further proceeding under this Act, the authorised officer shall stay the recovery of such part of the amount of the certificate as pertains to the said reduction for the period for which the appeal or other proceeding remains pending" [Section 8-E (3)].

(4) "Where a certificate for the recovery of amount has been issued and subsequently the amount of the outstanding demand is reduced as a result of an appeal or other proceeding under this Act, the authorised officer shall, when the order which was the subject-matter of such appeal or other proceeding has become final and conclusive, amend the certificate or withdraw it, as the case may be" [Section 8-E (4)].

1.8.7 Other Modes of Recovery

(1) Notwithstanding the issue of a certificate to the Recovery Officer under section 8-B, the Central Provident Fund Commissioner or any other officer authorised by the Central Board may recover the amount by any one or more of the modes provided in this section [Section 8-F (1)].

(2) If any amount is due from any person to any employer who is in arrears, the Central Provident Fund Commissioner or any other officer authorised by the Central Board in this behalf may require such person to deduct from the said amount the arrears due from such employer under this Act and such person shall comply with any such requisition and shall pay the sum so deducted to the credit of the Central Provident Fund Commissioner or the officer so authorised, as the case may be" [Section 8-F (2)].

It is provided that nothing in this sub-section shall apply to any part of the amount exempt from attachment in execution of a decree of a Civil Court under section 60 of the Code of Civil Procedure, 1908 (5 of 1908) [Proviso to Section 8-F (2)].

(3) (i) The Central Provident Fund Commissioner or any other officer authorised by the Central Board in this behalf may, at any time or from time to time, by notice in writing, require any person from whom money is due or may become due to the employer or, as the case may be, the establishment, or any person who holds or may subsequently hold money for or on account of the employer or, as the case may be, the establishment to pay to the Central Provident Fund Commissioner either forthwith upon the money becoming due or being held or at or within the time specified in the notice (not being before the money becomes due or is held) so much of the money as is sufficient to pay the amount due from the employer in respect of arrears or the whole of the money when it is equal to or less then that amount.

(ii) A notice under this sub-section may be issued to any person who holds or may subsequently hold any money for or on account of the employer jointly with any other person and for the purposes of this sub-section, the shares of the joint holders in such account shall be presumed, until the contrary is proved, to be equal.

(iii) A copy of the notice shall be forwarded to the employer at his last address known to the Central Provident Fund Commissioner, or as the case may be the officer so authorised and in the case of a joint account to all the joint-holders at their last addresses known to the Central Provident Fund Commissioner or the officer so authorised.

(iv) Save as otherwise provided in this sub-section, every person to whom a notice is issued under this sub-section shall be bound to comply with such notice, and, in particular, where any such notice is issued to a post office bank or an insurer, it shall not be necessary for any pass book, deposit receipt, policy or any other document to be produced for the purpose of any entry, endorsement or the like being made before payment is made notwithstanding any rule, practice or requirement to the contrary.

(v) Any claim respecting any property in relation to which a notice under this sub-section has been issued arising after the date of the notice shall be void as against any demand contained in the notice.

(vi) Where a person to whom a notice under this sub-section is sent objects to it by a statement on oath that the sum demanded or any part thereof is not due to the employer or that he does not hold any money or on account of the employer, then, nothing contained in this sub-section shall be deemed to require such person to pay any such sum or part thereof, as the case may be, but if it is discovered that such a statement was false in any material particular, such person shall be personally liable to the Central Provident Fund Commissioner or the officer so authorised to the extent of his own liability to the employer on the date of the notice, or to the extent of the employer's liability for any sum due under this Act, whichever is less.

(vii) The Central Provident Fund Commissioner or the officer so authorised may, at any time or from time to time, amend or revoke any notice issued under this sub-section or extend the time for making any payment in pursuance of such notice.

(viii) The Central Provident Fund Commissioner or the officer so authorised shall grant a receipt for any amount paid in compliance with a notice issued under this sub-section, and the person so paying shall be fully discharged from his liability to the employer to the extent of the amount so paid.

(ix) Any person discharging any liability to the employer after the receipt of a notice under this sub-section shall be personally liable to the Central Provident Fund Commissioner or the officer so authorised to the extent of his own liability to the employer so discharged or to the extent of the employer's liability for any sum due under this Act, whichever is less.

(x) If the person to whom a notice under this sub-section is sent fails to make payment in pursuance thereof to the Central Provident Fund Commissioner or the officer so authorised, he shall be deemed to be an employer in default in respect of the amount specified in the notice and further proceedings may be taken against him for the realisation of the amount as if it were an arrear due from him, in the manner provided in sections 8-B to 8-E and the notice shall have the same effect as an attachment of a debt by the Recovery Officer exercise of his powers under section 8-B [Section 8-F (3)].

(4) "The Central Provident Fund Commissioner or the officer authorised by the Central Board in this behalf may apply to the court in whose custody there is money belonging to the employer for payment to him of the entire amount of such money, or if it is more than the amount due, an amount sufficient to discharge the amount due" [Section 8-F (4)].

(5) The Central Provident Fund Commissioner or any officer not below the rank of Assistant Provident Fund Commissioner may, if so authorised by the Central Government by general or special order, recover any arrears of amount due from an employer or, as the case may be, from the establishment by distraint and sale of his or its movable property in the manner laid down in the Third Schedule to the Income-tax Act, 1961 (43 of 1961) [Section 8-F (5)].

1.8.8 Application of Certain Provisions of Income Tax Act of 1961 [Section 8-G]

The provisions of the Second and Third Schedules to the Income-tax Act, 1961 (43 of 1961) and the Income-tax (Certificate Proceeding) Rules, 1962, as in force from time to time, shall apply with necessary modifications as if the said provisions and the rules referred to the arrears of the amount mentioned in section 8 of this Act instead of to the income-tax" [Section 8-G].

It is provided that any reference in the said provisions and the rules to the "assessee" shall be construed as a reference to an employer as defined in this Act [Proviso to Section 8-G].

1.8.9 Fund to be Recognised under the Act of 1922 [Section 9]

"For the purposes of the Indian Income-tax Act, 1922 (11 of 1922), the Fund shall be deemed to be a recognised Provident Fund within the meaning of Chapter IX-A of that Act" [Section 9].

It is provided that "nothing contained in the said Chapter shall operate to render ineffective any provision of the Scheme (under which the Fund is established) which is repugnant to any of the provisions of that Chapter or of the rules made there under" [Proviso to Section 9].

1.8.10 Protection against Attachment [Section 10]

(1) "The amount standing to the credit of any member in the Fund or of any exempted employee in a Provident Fund shall not in any way be capable of being assigned or charged and shall not be liable to attachment under any decree or order of any Court in respect of any debt or liability incurred by the member or the exempted

employee, and neither the official assignee appointed under the Presidency Towns Insolvency Act, 1909 (3 of 1909) nor any receiver appointed under the Provincial Insolvency Act, 1920 (5 of 1920), shall be entitled to, or have any claim on any such amount [Section 10 (1)].

(2) "Any amount standing to the credit of a member in the fund or of an exempted employee in a Provident Fund at the time of his death and payable to his nominee under the Scheme or the rules of the Provident Fund shall subject to any deduction authorised by the said Scheme or rules, vest in the nominee and shall be free from any debt or other liability incurred by the deceased or the nominee before the death of the member or of the exempted employee, and shall also not be liable to attachment under any decree or order of any Court" [Section 10 (2)].

(3) "The provisions of sub-section (1) and sub-section (2) of Section 10 shall, so far as may be, apply in relation to the Pension or any other amount payable under the Pension Scheme and also in relation to any amount payable under the Insurance Scheme as they apply in relation to any amount payable out of the Fund [Section 10 (3)].

1.8.11 Priority of Payment of Contributions over Other Debts [Section 11]

(1) Where any employer is adjudicated insolvent or, being a Company, an order for winding up is made, the amount due –

(a) from the employer in relation to establishment to which any Scheme or the Insurance Scheme applies in respect of any contribution payable to the Fund or, as the case may be, the Insurance Fund damages recoverable under section 14-B, accumulations required to be transferred under sub- section (2) of section 15 or any charges payable by him under any other provision of this Act or of any provision of the Scheme or the Insurance Scheme; or

(b) from the employer in relation to an exempted "establishment in respect of any contribution to the Provident Fund or any insurance fund (in so far as it relates to exempted employees), under the rules of the Provident Fund or any insurance fund, any contribution payable by him towards the 'Pension Fund under sub-section (6) of section 17, damages recoverable under section 14-B or any charges payable by him to the appropriate Government under any provision of this Act or under any of the condition specified under section 17, shall, where the liability therefore has accrued before the order of adjudication or winding up is made, be deemed to be included among the debts which under section 49 of the Presidency Towns Insolvency Act, 1909 (3 of 1909, 1 or under section 61 of the Provincial Insolvency Act, 1920 (5 of 1920) or under 61 section 530 of the Companies Act, 1956 (1 of 1956), are to be paid in priority to all other debts in the distribution of the property of the insolvent or the assets of the company being wound up, as the case may be [Section 11 (1)].

In this sub-section and in section 17, "Insurance Fund" means any fund established by an employer under any Scheme for providing benefits in the nature of life insurance to employees, whether linked to their deposits in Provident Fund or not, without payment by the employees of any separate contribution or premium in that behalf [Explanation to Section 11 (1)].

(2) Without prejudice to the provisions of sub-section (1) of Section 11, if any amount is due from an employer 3, whether in respect of the employee's contribution (deducted from the wages of the employee) or the employer's contribution, the amount so due shall be deemed to be the first charge an the assets of the establishment, and shall, notwithstanding anything contained in any other law for the time being in force, be paid in priority to all other debts [Section 11 (2)].

1.8.12 Employer not to Reduce Wages, etc.

"No employer in relation to an establishment to which any scheme or Insurance Scheme applies shall, by reason only of his liability for the payment of any contribution to the Fund or the Insurance Fund or any charges under this Act or the Scheme or the Insurance Scheme reduce whether directly or indirectly, the wages of any employee to whom the Scheme or the Insurance Scheme applies or the total quantum of benefits in the nature of old age pension, gratuity, provident fund or Life Insurance to which the employee is entitled under the terms of his employment, express or implied. [Section 12].

1.9 Appointments and Powers of the Inspectors Appointed under this Act [Section 13]

[1] Appointment of the Inspectors under this Act:

The appropriate Government is empowered to appoint the inspectors by giving them certain powers for the purpose of this Act, schemes and also to define their jurisdiction. It is stated in Section 13 (1) of the Act which is related to the appointment of the Inspectors that, "The appropriate Government may, by notification in the Official Gazette, appoint such persons as it thinks fit to be Inspectors for the purposes of this Act, the Scheme, the Pension Scheme or the Insurance Scheme and may define their jurisdiction".

[II] Powers of the Inspectors appointed under this Act [Section 13 (2)]:

(1) "Any Inspector appointed under sub-section (1) of Section 13 may, for the purpose of inquiring into the correctness of any information furnished in connection with this Act or with any Scheme or the Insurance Scheme or for the purpose of ascertaining whether any of the provisions of this Act or of any Scheme or the Insurance Scheme have been complied with in respect of an establishment to which any scheme or the Insurance Scheme applies or for the purpose of ascertaining whether the provisions of this Act or any Scheme or the Insurance Scheme are applicable to any establishment to which the Scheme or the Insurance Scheme has not been applied or for the purpose of determining whether the conditions subject to which exemption was granted under section 17 are being complied with by employer in relation to an exempted establishment given as follows.

(a) require an employer or any contractor from whom any amount is recoverable under Section 8-A to furnish such information as he may consider necessary,

(b) at any reasonable time and with such assistance, if any, as he may think fit, enter and search any establishment or any premises connected therewith and require any one found in charge thereof to produce before him for examination any accounts, books, registers and other documents relating to the employment of persons or the payment of wages in the establishment;

(c) examine, with respect to any matter relevant to any of the purposes aforesaid, the employer or any contractor from whom any amount is recoverable under section 8-A, his agent or servant or any other person found incharge of the establishment or any premises connected therewith or whom the Inspector has reasonable cause to believe to be or have been an employee in the establishment;

(d) make copies of, or take extracts from, any book, register or other document maintained in relation to the establishment and, where he has reason to believe that any offence under this Act has been committed by an employer, seize with such assistance as he may think fit, such book, register or other document or portions thereof as he may consider relevant in respect of that offence;

(e) exercise of such other powers as the Scheme or the Insurance Scheme may provide [Section 13 (2)].

(2) Any Inspector appointed under sub-section (1) of Section 13 may, for the purpose of inquiring into the correctness of any information furnished in connection with the Pension Scheme or for the purpose of ascertaining whether any of the provisions of this Act or of the Pension Scheme have been complied with in respect of an establishment to which the Pension Scheme applies, exercise all or any of the powers conferred on him under clause (a), clause (b), clause (c) or clause (d) of sub-section (2) [Section 13 (2-A)].

(3) The provision of the Code of Criminal Procedure, 1898 (5 of 1898) shall, so far as may be, apply to any search or seizure under sub-section (2) or under sub-section (2A), as the case may be, as they apply to any search, or seizure made under the authority of a warrant issued under section 98 of the said Code [Section 13 (2-B)].

1.10 Penalties and Offences [Section 14]

For the contravention of the provisions of the Act by an employer or by any other person, stringent penal provisions have been made in Section 14. The provisions of Section 14 relating to penalties are given below:

(1) Whoever, for the purpose of avoiding any payment to be made by himself under this Act, the Scheme the Pension Scheme or the Insurance Scheme or of enabling any other person to avoid such payment, knowingly makes or causes to be made any false statement or false representation shall be punishable with imprisonment for a term which may extend to one year, or with fine of five thousand rupees, or with both [Section 14 (1)].

(2) An employer who contravenes, or makes default in complying with, the provisions of section 6 or clause (a) of sub- section (3) of section 17 in so far as it relates to the payment of inspection charges, or paragraph 38 of the Scheme in so far as it relates to the payment of administrative charges, shall be punishable with imprisonment for a term which may extend to three years but –

- (a) which shall not be less than one year and a fine of ten thousand rupees in case of default in payment of the employees contributions which has been deducted by the employer from the employees' wages;
- (b) which shall not be less than six months and a fine of five thousand rupees in any other case [Section 14 (1-A)].

It is also provided that the Court may, for any adequate and special reasons to be recorded in the judgement, impose a sentence of imprisonment for a lesser term [Proviso to Section 14 (1-A)].

(3) An employer who contravenes, or makes default in complying with the provisions of section 6-C, or clause (a) of sub-section (3-A) of section 17 in so far as it relates to the payment of inspection charges, shall be punishable with imprisonment for a term which may extend to one year but which shall not be less than six months and shall also be liable to fine which may extend to Five thousand rupees [Section 14-(1-B)].

It is provided that the Court may, for any adequate and special reasons to be recorded in the judgement, impose a sentence of imprisonment for a lesser term [Proviso to Section 14 (1-B)].

(4) Subject to the provisions of this Act, the Scheme, the Pension Scheme or the Insurance Scheme may provide that any person who contravenes, or makes default in complying with, any of the provisions thereof shall be punishable with imprisonment for a term which may extend to one year, or with fine which may extend to four thousand rupees, or with both [Section 14 (2)].

(5) Whoever contravenes or makes default in complying with any provision of this Act or of any condition subject to which exemption was granted under section 17 shall, if no other penalty is elsewhere provided by or under this Act for such contravention or non-compliance, be punishable with imprisonment which may extend to six months, but which shall not be less than one month, and shall also be liable to fine which may extend to five thousand rupees [Section 14 (2-A)].

1.10.1 Offences by Companies [Section 14-A]

(1) "If the person committing an offence under this Act, the Scheme or, the Pension Scheme or the Insurance Scheme is a company, every person, who at the time the offence was committed was in charge of, and was responsible to, the company for the conduct of the business of the Company, as well as the company, shall be deemed to be guilty of the offence and shall be liable to be proceeded against and punished accordingly [Section 14-A (1)].

It is provided that nothing contained in this sub-section shall render any such person liable to any punishment, if he proves that the offence was committed without his knowledge or that he exercised all due diligence to prevent the commission of such offence [Proviso to Section 14-A (1)].

(2) Notwithstanding anything contained in sub-section (1) of Section 14-A, where an offence under this Act, the Scheme or the Pension Scheme or the Insurance Scheme has been committed by a company and it is proved that the offence has been committed with the consent or connivance of, or is attributable to, any neglect on the part of, any director or manager, secretary or other officer of the company, such director, manager, secretary or other officer shall be deemed to be guilty of that offence and shall be liable to be proceeded against and punished accordingly [Section 14-A (2)].

For the purposes of this section –
- (i) "company" means any body corporate and includes a firm and other association of individuals; and
- (b) "director" in relation to a firm, means a partner in the firm [Explanation to Section 14-A (2)].

1.10.2 Enhanced Punishment in Certain Cases after Previous Conviction

Whoever, having been convicted by a Court of an offence punishable under this Act, the Scheme or, the Pension Scheme or the Insurance Scheme, commits the same offence shall be subject for every such subsequent offence to imprisonment for a term which may extend to five years, but which shall not be less than two years, and shall also be liable to a fine of twenty-five thousand rupees [Section 14-AA].

1.10.3 Certain Offences to be Cognizable

Notwithstanding anything contained in the Code of Criminal Procedure, 1898 (5 of 1898) an offence relating to default in payment of contribution by the employer punishable under this Act shall be cognizable [Section 14-AB].

1.10.4 Cognizance and Trial of Offences

(1) No court shall take cognizance of any offence punishable under this Act, the Scheme, or the 'Pension Scheme or the Insurance Scheme, except on a report in writing of the facts constituting such offence made with the previous sanction of the Central Provident Fund Commissioner or such other officer as may be authorised by the Central Government, by notification in the Official Gazette, in this behalf, by an Inspector appointed under Section 13" [Section 14 (AC) (1)].

(2) "No court inferior to that of a Presidency Magistrate or a Magistrate of the first class shall try any offence under this Act or the Scheme or, the Pension Scheme or the Insurance Scheme" [Section 14 (AC) (2)].

1.10.5 Power to Recover Damages

(1) Where an employer makes default in the payment of any contribution to the Fund, the Pension Fund or the Insurance Fund or in the transfer of accumulations required to be transferred by him under sub-section (2) of section 15 or sub-section (5) of section 17 or in the payment of any charges payable under any other provision of this Act or of any Scheme or Insurance Scheme or under any of the conditions specified under section 17, the Central Provident Fund Commissioner or such other officer as may be authorised by the Central Government, by notification in the Official Gazette, in this behalf may recover from the employer (by way of penalty) such damages, not exceeding the amount of arrears, as may be specified in the scheme [Section 14-B].

"It is provided that before levying and recovering such damages, the employer shall be given a reasonable opportunity of being heard" [Proviso to Section 14-B].

It is further provided that the Central Board may reduce or waive the damages levied under this section in relation to an establishment which is a sick industrial company and in respect of which a scheme for rehabilitation has been sanctioned by the Board for Industrial and Financial Reconstruction established under section 4 of the Sick Industrial Companies (Special Provisions) Act, 1985, (I of 1986) subject to such terms and condition as may be specified in the Scheme [Proviso 2 to Section 14-B].

1.10.6 Power of Court to Make Orders

(1) Where an employer is convicted of an offence of making default in the payment of any contribution to the Fund, the Pension Fund or the Insurance Fund or in the transfer of accumulations required to be transferred by him under sub-section (2) of section 15 or sub- section (5) of section 17, the court may, in addition to awarding any punishment, by order in writing require him within a period specified in the order (which the court may, if it thinks fit and on application in that behalf, from time to time, extend), to pay the amount of contribution or transfer the accumulations, as the case may be, in respect of which the offence was committed [Section 14-C (1)].

(2) Where an order is made under sub-section (1) of Section 14-C, the employer shall not be liable under this Act in respect of the continuation of the offence during the period or extended period, if any, allowed by the court, but if, on the expiry of such period or extended period, as the case may be, the order of the Court has not been fully complied with, the employer shall be deemed to have committed a further offence and shall be punished with imprisonment in respect thereof under section 14 and shall also be liable to pay fine which may extend to one hundred rupees for every day after such expiry on which the order has not been complied with" [Section 14-C (2)].

1.11 Other Miscellaneous Provisions of the Act [Sections 15, 16, 17, 18, 19, 20, 21 and 22]

1.11.1 Special Provisions Relating to Existing Provident Funds

(1) Subject to the provisions of Section 17, every employee who is a subscriber to any Provident Fund of an establishment to which this Act applies shall, pending the application

of a Scheme to the establishment in which he is employed, continue to be entitled to the benefits accruing to him under the Provident Fund, and the Provident Fund shall continue to be maintained in the same manner and subject to the same conditions as it would have been if this Act had not been passed [Section 15 (1)].

(2) On the application of any scheme to an establishment, the accumulations in any Provident Fund of the establishment, standing to the credit of the employees who become members of the Fund established under the Scheme shall, notwithstanding anything to the contrary contained in any law for the time being in force or in any deed or other instrument establishing the Provident Fund but subject to the provisions, if any, contained in the Scheme, be transferred to the fund established under the Scheme, and shall be credited to the accounts of the employees entitled thereto in the Fund [Section 15 (2)].

1.11.2 Act not to Apply to Certain Establishments

(1) This Act shall not apply –
   (a) to any establishment registered under the Co-operative Societies Act, 1912 (2 of 1912), or under any other law for the time being in force in any State relating to co-operative societies, employing less than fifty persons and working without the aid of power; or
   (b) to any other establishment belonging to or under the control of the Central Government or a State Government and whose employees are entitled to the benefit of contributory provident fund or old age pension in accordance with any Scheme or rule framed by the Central Government or the State Government governing such benefits; or
   (c) to any other establishment set up under any Central, Provincial or State Act and whose employees are entitled to the benefits of contributory provident fund or old age pension in accordance with any scheme or rule framed under that Act governing such benefits [Section 16 (1)].

(2) If the Central Government is of opinion that having regard to the financial position of any class of establishments or other circumstances of the case, it is necessary or expedient so to do, it may, by notification in the Official Gazette, and subject to such conditions, as may be specified in the notification, exempt, whether prospectively or retrospectively, that class of establishments from the operation of this Act for such period as may be specified in the notification [Section 16 (2)].

1.11.3 Authorising Certain Employers to Maintain Provident Fund Accounts

(1) The Central Government may, on an application made to it in this behalf by the employer and the majority of employees in relation to an establishment employing one hundred or more persons, authorise the employer, by an order in writing, to maintain a provident fund account in relation to the establishment, subject to such terms and conditions as may be specified in the Scheme [Section 16-A (1)].

It is provided that, "No authorisation shall be made under this sub-section if the employer of such establishment had committed any default in the payment of provident fund contribution or had committed any other offence under this Act during the three years immediately preceding the date of such authorisation" [Proviso to Section 16-A (1)].

(2) "Where an establishment is authorised to maintain a Provident Fund account under sub-section (1) of Section 16, the employer in relation to such establishment shall maintain such account, submit such return, deposit the contribution in such manner, provide for such facilities for inspection, pay such administrative charges, and abide by such other terms and conditions, as may be specified in the Scheme" [Section 16 (2)].

(3) "Any authorisation made under this section may be cancelled by the Central Government by order in writing if the employer fails to comply with any of the terms and conditions of the authorisation or where he commits any offence under any provision of this Act" [Section 16 (3)].

"It is also provided that before cancelling the authorisation, the Central Government shall give the employer a reasonable opportunity of being heard" [Proviso to Section 16 (3)].

1.11.4 Power to Exempt

(1) The appropriate Government may by notification in the Official Gazette, and subject to such conditions as may be specified in the notification, exempt, whether prospectively or retrospectively, from the operation of all or any of the provisions of any Scheme –

    (a) any establishment to which this Act applies if, in the opinion of the appropriate Government, the rules of its Provident Fund with respect to the rates of contribution are not less favourable than those specified in section 6 and the employees are also in enjoyment of other Provident Fund benefits which on the whole are not less favourable to the employees than the benefits, provided under this Act or any Scheme- in relation to the employees in any other establishment of a similar character; or

    (b) any establishment if the employees of such establishment are in enjoyment of benefits in the nature of Provident Fund, pension or gratuity and the appropriate government is of opinion that such benefits, separately or jointly, are on the whole not less favourable to such employees than the benefits provided under this Act or any Scheme in relation to employees in any other establishment of a similar character [Section 17 (1)].

It is also provided that no such exemption shall be made except after consultation with the Central Board which on such consultation shall forward its views on exemption to the appropriate Government within such time limit as may be specified in the Scheme" [Proviso to Section 17 (1)].

(2) "Where an exemption has been granted to an establishment under clause (a) of sub-section (1), of Section 17 –

    (a) the provisions of sections 6, 7, 8 and 14-B shall, so far as may be, apply to the employer of the exempted establishment in addition to such other conditions as may be specified in the notification granting such exemption, and where such employer contravenes, or makes default in complying with any of the said provisions or conditions or any other provisions of this Act, he shall be punishable under section 14 as if the said establishment had not been exempted under the said clause (a);

(b) the employer shall establish a Board of Trustees for the administration of the Provident Fund consisting of such number of members as may be specified in the Scheme;

(c) the terms and conditions of service of members of the Board of Trustees shall be such as may be specified in the Scheme;

(d) the Board of Trustees constituted under clause (b) shall –
   (i) maintain detailed accounts to show the contributions credited, withdrawals made and interest accrued in respect of each employee;
   (ii) submit such returns to the Regional Provident Fund Commissioner or any other officer as the Central Government may direct from time to time;
   (iii) invest the Provident Fund monies in accordance with the directions issued by the Central Government from time to time;
   (iv) transfer, where necessary, the Provident Fund account of any employee; and
   (v) perform such other duties as may be specified in the Scheme [Section 17 (1-A)].

(3) "Where the Board of Trustees established under clause (b) of sub-section (1-A) contravenes, or makes default in complying with, any provisions of clause (d) of that sub-section, the Trustees of the said Board shall be deemed to have committed an offence under sub-section (2-A) of Section 14 and shall be punishable with the penalties provided in that sub-section" [Section 17 (1-b)].

(4) "The appropriate Government may, by notification in the Official Gazette, and subject to the condition on the pattern of investment of Pension Fund and such other conditions as may be specified therein, exempt any establishment or class of establishments from the operation of the Pension Scheme, if the employees of such establishment or class of establishments are either members of any other Pension Scheme or propose to be members of such Pension Scheme, where the pensionary benefits are at par or more favourable than the Pension Scheme under this Act" [Section 17 (1-C)].

(5) "Any Scheme may make provision for exemption of any person or class of persons employed in any establishment to which the Scheme applies from the operation of all or any of the provisions of the Scheme, if such person or class of persons is entitled to benefits in the nature of provident fund, gratuity or old age pension and such benefits, separately or jointly, are on the whole not less favourable than the benefits provided under this Act or the Scheme" [Section 17 (2)].

It is provided that, "No such exemption shall be granted in respect of a class of persons unless the appropriate Government is of opinion that the majority of persons constituting such class desire to continue to be entitled to such benefits" [Proviso to Section 17 (2)].

(6) "The Central Provident Fund Commissioner may, if requested so to do by the employer, by notification in the Official Gazette, and subject to such conditions as may be specified in the notification, exempt whether prospectively or retrospectively, any establishment from the operation of all or any of the provisions of the Insurance Scheme, if he is satisfied that the employees of such establishment are, without making any separate contribution or payment of premium, in enjoyment of benefits in the nature of life insurance, whether linked to their deposits in Provident Fund or not, and such benefits are more favourable to such employees than the benefits admissible under the Insurance Scheme" [Section 17 (2-A)].

(7) "Without prejudice to the provisions of sub-section (2-A) of Section 17, the Insurance Scheme may provide for the exemption of any person or class of persons employed in any establishment and covered by that scheme from the operation of all or any of the provisions thereof, if the benefits in the nature of life insurance admissible to such person or class of persons are more favourable than the benefits provided under the Insurance Scheme" [Section 17 (2-B)].

(8) Where in respect of any person or class of persons employed in an establishment an exemption is granted under this section from the operation of all or any of the provisions of any Scheme (whether such exemption has been granted to the establishment wherein such person or class of persons employed, or to the person or class or persons as such), the employer in relation to such establishment –

    (a)   shall, in relation to the provident fund, pension and gratuity to which; any such period or class of persons is entitled maintain such accounts, submit such returns, make such investment, provide for such facilities for inspection and pay such inspection charges, as the Central Government may direct;

    (b)   shall not, at any time after the exemption, without the leave of the Central Government, reduce the total quantum of benefits in the nature of pension, gratuity or provident fund to which any such person or class of persons was entitled at the time of the exemption; and

    (c)   shall, where any such person leaves his employment and obtains re-employment in another establishment to which this Act applies, transfer within such time as may be specified in this behalf by the Central Government, the amount of accumulations to the credit to that person's account in the Provident Fund of the establishment in which he is re-employed or, as the case may be, in the fund establishment under the Scheme applicable to the establishment" [Section 17 (3)].

(9) "Where, in respect of any person or class of persons employed in any establishment, an exemption is granted under sub-section (2-A) or subsection (2-B) of Section 17 from the operation of all or any of the provisions of the Insurance Scheme (whether such exemption is granted to the establishment wherein such person or class of persons is employed or to the person or class of persons as such), the employer in relation to such establishment –

    (a)   shall, in relation to the benefits in the nature of life insurance, to which any such person or class of persons is entitled, or any insurance fund, maintain such accounts, submit such returns, make such investments, provide for such facilities for inspection and pay such inspection charges, as the Central Government may direct;

(b) shall not, at any time after the exemption without the leave of the Central Government, reduce the total quantum of benefits in the nature of life insurance to which any such person or class of persons was entitled immediately before the date of the exemption [Section 17 (3-A)].

(10) Ground for cancellation of exemption

"Any exemption granted under this section may be cancelled by the authority which granted it, by order in writing, if an employer fails to comply –

- (a) in the case of an exemption granted under sub-section (1), with any of the conditions imposed under that subsection or sub-section (1-A) or with any of the provisions of sub-section (3); (Section 17);
- (aa) in the case of an exemption granted under sub-section (1-C) with any of the conditions imposed under that subsection; and
- (b) in the case of an exemption granted under sub-section (2), with any of the provisions of sub-section (3) of Section 17;
- (c) in the case of an exemption granted under sub-section (2-A), with any of the conditions imposed under that sub-section or with any of the provisions of sub-section (3-A) of Section 17;
- (d) in the case of an exemption granted under sub-section (2-B) with any of the provisions of sub-section (3-A) of Section 17" [Section 17 (4)].

(11) "Where any exemption granted under sub-section (1), sub-section (1-C) sub-section (2), sub-section(2-A) or sub-section (2-B) of Section 17 is cancelled, the amount of accumulations to the credit of every employee to whom such exemption applied, in the Provident Fund, the Pension Fund or the Insurance Fund of the establishment in which he is employed together with any amount forfeited from the employer's share of contribution to the credit of the employee who leaves the employment before the completion of the full period of service shall, be transferred within such time and in such manner as may be specified in the Scheme or the Pension Scheme or the Insurance Scheme to the Credit of his account in the Fund or the Pension Fund or the Insurance Fund, as the case may be [Section 17 (5)].

(12) Subject to the provisions of sub-section (1-C), the employer of an exempted establishment or of an exempted employee of an establishment to which the provisions of the Pension Scheme apply shall, notwithstanding any exemption granted under sub-section (1) or subsection (2) of Section 7, pay to the Pension Fund such portion of the employer's contribution to its Provident Fund within such time and in such manner as may be specified in the Pension Scheme [Section 17].

1.11.5 Transfer of Accounts

(1) "Where an employee employed in an establishment to which this Act applies leaves his employment and obtains re-employment in another establishment to which this Act does not apply, the amount of accumulations to the credit of such employee in the Fund, or as the case may be, in the Provident Fund of the establishment left by him shall be transferred, within such time as may be specified by the Central Government in this behalf,

to the credit of his account in the Provident Fund of the establishment in which he is re-employed, if the employee so desires and the rules in relation to that Provident Fund permit such transfer" [Section 17-A (1)].

(2) "Where an employee employed in an establishment to which this Act does not apply leaves his employment and obtains re-employment in another establishment to which this Act applies, the amount of accumulations to the credit of such employee in the Provident Fund of the establishment left by him may, if the employee so desires and the rules in relation to such provident fund permit, be transferred to the credit of his account in tile Fund or, as the case may be, in the Provident Fund of the establishment in which is re-employed" [Section 17-A (2)].

1.11.6 Act to Have Effect Notwithstanding Anything Contained in Act 31 of 1956

The provisions of this Act shall have effect notwithstanding anything inconsistent therewith contained in the Life Insurance Corporation Act, 1956 (31 of 1956). [Section 17 A-A].

1.11.7 Liability in Case of Transfer of Establishment

"Where an employer, in relation to an establishment, transfers that establishment in whole or in part, by sale, gift, lease or license or in any other manner whatsoever, the employer and the person to whom the establishment is so transferred shall jointly and severally be liable to pay the contribution and other sums due from the employer under any provision of this Act or the Scheme or the Pension Scheme or the Insurance Scheme as the case may be, in respect of the period up to the date of such transfer" [Section 17-B]

It is provided that the liability of the transferee shall be limited to the value of the assets obtained by him by such transfer [Proviso to Section 17-B].

1.11.8 Protection of Action taken in Good Faith

"No suit, prosecution or other legal proceeding shall lie against the Central Government, a State Government, the Presiding Officer of a Tribunal, any authority referred to in section 7-A, an Inspector or any other person for anything which is in good faith done or intended to be done in pursuance of this Act, the Scheme, the Pension scheme or the Insurance scheme" [Section 18].

1.11.9 Presiding Officer and Other Officers to be Public Servants

"The Presiding Officer of a Tribunal, its officers and other employees the authorities referred to in Section 7-A and every Inspector shall be deemed to be public servants within the meaning of Section 21 of the Indian Penal Code (45 of 1860)" [Section 18-A].

1.11.10 Delegation of Powers

The appropriate Government may direct that any power or authority or jurisdiction exercisable by it under this Act, the Scheme, the Pension Scheme or the Insurance Scheme shall, in relation to such matters and subject to such conditions, if any, as may be specified in the direction, be exercisable also –

(a) where the appropriate Government is the Central Government, by such officer or authority subordinate to the Central Government or by the State Government, or by such officer or authority subordinate to the State Government, as may be specified in the notification; and

(b) where the appropriate Government is a State Government, by such officer or authority subordinate to the State Government as may be specified in the notification [Section 19].

1.11.11 Power of Central Government to give directions

"The Central Government may, from time to time, give such directions to the Central Board as it may think fit for the efficient administration of this Act and when any such direction is given, the Central Board shall comply with such direction" [Section 20].

1.11.12 Power to Make Rules

(1) The Central Government may, by notification in the Official Gazette, make rules to carry out the provisions of this Act [Section 21 (1)].

(2) Without prejudice to the generality of the foregoing power, such rules may provide for all or any of the following matters, namely –

(a) "the salary and allowances and other terms and conditions of service of the Presiding Officer and the employees of a Tribunal;

(b) the form and the manner in which, and the time within which, an appeal shall be filed before a Tribunal and the fees payable for filing such appeal;

(c) the manner of certifying the copy of the certificate to be forwarded to the Recovery Officer under sub-section (2) of section 8-C; and

(d) any other matter, which has to be, or may be, prescribed by rules under this Act" [Section 21 (2)].

(3) "Every rule made under this Act shall be laid, as soon as may be after it is made, before each House of Parliament, while it is in session, for a total period of thirty days which may be comprised in one session or in two or more successive sessions, and if, before the expiry of the session immediately following the session or the successive sessions aforesaid, both Houses agree in making any modification in the rule or both Houses agree that the rule should not be made, the rule shall thereafter have effect only in such modified form or be of no effect, as the case may be, so, however, that any such modification or annulment shall be without prejudice to the validity of anything previously done under that rule" [Section 21 (3)].

1.11.13 Power to remove difficulties

(1) If any difficulty arises in giving effect to the provisions of this Act, as amended by the Employees Provident Funds and Miscellaneous Provisions (Amendment) Act, 1988, the Central Government may, by order published in the Official Gazette, make such provisions, not inconsistent with the provisions of this Act, as appear to it to be necessary or expedient for the removal of the difficulty" [Section 21 (1)].

It is provided that, "no such order shall be made after the expiry of a period of three years from the date on which the said Amendment Act receives the assent of the President" [Proviso to Section 22 (1)].

(2) "Every order made under this section shall, as soon as may be after it is made, be laid before each House of Parliament" [Section 22 (2)].

Questions For Discussion

1. Explain the object and scope of the EPF Act.
2. To whom is the EPF Act applicable? In what manner can the Central Government apply the provisions of the Act to other establishments?
3. What is 'Base Wage' under this Act? State what are specifically exempted from basic wages under this Act?
4. Define the following terms as used in the EPF Act.
   (a) Employee, (b) Exempted Employee and Establishment, (c) Manufacturing Process, (d) Controlled Industry.
5. Which establishments may be exempted from the operation of the EPF Act, 1952?
6. Who is 'Employer' EPF Act, 1952? Explain the powers and duties of the employer under this Act.
7. Explain the provisions of Section 16 of the Act. Does this Act cease to apply if at any time the number of employees in an establishment to which this Act applies falls below twenty?
8. Explain the provisions of the Act relating to the Constitution of Employees' Provident Fund Scheme and Pension Scheme.
9. Explain fully the provisions relating to the Employees' Deposit-Linked Insurance Scheme.
10. State the rules for recovery of money under the Employees' Deposit-Linked Insurance Scheme.
11. State the rules as to the payment and recovery of contributions by an employer.
12. Explain the modes of recovery of moneys due from employees under the EPF Act of 1952.
13. What is 'Employees' Provident Fund'? How is the Fund created? Explain the benefits of the fund.
14. What is 'Pension Fund'? State the rules relating to the contribution of the Pension Fund.
15. State the rules relating to 'Exempted Establishment'.
16. Explain the provisions of EPF Act relating to the protection of Provident Fund money against attachment.
17. Is an employer empowered to reduce wages of his employees by reason of their liability for the payment of any contribution to the Provident Fund?
18. Explain the provisions of the Act relating to the appointment, functions and powers of the inspectors appointed under EPF Act of 1952.
19. Explain the provisions of the Act relating to the penalties to be imposed for various offences.
20. Write notes on the following:
    (a) Various offences and penalties under the Act
    (b) Priority of payment of contribution over debts
    (c) Employees' Provident Fund Scheme
    (d) Employees' Pension Scheme
    (e) Employees' Deposit-Linked Insurance Scheme
    (f) Administration of Schemes
    (g) Constitution of functions of Central Board.

***

Chapter 2...

The Employees' State Insurance Act, 1948

Contents ...

2.1 Applicability and Main Object of the Employees' State Insurance Act, 1948
2.2 Exemptions
2.3 Definitions
2.4 The Employees' State Insurance Corporation
2.5 Employees' State Insurance Fund
2.6 Contributions
2.7 Various Benefits under the Act
2.8 Important Duties of an Employer under this Act
2.9 Constitution of Employees' Insurance Court
2.10 Penalties
2.11 Miscellaneous Provisions of the Act
• Questions for Discussion

There is a network of laws or Acts in India which provide social security for workers to whom those laws are applicable. These Acts include:
(a) The Workmen's Compensation Act of 1923;
(b) The Employees' State Insurance Act of 1948;
(c) The Employees' Provident Fund and Miscellaneous Provisions Act of 1952;
(d) The Maternity Benefit Act of 1961; and
(e) The Payment of Gratuity Act of 1972.

The above mentioned Acts provide for various social security schemes in Modern India. As the directive principles of the State Policy as embodied in the Constitution of India lay special stress on the goal of a Welfare State, the States have been directed to follow certain principles which are essential to secure a social order for the promotion of the welfare of Indians.

Considering this, various Acts have been passed and the Employees' State Insurance Act of 1948 is one of them which had been passed. It came into existence on 19th April 1948. This Act mainly provides certain benefits to the employees of various establishments in case of sickness, maternity, employment, injuries etc. and also makes provisions for certain other matters in relation thereto.

The Employees' State Insurance Act of 1948 is the first Act of its kind passed in 1948. It has been passed to introduce a compulsory integrated system of social insurance covering health, maternity, accident and certain other benefits. The administration of the Insurance Scheme framed under this Act has been entrusted to an autonomous body known as "The Employees' State Insurance Corporation". In Chapter II of the Act [Sections from 3 to 25], we find the provisions relating to the establishment of the Employees' State Insurance Corporation, its constitution, constitution of Medical Benefit Council, Standing Committee etc.

The important benefits which have been provided under this Act are as follows:
1. Sickness benefit;
2. Maternity benefit;
3. Disablement benefit;
4. Dependent's benefit; and
5. Medical benefit.

Out of the above mentioned five benefits, the first four benefits are paid in cash. But so far as medical benefit is concerned, it is not paid in cash. An insured person or where such medical benefit is extended, his family, a member of his family whose condition requires a medical treatment and attendance, is entitled to receive medical benefit under this insurance scheme. But such medical treatment is given either in the form of out-patient treatment and attendance in a hospital or dispensary, clinic or other institutions or by visit to the home of the insured person or treatment as in-patient in a hospital or other institutions [Section 58 (1) & (2)].

Besides these benefits, the Act has also provided for funeral expenses not exceeding one thousand five hundred rupees. Previously, the amount of funeral expenses prescribed was ₹ 1000. But this limit has been increased to ₹ 1500 with effect from 16th November 1996.

There are certain difficulties in extending these schemes of insurance over a wide area. The practical difficulty in implementing the scheme has been the shortage of medical personnel and difficulty in finding suitable accommodation in hospitals or dispensaries. However, it is considered as the best effort to provide covering sickness, maternity, disablement, dependents' and medical benefits.

Now let us consider various provisions of the Employees' State Insurance Act of 1948 to get a better idea about the insurance scheme and other related matter. But before that, let us try to know the applicability of the Act provisions relating to exemption and definitions of terms, words concepts etc. as given in Section 2 of the Act.

2.1 Applicability and Main Object of the Employees' State Insurance Act, 1948

2.1.1 Short Title, Extent, Commencement and Application

Section 1 of the Act throws light on the extent application etc. of the Act. It states that,

"(1) This Act may be called the Employees' State Insurance Act, 1948 [Section 1 (1)].

(2) It extends to the whole of India [Section 1 (2)].

(3) It shall come into force on such date or dates as the Central Government may, by notification in the Official Gazette, appoint, and different dates may be appointed for different provisions of this Act or different States or for different part thereof [Section 1 (3)].

(4) It shall apply, in the first instance, to all factories, (including factories belonging to the Government) other than seasonal factories [Section 1 (4)].

It is provided that nothing contained in this sub-section shall apply to a factory or establishment belonging to or under the control of the Government whose employees are otherwise in receipt of benefits substantially similar or superior to the benefits provided under this Act [Proviso to Section 1 (4)].

(5) The appropriate Government may, in consultation with the Corporation and where the appropriate Government is a State Government, with the approval of the Central Government, after giving six months notice of its intention of doing so by notification in the Official Gazette, extend the provisions of this Act or any of them, to any other establishment or class of establishment, industrial, commercial, agricultural or otherwise [Section 1 (5)].

It is provided that where the provisions of this Act have been brought into force in any part of the State, the said provisions shall stand extended to any such establishment or class of establishments within that part if the provisions have already been extended to similar establishment or class of establishments in another part of that State. [Proviso to Section 1 (5)].

(6) A factory or an establishment to which this Act applies shall continue to be governed by this Act, notwithstanding that the number of persons employed therein at any time, falls below the limit specified by or under this Act or the manufacturing process therein ceases to be carried on with the aid of power [Section 1 (6)].

Following are the important points which become clear from the provisions of Section 1 reproduced above.

(a) This Act extends to the whole of India. In the beginning, it was extended to the whole of India except Jammu and Kashmir. But, later on it was extended to Jammu and Kashmir by the Central Labour Laws [Extension to Jammu and Kashmir) Act, 1970. Thus, at present this Act applies to all factories, including factories belonging to the Government, other than seasonal factories. However, provisions of Section 1 (4) are not applicable to a factory or establishment belonging to or under the control of the Government, whose employees are otherwise in receipt of the benefits substantially similar or superior to the benefits available under this Act.

(b) The appropriate Government, in consultation with the Employees' State Insurance Corporation which is constituted under Section 3 of this Act and where the appropriate Government is the State Government, with the approval of the Central Government, may extend the provisions of this Act, or any of them, to any establishment or class of establishments, may it be commercial, industrial, agricultural or otherwise. However, before extending the Act to these establishments, the appropriate Government has to give six months notice of its intention to do so by notifying the same in the Official Gazette.

(c) It has been made also clear that where the provisions of this Act have been brought into force in any part of any State, these provisions stand extended to the establishments to which this Act has been made applicable. The important point in this context is that a factory or any establishment to which this Act applies shall continue to apply, notwithstanding that the number of persons employed therein at any time falls below the limit specified by or under this Act or the manufacturing process therein ceases to be carried on with the help of power.

2.1.2 Main Objectives of the Act

This Act is a piece of social security legislation and is a landmark for compulsion of social security in India. It provides for compulsory State Insurance to the employees of organisations to which this Act is applicable and makes available certain benefits such as sickness benefit, maternity benefit, disablement benefit and medical benefits. However, these benefits are secured by financial contributions to the scheme, both by employers as well as employees. The main objective of the Act is to introduce social insurance by providing for these benefits to the employees covered by this Act and also for certain other matters in relation thereto. It should also be noted that the scope of coverage under this Act is much wider, than under the Workmen's Compensation Act of 1923.

The Act has been amended many times. The recent amendment has been made in Nov. 1996. The main aims of amending the Act are to extend the provisions of this Act to more factories and establishments to makes its base broad and also to make the existing penal provisions more stringent.

2.2 Exemptions

The appropriate Government is empowered to exempt any factory or establishment, class of factories or class of establishments or any person or class of persons by notification in the Official Gazette and subject to such conditions as may be prescribed from the operation of the provisions of this Act. Provisions relating to such exemption have been made in Sections 87, 88, 89, 90, 91, and 91A of Chapter VIII (Miscellaneous) of this Act. These sections are as under:

Section 87 Exemption of a factory or establishment or class of factories or establishments:

The appropriate Government may, by notification in the Official Gazette and subject to such conditions as may be specified in the notification, exempt any factory or establishment or class of factories or establishments in any specified area from the operation of this Act for a period, not exceeding one year and may from time to time by like notification, renew any such exemption for periods not exceeding one year at a time.

Section 88 Exemption of persons or class of persons:

The appropriate Government may, by notification in the Official Gazette and subject to such conditions as it may deem fit to impose, exempt any persons or class of persons employed in any factory or establishment or class of factories or establishments to which this Act applies from the operation of the Act.

Section 89 Corporation to make representation:

No exemption shall be granted or renewed under Section 87 or Section 88, unless a reasonable opportunity has been given to the Corporation to make any representation it may wish to make in regard to the proposal and such representation has been considered by the appropriate Government.

Section 90 Exemption of factories or establishments belonging to Government or any local authority:

The appropriate Government may, after consultation with the Corporation, by notification in the Official Gazette and subject to such conditions as may be specified in the notification, exempt any factory or establishment belonging to any local authority from the operation of this Act, if the employees in any such factory of establishment and otherwise in receipt of benefits substantially similar or superior to the benefits provided under this Act.

Section 91 Exemption from one or more provisions of the Act:

The appropriate Government may, with the consent of the Corporation, by notification in the Official Gazette, exempt any employees or class of employees in any factory or establishment or class of factories or establishments from one or more of the provisions relating to the benefits provided under this Act.

Section 91A: Exemption to be either prospective or retrospective:

Any notification granting exemption under Section 87, Section 88, Section 90 or Section 91 may be issued so as to take effect either prospectively or retrospectively on such date as may be specified therein.

For the purpose of granting exemption under Sections 90 and 91, the appropriate Government has to take consent of the Employees' State Insurance Corporation. For granting exemption under Sections 87, 88, 90 or 91, the appropriate Government is empowered to grant exemption by notification in the Official Gazette so as to take effect either prospectively or retrospectively on such date as may be specified in the notification.

This Act is not applicable to the following factories, persons etc.

(1) All seasonal factories [Section 1 (4)].
(2) All factories or establishments belonging either to the Government or under the control of the Government whose employees are otherwise in receipt of benefits substantially similar or superior to the benefits provided under this Act [Proviso to Section 1 (4)].
(3) Any of the members of the Indian Naval, Military or Air Force [Section 2 (9) (a)].
(4) Any employed person whose wages, excluding the remuneration for overtime work, exceed such wages as may be prescribed by the Central Government [Section 2 (9) (b].
(5) Mines subject to the operation of the Mines Act of 1952 [Section 2 (12)].
(6) Railway Running Sheds [Section 2 (1)].

2.3 Definitions

Definitions of certain words, terms, concepts, etc. which have been used in the Act are given in Section 2 of the Act. These definitions are given below:

(1) Appropriate Government [Section 2 (1)]:
"Appropriate Government" means, in respect of establishment under the control of the Central Government or a railway administration or a major port or a mine or oil field, the Central Government, and in all other cases, the State Government;

(2) Confinement [Section 2 (3)]:
"Confinement" means labour resulting in the issue of a living child, or labour after twenty-six weeks of pregnancy resulting in the issue of a child whether alive or dead;

(3) Contribution [Section 2 (4)]:
"Contribution" means the sum of money payable to the Corporation by the principal employer in respect of an employee and includes any amount payable or on behalf of the employee in accordance with the provisions of this Act;

(4) Corporation [Section 2 (6)]:
"Corporation" means the Employees' State Insurance Corporation set up under this Act;

(5) Dependent [Section 2 (6-A):
"Dependent" means any of the following relatives of a deceased insured person, namely
- (i) a widow, a minor legitimate or adopted son, an unmarried legitimate or adopted daughter;
- (ia) a widowed mother;
- (ii) if wholly dependent on the earnings of the insured person at the time of his death, a legitimate or adopted son or daughter who has attained the age of eighteen years and is infirm;
- (iii) if wholly or in part dependent on the earnings of the insured person at the time of his death.
  - (a) a parent other than a widowed mother,
  - (b) a minor illegitimate son, an unmarried illegitimate daughter or a daughter legitimate or adopted or illegitimate if married and a minor or if a widowed and a minor,
  - (c) a minor brother or an unmarried sister or a widowed sister if a minor,
  - (d) a widowed daughter-in-law,
  - (e) a minor child of a pre-deceased son,
  - (f) a minor child of a pre-deceased daughter where no parent of the child is alive, or
  - (g) a paternal grand-parent if no parent of the insured person is alive.

(6) Duly Appointed [Section 2 (7)]:
"Duly appointed" means appointed in accordance with the provisions of this Act or with the rules or regulations made thereunder;

(7) Employment Injury [Section 2 (8)]:
"Employment injury" means a personal injury to an employee caused by accident or an occupational disease arising out of and in the course of his employment, being an insurable

employment, whether the accident occurs or the occupational disease contracted within or outside the territorial limits of India;

Injury here does not mean merely visible injury in the shape of some wound, such a meaning of injury would be narrow and would be inconsistent with the purpose of the Act, as this act provides for certain benefits to employees in case of sickness, maternity etc.

The words in the course of employment and 'arising out of employment' used in the definition of 'Employment Injury' suggest casual relationship between the accident and the employment 'Mackinnon Mackenzie Vs. Ibrahim M. Issak case (1969), 2 SCC – 607 – 1970 – Lab – IC – 1413]. A person, who was employed to load and unload the goods of a manufacturing company, while accompanying their truck, tried to cross over the railway line to buy some bidis for himself from the shop which was on the other side. While doing so, he received the serious injury from a railway train and as a result, he suffered an employment injury (E.S.I.C.V Gulab Bux Mulla case – (1986) 2 LLN 503 (Bombay) 1987 Lab IC 14) Employment injury also includes death [Annapurna V. G. M. Karnataka SRTC case (1984) Lab I.C. 1356]. These cases make clear the meaning and nature of employment injury.

(8) Employee [Section 2 (9)]:

"Employee" means any person employed for wages in or in connection with the work of a factory or establishment to which this Act applies and

(i) who is directly employed by the principal employer on any work of, or incidental or preliminary to or connected with the work of the factory or establishment, whether such work is done by the employee in the factory or establishment or elsewhere; or

(ii) who is employed by or through an immediate employer on the premises of the factory or establishment or under the supervision of the principal employer or his agent on work which is ordinarily part of the work of the factory or establishment or which is preliminary to the work carried on in or incidental to the purpose of the factory or establishment; or

(iii) whose services are temporarily lent or let on hire to the principal employer by the person with whom the person whose services are so lent or let on hire has entered into a contract of service;

and includes any person employed for wages on any work connected with the administration of the factory or establishment or any part, department or branch thereof, or with the purchase of raw materials for, or the distribution or sale of the products of, the factory or establishment; or any person engaged as an apprentice, not being an apprentice engaged under the Apprentices Act, 1961, (52 of 1961) or under the standing orders of the establishment; but does not include -

(a) any member of the Indian naval, military or air force; or

(b) any person so employed whose wages (excluding remuneration for overtime work) exceed such wages as may be prescribed by the Central Government;

Provided that an employee whose wages (excluding remuneration for overtime work) exceed such wages as may be prescribed by the Central Government a month at any time after (and not before) the beginning of the contribution period, shall continue to be an employee until the end of that period; [Proviso to Section 8 (iii)].

The term 'Employee' is not merely confined to persons actually working on the floor of a factory. But even persons doing something incidental or preliminary to or connected with the work of the factory are also employees. The wage limit prescribed by the Central Government is now ₹ 6500 per month. Previously, it was ₹ 3000.

(9) Exempted Employee [Section 2 (10)]:

"Exempted employee" means an employee who is not liable under this Act to pay the employee's contribution;

(10) Family [Section 2 (11):

"Family" means all or any of the following relatives of an insured person, namely:
(i) a spouse:
(ii) a minor legitimate or adopted child dependent upon the insured person;
(iii) a child who is wholly dependent on the earnings of the insured person and who is
   (a) receiving education, till he or she attains the age of twenty-one years,
   (b) an unmarried daughter;
(iv) a child who is infirm by reason of any physical or mental abnormality or injury and is wholly dependent on the earnings of the insured person, so long as the infirmity continues;
(v) dependent parents;

(11) Factory [Section 2 (12)]:

The term 'factory' is defined in the same way in the Employees' State Insurance Act of 1948 as it is defined under the Factories Act of 1948.

According to Section 2 (12) of the Employees' State Insurance Act, "Factory" means any premises including the precincts thereof –
(a) whereon ten or more persons are employed or were employed for wages on any day of the preceding twelve months, and in any part of which a manufacturing process is being carried on with the aid of power or is ordinarily so carried on, or
(b) whereon twenty or more persons are employed or were employed for wages on any day of the preceding twelve months, and in any part of which a manufacturing process is being carried on without the aid of power or is ordinarily so carried on, but does not include a mine, subject to the operation of the Mines Act, 1952 (35 of 1952) or a railway running shed.

In the Factories Act of 1948, Factory is defined in Section 2 (m) as follows:

"Factory" means any premises including the precincts thereof:
(i) Whereon ten or more workers are working, or were working on any day of the preceding twelve months, and in any part of which a manufacturing process is being carried on with the aid of power, or is ordinarily so carried on, or

(ii) Whereon twenty or more workers are working, or were working on any day of the preceding twelve months, and in any part of which a manufacturing process is being carried on without the aid of power, or is ordinarily so carried on – but it does not include a mine which is subject to the operation of the Mines Act of 1952, or a mobile unit belonging to the armed-forces of the Union, a railway running shed or a hotel, restaurant or any eating house or place.

For the purpose of computing the number of workers, all the workers in different groups and relays in a day are to be taken into account [Section 1 to Section 2 (m) of the Act].

In short, a factory is any premises whereon ten or more persons are engaged, if power is used or twenty or more persons are engaged in any manufacturing process if power is not used. The mine, a mobile unit of the Armed-Forces of the Union, a railway running shed, a hotel, restaurant, eating place are excluded. For understanding properly the meaning of the term 'factory', the following points must be clearly understood.

1. **Meaning of precincts:**

A factory must occupy a fixed site or place or premises which include lands and buildings. Precincts are usually understood as a space enclosed by fences or walls or by any other means. Where premises are buildings, they would include precincts, but where premises are lands, they would have no precincts. What are the precincts of particular premises is a question of fact and it is to be determined according to the circumstances of each case. The word premises should not be confined in its meaning to buildings alone. According to the definition of a factory [2 (m)] of the Act, the word premises includes precincts thereof and therefore buildings and lands are also covered by the term 'factory'.

2. **Number of Workers:**

For computing the number of workers, all workers working in different relays in a day or throughout the day must be taken into account.

3. **Use of power:**

The fact that the power is used in the premises is not the deciding factor but the power used must be in the aid of the manufacturing process.

4. **Manufacturing process:**

To be a factory, a manufacturing process [Section 2 (k)] must be carried on with or without the aid of power. If a manufacturing process is carried on at two different places, they are factories [V.K. Press V/s. Authority].

5. **Tests to determine whether an establishment is a factory?**

In order to determine whether any establishment is a factory or not, the following two things must be proved.
    (a) that a manufacturing process is being carried on in any of the parts of the premises of that establishments; and
    (b) that there are prescribed number of workers employed, where the manufacturing process is carried on.

The following illustrations make the term 'factory' more clear.
   (a) A premises where the manufacturing process was carried on with the help of seven persons who were permanently employed and three other persons temporarily employed for the purpose of repairing the parts of machinery, it was held that such premises was a factory [Hari Kishan V/s. State].
   (b) Salt works merely consisting of open stretches of land with some temporary shelters were treated as a factory Bhiwandiwala V/s. Bombay State, [A.I.R. (1962)S.C.29].
   (c) It was held in one case that a sub-station converting high voltage electricity into low voltage electricity with the help of transformers is not a factory, because the conversion process is not the same as the power generation process [Gujarat State V/s. Gujarat Electricity Board].
   (d) Hospital is not a factory within the meaning of this Act and therefore, any department attached to the hospital, even the laundry attached to the hospital cannot be segregated (isolated) to bring it within the purview of the definition of a factory under this Act [Dr. Rao V/s. Inspector of Factories].
   (e) The premises on which the ginning and pressing cotton processes are carried on is considered as a factory.

(12) Seasonal Factory [Section 2 (19 a)]:

"Seasonal factory" means a factory which is exclusively engaged in one or more of the following manufacturing processes, namely, cotton ginning, cotton or jute pressing, decortication of groundnuts, the manufacture of coffee, indigo, lac, rubber, sugar (including gur) or tea or any manufacturing process which is incidental to or connected with any of the aforesaid processes and includes a factory which is engaged for a period not exceeding seven months in a year
   (a) in any process of blending, packing or repacking of tea or coffee; or
   (b) in such other manufacturing process as the Central Government may, by notification in the Official Gazette, specify

(13) Manufacturing Process [Section 2 (14 AA)]:

"Manufacturing Process" shall have the same meaning assigned to it in the Factories Act, 1948.

The meaning of manufacturing process according to Section 2 (k) of the Factories Act of 1948 is as follows:

Manufacturing Process means any process for:
(i) making, altering, repairing, ornamenting, finishing, packing, oiling, washing, cleaning, breaking up, demolishing, or otherwise treating or adapting any article or substance with a view to its use, sale, transport, delivery or disposal, or
(ii) pumping oil, water, sewage or any other substance, or
(iii) generating, transforming or transmitting power, or

(iv) composing types for printing, binding by letter press, lithography, photogravure or any other similar process or book binding; or
(v) constructing, reconstructing, repairing, refilling, finishing or breaking up ships or vessels or
(vi) preserving or storing any article in cold storage.

The above mentioned definition makes clear the meaning of the manufacturing process. In deciding whether a particular business or process is a manufacturing process or not, the circumstances of each particular case must be considered. To constitute a manufacturing process, it is very essential that there must be some sort of transformation of articles.

This means the articles must be transformed into any other form or into a finished product and the articles must become commercially as something different or as another from which it acquires its existence.

Following processes have been held to be manufacturing processes:
(1) Bidi making [Chintaman Rao V/s. M.P. State].
(2) The work of composition in printing business.
(3) Moulding and transformation of raw cinematography films into a finished product [Gemini Studio V/s. State].
(4) Use of electric motor for lifting water.
(5) The scrapping of salt and its gradation. Salt work which consists of converting sea-water into salt (Bhivandiwala V/s. Bombay State].
(6) Use of refrigerators for treating or adapting any article with a view to its sale [New Taj Mahal V/s. Inspector of Factories].
(7) Activities of a petrol pump [Gateway Auto Service V/s. Regional Director].
(8) In one case, it was held that washing process and cleaning of pepper while packing the same with a view to its sale is a manufacturing process.
(9) In another interesting case, the Supreme Court discussed the scope of the expression of manufacturing process. In the premises of a company, cured [preserved] tobacco leaves purchased from the tobacco growers were subjected to the processes of moistening, stripping and packing. The stems were stripped from the leaves and the leaves were packed in gunny bags by bundling the same properly. It was held that all these processes were the manufacturing processes within the meaning of the Section 2 (k) (i) of the Act [Gopal Rao V/s. Public prosecutor].

(14) Immediate Employer [Section 2 (13)]:

"Immediate employer", in relation to employees employed by or through him, means a person who has undertaken the execution, on the premises of a factory, or an establishment to which this Act applies or under the supervision of the principal employer or his agent, of the whole or any part of any work which is ordinarily part of the work of the factory or establishment of the principal employer or is preliminary to the work carried on in, or incidental to the purpose of, any such factory or establishment, and includes a person by whom the services of an employee who has entered into a contract of service with him are temporarily lent or let on hire to the principal employer and includes a contractor".

Thus, immediate employer in relation to employees employed by or through him is a person who has undertaken the execution of the whole or any part of any work which is ordinarily part of the work of the factory or establishment of the principal employer or is preliminary to the work carried on in, or incidental to the purpose of any such factory or establishment to which this Act applies. Such person who has been employed may have undertaken the execution of the work independently or even under the supervision of the principal employer or his agent. He may have undertaken the execution of the whole or any part of any work which is ordinarily considered as the part of the factory or establishment of the principal employer or is preliminary to the work carried on in, or even incidental to the purpose of any such factory or establishment. The immediate employer also includes a person by when the services of an employee who has entered into contract of service with him are temporarily lent or let on hire to the principal employer and includes even a contractor. There should be some sort of control or understanding relating to the business of the establishment of the principal employer between the principal employer and the immediate employer. This Act has been amended in 1989 to include a contractor in the definition of immediate employer. In one case [B.M. Lakshamanamurthy Vs. The Employees' State Insurance Corporation, Bangalore, AIR (1974) – Supreme Court – 759], the work was undertaken by contractors through their labour in the factory which was forming the part of the work of the principal factory. Both the factories were on the same leased land. The contractors were held immediate employers in that case.

The definitions of 'Principal Employer' and 'Managing Agent's' are given in Section 2 (17) and (14-A) respectively in the Act which are as follows.

(15) Managing Agent [Section 2 (14-A)]:

"Managing Agent" means any person appointed or acting as the representative of another person for the purpose of carrying on such other person's trade or business, but does not include an individual manager subordinate to an employer".

(16) Principal Employer [Section 2 (17)]:

"Principal Employer" means –
(i) in a factory, the owner or occupier of the factory and includes the managing agent or such owner or occupier, the legal representative of a deceased owner or occupier, and where a person has been named as the manager of the factory under the Factories Act, 1948 (63 of 1948) the person so named;
(ii) in any establishment under the control of any department of Government of India, the authority appointed by such Government in this behalf or where no authority is so appointed, the head of the department;
(iii) in any establishment, any person responsible for the supervision and control of the establishment;

In B. M. Chatterjee vs. State of Bengal [A.I.R. - 1970 - Cal. 290] case, the Calcutta High Court held that a director of a limited company responsible for the supervision and control of the company was the principal employer within the meaning of Section 2 (17) and (iii). But the Bombay High Court did not agree with this view and in Suresh Vs. Collector of Bombay [Lab. I.C. – 1615 (1984)], Case the Bombay High Court held that the director of a company, by virtue of being a director, was not a principal employer. Hence, he was not personally liable to pay employer's contribution under this Act.

(17) Insurable Employment [Section 2 (13-A)]:

"Insurable employment" means an employment in a factory or establishment to which this Act applies;

(18) Insured Person [Section 2 (14)]:

"Insured person" means a person who is or was an employee in respect of whom contributions are or were payable under this Act and who is, by reason thereof, entitled to any of the benefits provided by this Act;

(19) Miscarriage [Section 2 (14 B)]:

"Miscarriage" means expulsion of the contents of a pregnant uterus at any period prior to or during the twenty-six weeks of pregnancy, but does not include any miscarriage, the causing of which is punishable under the Indian Penal Code (45 of 1860).

(20) Occupier [Section 2 (15)]:

Occupier of the factory shall have the same meaning assigned to it in the Factories Act of 1948.

The term 'Occupier' is defined in Section 2 (n) of the Factories Act, 1948 as follows:

Occupier of a factory is the person who has ultimate control over the affairs of the factory. Provided that:

(i) In the case of a firm or any other association of individuals, any one of the individual partners or members thereof shall be deemed to be the occupier;

(ii) If it is a company, any one of the directors shall be deemed to be the occupier;

(iii) In the case of a factory which is owned and/or controlled by the Central Government or any State Government, or any local authority, the person or persons appointed to manage the affairs of the factory by the Central Government or the State Government or the local authority, as the case may be, shall be deemed to be the occupier.

It is provided further that in the case of a ship which is being repaired, or on which maintenance work is being carried out, in a dry dock which is available for hire;

1. The owner of the dock shall be deemed to be the occupier for the purposes of any matter provided by or under (a) sections 6, 7, 7–A, 7–B, 11 or 12 (b) Section 17, in so far as it relates to the providing and maintaining sufficient and suitable lighting in and/or around the dock (c). Sections 18, 19, 42, 47 or 49 in relation to workers employed on such repairs and maintenance.

2. The owner of the ship or his agent or master or other officer-in-charge of the ship or any other person who enters into contract with such owner, agent, master, or any other officer-in-charge to carry out the repair or maintenance work, shall be deemed to be the occupier for the purposes of any matter provided for by or under sections 13, 14, 16 or 17, save as otherwise provided in this proviso or chapter IV (except Section 27) or Sections 43, 44 or 45, chapters VI, VII, VIII or IX or sections 108, 109 or 110 in relation to (a) the workers employed directly by him or by or through any agency; and (b) the machinery, plant or premises in use for the purpose of carrying out such repair or maintenance work by such owner, agent, master or any other person or other officer-in-charge.

From the above mentioned definitions of 'Occupier', we come to know that:

1. Occupier of a factory means the person who has ultimate control over the affairs of the factory. Where the said 'affairs' are entrusted to a managing agent, such agent is deemed to be the occupier of the factory.
2. Occupier is not synonymous with owner. The ultimate control over the working of a factory is the important and deciding factor in determining whether the owner, licensee, lessee or any other person is the occupier of the factory.
3. Such person is the occupier who is in possession of the factory and who controls the working of the factory. A servant who is entrusted with some specific duties in regard to the control of the machinery, workmen or office is not the occupier. Managers of a factory staying in some part of the premises of the factory are not an occupier within the meaning of this Act.
4. Occupier may be a partnership firm or association of individuals, or a company, Lessee or even licensee having a right to occupy and control the affairs of the factory and dictate the terms of management.
5. In case of a firm or association of individuals, any one of the partners or members is deemed to be the occupier. If it is a company, anyone of the directors is deemed to be the occupier. In the case of the factory owned or controlled by the Central or State Government, the person or persons appointed to manage the affairs, shall be deemed to be the occupier and therefore these persons (occupiers) can be prosecuted and punished for any offence for which the occupier of the factory is punishable.

(21) Power [Section 2 (15-c)]:

"Power shall have the same meaning assigned to it in the Factories Act, 1948". Section 2 (g) of the Factories Act, 1948 defines power as "electrical energy or any other form of energy which is mechanically transmitted and is not generated by human or animal energy".

(22) Sickness [Section 2 (20)]:

"Sickness" means a condition which requires medical treatment and attendance and necessitates abstention from work on medical grounds.

(23) Meaning and Definitions of "Temporary Disablement"; 'Permanent Partial Disablement' and Permanent Total Disablement:

Disablements can be temporary disablement as well as permanent disablement. Permanent disablement can be either 'permanent total disablement' or 'permanent partial disablement'. Definitions of all these types of disablements are given in this Act which are as follows:

[A] Temporary Disablement [Section 2 (21)]:

"Temporary disablement" means a condition resulting from an employment injury which requires medical treatment and renders an employee, as a result of such injury, temporarily incapable of doing the work which he was doing prior to or at the time of injury.

[B] Permanent Total Disablement [Section 2 (15-B):

"Permanent total disablement" means such disablement of a permanent nature as incapacitates an employee for all work which he was capable of performing at the time of the accident resulting in such disablement.

It is also provided that permanent total disablement shall be deemed to result from every injury specified in Part I of the Second Schedule or from any combination of injuries specified in Part II thereof, where the aggregate percentage of the loss of earning capacity, as specified in the said Part II against those injuries, amounts to one hundred per cent or more.

[C] Permanent Partial Disablement [Section 2 (15-A)]:

"Permanent partial disablement" means such disablement of a permanent nature, as reduces the earning capacity of an employee in every employment, which he was capable of undertaking at the time of the accident resulting in the disablement.

It is also provided that every injury in Part II of the Second Schedule shall be deemed to result in permanent partial disablement.

Thus, from the definitions of permanent total disablement and permanent partial disablement as given Section 2 [15-A and 15-B] of the Act, it becomes clear that permanent total disablement is such disablement of a permanent nature which incapacitates an employee for all works which he was capable of performing at the time of the accident resulting in such disablement. Permanent total disablement is deemed to result from every injury specified in the Second Schedule – Part I or from any combination of injuries specified in Part II of that Second Schedule thereof, where the aggregate percentage of loss of earning capacity amounts to 100% or more. While permanent partial disablement is such disablement of a permanent nature which reduces the earning capacity of an employee in every employment which he is capable of undertaking at the time of the accident resulting in the disablement. Every injury specified in the Second Schedule-Part II is deemed to result in the permanent partial disablement.

(24) Wages [Section 2 (22)]:

"Wages" means all remuneration paid or payable in cash to employee, if the terms of the contract of employment, express or implied, were fulfilled and includes any payment to an employee in respect of any period of authorised leave, lockout, strike, which is not illegal

or layoff and other additional remuneration, if any, paid at intervals not exceeding two months, but does not include –
  (a) any contribution paid by the employer to any person fund or provident fund, under this Act;
  (b) any travelling allowance or the value of any travelling concession;
  (c) any sum paid to the person employed to defray special expenses entailed on him by the nature of his employment; or
  (d) any gratuity payable on discharge".

Thus, the term 'Wages' as defined in this Act makes clear as to what is included in wages and what is not included in wages. Accordingly 'wages', include any payment to an employee in respect of any period of
  (1) authorised a leave;
  (2) lock-out or strike which is not illegal or lay-off and
  (3) any other additional remuneration, if any, paid at intervals not exceeding two months. This implies that wages must be a payment for service given or to be given to the employee by his employer. The term 'Wages' also includes compensation for lay-off and bonus also. But the wages according to Section 2 (22) do not include the following:
  (a) Any contribution paid towards any pension fund or provident fund under this Act; or
  (b) Any travelling allowance or value of any travelling concession; or
  (c) Any amount paid to the person employed to defray special expenses entailed on him by the nature of his employment; or
  (d) Any gratuity payable on discharge of an employee.

(25) Wage Period [Section 2 (23)]:
"Wage period" in relation to an employee means the period in respect of which wages are ordinarily payable to him, whether in terms of the contract of employment, express or implied or otherwise".

(26) Meaning of all other words, expressions used in the Act but not defined:
Section 2 (24) states that, "all other words and expressions used but not defined in this Act and defined in the Industrial Disputes Act, 1947 shall have the meanings respectively assigned to them in that Act".

(27) An Insurable Workman [Section 38]:
According to Section 38 of this Act, "subject to the provisions of this Act, all employees in factories or establishments to which this Act applies, shall be insured in the manner provided by this Act". This means that every employee of a factory or an establishment to which this Act applies is an insurable workman. We have already considered the definitions of the terms 'employee' and 'factory'. Considering the meaning of these definitions, it can be said that an insurable workman is one who is employed directly or through an intermediate employer or is let on hire to an employer and the factory or establishment must be one to which this Act applies. This Act does not confer any benefit on the following persons, as this Act does not apply to them and hence, they are not insurable under this Act.

(1) Workers in railway's running sheds [Section 2 (12)].

(2) Workers in mines subject to the Mines Act of 1952 [Section 2 (12)].

(3) Members of the Indian Naval, Military or Air Force [Section 2 (9)].

(4) Workers whose wages (excluding remuneration for overtime) exceed such wages as may be prescribed by the Central Government [Section 2 (9)].

(5) Workers in seasonal factories.

Mines, railway running sheds, seasonal factories etc. are not included within the term 'Factory' as defined in this Act. While workmen coming under items No. 3 and 4 mentioned above are not included within the term 'Employees' as defined in this Act.

(28) Prescribed [Section 2 (16)]:

'Prescribed' means prescribed by rules under this Act. In exercise of the powers conferred by Section 95 of this Act, the Central Government has made certain rules which have been included in the Employees' State Insurance (Central) Rules of 1950. These rules make clear the procedure of implementing certain provisions of this Act.

(29) Regulation [Section 2 (18)]:

'Regulation' means a regulation made by the Corporation [i.e. The Employees' State Insurance Corporation]. In exercise of the powers conferred by Section 97 of this Act, the Employees' State Insurance Corporation has made certain regulations – The Employees' State Insurances [General] Regulation of 1950 pertaining to contributions, benefits and benefit periods, Regional Boards, Collection of contributions, etc.

(30) Registration of Factories and Establishments under this Act [Section 2-A]:

Section 2-A of the Act provides for the registration of factories and establishments. Section 2-A is as follows:

Section 2-A Registration of factories and establishments:

Every factory or establishment to which this Act applies shall be registered within such time and in such manner as may be specified in the regulations made in this behalf.

Regulation 10-B of the Employees' State Insurance (General) Regulations of 1950 makes clear the procedure of registration of factories and establishment under this Act. Regulation 10-B is given below.

Regulation 10-B Registration of Factories or Establishments:

(a) The employer in respect of a factory or an establishment to which the Act applies for the first time and to which an Employer's Code Number is not yet allotted and the employer in respect of a factory or an establishment to which the Act previously applied, but has ceased to apply for the time being, shall furnish to the appropriate Regional Office not later than 15 days after the Act becomes applicable, as the case may be, to the factory or establishment, a declaration of registration in writing in Form 01 (hereinafter referred to as Employer's Registration Form).

(b) The employer shall be responsible for the correctness of all the particulars and information required for and furnished on the Employer's Registration Form.
(c) The appropriate Regional Office may direct the employer who fails to comply with the requirements of paragraph (a) of this regulation within the time stated therein, to furnish to that office Employer's Registration Form duly completed within such further time as may be specified and such employer shall, thereupon comply with the instructions issued by that office in this behalf.
(d) Upon receipt of the completed Employer's Registration Form, the appropriate Regional Office shall, if satisfied that the factory or the establishment is one to which the Act applies, allot to it an Employer's Code Number (unless the factory or the establishment had already been allotted an Employer's Code Number) and shall inform the employer of that number.
(e) The employer shall enter the Employer's Code Number on all documents prepared or completed by him in connection with the Act, the rules and regulations in all correspondence with the appropriate office.

2.4 The Employees' State Insurance Corporation

The administration of the scheme of insurance contained in this Act which has been in the Employees' State Insurance Corporation, which has been set up by the Central Government, according to the provisions of Section 3 of this Act. This Corporation (ESIC) is a body corporate and it has perpetual succession and a common seal. It can sue and be sued by its name [Section 3 (2)]. It is a statutory body which has been created under this Act to administer and execute the scheme of the Employer's State Insurance, in accordance with the provisions of this Act [Section 3 (1)].

A Standing Committee has been set up to act as an executive body from among the members of the E.S.I. Corporation for administering the insurance scheme under the general superintendent and control of the E.S.I. Corporation. Besides this Committee, Medical Benefit Council also has been set up under this Act to advice the E.S.I. Corporation on medical questions.

The E.S.I. Corporation has been given the powers to appoint Regional Boards, Local Committees, Regional and Local Medical Benefit Councils in such areas and in such manner, and delegate to them such powers and also functions as may be provided by the regulation made by the E.S.I. Corporation in that behalf. The provisions also have been made to appoint Inspectors by the E.S.I. Corporation for the purposes of this Act.

2.4.1 The Employees' State Insurance Corporation [E.S.I. Corporation]

Provisions relating to the constitution, powers and duties of the E.S.I. Corporation have been made in this Act which are as follows:

(A) Constitution of the E.S.I. Corporation [Section 4]

The Corporation shall consist of the following members, namely:
(a) a Chairman to be appointed by the Central Government;
(b) a Vice-Chairman to be appointed by the Central Government;

(c) not more than *five persons* to be appointed by the Central Government;
(d) one person each, representing each of the States in which this Act is in force to be appointed by the State Government concerned;
(e) one person to be appointed by the Central Government to represent the Union territories.
(f) *ten persons* representing employers to be appointed by the Central Government in consultation with such organisation of employers as may be recognised for the purpose by the Central Government.
(g) *ten persons* representing employees to be appointed by the Central Government in consultation with such organisations of medical practitioners as may be recognised for the purpose by the Central Government;
(h) *two persons* representing the medical profession to be appointed by the Central Government in consultation, with such organisations of medical practitioners as may be recognised for the purpose by the Central Government;
(i) *three members* of Parliament of whom two shall be members of the House of the People (Lok Sabha) and one shall be member of the Council of States (Rajya Sabha) elected respectively by the members of the House of the People and the members of the Council States; and
(j) the Director General of the Corporation, ex-officio;

(B) Term of office of members of the Corporation

(1) Save otherwise expressly provided in this Act, the term of office of member of the Corporation, other than the members referred to in clauses (a), (b), (c), (d) and (e) of Section 4 and the ex-officio member shall be four years commencing from the date on which their appointment or election is notified [Section 5 (1)].

It is provided that a member of the Corporation referred to in clauses (a), (b), (c), (d) and (e) of Section 4 shall hold office during the pleasure of the Government appointing them [Section 5 (2)].

(C) Eligibility for re-appointment or re-election

An outgoing member of the Corporation, the Standing Committee, or the Medical Benefit Council shall be eligible for re-appointment or re-election as the case may be [Section 6].

(D) Authentication of orders, decisions, etc.

All orders and decisions of the Corporation shall be authenticated by the signature of the Director General of the Corporation and all other instruments by the Corporation shall be authenticated by the signature of the Director General or such other officer of the Corporation as may be authorised by him. Corporation and all other instruments issued by the Corporation shall be authenticated by the signature of the Director General or such other officer of the Corporation as may be authorised by him [Section 7].

An outgoing member of the corporation is eligible for re-appointment or re-election as the case may be (Sec. 6).

(E) Principal Officers of the Corporation [Section 16]
   (1) The Central Government may, in consultation with the Corporation, appoint a Director General and a Financial Commissioner.
   (2) The Director General shall be the Chief Financial Executive Officer of the Corporation.
   (3) The Director General and the Financial Commissioner shall be whole-time officers of the Corporation and shall not undertake any work unconnected with their office without the sanction of the Central Government and of the Corporation.
   (4) The Director General or Financial Commissioner shall hold office for such period, not exceeding five years, as may be specified in the order appointing him. An outgoing Director General or Financial Commissioner shall be eligible for re-appointment if he is otherwise qualified.
   (5) The Director General or the Financial Commissioner shall receive such salary and allowances as may be prescribed by the Central Government.
   (6) A person shall be disqualified from being appointed as or for being the Director General or the Financial Commissioner, if he is subject to any of the disqualifications specified in Section 13.
   (7) The Central Government may at any time remove the Director General or the Financial Commissioner from office and shall do so, if such removal is recommended by a resolution of the Corporation, passed at a special meeting called for the purpose and supported by the votes of not less than two-thirds of the total strength of the Corporation.

(F) Status of the Officers and Servants of the Corporation
All officers and servants of the Corporation are deemed to be the public servants within the meaning of Section 21 of the Indian Penal Code of 1860 [Section 93].

(G) Powers of the Corporation

[I] Power to appoint staff [Section 17]:
Section 17 of the Act empowers the Corporation to appoint or employ necessary staff or officers for efficiently carrying on the business, transactions etc. of the Corporation. Section 17 is as follows:
   (1) The Corporation may employ such other staff of officers and servants as may be necessary for the efficient transaction of its business, provided that the sanction of the Central Government shall be obtained for the creation of any post, the maximum monthly salary of which exceeds such salary as may be prescribed by the Central Government [Section 17 (1)].
   (2) (a) The method of recruitment, salary and allowances, discipline and other conditions of service of the members of the staff of the Corporation shall be such, as may be specified in the regulations made by the Corporation in accordance with the rules and orders applicable to the officers and employees of the Central Government drawing corresponding scales of pay; [Section 17 (2) (a)].

It is also provided that where the Corporation is of the opinion that it is necessary to make a departure from the said rules or orders in respect of any of the matters aforesaid, it shall obtain the prior approval of the Central Government [Proviso to Section 17 (20)].

    (b) In determining the corresponding scales of pay of the matters of the staff under clause (a) the Corporation shall have regard to the educational qualifications, methods of recruitment; duties and responsibilities of such officers and employees under the Central Government and in case of any doubt, the corporation shall refer the matter to the Central Government whose decision thereon shall be final [Section 17 (2) (b)].

(3) Every appointment to posts other than medical posts corresponding to Group A and Group B posts under the Central Government, shall be made in consultation with the Union Public Service Commission [Section 17 (3)].

It is provided that this sub-section shall not apply to an officiating or temporary appointment for a period not exceeding one year [Proviso 2 to Section 17 (3)].

It is provided further that any such officiating or temporary appointment shall not confer any claim for regular appointment and the services rendered in that capacity shall not count towards seniority or minimum qualifying service specified in the regulations for promotion to next higher grade [Proviso 2 to Section 17 (3)].

(4) If any question arises whether a post corresponds to Group A and Group B post under the Central Government, the question shall be referred to that Government whose decisions thereon shall be final [Section 17 (4)].

[II] Powers of the Corporation in respect of measures for health:

The Corporation may, in addition to the scheme of benefits in this Act, promote measures for the improvement of the health and welfare of insured persons and for the rehabilitation and re-appointment of insured persons who have been disabled or injured and may incur in respect of such measures, expenditure from the funds and the Corporation within such limits as may be prescribed by the Central Government [Section 19].

[III] Powers of the Corporation to hold property, to invest its money and to raise loans:

(1) The Corporation may, subject to such conditions as may be prescribed by the Central Government, acquire and hold property, both movable and immovable, sell or otherwise transfer any movable or immovable property which may have become vested in or have acquired by it and do all things necessary for the purpose for which the Corporation is established [Section 29 (1)].

(2) Subject to such conditions as may be prescribed by the Central Government, the Corporation may from time to time invest any moneys which are not immediately required for expenses properly defrayable under this Act and may, subject as aforesaid from time to time re-invest or realise such investments [Section 29 (2)].

(3) The Corporation may, with the previous sanction of the Central Government and on such terms as may be prescribed by it, raise loans and take measures for discharging such loans [Section 29 (3)].

[IV] Power of the Corporation to constitute Provident Fund or Benefit Fund

The Corporation may constitute for the benefit of its staff or any class of them, such provident or other benefit fund as it may think [Section 29 (4)].

[V] Power of the Corporation to appoint Inspectors

According to Section 45 (1), "the Corporation is empowered to appoint such persons as Inspectors as it thinks fit for the purposes of this Act within such local limits as it may assign to them".

[VI] Power of the Corporation to determine the amount of contributions

Under Section 45-A, "the Corporation, on the basis of information available to it, is empowered to determine, by order, the amount of contribution payable in respect of employees of a factory or an establishment in respect of which no particulars, registers or records are submitted, maintained or furnished".

[VII] Power of the Corporation to write-off of the losses [Rule 53]

Rule 53 of the Employees' State Insurance (Central) Rules of 1950 empowers the E.S.I. Corporation to write-off of losses. It states that, "where the Corporation is of the opinion that the amount of contributions, interest and damages due to the Corporation has become irrecoverable, the Corporation or any other officer authorised by it in this behalf may sanction the writing off of the said amount, subject to the following conditions, namely:

(i) establishment or factory has been closed for more than five years and the whereabouts of the employer cannot be ascertained, despite all possible efforts;

(ii) decree obtained by the Corporation could not be executed successfully for want of sufficient assets of the defaulting employer; or
   (a) the Official Liquidator in the event of factories, establishments having gone into liquidation; or
   (b) the Commissioner of payments in the event of unit being nationalised or taken over by the Government".

[H] Duties of the Corporation

Following are the important duties of the Corporation:

(1) Framing of Budget Estimates [Section 32]:

According to Section 32, "it is the duty of the Corporation to frame or prepare the budget and submit a copy of the budget for approval to the Central Government before such date as may be fixed". Section 32 states that, "the Corporation shall in each year frame a budget showing the probable receipts and the expenditure which it proposes to incur during the following year and shall submit the copy of the budget for the approval of the Central Government before such date as may be fixed by it in that behalf. The budget shall contain provisions adequate in the opinion of the Central Government for the discharge of the liabilities incurred by the Corporation and for the maintenance of the working balance".

(2) To maintain the accounts [Section 33]:

According to the provisions of Section 33, "it is the duty of the Corporation to maintain correct accounts of its income and expenditure in such form and in such manner as may be prescribed by the Central Government".

(3) To get the accounts audited [Section 34]:

The accounts maintained by the Corporation must be duly audited. It is the duty of the Corporation to get the accounts audited in the manner prescribed in Section 34 which is as follows:

(i) The accounts of the Corporation shall be audited annually by the Comptroller and Auditor General of India and any expenditure incurred by him in connection with such audit shall be payable by the Corporation to the Comptroller and Auditor-General of India [Section 34 (1)].

(ii) The Comptroller and Auditor General of India and any person appointed by him in connection with the audit of the accounts of the Corporation shall have the same rights and privileges and authority in connection with such audit as the Comptroller and Auditor General has in connection with the audit of Government accounts and, in particular shall have the right to demand the production of books of accounts, connected vouchers and other documents and papers and to inspect any of the Offices of the Corporation [Section 34 (2)].

(iii) The accounts of the Corporation as certified by the Comptroller and Auditor-General of India or any other person appointed by him in this behalf together with the audit report thereon shall be forwarded to the Corporation which shall forward the same to the Central Government along with its comments on the report of the Comptroller and Auditor-General [Section 34 (3)].

(4) Submission of Annual Report [Section 35]:

It is the duty of the Corporation to submit to the Central Government an annual report of its work and activities [Section 35].

The annual report, the audited accounts of the Corporation, together with the report of the Comptroller and Auditor-General of India thereon and the comments of the Corporation on such reports under Section 34 and the budget as finally adopted by the Corporation shall be placed before Parliament [Section 36].

(5) Valuation of Assets and Liabilities [Section 37]:

It is the duty of the Corporation to valuate its assets and liabilities at the intervals of five years.

According to Section 37, "The Corporation shall, at intervals of five years, have a valuation of its assets and liabilities made by the valuer appointed with the approval of the Central Government". However, it is also provided that it shall be open to the Central Government to direct a valuation to be made at such other times as it may consider necessary [Proviso to Section 37].

2.4.2 Standing Committee

The Standing Committee has been set up under this Act to administer the affairs of the E.S.I. Corporation with certain powers. Provisions relating to its constitutions, powers, duties etc. have been made in this Act which are as follows:

[A] Constitution of Standing Committee [Section 8]

Section 8 of this Act provides for the creation of a Standing Committee from among the members of the E.S.I. Corporation. The Standing Committee is constituted as follows:

(a) a Chairman, appointed by the Central Government; [Section 8 (a)]

(b) three members of the Corporation, appointed by the Central Government; [Section 8 (b)]

(bb) three members of the Corporation representing such three State Governments thereon as the Central Government may, by notification in the Official Gazette, specify from time to time; [Section 8 (bb)]

(c) eight members elected by the Corporation as follows:
   (i) three members from among the members of the Corporation representing employees;
   (ii) three members from among the members of the Corporation representing employers;
   (iii) one member from among the members of the Corporation representing the medical profession; and
   (iv) one member from among the members of the Corporation elected by Parliament

(d) the Director General of the Corporation, ex-officio [Section 8 (d)].

[B] Term of Office of the Members of Standing Committee [Section 9]

Section 9 states that, "(1) Save as otherwise expressly provided in this Act, the term of office of a member of the Standing Committee, other than a member referred to in clause (a) or clause (b) or clause (bb) of section 8, shall be two years from the date on which his election is notified [Section 9 (1)].

It is provided that a member of the Standing Committee shall, notwithstanding the expiry of the said period of two years, continue to hold office until the election of his successor is notified [Proviso 1 to Section 9].

It is provided further that a member of the Standing Committee shall cease to hold office when he ceases to be a member of the Corporation [Proviso to Section 9].

(2) A member of the Standing Committee referred to in clause (a) or clause (b) or clause (bb) of section 8 shall hold office during the pleasure of the Central Government [Section (2)].

An outgoing member of the Standing Committee is eligible for re-appointment or re-election as the case may be [Section 6].

Thus, the provisions of Section 9 make clear the term of office of the members of the Standing Committee.

[C] Powers and Duties of the Standing Committee [Section 18]

Important powers and duties of the Standing Committee are made clear in Section 18 which are as follows:

(1) Subject to the general superintendent, affairs of the Corporation, the Standing Committee shall administer the affairs of the Corporation and may exercise any of the powers and perform any of the functions of the Corporation [Section 18 (1)].

(2) The Standing Committee shall submit for the consideration and decision of the Corporation all such cases and matters as may be specified in the regulations made in this behalf [Section 18 (2)].

(3) The Standing Committee, in its discretion, submits any other case or matter for the decision of the Corporation [Section 18 (3)].

2.4.3 Medical Benefit Council

Medical Benefit Council has been set up under this Act to advice the E.S.I. Corporation on the medical side of its operations. Provisions relating to the constitution of Medical Benefit Councils are found in Section 10 of the Act which is reproduced below.

[A] Constitution of Medical Benefit Council [Section 10]

(1) **Medical Benefit Council:** The Central Government shall constitute a Medical Benefit Council consisting of –

(a) the Director General, Health Service ex-officio, as Chairman.

(b) a Deputy Director General, Health Services, to be appointed by the Central Government;

(c) the Medical Commissioner of the Corporation, ex-officio.

(d) one member each representing each of the State (other than Union territories) in which this Act is in force) to be appointed by the State Government concerned;

(e) *three members* representing employers to be appointed by the Central Government in consultation with such organisations of employers as may be recognised for the purpose by the Central Government; and

(f) *three members* representing employees to be appointed by the Central Government in consultation with such organisations employees as may be recognised for the purpose by the Central Government; and

(g) *three members*, of whom not less than one shall be a woman, representing the medical profession, to be appointed by the Central Government in consultation with such organisations of medical practitioners as may be recognised for the purpose by the Central Government.[Section 10 (1)].

[B] Term of Office:

Save as otherwise expressly provided in this Act, the term of office of a member of the Medical Benefit Council, other than a member referred to any of the clauses (a) to (d) of sub-section (1), shall be four years from the date on which his appointment is notified [Section 10 (2)].

It is provided that a member of the Medical Benefit Council shall, notwithstanding the expiry of the said period of four years continue to hold office until the appointment of his successor is notified [Proviso to Section 10 (2)].

A member of the Medical Benefit Council referred to in clauses (b) and (d) of Section 10 (1) shall hold office during the pleasure of the Government appointing him. [Section 10 (3)].

An outgoing member of the Medical Benefit Council constituted under this Act is eligible for re-appointment or re-election as the case may be [Section 6].

[C] Powers and Duties of the Medical Benefit Council [Section 22]

The powers and duties of the Medical Benefit Council constituted under this Act are laid down in Section 22 which is as under:

(1) The Medical Benefit Council shall advise the Corporation and the Standing Committee on matters relating to the administration of medical benefit, the certification for purposes of the grant of benefits and other connected matters; [Section 22 (a)].

(2) The Medical Benefit Council shall have such powers and duties of investigation as may be prescribed in relation to complaints against medical practitioners in connection with medical treatment and attendance; [Section 22 (b)].

(3) The Medical Benefit Council performs such other duties in connection with the medical treatment and attendance as may be specified in the regulations [Section 22 (c)].

The powers and duties of the Medical Benefit Council have also been made clear in Rule 14 of the Employees' State Insurance (General) Rules of 1950 which are as follows:

The powers and duties of the Medical Benefit Council shall be –

(1) to advise the Corporation in regard to the constitution, setting up, duties and powers of the Regional and Local Medical Benefit Councils;

(2) to make recommendations to the Corporation in regard to
   (i) the scale and nature of medical benefit provided at hospitals, dispensaries, clinics and other institutions and the nature and the extent of the medicines, staff and equipment which shall be maintained at such institutions and the extent to which these fall short of the desired standard;
   (ii) the medical formulary for use in connection with the medical benefit provided under the Act;
   (iii) medical certification, including the procedure and the forms for such certification, statistical returns, registers and other medical records;
   (iv) measures undertaken for the improvement of the health and welfare of insured persons, and the rehabilitation and re-employment of insured persons, disabled or injured.

(3) to advise the Corporation on any matter relating to the professional conduct of any medical practitioner employed for the purpose of providing medical benefit under the Act.

2.4.4 Appointment of Regional Boards, Local Committees, Regional Local Medical Benefit Councils

Section 25 of the Act provides for the appointment of Regional Boards, Local Committees, Regional and Local Medical Benefit Councils. It states that, "The Corporation may appoint Regional Boards, Local Committees and Regional and Local Medical Benefit Councils in such areas and in such manner, and delegate to them such powers and functions, as may be provided by the regulations".

2.4.5 Officers and Staff

[A] Principal Officers of the E.S.I. Corporations

Section 16 empowers the Central Government to appoint in consultation with the Corporation two principal officers i.e. Director General of the Corporation and a Financial Commissioner. The Director General appointed under this Section 16 works as the Chief Executive Officer of the Corporation. Both these officers are the whole-time officers of the Corporation. Provisions relating to their appointments, term of office, removals etc. have been in Section 16.

[I] Director General of the E.S.I. Corporation

The Director-General is the Chief Executive Officer of the Corporation. He is not supposed to undertake any work unconnected with his office without the prior sanction of the Central Government and also of the E.S.I. Corporation. He holds the office for a period not exceeding five years. However, he is eligible for re-appointment if otherwise eligible. He is entitled to receive such salary and allowances as may be prescribed by the Central Government. A person is considered to be disqualified from being appointed the Director General if he is subject to any of the disqualification specified in Section 13 of this Act. Provisions of Section 13 are given under the heading 'Rules regarding membership and general provisions'. The Central Government is empowered to remove the Director General at any time. But if his removal is recommended by a resolution of the E.S.I. Corporation passed in a special meeting called for the purpose and supported by the votes of not less than the two thirds of the total strength of the E.S.I. Corporation, the Central Government has to remove the Director-General [Section 16].

Power and Duties of the Director General:

The provisions of Section 23 make it clear that the "Director General shall exercise such powers and discharge such duties as may be prescribed. He has to perform all such functions as may be specified in the rules and regulations.

Rule 16 of the Employees' State Insurance (Central) Rules of 1950 states the powers and duties of the Director General. It lays down that,

"(1) The powers and duties of the Director-General shall be –
- (i) to act as the Chief Executive Officer of the Corporation;
- (ii) to convene, under the orders of the Chairman, meetings of the Corporation, the Standing Committee and the Medical Benefit Council in accordance with the Act and the Rules and to implement the decisions reached at the meetings;

(iii) to enter into contracts on behalf of the Corporation in accordance with the Act or the Rules or Regulations made thereunder, or the general or special instructions of the Corporation or the Standing Committee;

(iv) to furnish all returns and documents required by the Act or the Rules to the Central Government upon all matters concerning the Corporation;

(v) to undertake such other duties and to exercise such other powers as may, from time to time be entrusted or delegated to him.

(2) The Director-General may, with the approval of the Standing Committee, by general or special order, delegate any of his powers or duties under the Rules or Regulations or under any resolution of the Corporation or the Standing Committee, as the case may be, to any person subordinate to him. The exercise or discharge of any of the powers or duties so delegated shall be subjected to such restrictions, limitations and conditions, if any, as the Director-General may, with the approval of the Standing Committee impose.

[II] Financial Commissioner

The Central Government is empowered to appoint a Financial Commissioner in consultation with the E.S.I. Corporation. He is the whole-time officer of the Corporation. He is not allowed to undertake any work not connected with his office without the prior permission of the Central Government as well as the E.S.I. Corporation. He holds the office for a period not exceeding five years but is eligible for re-appointment if otherwise eligible. He is entitled to receive such salary and allowances as may be prescribed by the Central Government. A person is considered disqualified from being appointed as the Financial Commissioner if he is subject to any of the disqualifications specified in Section 13 of this Act. The provisions of Section 13 are given under the heading 'Rules regarding membership and general provisions'. The Central Government may at any time remove the Financial Commissioner from his office. However, if his removal is recommended by a resolution of the E.S.I. Corporation passed in a special meeting called for the purpose and supported by the votes of not less than two thirds of the total strength of the E.S.I. Corporation, the Central Government has to remove him from his office [Section 16].

Powers and Duties of the Financial Commissioner:

The Financial Commissioner has to exercise all such powers and discharge all such duties as may be prescribed. He has also to perform such other functions as may be specified in the Rules and Regulations [Section 23].

Rule 19 of the Employees' State Insurance (Central) Rules, 1950 specifies the powers and duties of the Financial Commissioner. It lays down that, "the powers and duties of the Financial Commissioner shall be subject to the control of the Director-General –

(i) To maintain the accounts of the Corporation and to arrange for the compilation of accounts by the collection of returns from the Centres and Regions;

(ii) To prepare the budget of the Corporation;

(iii) To arrange for internal audit of the accounts of the Centres and Regions and of the receipt and payments thereat;

(iv) To make recommendations for the investment of the funds of the Corporation; and
(v) To undertake such other duties and to exercise such other powers as may, from time to time, be entrusted or delegated to him.

[B] Staff of the Corporation

Section 17 of the Act provides for the employment of staff of officers and servants. Section 17 empowers the E.S.I. Corporation to employ such staff of officers and servants as may be necessary for efficiently carrying on the transactions of its business. However, for creating any post with the maximum monthly salary which exceeds such salary as may be prescribed by the Central Government, the prior sanction of the Central Government is required to be obtained [Section 17 (1)].

The method of recruitment, salary, allowances, discipline and other conditions of service of the members of the staff of the Corporation are such as are specified in the regulations made by the Corporation. The E. S. I. Corporation has made these rules and regulations in accordance with the rules and orders applicable to the officers and employees i.e. staff of the Central Government drawing corresponding pay scales. However, for any departure from the said rules or orders, as the case may be, in any of the matters aforesaid, the Corporation has to obtain the prior approval of the Central Government. The Corporation has to take into consideration the educational qualifications, method of recruitment, duties, responsibilities, etc. of such officers and employees under the Central Government while determining the corresponding scales of pay of its members of the staff. In case of any doubt, the Corporation refers the matter to the Central Government whose decision thereon is final [Section 17 (2)].

All the officers and servants of the E.S.I. Corporation are deemed to be the public servants within the meaning of Section 21 of the Indian Penal Code of 1860 [Section 93].

[C] Inspectors

The E.S.I. Corporation is empowered to appoint inspectors under Section 45 (1). Section 45 (1) lays down that, "the Corporation may appoint such persons as Inspectors as it thinks fit for the purpose of this Act and within such local limits as it may assign to them".

The Inspectors thus appointed have to perform such functions and duties as may be specified in the regulations passed in this behalf. The powers and duties of the Inspectors appointed under this Act are made clear in Section 45 (2) and 45 (3).

Section 45 (2) states that, "Any Inspector appointed by the Corporation under sub-section (1) thereinafter referred to as Inspectors, or other official of the Corporation authorised in this behalf by it, may for purposes of enquiring into the correctness of any of the particulars stated in any return referred to in Section 44 or for the purpose of ascertaining whether if any provisions of this Act has been complied with –

(a) require any principal or immediate employer to furnish to him such information as he may consider necessary for the purposes of this Act; or
(b) at any reasonable time enter any office, establishment, factory or other premises occupied by such principal or immediate employer and require any person found

in charge thereof to produce to such Inspector or other official and allow him to examine such accounts, books and other documents relating to the employment of persons and payment of wages or to furnish to him such information as he may consider necessary; or

(c) examine with respect to any matter relevant to the purpose aforesaid, the principal or immediate employer, his agent or servant, or any person found in such factory, establishment, office or other premises, or any person whom the said Inspector or other official, has reasonable cause to believe to be or to have been an employee.

(d) make copies, or take extracts from, any register, account book or other document maintained in such factory, establishment, office or other premises;

(e) exercise such other powers as may be prescribed.

According to Section 45 (3), "An inspector shall exercise such functions and perform such duties as may be authorised by the Corporation or as may be specified in the regulations".

2.4.6 Rules Regarding Membership and Other General Provisions of the Act

Certain general provisions regarding eligibility for re-appointment, re-election, resignation of membership, cessation of membership etc. in relation to the Corporation the Standing Committee and the Medical Benefit Council have been made in Chapter 1] of the Act. They are enumerated below.

(1) Eligibility for re-appointment or re-election [Section 6]:

An outgoing member of the Corporation, or the Standing Committee, or the Medical Benefit is considered eligible for re-appointment or re-election as the case may be.

(2) Resignation of Membership [Section 11]:

Provisions have been made in Section 11 of this Act regarding the resignation of the membership of the Corporation, or the Standing Committee, or the Medical Benefit Council. Section 11 states that, "A member of the Corporation, the Standing Committee or the Medical Benefit Council may resign his office by notice in writing to the Central Government and his seat shall fall vacant on the acceptance of the resignation by that Government."

(3) Cessation of Membership [Section 12]:

So far as the cessation of the membership of the Corporation, or the Standing Committee, or the Medical Benefit Council is concerned, the Section 12 lays down that, "(1) A member of the Corporation, the Standing Committee or the Medical Benefit Council shall cease to be a member of that body if he fails to attend three consecutive meeting thereof [Section 21 (1)].

It is provided that the Corporation, the Standing Committee or the Medical Benefit Council, as the case may be, may subject to rules made by the Central Government in this behalf, restore him to membership [Proviso to Section 12 (1)].

(2) Where in the opinion of the Central Government any person appointed, or elected to represent employers, employees or the medical profession on the Corporation, the

Standing Committee or the Medical Benefit Council, as the case may be, has ceased to represent such employers, employees or the medical profession, the Central Government may, by notification in the Official Gazette, declare that with effect from such date as may be specified thereon such person shall cease to be a member of the Corporation, Standing Committee or the Medical Benefit Council, as the case may be [Section 12 (12)].

(3) A person referred to in clause (i) of Section 4 shall cease to be a member of the Corporation when he ceases to be a Member of Parliament [Section 12 (3)].

The provisions of Section 4 have been already given under the heading 'Constitution of the Corporation'.

(4) Disqualification [Section 13]:

A person shall be disqualified for being chosen as or for being a member of the Corporation, the Standing Committee or the Medical Benefit Council –

  (a) if he is declared to be of unsound mind by a competent Court; or
  (b) if he is an undischarged insolvent; or
  (c) if he has directly or indirectly by himself or by his partner any interest in subsisting contract with, or any work being done for, the Corporation except as a medical practitioner or as a shareholder (not being a Director) of company; or
  (d) if before or after the commencement of this Act, he has been convicted of an offence involving moral turpitude.

(5) Filling of Vacancies [Section 14]:

(1) Vacancies in the office appointed or elected members of the Corporation, the Standing Committee and the Medical Benefit Council shall be filled by appointment or election, as the case may be [Section 14 (1)].

(2) A member of the Corporation, the Standing Committee or the Medical Benefit Council appointed or elected to fill a casual vacancy shall hold office only so long as the member in whose place he is appointed or elected would have been entitled to hold office if the vacancy had not occurred [Section 14 (2)].

(6) Fees and Allowances [Section 15]:

Members of the Corporation; the Standing Committee and the Medical Benefit Council shall receive such fees and allowances as may from time to time be prescribed by the Central Government [Section 15].

(7) Meetings of Corporation, Standing Committee and Medical Benefit:

Subject to any rules made under this Act, the Corporation, the Standing Committee and the Medical Benefit Council shall meet at such times and places and shall observe such rules or procedure in regard to transaction of business at their meetings as may be specified in the regulations made in this behalf.

(8) Supersession of the Corporation and Standing Committee [Section 21]:

If in the opinion of the Central Government; the Corporation or the Standing Committee persistently makes default in performing the duties imposed on it by or under this Act or abuses its powers, that Government may, by notification in the Official Gazette, supersede the Corporation, or in the case of the Standing Committee supersede, in consultation with the Corporation, the Standing Committee. [Section 21 (1)].

It is provided that before issuing a notification under this sub-section, the Central Government shall give a reasonable opportunity to the Corporation or the Standing Committee, as the case may be, to show cause why it should not be superseded and shall consider the explanations and objection, if any, of the Corporation or the Standing Committee, as the case may be [Proviso to Section 21 (1)].

(2) Upon the publication of a notification under sub-section (1) superseding the Corporation or the Standing Committee, all the members of the Corporation or the Standing Committee, as the case may be, shall, as from the date of such publication, be deemed to have vacated their offices [Section 21 (2)].

(3) When the Standing Committee has been superseded, a new Standing Committee shall be immediately constituted in accordance with Section [Section 21 (3)].

(4) When the Corporation has been superseded, the Central Government may –
    (a) immediately
    (b) in its discretion, appoint such agency, for such period as it may think fit, to exercise the powers and perform the functions of the Corporation and such agency shall be competent to exercise all the powers and perform all the functions of the Corporation [Section 21 (4)].

(5) The Central Government shall cause a full report of any action taken under this Section and the circumstances leading to such action to be laid before the Parliament at the earliest opportunity and in any case not later than three months from the date of the notification superseding the Corporation or the Standing Committee, as the case may be.

(9) Acts of Corporation, etc., not invalid by reason of defect in constitution:

No act of the Corporation, the Standing Committee or the Medical Benefit Council shall be deemed to be invalid by reason of any defect in the constitution of the Corporation, the Standing Committee or the Medical Benefit Council, or on the ground that any member thereof was not entitled to hold or continue in office by reason of any disqualification or of any irregularity in his appointment or election, or by reason of such act having been done during period of any vacancy in the office of any member of the Corporation, the Standing Committee or the Medical Benefit Council [Section 24].

2.5 Employees' State Insurance Fund

Provisions have been made in the Act to create a Fund called as the Employees' State Insurance Fund. This E.S.I. Fund is basically created for (a) payment of benefits to the insured persons according to the provisions of this Act and rules, regulations made in their behalf. (b) meeting the cost of the administration, and (c) making provisions for other authorised purposes. The provisions relating to E.S.I. Fund are made in Sections 26 to 37 (Chapter III of the Employees' State Insurance Act of 1948). These provisions are as under:

2.5.1 Raising of E.S.I. Fund

The E.S.I. Fund is mainly raised by way of contributions from employers as well as from employees. However, the Corporation is allowed to accept grants, donations, gifts from the local authority, or any individual or body of the individuals, whether incorporated or not, for all or any of the purposes of the Act. Provisions relating to raising of funds, crediting the amounts of fund, operations of fund etc. have been made in Section 26 of the Act. Section 26 lays down that, (1) All contributions paid under this Act and all other moneys received on behalf of the Corporation shall be paid into a fund called the Employees' State Insurance Fund which shall be held and administered by the Corporation for the purposes of this Act [Section 26 (1)].

(2) The Corporation may accept grants, donations and gifts from the local authority, or any individual or body whether incorporated or not, for all or any of the purposes of this Act [Section 26 (2)].

(3) Subject to the other provisions contained in this Act and to any rules or regulations made in this behalf, all moneys accruing or payable to the said Fund shall be paid into the Reserve Bank of India or such other bank as may be approved by the Central Government to the credit of an account styled the account of the Employees' State Insurance Fund [Section 26 (3)].

(4) Such account shall be operated on by such officers as may be authorised by the Standing Committee with the approval of the Corporation [Section 26 (4)].

2.5.2 Procedure for Crediting Moneys to the Banks

Rules 21 and 22 of the Employees' State Insurance (General) Rules of 1950 pertain to depositing of fund and procedure for crediting money to the banks which are as follows:

Rule 21 Bank or Banks for depositing the fund:

(1) All the money accruing or payable to the Fund shall be received by such officers of the Corporation as may be authorised by it in this behalf. The amounts so received shall as soon as practicable be acknowledged by a receipt in Form I and deposited in the Reserve or the State Bank of India or any of its subsidiaries for the Nationalised Banks into the account of the Fund.

Provided that any money may also be paid directly to the account of the Fund in any such bank.

Explanation:

"Nationalised Bank" means a corresponding new bank specified 'in the First Schedule to the Banking Companies (Acquisition and Transfer of Undertakings) Act, 1970 (5 of 1970), a corresponding new bank specified in the First Schedule to the Banking Companies (Acquisition and Transfer of Undertakings) Act, 1980 (40 of 1980)].

(2) The receipt book in Form I shall be numbered serially by machine and the unused forms shall be kept in the custody of the Financial Commissioner or such other officer of the Corporation as may be authorised by the Corporation in this behalf.

Rule 22 Procedure for crediting moneys to the Banks:

(1) All moneys accruing or payable to the Corporation shall be credited to the approved bank and not utilised directly for any purpose.

(2) The bank or banks shall be required at the end of every calendar month to furnish to the Corporation or such officer as may be authorised by it in this behalf, a statement of the amounts deposited in and withdrawn from the Fund during the month. These statements shall be examined by the Director-General before the expiry of a period of two months following the period to which the statements relate.

2.5.3 Purpose for which the Fund may be expanded

Purposes for which the Fund may be expended are enumerated in Section 28 of this Act, Section 28 states that, "Subject to the provisions of this Act and of any rules made by the Central Government in that behalf, the Employees' State Insurance Fund shall be expended only for the following purposes, namely –

(i) Payment of benefits and provision of medical treatment and attendance to insured persons and, where the medical benefit is extended to their families, the provision of such medical benefit to their families, in accordance with the provisions of this Act and defraying the charges and costs in connection therewith;

(ii) Payment of fees and allowances to members of the Corporation, the Standing Committee and the Medical Benefit Council, the Regional Boards Local Committees and Regional and Local Medical Benefit Councils;

(iii) Payment of salaries, leave and joining time allowances, travelling and compensatory allowances, gratuities and compassionate allowances, pensions, contributions to provident or other benefit fund of officers and servants of the Corporation and meeting the expenditure in respect of officers and other services set up for the purpose of giving effect to the provisions of this Act;

(iv) Establishment and maintenance of hospitals, dispensaries and other institutions and the provisions of medical and other ancillary services for the benefit of insured persons and, where the medical benefit is extended to their families;

(v) Payment of contributions to any State Government, local authority or any private body or individual, towards the cost of medical treatment and attendance provided to insured persons and, where the medical benefit is extended to their families, the cost of any building and equipment in accordance with any agreement entered into by the Corporation;

(vi) Defraying the cost (including all expenses) of auditing the accounts of the Corporation and of the valuation of its assets and liabilities;

(vii) Defraying the cost (including all expenses) of the Employees' Insurance Courts set up under this Act;

(viii) Payment of any sums under any contract entered into for the purposes of this Act by the Corporation or the Standing Committee or by any officer duly authorised by the Corporation or the Standing Committee in that behalf;

(ix) Payment of sums under any decree, order or award of any Court or Tribunal against the Corporation or any of its officers or servants for any act done in the execution of his duty or under a compromise or settlement of any suit or other legal proceeding or claim instituted or made against the Corporation;

(x) Defraying the cost and other charges of instituting or defending any civil or criminal proceedings arising out of any action taken under this Act;

(xi) Defraying expenditure, within the limits prescribed, on measures for the improvement of the health and welfare of insured persons and for the rehabilitation and re-employment of insured persons who have been disabled or injured; and

(xii) Such other purposes as may be authorised by the Corporation with the previous approval of the Central Government.

2.5.4 Administrative Expenses [Section 28-A]

Section 28-A says that, "the types of expenses which may be termed as administrative expenses and the percentage of the income of the Corporation Central Government and the Corporation shall keep its administrative expenses within the limit so prescribed by the Central Government;

2.5.5 Investment, Transfer or Realisation of the Fund [Rule 27]

Following are the rules embodied in Rule 27 of the Employees' State Insurance Fund:

(1) All the money belonging to the Fund which are not immediately required for expenses properly defrayable under the Act, may, subject to the approval of the Standing Committee, be invested by the Director-General –
   (i) In Government securities including Treasury Deposit Receipts; or
   (ii) In securities mentioned or referred to Clauses (a) to (d) of Section 20 of the Indian Trusts Act, 1882 (II of 1882); or
   (iii) As fixed deposit in the Reserve or the State Bank of India or any of its subsidiaries, or a corresponding new banks constituted under S.3 of the Banking Companies (Acquisition and Transfer of Undertakings) Act, 1970 (5 of 1970).

(2) Money belonging to the Fund shall not be invested in any other manner except with the prior approval of the Central Government.

(3) Any investment made under this rule may, subject to the provisions of sub-rules (1) and (2), be varied, transposed, or realised from time to time.

Provided, however, that if such variation, transposition or realisation is likely to result in loss, the prior approval of the Central Government shall be obtained.

Explanation: The approval of the Central Government shall not be required merely on the ground that the value of the security on its maturity is less than the price at which it was purchased.

(4) The Central Government may, at any time, direct the vacation in part or in whole, or prohibits investment, in any security or class of securities or any land or building.

(5) All dividends, interest or other sums received in respect of any investment, shall, as soon as possible after receipt, be paid into or credited to the account of the Fund.

(6) The expenses of, or the loss, if any arising from any investment shall be charged to the Fund and the profit, if any, from the sale of any investment shall also accrue to the Fund.

(7) The approval under sub-rules (1) and (2) of the Standing Committee or the Central Government, as the case may be, may be given with or without any conditions either generally or in any particular case.

2.6 Contributions

So far as the Employees' State Insurance Act of 1948 is concerned, contribution means the sum of money payable to the E.S.I. Corporation by the principal employer in respect of his employees and it includes any amount payable by or on behalf of the employees in accordance with the provisions of the Act.

Subject to the provisions of this Act, all the employees employed in factories, or establishments to which this Act applies must be insured in the manner provided by this Act [Section 38]. This scheme of Employees' State Insurance is contributory and therefore, the employers as well as their employees have to pay their contributions according to the provisions of this Act. Obviously, the contributions payable to the employers are known as 'Employers' contributions while the contributions payable by employees are known as 'Employees contribution'. All these contributions are required to be paid to the E.S.I. Corporation.

Provisions relating to contributions are included in Chapter IV under the heading "Corporation". The relevant sections are given below for your information.

Section 39. Contributions:
  (1) The contributions payable under this Act in respect of an employee shall comprise contribution payable by the employer (hereinafter referred to as the employer's contribution) and contribution payable by the employee (hereinafter referred to as the employee's contribution) and shall be paid to the Corporation [Section 39 (1)].
  (2) The contribution shall be paid at such rates as may be prescribed by the Central Government [Section 39 (2)].

It is provided that the rates so prescribed shall not be more than the rates which were in force immediately before the commencement of the Employees' State Insurance (Amendment) Act, 1989 [Proviso to Section 39 (2)].

  (3) The wage period in relation to an employee shall be the unit in respect of which all contributions shall be payable under this Act [Section 39 (3)].
  (4) The contributions payable in respect of each wage period shall ordinarily fall due on the last day of the wage period and where an employee is employed for part of the wage period or is employed under two or more employers during the same wage period, the contributions shall fall due on such days as may be specified in the regulations [Section 39 (4)].
  (5) (a) If any contribution payable under this Act is not paid by the principal employer on the date on which such contribution has become due, he shall be liable to pay simple interest at the rate of twelve per cent per annum or at such higher rate as may be specified in the regulations till the date of its actual payment [Section 39].

It is provided that higher interest specified in the regulations shall not exceed the lending rate of interest charged by any schedule bank [Proviso to Section 39 (5)].

(b) Any interest recoverable under clause (a) may be recovered as an arrear of land revenue or under Section 45-C to Section 45-I.

Explanation:

In this sub-section "schedule bank" means a bank for the time being included in the Second Schedule to the Reserve Bank of India Act, 1934 (2 of 1934). (Explanation to Sec. 39 (15)].

Sections 45-A Determination of the contributions in certain cases:

(1) Where in respect of a factory or establishment no returns, particulars, registers, or records are submitted, furnished or maintained in accordance with the provisions of Sec. 44 or any Inspector or other official of the Corporation referred to in sub-sec. (2) of Section 45 is prevented in any manner by the principal or immediate employer or any other person in exercising his functions or discharging his duties under Section 45, the Corporation may, on the basis of information available to it, by order determine the amount of contributions payable in respect of the employees of that factory or establishment.

It is provided that no such order shall be passed by the Corporation unless the principal or immediate employer or the person in charge of the factory or establishment has been given a reasonable opportunity of being heard.

(2) An order made by the Corporation under sub-section (1) shall be sufficient proof of the claim of the Corporation under Section 75 or for recovery of the amount determined by such order as an arrear of land revenue under Section 45-B for the recovery under Section 45-C to Section 45-1.

Section 45-B Recovery of contribution:

Any contribution payable under this Act may be recovered as an arrear of land revenue.

Section 45-C Issue of the Certificate to the Recovery Officer:

(1) Where any amount is in arrears under this Act, the authorised officer may issue to the Recovery Officer, a certificate under his signature specifying the amount of arrears and the Recovery Officer, on receipt of such certificate, shall proceed to recover the amount specified therein from the factory or establishment or as the case may be, the principal or immediate employer by one or more of the modes mentioned below:

(a) attachment and sale of the movable or immovable property of the factory or establishment or, as the case may be, the principal or immediate employer;

(b) arrest of the employer and his detention in prison;

(c) appointing a receiver for the management of the movable or immovable properties of the factory or establishment or, as the case may be, the employer.

Provided that the attachment and sale of any property under this section shall first be effected against the properties of the factory or establishment and where such attachment and sale is insufficient for recovering the whole of the amount of arrears specified in the certificate, the Recovery Officer may take such proceedings against the property of the employer for recovery of the whole or any part of such arrears.

(2) The authorised officer may issue a certificate under sub-section (1) notwithstanding that proceedings for recovery of the arrears by any other mode have been taken.

Section 45-D Recovery Officer to whom the certificate is to be forwarded:

(1) The authorised officer may forward the certificate referred to the section 45-C to the Recovery Officer within whose jurisdiction the employer
   (a) carries on his business or profession or within whose jurisdiction the principal place of his factory or establishment is situated; or
   (b) resides or any movable or immovable property of the factory or establishment or the principal or immediate employer is situated.

(2) Where a factory or an establishment or the principal or immediate employer has property within the jurisdiction of more than one Recovery Officer and the Recovery Officer to whom a certificate is sent by the authorised officer
   (a) is not able to recover the entire amount by the sale of the property, movable or immovable, within his jurisdiction; or
   (b) is of the opinion that for the purpose of expediting or securing the recovery of the whole or any part of the amount, it is necessary so to do, he may send the certificate or, where only a part of the amount is to be recovered, a copy of the certificate certified in the manner prescribed by the Central Government and specifying the amount to be recovered to the Recovery Officer within whose jurisdiction the factory or establishment or the principal or immediate employer has property or the employer resides, and thereupon that Recovery Officer shall also proceed to recover the amount due under this section as if the certificate or the copy thereof had been the certificate sent to him by the authorised officer.

Section 45-E Validity of the certificate and amendment thereof:

(1) When the authorised officer issues a certificate to a Recovery Officer under Section 45-C, it shall not be open to the factory or establishment or the principal or immediate employer to dispute before the Recovery Officer the correctness of the amount, and no objection to the certificate on any other ground shall also be entertained by the Recovery Officer.

(2) Notwithstanding the issue of a certificate to a Recovery Officer, the authorised officer shall have power to withdraw the certificate or correct any clerical or arithmetical mistake in the certificate by sending an intimation to the Recovery Officer.

(3) The authorised officer shall intimate to the Recovery Officer any orders, withdrawing or cancelling a certificate or any correction made by him under sub-section (2) or any amendment made under sub-section (4) of Section 45-F.

Section 45-F Stay of proceedings under the certificate and amendment or withdrawal:

(1) Notwithstanding that a certificate has been issued to the Recovery Officer for the recovery of any amount, the authorised officer may grant time for the payment of the amount, and thereupon the Recovery Officer shall stay the proceedings until the expiry of the time so granted.

(2) Where a certificate for the recovery of amount has been issued, the authorised officer shall keep the Recovery Officer informed of any amount paid or home granted for payment, subsequent to the issue of such certificate.

(3) Where the order giving rise to demand of amount for which a certificate for recovery has been issued has been modified in appeal or other proceedings under this Act, and, as a consequence thereof, the demand is reduced but the order is the subject-matter of a further proceeding under this Act, the authorised officer shall stay the recovery of such part of the amount of the certificate as pertains to the said reduction for the period for which the appeal or other proceeding remains pending.

(4) Where a certificate for the recovery of amount has been issued and subsequently the amount of the outstanding demand is reduced as a result of an appeal or other proceedings under this Act, the authorised officer shall, when the order which was the subject-matter of such appeal or other proceeding has become final and conclusive, amend the certificate or withdraw it, as the case may be.

Section 45-G Other modes of recovery:

(1) Notwithstanding the issue of a certificate in the Recovery Officer under Section 45-C, the Director General or any other officer authorised by the Corporation may recover the amount by any one or more of the modes provided in this section.

(2) If any amount is due from any person to any factory or establishment or, as the case may be the principal or immediate employer who is in arrears, the Director General or any other officer authorised by the Corporation in this behalf may require such person to deduct from the said amount the arrears due from such factory or establishment or, as the case may be, the principal or immediate employer under this Act and such person shall comply with any such requisition and shall pay the sum so deducted to the credit of the Corporation.

It is provided that nothing in this sub-section shall apply to any part of the amount exempt from attachment in execution of a decree of a civil court under Section 60 of the Code of Civil Procedure, 1908 (5 of 1908).

(3) (i) The Director General or any other officer authorised by the Corporation in this behalf may, at any time or from time to time, by notice in writing, require any person from whom money is due or may become due to the factory or

establishment or, as the case may be, the principal or immediate employer, or any person who holds or may subsequently hold money for or on account of the factory or establishment or, as the case may be, the principal or immediate employer, to pay to the Director General either forthwith upon the money becoming due or being held or at or within the time specified in the notice (not being before the money becomes due or is held) so much of the money as is sufficient to pay the amount due from the factory or establishment or, as the case may be, the principal or immediate employer in respect of arrears or the whole of the money when it is equal to or less than that amount.

(ii) A notice under this sub-section may be issued to any person who holds or may subsequently hold any money for or on account of the principal or immediate employer jointly with any other person and for the purposes of this sub-section, the shares of the joint holders in such account shall be presumed, until the contrary is proved to be equal.

(iii) A copy of the notice shall be forwarded to the principal or immediate employer at his last address known to the Director General or as the case may be the officer so authorised and in the case of a joint account to all the joint-holders at their last address known to the Director General or the officer so authorised.

(iv) Save as otherwise provided in this sub-section, every person to whom a notice is issued under this sub-section shall be bound to comply with such notice and, in particular, where any such notice is issued to a post office, bank or an insurer, it shall not be necessary for any pass book, deposit receipt, policy or any other document to be produced for the purpose of any entry, endorsement or the like being made before payment is made notwithstanding any rule, practice or requirement to the contrary.

(v) Any claim respecting any property in relation to which a notice under this sub-section has been issued arising after the date of the notice shall be void as against any demand contained in the notice.

(vi) Where a person to whom a notice under this sub-section is sent objects to it by a statement on oath that the sum demanded or any part thereof is not due to the principal or immediate employer or that he does not hold any money for or on account of the principal or immediate employer, then, nothing contained in this sub-section shall be deemed to require such person to pay any such sum or part thereof, as the case may be, but if it is discovered that such statement was false in any material particular, such person shall be personally liable to the Director General or the officer so authorised to the extent of his own liability to the principal or immediate employer on the date of the notice, or to the extent of the principal or immediate employer's liability for any sum due under this Act, whichever is less.

(vii) The Director General or the officer so authorised may, at any time or from time to time amend or revoke any notice issued under this sub-section or extend the time for making any payment in pursuance of such notice.

(viii) The Director General or the officer so authorised shall grant a receipt for any amount paid in compliance with a notice issued under this sub-section and the person so paying shall be fully discharged from his liability to the principal or immediate employer to the extent of the amount so paid.

(ix) Any person discharging any liability to the principal or immediate employer after the receipt of a notice under this sub-section shall be personally liable to the Director General or the officer so authorised to the extent of his own liability to the principal or immediate employer so discharged or to the extent of the principal or immediate employers liability for any sum due under this Act, whichever is less.

(x) If the person to whom a notice under this sub-section is sent fails to make payment in pursuance thereof to the Director General or the officer so authorised he shall be deemed to be a principal or immediate employer in default in respect of the amount specified in the notice and further proceeding may be taken against him for the realisation of the amount as if it were an arrear due from him, in the manner provided in Sections 45-C to 45-F and the notice shall have the same effect as an attachment of a debt by the Recovery Officer in exercise of his powers under Section 45-C.

(4) The Director General or the officer authorised by the Corporation in this behalf may apply to the court in whose custody there is money belonging to the principal or immediate employer for payment to him of the entire amount of such money, or if it is more than the amount due, an amount sufficient to discharge the amount due.

(5) The Director General or any officer of the Corporation may, if so authorised by the Central Government by general or special order, recover any arrears of amount due from a factory or an establishment or, as the case may be, from the principal or immediate employer by distraint and sale of its or his movable property in the manner laid down in the Third Schedule to the Income-Tax Act, 1961 (43 of 1961).

Section 45-H: Application of certain provisions of the Income-Tax Act:

The provisions of the Second and Third schedule to the 'Income Tax' Act, 1961 (43 of 1961) and the Income Tax (Certificate Proceedings) Rules, 1962, as in force from time to time, shall apply with necessary modifications, as if the said provisions and the rules referred to the arrears of the amount of contributions, interests or damages under this Act instead of to the income-tax:

Provided that any reference in the said provisions and the rules to the "assessee" shall be construed as a reference to a factory or an establishment or the principal or immediate employer under this Act.

Section 45-I: Definitions: For the purposes of Sections 45-C to 45-H
   (a) "Authorised officer" means the Director General, Insurance Commissioner, Joint Insurance Commissioner, Regional Director or such other officer as may be authorised by the Central Government, by notification in the Official Gazette;
   (b) "Recovery Officer" means any officer of the Central Government, State Government or the Corporation, who may be authorised by the Central Government, by notification in the Official Gazette, to exercise the powers of a Recovery Officer under this Act.

2.6.1 Responsibility of the Principal Employer to Pay the Contributions in the First Instance [Section 40]

It is the responsibility of the principal employer to pay the contributions in the first instance. Section 40 states that, "(1) The principal employer shall pay in respect of every employee, whether directly employed by him or by or through an immediate employer, both the employer's contribution and the employee's contribution [Section 40 (1)].

   (2) Notwithstanding anything contained in any other enactment but subject to the provisions of this Act and the regulations, if any, made thereunder the principal employer shall, in the case of an employee directly employed by him (not being an exempted employee), be entitled to recover from the employee the employee's contribution by deduction from his wages and not otherwise [Section 40 (2)].

It is provided that no such deduction shall be made from any wages other than such as relate to the period or part of the period in respect of which the contribution is payable, or in excess of the sum representing the employee's contribution for the period [Proviso to Section 40 (2)].

   (3) Notwithstanding any contract to the contrary, neither the principal employer nor the immediate employer shall be entitled to deduct the employer's contribution from any wage payable to an employee or otherwise to recover it from him [Section 40 (3)].
   (4) Any sum deducted by the principal employer from wages under this Act, shall be deemed to have been entrusted to him by the employee for the purpose of paying the contribution in respect of which, it was deducted [Section 40 (4)].
   (5) The principal employer shall bear the expenses of remitting the contributions to the Corporation [Section 40 (5)].

2.6.2 Recovery of Contributions from Immediate Employer [Section 41]

Provisions have also been made in section 41 of this Act to recover the amount of contributions paid by the principal employer from the immediate employer.

These provisions are given below:
   (1) A principal employer, who has paid contribution in respect of an employee employed by or through an immediate employer, shall be entitled to recover the

amount of the contribution so paid (that is to say the employer's contribution as well as the employee's contribution, if any) from the immediate employer, either by deduction from any amount payable to him by the principal employer under any contract or as a debt payable by the immediate employer [Section 41 (1)].

(1-A) The immediate employer shall maintain a register of employees employed by or through him as provided in the regulations and submit the same to the principal employer before the settlement of any amount payable under sub-section (1). [Section 41 (1-A)].

(2) In the case referred to in sub-section (1), the immediate employer shall be entitled to recover the employee's contribution from the employee employed by or through him by deduction from wages and not otherwise, subject to the conditions specified in the proviso to sub-section (2) of Section 40. [Section 41 (2)].

2.6.3 General Provisions as to the Payment of Contributions [Section 42]

(1) No employee's contribution shall be payable by or on behalf of an employee whose average daily wages during a wage period are below such wages as may be prescribed by the Central Government [Explanation to Section 42 (1)].

Explanation:

The average daily wages of employees shall be calculated in such a manner as may be prescribed by the Central Government [Section 42 (1)].

(2) Contribution (both the employer's contribution and the employee's contribution) shall be payable by the principal employer for each wage period in respect of the whole or part of which wages are payable to the employee and not otherwise. [Section 42 (2)].

2.6.4 Method of Payment of Contributions of

Subject to the provisions of this Act, the Corporation may make regulations for any matter relating or incidental to the payment and collection of contribution payable under this Act and without prejudice to the generality of the foregoing power; such regulations may provide for:

(a) the manner and time of payment of contributions;

(b) the payment of contributions by means of adhesive or other stamps affixed to or impressed upon books, cards or otherwise and regulating the manner, times and conditions in, at and under which, such stamps are to be affixed or impressed;

(bb) the date by which evidence of contributions having been paid is to be received by the Corporation;

(c) the entry in or upon books or cards of particulars of contributions paid and benefits distributed in the case of the insured person to whom such books or cards relate; and

(d) the issue, sale, custody, production, inspection and delivery of books or cards and the replacement of books or cards which have been lost, destroyed or defaced [Section 43].

2.6.5 Employers to Furnish Returns and Maintain Registers in Certain Cases [Section 44]

(1) Every principal and immediate employer shall submit to the Corporation or to such officer of the Corporation as it may direct such returns in such form and containing such particulars related to persons employed by him or to any factory or establishment in respect of which he is the principal or immediate employer as may be specified in regulations made in this behalf [Section 44 (1)].

(2) Where in respect of any factory or establishment, the Corporation has reason to believe that a return should have been submitted under sub-section (1) but has not been so submitted, the Corporation may require any person in charge of the factory or establishment to furnish such particulars as it may consider necessary for the purpose of enabling the Corporation to decide whether the factory or establishment is a factory or establishment to which this Act applies [Section 44 (2)].

(3) Every principal and immediate employer shall maintain such registers or records in respect of his factory or establishment as may be required by regulations made in this behalf. [Section 44 (3)].

2.6.6 Rates of Contribution

The employer's contribution was linked to the employee's contribution before 1984. The employees were divided into nine groups and their contribution varied according to their wages. The employer's contribution was exactly double the contribution of an employee. But, the Act was amended in 1984, which delinked the employer's contribution from the employee's contribution.

At present, according to the Rule 51 of the Employee's State Insurance (Central) Rules of 1950, the amount of contribution for a wage period is as follows:

(a) **Employer's contribution:** a sum (rounded off to the next higher multiple of five paise) equal to four and three-fourth per cent of the wages payable to an employee; and

(b) **Employees' contribution:** a sum (rounded off to the next higher multiple of five paisa) equal to one and three-fourth per cent of the wages payable to an employee.

Rule 50 fixes wage limit for coverage of an employee under this Act. Accordingly, "the wage limit for coverage of an employee under sub-clause (b) of clause (9) of Section 2 of the Act shall be six thousand and five hundred rupees a month".

It is also provided that an employee whose wages (excluding remuneration for overtime work) exceed six thousand and five hundred rupees a month at any time after and not before the beginning of the contribution period, shall continue to be an employee until the end of that period.

We have already considered the Section 2 (9) (b) under the heading definitions.

Exemption:

Section 42 of the Act provides that, "No employee's contribution shall be payable by or on behalf of an employee, whose average daily wages during a wage period are below such wages, as may be prescribed by the Central Government. The average daily wages of an employee shall be calculated in such manner as may be prescribed by the Central Government". Rule 52 provides the manner in which the average daily wages of an employee are to be calculated. Rule 52 states that, "the average daily wages during a wage period for exemption from payment of employees' contribution under Section 42 shall be upto and inclusive of rupees 'twenty five'".

This implies that employees whose average daily wages during a wage period are less than ₹ Twenty Five are exempted for making any contribution.

Meaning of 'Average Daily Wages during a contribution period' and 'Average Daily Wages during a wage period' is given in Rule 2 (1-A) and 2 (1-B) of the Employees' State Insurance (Central) Rules of 1950 as under:

Average Daily Wages during a Contribution Period:

"Average daily wages during a 'contribution period' means, in respect of any employee for the purpose of the daily rate of sickness benefit, maternity benefit, disablement benefit and dependent's benefit, the sum equal to one hundred and fifteen per cent of the aggregate amount of wages payable to him during that period, divided by the number of days (including paid holidays and leave days) for which such wages were payable.

Average Daily Wages during a Wage Period:

"Average daily wages during a wage period" means:

(a) in respect of an employer who is employed on time-rate basis, the amount of wages which would have been payable to him for the complete wage period had he worked on all the working days in that wage period, divided by 26 if he is monthly rated, 13 if he is fortnightly rated, 6 if he is weekly rated and 1 if he is daily rated;

(b) in respect of an employee employed on any other basis, the amount of wages earned during the complete wage period in the contribution period divided by the member of days in full or part for which he has worked for wages in that wage period.

It is also provided that where an employee receives wages without working on any day during such wage period, be shall be deemed to have worked for 26, 13, 6 or I days or day if his wage period be a month, a fortnight, a week or a day, respectively.

Explanation:

Where any night shift continues beyond midnight, the period of the night shift after midnight shall be counted for reckoning the day worked as part of the day preceding.

2.7 Various Benefits Under the Act

This Employees' State Insurance Act of 1948 provides the following six types of benefits to which the insured persons, or their dependents, or certain other persons who are covered under this Act are entitled.

[A] Sickness Benefit,
[B] Maternity Benefit,
[C] Disablement Benefit,
[D] Dependant's Benefit,
[E] Medical Benefit,
[F] Benefit in respect of funeral expenses.

All the above mentioned benefits except the medical benefit are monetary benefits. The provisions, rules and regulations regarding these benefits are contained in Sections 46 to 58 [Chapter V] of the Employees' State Insurance Act of 1948, in Rules 55 to 62 [Chapter V] of the Employees' State Insurance (Central) Rules to 1950 and in Regulations 44 to 95 [Chapter III] of the Employees' State Insurance (General) Regulations of 1950. Now, let us consider important provisions, rules and regulations pertaining to these benefits.

2.7.1 Benefits [Section 46]

Section 46 states that,

"(1) Subject to the provisions of this Act, the Insured persons, their dependents or the persons hereinafter mentioned, as the case may be, shall be entitled to the following benefits, namely:

(a) periodical payments to any insured person in case of his sickness certified by a duly appointed medical practitioner or by any other person possessing such qualifications and experience as the Corporation may, by regulations, specify in this behalf, hereinafter referred to as 'sickness benefit'.

(b) periodical payments to an insured woman in case of confinement or miscarriage or sickness arising out of pregnancy, confinement, premature birth of child or miscarriage, such woman being certified to be eligible for such payments by an authority specified in this behalf by the regulations (hereinafter referred to as maternity benefit).

(c) periodical payments to an insured person suffering from disablement as a result of an employment injury sustained as an employee under this Act and certified to be eligible for such payments by an authority, specified in this behalf by the regulations (hereinafter referred to as disablement benefit).

(d) periodical payments to such dependants of an insured person who dies as a result of an employment injury sustained as an employee under this Act, as are entitled to compensation under this Act (hereinafter referred to as dependant's benefit).

(e) medical treatment for an attendance on insured persons (hereinafter referred to as medical benefit); and

(f) Payment to the eldest surviving member of the family of an insured person who has died, towards the expenditure on the funeral of the deceased insured person or, where the insured person did not have a family or was not living with his family at the time of his death, to the person who actually incurs the expenditure on the funeral of the deceased insured person to be known as funeral expenses [Section 46 (1)].

It is also provided that the amount of such payment shall not exceed such amount as may - be prescribed by the Central Government and the claim for such payment shall be made within three months of the death of the insured person or within such extended period as the Corporation or any officer of authority authorised by it in this behalf may allow [Proviso to Section 46 (1)].

(2) The Corporation may, at the request of the appropriate Government, and subject to such conditions as may be laid down in the regulations, extend the medical benefits to the family of an insured person [Section 46 (2)].

2.7.2 Sickness Benefit

For the purpose of this Act, sickness means a condition which requires medical treatment and attendance and necessitates abstention i.e. to keep away from work on medical ground.

The qualification of a person to claim sickness benefit, the conditions subject to which such benefit may be given, the rate and period thereof shall be as may be prescribed by the Central Government [Section 49].

2.7.3 When is a Person Eligible for a Sickness Benefit?

A recipient of sickness or disablement benefit has to observe certain conditions. These conditions are stated in the provisions of Section 64 of the Act. Section 64 states that, "A person who is in receipt of sickness benefit or disablement benefit (other than benefit granted on permanent disablement) –

- (a) shall remain under medical treatment at a dispensary, hospital, clinic, or other institution provided under this Act and shall carry out the instructions given by the medical officer or medical attendant in charge thereof;
- (b) shall not, while under treatment, do anything which might retard or prejudice his chances of recovery;
- (c) shall not leave the area in which medical treatment provided by this Act is being given, without the permission of the medical officer, medical attendant or such other authority as may be specified in this behalf by the regulations; and
- (d) shall allow himself to be examined by and duly appointed medical officer or other person authorised by the Corporation in this behalf".

Section 65 makes it clear that an insured person is not entitled to receive certain benefits for the same period. Section 65 lays down that,

"(1) An insured person shall not be entitled to receive for the same period –
- (a) both sickness benefit and maternity benefit; or

(b) both sickness benefit and disablement benefit for temporary disablement; or
(c) both maternity benefit and disablement benefit or temporary disablement [Section 65 (1)].

(2) Where a person is entitled to more than one of the benefits mentioned in sub-section (1), he shall be entitled to choose which benefit he shall receive [Section 65 (2)]."

2.7.4 Maternity Benefit

Meaning of Maternity Benefit:

Maternity Benefits are periodical payments to an insured person in case of confinement or miscarriage or sickness arising out of pregnancy, confinement, premature birth of a child, or miscarriage; such insured woman being certified to be eligible for such payments by an authority specified in this behalf by the regulations. According to Section 2 (3), confinement means labour resulting in the issue of a living child, in the issue of a child whether alive or dead. While Section 2 (14-B) defines miscarriage as the expulsion of the contents of a pregnant uterus at any period prior to or during the twenty sixth week of pregnancy, but does not include any miscarriage, the causing of which is punishable under the Indian Penal Code.

Thus, an insured woman is entitled to the maternity benefit in case of (1) confinement, or (2) miscarriage, or (3) sickness arising out of pregnancy, confinement, premature birth of a child or miscarriage. However, before an insured woman is entitled to this benefit under this Act, she must be certified to be eligible for such payment by an authority specified in this behalf. Section 50 of the Act states that, "the qualification of an insured woman to claim maternity benefit, the conditions subject to which such benefit may be given, the rates and period thereof shall be such as may be prescribed by the Central Government".

2.7.5 Disablement Benefit

Disablement benefit is nothing but the periodical payments made to an insured person suffering from disablement, as a result of an **employment injury** sustained as an employee under this Act and certified to be eligible for such periodical payments by an authority, specified in this behalf by the regulations made for this purpose [Section 46 (c)]. The term employment injury used above means a personal injury to an employee caused by accident or an occupational disease arising out and in the course of his employment, being an insurable employment, whether the accident occurs or the occupational disease is contracted with or outside the territorial limits of India.

Disablement can be temporary disablement, permanent partial disablement or permanent total disablement. All these three types of disablements are defined in Section two of the Act in the following way:

"Temporary disablement" means a condition resulting from an employment injury which requires medical treatment and renders an employee, as a resultant of such injury, temporarily incapable of doing the work which he was doing prior to or at the time of injury [Section 2 (21)].

"Permanent partial disablement" means such disablement of a permanent nature, as reduces the earning capacity of an employee in every employment which he was capable of undertaking at the time of the accident, resulting in the disablement [Section 2 (15-A)]. Every injury specified in Part II of the Second Schedule is deemed to result in permanent partial disablement. The second schedule is already given elsewhere.

"Permanent total disablement" means such disablement of a permanent nature that incapacitates an employee for all work which he was capable of performing at the time of accident, resulting in such disablement [Section 2 (15-B)]. Permanent total disablement is deemed to result from every injury specified in Part I of the Second Schedule or from any combination of injuries specified in Part II thereof, where the aggregate percentage of the loss of earning capacity, as specified in the said Part II against those injuries, amounts to one hundred per cent or more.

[A] Who is entitled to receive periodical payment in respect of disablement benefit?

Subject to the provisions of this Act –

(a) a person who sustains temporary disablement for not less than three days (excluding the day of accident), shall be entitled to periodical payment at such rates and for such period and subject to such conditions as may be prescribed by the Central Government [Section 51 (a)].

(b) a person who sustains permanent disablement, whether total or partial, shall be entitled to periodical payment at such rates and for such period and subject to such conditions as may be prescribed by the Central Government. [Section 51 (b)].

[B] Presumption as to accident arising in course of employment

For the purpose of this Act, an accident arising in the course of an insured person's employment shall be presumed, in the absence of evidence to the contrary, also to have arisen out of that employment [Section 51-A].

[C] Accidents happening while acting in breach of regulations, etc.

An accident shall be deemed to arise out of and in the course of an insured person's employment, notwithstanding that he is at the time of the accident acting in contravention of the provisions of any law applicable to him, or of any orders given by or on behalf of his employer or that he is acting without instructions from his employer, if –

(a) the accident would have been deemed so to have arisen and the act not been done in contravention as aforesaid or without instructions from his employer, as the case may be; and

(b) the act is done for the purpose of and in connection with the employer's trade or business [Section 51-B].

[D] Accidents happening while travelling in employer's transport

(1) An accident happening while a person is, with the express or implied permission of his employer, travelling as a passenger by any vehicle to or from his place of work shall,

notwithstanding that he is under no obligation to his employment to travel by that vehicle, be deemed to arise out of and in the course of his employment, if –

- (a) the accident would have been deemed so to have arisen had been under such obligation; and
- (b) at the time of the accident, the vehicle –
    - (i) is being operated by or on behalf of his employer or some other person by whom it is provided in pursuance of arrangements made with his employer, and
    - (ii) is not being operated in the ordinary course of public transport service [Section 51 (c)].
- (2) In this section "vehicle" includes a vessel and an aircraft [Section 51 (c) (2)].

[E] Accidents happening while meeting emergency

An accident happening to an insured person in or about any premises at which he is for the time being employed for the purpose of his employer's trade or business, shall be deemed to arise out of and in the course of his employment, if it happens while he is taking steps, on an actual or supposed emergency at those premises, to rescue, succor or protect persons who are, or are thought to be, or possibly to be, injured or impended, or to minimize serious damage to property [Section 51-D].

[F] Occupational Disease

Section 52-A throws light on the occupational disease. The term 'occupational disease' has not been defined in this Act. But Third Schedule appended to this Act specified certain diseases as occupational diseases. The Third Schedule is given below after the provisions of Section 52-A. Following are the provisions of Section 52-A.

(1) If an employee employed in any employment specified in Part A of the Third Schedule contracts any disease specified therein as an occupational disease peculiar to that employment, or if an employee employed in the employment specified in Part B of that Schedule for a continuous period of not less than six months, contracts any disease specified therein as an occupational disease, peculiar to that employment or if an employee employed in any employment specified in Part C of that Schedule for such continuous period as the Corporation may specify in respect of each such employment, contracts any disease specified therein as an occupational disease, peculiar to that employment, the contracting of the disease shall, unless the contrary is proved, be deemed to be an "employment injury" arising out of and in the course of employment [Section 52-A (1)].

- (2) (i) Where the Central Government or a State Government as the case may be adds any description of employment to the employments specified in Schedule III to the Workmen's Compensation Act, 1923 (8 of 1923) by virtue of the powers vested in it under sub-section (3) of Section 3 of the said Act, the said description of employment and the occupational diseases specified under that sub-section as peculiar to that description of employment, shall be deemed to form part of the Third Schedule.

(ii) Without prejudice to the provisions of clause (i), the Corporation after giving, by notification in the Official Gazette, not less than three months' notice of its intention so to do, may by a like notification, add any description of employment to the employments specified in the Third Schedule and shall specify in the case of employments so added the diseases which shall be deemed for the purposes of this section to be occupational diseases, peculiar to those employments respectively and thereupon the provisions of this Act shall apply, as if such diseases had been declared by this Act to be occupational diseases, peculiar to those employments [Section 52-A (2)].

(3) Save as provided by sub-sections (1) and (2), no benefit shall be payable to an employee in respect of any disease, unless the disease is directly attributable to a specific injury by accident arising out of and in the course of his employment. [Section 52-A (3)].

(4) The provisions of Section 51-A shall not apply to the cases to which this section applies [Section 52-A (4)].

[G] Other provisions of the Act providing to disablement benefits

[I] Bar against receiving or recovery of compensation or damages under any other law: An insured person or his dependants shall not be entitled to receive or recover, whether from the employer of the insured person or from any other person, any compensation or damages under the Workmen's Compensation Act, 1923 (8 of 1923) or any other law for the time being in force or otherwise, in respect of an employment injury sustained by the insured person as an employee under this Act [Section 53].

[II] Determination of question of disablement: Any question –

(a) whether the relevant accident has resulted in permanent disablement; or

(b) whether the extent of loss of earning capacity can be assessed provisionally or finally; or

(c) whether the assessment of the proportion of the loss of earning capacity is provisional or final; or

(d) in the case of provisional assessment, as to the period for which such assessment shall hold good,

shall be determined by a medical board constituted in accordance with the provisions of the regulations and any such question shall hereinafter be referred to as the "disablement question." [Section 54].

[III] References to medical boards and appeals to medical appeal tribunals and Employees' Insurance Courts: (1) The case of any insured person for permanent disablement benefit shall be referred by the Corporation to a medical board for determination of the disablement question and if, on that or any subsequent reference, the extent of loss of earning capacity of the insured person is provisionally assessed, it shall again be so referred to the medical board not later than the end of the period taken into account by the provisional assessment [Section 54-A (1)].

(2) If the insured person or the Corporation is not satisfied with the decision of the medical board, the insured person or the Corporation may appeal in the prescribed manner and within the prescribed time to
> (i) the medical appeal tribunal constituted in accordance with the provisions of the regulations with a further right of appeal in the prescribed manner and within the prescribed time to the Employees' Insurance Court, or
> (ii) the Employees' Insurance Court directly [Section 54-A (2)].

It is provided that no appeal by an insured person shall lie under this sub-section if such person has applied for commutation of disablement benefit on the basis of the decision of the medical board and received the commuted value of such benefit [Proviso 1 to Section 54-A (2)].

It is provided further that no appeal by the Corporation shall lie under this sub-section if the Corporation paid the commuted value of the disablement benefit on the basis of the decision of the medical board [Proviso 2 to Section 54-A (2)].

[IV] Review of decisions by medical board or medical appeal tribunal: (1) Any decision under this Act of a medical board or a medical appeal tribunal may be reviewed at any time by the medical board or the medical appeal tribunal, as the case may be, if it is satisfied by fresh evidence that the decision was given in consequence of the non-disclosure or misrepresentation by the employee or any other person of a material fact (whether the non-disclosure or misrepresentation was or was not fraudulent) [Section 55 (1)].

(2) Any assessment of the extent of the disablement resulting from the relevant employment injury may also be reviewed by a medical board, if it is satisfied that since the making of the assessment, there has been a substantial and unforeseen aggravation of the results of the relevant injury [Section 55 (2)].

It is provided that an assessment shall not be reviewed under this sub-section, unless the medical board is of opinion that is having regard to the period taken into account by the assessment and the probable duration of the aggravation aforesaid, substantial injustice will be done by not reviewing it [Proviso to Section 55 (2)].

(3) Except with the leave of a medical appeal tribunal, an assessment, shall not be reviewed under sub-section (2) on any application made less than five years, or in the case of a provisional assessment, six months, from the date thereof and on such a review the period to be taken into account by any revised assessment, shall not include any period before the date of the application [Section 55 (3)].

(4) Subject to the foregoing provisions of this section, a medical board may deal with a case of review in any manner in which it could deal with it on an original reference to it, and in particular may make a provisional assessment notwithstanding that the assessment under review was final; and the provisions of Section 54-A shall apply to an application for review under this section and to a decision of a medical board in connection with such application as they apply to a case for disablement benefit under this section and to a decision of the medical board in connection with such case [Section 55 (4)].

2.7.6 Dependent's Benefit

Periodical payments to such dependants of an insured person who dies as a result of an employment injury sustained as an employee under this Act, as are entitled to compensation under this Act [Section 46 (1) (d)]. Such dependants get the dependent's benefit.

According to Section 52 of this Act,

"(1) If an insured person dies as a result of an employment injury sustained as an employee under this Act (whether or not he was in receipt of any periodical payment for temporary disablement in respect of the injury) dependants' benefit shall be payable at such rates and for such period and subject to such conditions as may be prescribed by the Central Government to his dependants specified in sub-clause (i), sub-clause (i-a) and sub-clause (ii) of clause (6-A) of Section 2 [Section 52 (1)].

(2) In case the insured person dies without leaving behind him the dependants as aforesaid, the dependants' benefit shall be paid to the other dependants of the deceased at such rates and for such period and subject to such conditions as may be prescribed by the Central Government [Section 52 (2)]".

[A] Who are dependants?

According to Section 2 (6-A), dependant means any of the following relatives of a deceased insured person namely:

- (i) a widow, a minor legitimate or adopted son, an unmarried legitimate or adopted daughter;
- (ia) a widowed mother;
- (ii) if wholly dependent on the earnings of the insured person at the time of his death, a legitimate or adopted son or daughter who has attained the age of eighteen years and is infirm.
- (iii) if wholly or in part dependent on the earnings of the insured person at the time of his death –
    - (a) a parent other than widowed mother;
    - (b) a minor illegitimate son, an unmarried illegitimate daughter or a daughter legitimate or adopted or illegitimate, if married and a minor or if widowed and a minor;
    - (c) a minor brother or an unmarried sister or a widowed sister, if a minor;
    - (d) a widowed daughter-in-law;
    - (e) a minor child of a pre-deceased son;
    - (f) a minor child of a pre-deceased daughter where no parent of the child is alive; or
    - (g) a paternal grand-parent, if no parent of the person is alive.

The relations mentioned above in group (i) are entitled to claim the dependant's benefits under this Act by virtue of their relationship with the insured person.

While the relations mentioned above in groups (ii) and (iii) have to prove their dependence on the insured person in order to claim the benefits under this Act.

[B] Rules of the Employees' State Insurance (Central) Rules of 1950 regarding the scale of dependant's benefits

Rule 58 of the Employees' State Insurance (Central) Rules of 1950 throws light on the scale of dependent's benefits. These rules are given below.

Dependant's benefits:

(1) Dependants benefit shall be paid to the dependents of the Insured person who dies as a result of an employment injury, in the following manner –

(A) In the case of death of the insured person, the dependants' benefit shall be payable to his widow and children as follows:

    (a) to the widow during life until remarriage, an amount equivalent to three fifth of the full rate and, if there are two or more widows, the amount payable to the widow as aforesaid shall be divided equally between the widows;

    (b) to each legitimate or adopted son, an amount equivalent to two-fifths of the full rate until he attains the age of eighteen years;

Provided that in the case of a legitimate son who is infirm and who is wholly dependant on the earnings of the insured person at the time of his death, dependants benefits shall continue to be paid while the infirmity lasts;

    (c) to each legitimate or adopted unmarried daughter, an amount equivalent to two-fifth of the full rate until she attains the age of eighteen years or until marriage, whichever is earlier.

Provided that in the case of legitimate or adopted unmarried daughter who is wholly dependant on the earnings of the insured person at the time of his death, dependants' benefit shall continue to be paid, while the infirmity lasts and she continues to be unmarried;

Provided further that if the total of the dependants' benefits distributed among the widow or widows and legitimate or adopted children of the deceased person as aforesaid exceeds at any time the full rate, the share of each of the dependents shall be proportionately reduced, so that the total amount payable to them does not exceed the amount of disablement benefits at the full rate.

(B) In case the deceased person does not leave a widow or legitimate or adopted child, dependents' benefit shall be payable to other dependents as follows:

    (a) to a parent or grand-parent, for life, at an amount equivalent to three tenth of the full rate and if there are two or more parents or grand-parents, the amount payable to the parents or grand-parents as aforesaid shall be equally divided between them;

    (b) to any other-

        (i) male dependent, until he attains the age of eighteen years,

        (ii) female dependent, until she attains the age of eighteen years or until marriage, whichever is earlier or if widowed, until she attains eighteen years of age or remarriage whichever is earlier; at an amount equivalent to two tenth of the full rate.

Provided that if there be more than one dependent under clause (b) the amount payable under this clause shall be equally divided between them.

(2) (a) The daily rate of dependants' benefit shall be forty per cent more than the "standard benefit rate" specified in rule 54 rounded to the next higher multiple of five paise, corresponding to the average daily wages in the contribution period corresponding to the benefit period in which the employment injury occurs.

(b) Where an employment injury occurs before the commencement of the first benefit period in respect of a person, the daily rate of dependent's benefit shall be
(i) where a person sustains employment injury after the expiry of the first wage period in the contribution period in which the injury occurs, the rate, forty per cent more than the standard benefit rate rounded to the next higher multiple of five paisa corresponding to the wage group in which his average daily wages during that wage period fall;
(ii) where a person sustains employment injury before the expiry of the first wage period in the contribution period in which the injury occurs, the rate, forty per cent more than the standard benefit rate, rounded to the next higher multiple of five paisa corresponding to the group in which wages actually earned or which would have been earned he worked for a full day on the date of accident fall.

Explanation:
The dependent's benefit rate calculated as aforesaid shall be called the "full rate".

[C] Review of Dependent's Benefit [Section 55-A]
(1) Any decision awarding dependants benefit under this Act may be reviewed at any time by the Corporation, if it is satisfied by fresh evidence that the decision was given in consequence of non-disclosure or misrepresentation by the claimant or and other person of a material fact (whether the non-disclosure or misrepresentation was not fraudulent) or that the decision is no longer in accordance with this Act due to any birth or death or due to the marriage, re-marriage or cesser of infirmity of, or attainment of the age of eighteen years by claimant [Section 55 (1)].
(2) Subject to the provisions of this Act, the Corporation may, on such review as aforesaid, direct that the dependants, benefit be continued, increased, reduced or discontinued [Section 55 (2)].

[D] Regulations of the Employees' State Insurance (General) Regulations of 1950 relating to Dependent's Benefits

Regulations from 77 to 86 of the Employees' State Insurance (General) Regulations of 1950 are related to the dependent's benefits. These regulations are given below for your information.

(1) Report of death of insured person by employment injury:

In case of death of an insured person as a result of an employment injury
   (a) if the death occurs at the place of employment the employer shall, and
   (b) if the death occurs at any other place, a dependant intending to claim dependants' benefit shall, or
   (c) any other person present at the time of death may, immediately report the death to the nearest Local Office and to the nearest dispensary, hospital, clinic or other institution where medical benefit under the Act is available [Regulation 77].

(2) Disposal of body of an insured person dying by employment injury:

Where an insured person dies as a result of an employment injury sustained as an employee under the Act, the body of the insured person shall not be disposed of until the body has been examined by an Insurance Medical Officer, who will also arrange a post-mortem examination, if considered necessary, in co-operation with any other existing agency [Regulation 78].

It is also provided that if an Insurance Medical Officer is unable to arrive for the examination within 12 hours of such death, the body may be disposed of after obtaining a certificate from such medical officer or practitioner as may be available [Proviso 1 to Regulation 78].

It is also provided further that nothing contained in this regulation shall be in derogation of any power conferred on a Coroner under any law for the time being in force or on the officer-in-charge of a police station or some other police officer under Section 174 of the Code of Criminal Procedure 1973 (2 of 1974) [Proviso to Regulation 78].

(3) Issue of death certificate:

An Insurance Medical Officer attending the disabled person at the time of his death or the Insurance Medical Officer who examines the body after the death or the Medical Officer who attended the insured person in a hospital or other institution where such disabled person died, shall issue free of charge, a death certificate in Form 17 to the dependants of the deceased and shall send a report to the appropriate Regional Office [Regulation 79].

(4) Submission of claim for dependants' benefit:
   (1) A claim for dependants' benefit shall be submitted to the appropriate Local Office by post or otherwise in Form 18 by the dependant or dependants concerned or by their legal representative or, in case of a minor, by his guardian, and such clause shall be supported by documents proving –
       (i) that the death is due to an employment injury;
       (ii) that the person claiming is a dependant entitled to claim as provided in Rule 58 of the Employees' State Insurance (Central) Rules, 1950.
       (iii) the age of the claimant;
       (iv) the infirmity of the dependant claiming to be infirm within the purview of Rule 58 of the Employees' State Insurance (Central) Rules, 1950 by a certificate of such medical or other authority as the Director-General may, by a general or special order in this behalf. [Regulation 80 (1)].

It is also provided that where the appropriate Regional Office is satisfied about the bonafides of the applicant or about the truth of the facts relating to any of the matters mentioned above, one or more of the documents may be dispensed with [Proviso to Regulation 80 (1)].

(2) The following may be accepted as proof of age –
  (a) Certified extract from an official record of births showing the date and place of birth and father's name;
  (b) Original horoscope prepared soon after birth;
  (c) Certified extract from baptismal register;
  (d) Certified extract from school record showing the date of birth and father's name;
  (e) Such other evidence as may be acceptable to the appropriate Regional Office in the circumstances of a particular case [Regulation 82 (2)].

(5) Notice for dependants' benefit:

On receipt of a claim or claims for dependants' benefit in respect of the death of an insured person, and, after making such inquiries as may be necessary about the circumstances and cause of death and about all persons who may be entitled to dependants' benefit, the appropriate Regional Office shall issue by registered post to such other persons, if any, as appear on enquiry to be entitled to dependants' benefit, and who have not yet submitted a claim for such benefit a notice for submission of claims for dependants' benefit within a period of thirty days from the date of such notice. The notice shall indicate, inter alia, the relevant provisions of the Act and regulations and the procedure for submission of a claim for dependants benefit [Regulation 81].

(6) Intimation of decision regarding dependants' benefit:

As soon as possible after the expiry of the period during which claims can be submitted in terms of the notice issued under Regulation 81, the appropriate Regional Office shall intimate by Registered Post, the decision of the Corporation in regard to the claim of each of the dependants in writing to the dependants concerned or to his legal representative, or, in the case of a minor, to his guardian [Regulation 82].

(7) Date of accrual of dependants' benefit:

The dependants' benefit shall accrue from the date of the death in respect of which the benefit is payable, or where disablement benefit was payable for that date from the date following the date of death [Regulation 83].

(8) Submission of claims for periodical payments of dependants' benefit:

Each dependant whose claim for dependant's benefit is admitted under Regulation 82, shall submit to the appropriate Local office, by post or otherwise, a claim covering, except in the case of first or final payment, a period of one or more complete calendar months in Form 18-A. Such claim may be made by the legal representative of a beneficiary or in the case of a minor by his guardian [Regulation 83-A].

(9) Review of dependants' benefit:

  (1) The amounts payable as dependants' benefit in respect of the death of any insured person may be reviewed, by the appropriate Regional Office at its own initiates,

and shall be so reviewed if an application is made to that effect, under any of the following circumstances –
(a) if any of the beneficiaries cease to be entitled to dependants' benefit by reason of marriage, re-marriage, death, age or otherwise, or
(b) if a fresh dependant is admitted to the claim for dependants benefit by the birth of a posthumous child, or
(c) if, after the previous decision as to the distribution of the dependants, benefit was taken, some facts materially affecting such distribution come to light [Regulation 84 (1)].
(2) Any review under this regulation shall be made after giving due notice by registered post to each of the dependants, stating therein the reasons for the proposed review and giving them an opportunity to submit objections, if any, to such review [Regulation 84 (2)].
(3) Subject to the provisions of the Act and these regulations, the appropriate Regional Office may, as a result of such review, commence, continue, increase reduce or discontinue from such date as it may decide the share of any of the dependants [Regulation 84 (3)].

(10) Appointment of another guardian:

If at any time the appropriate Regional Office is satisfied that a child who is in receipt of dependants' benefit is being neglected by his guardian, not being a guardian appointed under the Guardian and Wards Act, 1890, and the child's share of the dependants' benefit is not being properly spent on his or her maintenance, the appropriate Regional Office may direct that such share may be paid subject to such conditions as it may specify to such other person as it deems fit and as in its opinion would utilize it for the care and maintenance of the child [Regulation 86].

2.7.7 Medical Benefit

Medical benefit is a non-monetary benefit. A medical benefit is given either in the form of out patient treatment, and attendance in a hospital or dispensary, clinic or other institution or by visits to the home of the insured person or treatment as in-patient in a hospital or other institution. An insured person and where a medical benefit extended to the family of such insured person whose condition requires a medical treatment and attendance are entitled to receive medical benefits. According to the provisions of Section 46 (2), the E.S.I. Corporation is empowered, at the request of the appropriate Government and subject to such conditions as may be laid down in the regulations, to extend the medical benefits to the family of an insured person whom the provisions of this Act apply. The provisions in respect of medical benefits have been done in Sections 56, 57, 58 and 59 which are as follows:

[A] Medical benefit
(1) An insured person or (where such medical benefit extended to his family) a member of his family whose condition requires medical treatment and attendance, shall be entitled to receive medical benefit [Section 56 (1)].

(2) Such medical benefit may be given either in the form of out- patient treatment and attendance in a hospital or dispensary, clinic or other institution or by visits to the home of the insured person or treatment as in-patient in a hospital or other institution [Section 56 (2)].

(3) A person shall be entitled to medical benefit during any period for which contributions are payable in respect of him or in which he is qualified to claim sickness benefit or maternity benefit or is in respect of such disablement benefit as does not disentitle him to medical benefit under the regulations [Proviso 1 to Section 56 (3)].

It is provided that a person in respect of whom contribution ceases to be payable under this Act may be allowed medical benefit for such period of such nature as may be provided under the regulations [Proviso 2 to Section 56 (3)].

It is provided further that an insured person who ceases to be in insurable employment on account of permanent disablement shall continue, subject to payment of contribution and such other conditions as may be prescribed by the Central Government, to receive medical benefit till the date on which he would have vacated the employment on attaining the age of superannuation, had he not sustained such permanent disablement [Proviso 3 to Section 56 (4)].

It is provided also that an insured person, who has attained the age of superannuation, and his spouse shall be eligible to receive medical benefits subject to payment of contribution and such other conditions as may be prescribed by the Central Government [Proviso 3 to Section 56 (4)].

Explanation:

In this section, "superannuation" in relation to an insured person, means the attainment by that person of such age as is fixed in the contract or conditions of service as the age on the attainment of which he shall vacate the insurable employment or the age of sixty years where no such age is fixed and the person is no more in the insurable employment [Explanation to Section 56].

[B] Scale of medical benefit

(1) An insured person and (where such medical benefit is extended to his family) his family shall be entitled to receive medical benefit only of such kind and on such scale, as may be provided by the State Government or by the Corporation and an insured person or, where such medical benefit is extended to his family, his family shall not have a right to claim any medical treatment except such as is provided by the dispensary, hospital, clinic or other institution to which he or his family is allotted, or as may be provided by the regulations [Section 57 (1)].

(2) Nothing in this Act shall entitle an insured person and (where such medical benefit is extended to his family) his family to claim reimbursement from the Corporation of any expenses incurred in respect of any medical treatment, except as may be provided by the regulations [Section 57 (2)].

[C] Provision of medical treatment by State Government
   (1) The State Government shall provide for insured persons and (where such benefit is extended to their families) their families in the State, reasonable medical, surgical and obstetric treatment [Section 58 (1)].

It is provided that the State Government may, with the approval of the Corporation arrange for medical treatment at clinics of medical practitioners on such scale and subject to such terms and conditions as may be agreed upon [Proviso to Sec. 58 (1)].

   (2) Where the incidence of sickness benefit payment to insured persons in any State is found to exceed the all-India average, the amount of such excess shall be shared between the Corporation and the State Government in such proportion as may be fixed by agreement between them [Section 58 (2)].

It is provided that the Corporation may in any case waive the recovery of the whole or any part of the share which is to be borne by the State Government. [Proviso to Section 58 (2)].

   (3) The Corporation must enter into an agreement with a State Government in regard to the nature and scale of the medical treatment that should be provided to insured persons and (where such medical benefit is extended to the families) their families (including provision of buildings, equipment, medicines and staff and for the sharing of the cost thereof and of any excess in the incidence of sickness benefit to insured persons between the Corporation and the State Government [Section 58 (3)].
   (4) In default of agreement between the Corporation and any State Government as aforesaid, the nature and extent of the medical treatment to be provided by the State Government, and the proportion in which the cost thereof and of the excess in the incidence of sickness benefit shall be shared between the Corporation and the Government, shall be determined by an arbitrator (who shall be or shall have been a Judge of the High Court of a State) appointed by the Chief Justice of India (and the award of the arbitrator) shall be binding on the Corporation and the State Government [Section 58 (4)].

[D] Establishment and maintenance of hospitals, etc., by Corporation
   (1) The Corporation may, with the approval of the State Government, establish and maintain in a State, such as hospitals, dispensaries and other medical and surgical services as it may think fit for the benefit of insured persons and (where such medical benefit is extended to their families) their families [Section 59 (1)].
   (2) The Corporation may enter into agreement with any local authority, private body or individual in regard to the provision of medical treatment and attendance for insured persons and (where such medical benefit is extended to their families) their families, in any area and sharing the cost thereof. [Section 59 (2)].

[E] Provision of medical benefit by the Corporation in lieu of State Government
   (1) Notwithstanding anything contained in any other provision of this Act, the Corporation may, in consultation with the State Government, undertake the

responsibility for providing medical benefit to insured persons and where such medical benefit is extended to their families, to the families of such insured persons in the State subject to the condition that the State Government shall share the cost of such medical benefit in such proportion as may be agreed upon between the State Government and the Corporation [Section 59-A (1)].
(2) In the event of the Corporation exercising its power under sub-section (1), the provisions relating to medical benefit under this Act shall apply, so far as may be, as if a reference therein to the State Government were a reference to the Corporation [Section 59-A (2)].

2.7.8 Benefit in respect of Funeral Expenses

The Employees' State Insurance Act of 1948 was amended in 1966 which provided for the first time the payment of funeral expenses. Initially, the amount of the funeral expenses was fixed at ₹ 100. With effect from 22nd January 1991, it was increased upto ₹ 1000. Then, from 16th Nov. 1996, it was ₹ One thousand five hundred. They are ₹ 3,000 with effect from 01-12-2007.

If an insured person dies, the expenditure on his funeral i.e. funeral expenses are payable to the eldest surviving member of his family. But, if the decreased insured person did not have a family or was not living with his family at the time of his death, the funeral expenses are payable to the person who actually incurs the expenditure on the funeral of the deceased insured person. However, such amount does not exceed the amount as may be prescribed by the Central Government. The claim for the funeral expenses is required to be made within three months of the death of the insured person or within such extended period as the E.S.I. Corporation or any officer or authority authorised by the Corporation in this behalf may allow [Provisions of Section 46 (1) (f) of the Act and Rule of the Employees' State Insurance (Central) Rules of 1950.

2.7.9 General Provisions of the Act relating to Benefits

[I] Benefit not assignable or attachable
(1) The right to receive any payment of any benefit under this Act, shall not be transferable or assignable [Section 60 (1)].

[II] Bar of benefits under other enactments
When a person is entitled to any of the benefits provided by this Act, he shall not be entitled to receive any similar benefit admissible under the provisions of any other enactments [Section 61].

[III] Persons not to commute cash benefits
Save as may be provided in the regulations, no person shall be entitled to commute for a lump sum any disablement benefit admissible under this Act [Section 62].

[IV] Persons not entitled to receive benefit in certain cases
Save as may be provided in the regulations, no person shall be entitled to sickness benefit or disablement benefit for temporary disablement on any day on which he works or remains on leave or on a holiday in respect of which he receives wages or on any day on which he remains on strike [Section 63].

[V] Corporation's right where a principal employer fails or neglects to pay any contribution

(1) If any principal employer fails or neglects to pay any contribution under this Act, he is liable to pay in respect of any employee and by reason thereof such person becomes disentitled to any benefit or entitled to a benefit on lower scale, the Corporation may, on being satisfied that the contribution should have been paid by the principal employer, pay to the person the benefit at the rate to which he would have been entitled, if the failure or neglect had not occurred and the Corporation shall be entitled to recover from the principal employer either

   (i) the difference between the amount of benefit which is paid by the Corporation to the said person and the amount of the benefit which would have been payable on the basis of the contributions, which were in fact paid by the employer; or

   (ii) twice the amount of the contribution which the employer failed or neglected, whichever is greater [Section 68 (1)].

(2) The amount recoverable under this section may be recovered as if it were an arrear of land-revenue, or under Sections 45-C to 45-I [Section 68 (2)].

[VI] Liability of owner or occupier of factories, etc. for excessive sickness benefit

(1) Where the Corporation then considers that the incidence of sickness among insured persons is excessive by reason of

   (i) insanitary working condition in a factory or establishment or the neglect of the owner or occupier of the factory or establishment to observe any health regulations enjoined on him by or under any enactment, or

   (ii) insanitary conditions of any tenements or lodgings occupied by insured persons and such insanitary conditions are attributable to the neglect of the owner of the tenements or lodgings to observe any health regulations enjoined on him by or under any enactment,

the Corporation may send to the owner or occupier of the factory or establishment or to the owner of the tenements or lodgings, as the case may be, a claim for the payment of the amount of the extra expenditure incurred by the Corporation as sickness benefit; and if the claim is not settled by agreement, the Corporation may refer the matter, with a statement in support of its claim, to the appropriate Government [Section 69 (1)].

(2) If the appropriate Government is of the opinion that a prima facie case for inquiry is disclosed, it may appoint a competent person or persons to hold an inquiry into the matter [Section 69 (2)].

(3) If upon such inquiry it is proved to the satisfaction of the person or persons holding the inquiry that the excess in incidence of sickness among the insured persons is due to the default or neglect of the owner or occupier of the factory or establishment or the owner of the tenements or lodgings, as the case may be, the said person or persons shall determine the amount of the extra expenditure

incurred as sickness benefit, and the person or persons by whom the whole or any part of such amount shall be paid to the Corporation [Section 69 (3)].
- (4) A determination under sub-section (3) may be enforced as if it were a decree for payment of money passed in a suit by a Civil Court [Section 69 (4)].
- (5) For the purposes of this section, "owner" of tenements or lodgings shall include any agent of the owner and any person who is entitled to collect the rent of the tenements or lodgings as a lessee of the owner [Section 69 (5)].

[VII] Repayment of benefit improperly received
- (1) Where any person has received any benefit or payment under this Act when he is not lawfully entitled thereto, he shall be liable to repay to the Corporation the value of the benefit or the amount of such payment, or in the case of his death his representative shall be liable to repay the same from the assets of the deceased, if any, in his hands [Section 70 (1)].
- (2) The value of any benefits received other than cash payments shall be determined, such authority as may be specified in the regulations made in this behalf and the decision of such authority shall be final [Section 70 (2)].
- (3) The amount recoverable under this section may be recovered as if it were an arrear of land revenue for under Sections 45-C to 45-I [Section 70 (3)].

[VIII] Benefit payable up to and including day of death
If a person dies during any period for which he is entitled to a cash benefit under this Act, the amount of such benefit up to and including the day of his death shall be paid to any person nominated by the deceased person in writing in such form as may be specified in the regulations or, if there is no such nomination, to the heir or legal representative of the deceased person [Section 71].

[IX] Employer not to reduce wages, etc.
No employer by reason only of his liability for any contributions payable under this Act shall, directly or indirectly, reduce the wages of any employee, or except as provided by the regulations, discontinue or reduce benefits payable to him under the conditions of his service which are similar to the benefits conferred by this Act [Section 72].

[X] Employer not to dismiss or punish employee during period of sickness, etc.
- (1) No employer shall dismiss, discharge, or reduce or otherwise punish an employee during the period the employee is in receipt of sickness benefit or maternity benefit, nor shall he, except as provided under the regulations, dismiss, discharge or reduce or otherwise punish an employee during the period he is in receipt of disablement benefit for temporary disablement or is under medical treatment for sickness or is absent from work as a result of illness duly certified in accordance with the regulations to arise out of the pregnancy or confinement rendering the employee unfit for work. [Section 73 (1)].
- (2) No notice of dismissal or discharge or reduction given to an employee during the period specified in sub-section (1) shall be valid or operative. [Section 73 (2)].

[XI] Medical care for the benefit of insured persons

At any time when its funds so permit, the Corporation may provide or contribute towards the cost of medical care for the families of insured persons [Section 99]. Thus, this section 99 provides for the enactment of benefit.

[XII] Misuse of benefits

If the General-Government is satisfied that the benefits under this Act are being misused by insured persons in a factory or establishment, that Government may, by order, publish it in the official gazette, and disentitle such persons from such of the benefits at it thinks fit [Section 91-B].

It is provided that no such order shall be passed unless a reasonable opportunity of being heard is given to the concerned factory or establishment, insured persons and the trade unions registered under the Trade Unions Act, 1926 (16 of 1926 having members in the factory or establishment [Proviso to Section 91-B].

2.8 Important Duties of an Employer Under this Act

We have studied so far various important provisions of this Act. From these provisions, we come to know the duties of an employer. Following are the important duties of an employer.

(a) An employer has to pay his contribution of his employees to the local Corportaion office payable under this Act at such rates as prescribed by the Central Government [Section 39].

(b) The employer has to furnish returns to the Corporation or to such officer of the Corporation as it may direct in such form and containing such information and particulars relating to insured persons employed by him as may be specified in the regulations made in this behalf [Section 44 (1)].

(c) The employer has to keep the contribution cards under his safe custody. In case of destruction, loss or mutilation of cards, they must be replaced through the regional office of the Corporation.

(d) It is the duty of the employer to maintain such registers or records in respect of his factory or establishment as may be required by the regulations made in the behalf [Section 44 (3)].

(e) The employer has to produce all books, returns, registers, cards, etc. for the purpose of the inspection by an inspector appointed under this Act. [Section 45].

(f) The employees must be allowed to inspect their cards at reasonable hours.

2.9 Constitution of Employees' Insurance Court

This Act empowers the State Governments to constitute the courts for the purpose of deciding questions and disputes arising from the insurance of workmen. Such courts are known as Employees' Insurance Courts'. Section 74 and 75 of this Act lay down that where a dispute arises under the provisions of this act, the matter in that dispute shall be decided by the Employees' State Insurance Court constituted under Section 74 and not by a Civil Court.

For adjudication of dispute and claims, various provisions have been done in Sections 75 to 83 [Chapter VI] of this Act. Let us consider important various provisions relating to adjudication of disputes and claims.

[I] Constitution of Employees' Insurance Court

(1) The State Government shall, by notification in the Official Gazette, constitute an Employees' Insurance Court for such local area as may be specified in the notification [Section 74 (1)].

(2) The Court shall consist of such number of Judges as the State Government may think fit [Section 74 (2)].

(3) Any person who is or has been a judicial officer or is a legal practitioner of five years' standing shall be qualified to be a Judge of the Employees' Insurance Court [Section 74 (3)].

(4) The State Government may appoint the same Court for two or more local areas or two or more Courts for the same local area [Section 74 (4)].

(5) Where more than one Court has been appointed for the same local area, the State Government may, by general or special order, regulate the distribution of business between them [Section 85 (5)].

[II] Matters to be decided by Employees' Insurance Court

(1) if any question or dispute arises as to –
  (a) whether any person is an employee within the meaning of this Act or whether he is liable to pay the employee's contribution, or
  (b) the rate of wages or average daily wages of an employee for the purposes of this Act, or
  (c) the rate of contribution payable by a principal employer in respect of any employee, or
  (d) the person who is or was the principal employer in respect of any employee, or
  (e) the right of any person to any benefit and as to the amount and duration thereof, or
  (ee) any direction issued by the Corporation under Section 55-A on a review of any payment of dependants benefits, or
  (f) any other matter which is in dispute between a principal employer and the Corporation, or between a principal employer and an immediate employer, or between a person and the Corporation or between an employee and a principal or immediate employer, in respect of any contribution or benefit or other dues payable or recoverable under this Act, or any other matter required to be or which may be decided by the Employees' Insurance Court under this Act.

Such question or dispute subject to the provisions of sub-section (2-A), shall be decided by the Employees' Insurance Court in accordance with the provisions of this Act [Section 57 (1)].

(2) Subject to the provisions of sub-section (2-A), the following claims shall be decided by the Employees' Insurance Court, namely:
   (a) claim for the recovery of contribution from the principal employer;
   (b) claim by a principal employer to recover contributions from any immediate employer;
   (c) claim against a principal employer under Section 68;
   (d) claim under Section 70 for the recovery of the value or amount of the benefits received by a person when he is not lawfully entitled thereto; and
   (e) any claim for the recovery of any benefit admissible under this Act.
   [Section 75 (2)].

If in any proceedings before the Employees' Insurance Court, a disablement question arises and the question of a medical board or a medical appeal tribunal has not been obtained on the same and the decision of such question is necessary for the determination of the claim or question before the Employees' Insurance Court, that Court shall direct the Corporation to have the question decided by this Act and shall thereafter proceed with the determination of the claim or question before it in accordance with the decision of the medical board or the medical appeal tribunal, as the case may be, except where an appeal has been filed before the Employees' Insurance Court under sub-section (2) of Section 54-A in which case the Employees' Insurance Court may itself determine all the issues arising before it [Section 75 (2-A)].

(2-B) No matter which is in dispute between a principal employer and the Corporation in respect of any contribution or any other dues shall be raised by the principal employer in the Employees' Insurance Court unless he has deposited with the Court fifty per cent of the amount due from him as claimed by the Corporation. [Section 75 (2-B)].

It is provided that the Court may, for reasons to be recorded in writing waive or reduce the amount to be deposited under this sub-section [Proviso to Section 75 (2-B)].

(3) No Civil Court shall have jurisdiction to decide or deal with any question or dispute as aforesaid or to adjudicate on any liability which by or under this Act is to be decided by a medical board, or by a medical appeal tribunal or by the Employees' Insurance Court [Section 75 (3)].

[III] Powers of Employees' Insurance Court

(1) The Employees' Insurance Court shall have all the powers of a Civil Court for the purposes of summoning and enforcing the attendance of witnesses, compelling the discovery and production of documents and material objects, administering oath and recording evidence and such Court shall deemed to be a Civil Court within the meaning of Section 195 and Chapter XXVI of the Code of Criminal Procedure, 1973 (2 of 1974) [Section 78 (1)].

(2) The Employees' Insurance Court shall follow such procedure as may be prescribed by rules made by the State Government [Section 78 (2)].

(3) All costs identical to any proceeding before an Employees' Insurance Court shall, subject to such rules as may be made in this behalf by the State Government, be in the discretion of the Court [Section 78 (3)].

(4) An order of the Employees' Insurance Court shall be enforceable as if it were a decree passed in a suit by a Civil Court [Section 78 (4)].

2.9.1 Provisions Relating to Proceedings and Appeals

(A) Institution of proceedings etc.

Subject to the provisions of this Act and any rules made by the State Government, all proceedings before the Employees' Insurance Court shall be instituted in the Court appointed for the local area in which the insured person was working at the time the question or dispute arose [Section 76 (1)].

(2) If the Court is satisfied that any matter arising out of any proceeding pending before it can be more conveniently dealt with by any other Employees' Insurance Court in the same State, it may, subject to any rules made by the State Government in this behalf, order such manner to be transferred to such other Court for disposal and shall forthwith transmit to such other Court the records connected with that matter [Section 76 (2)].

(3) The State Government may transfer any manner pending before any Employees' Insurance Court in the State to any such Court in another State with the consent of the State Government of that State [Section 76 (3)].

(4) The Court to whom any matter is transferred under sub-section (2) or sub-section (3) shall continue the proceeding as if they had been originally instituted in it [Section 76 (4)].

(B) Commencement proceedings

(1) The proceedings before an Employees' Insurance Court shall be commenced by application [Section 77 (1)].

(1-A) Every such application shall be made within a period of three years from the date on which the cause of action arose [Section 77 (2)].

Explanation:

For the purpose of this sub-section,

(a) the cause of action in respect of a claim for benefit shall not be deemed to arise unless the insured person or in the case of dependants' benefit, the dependants of the insured person claims or claim that benefit in accordance with the regulations made in that behalf within a period of twelve months after the claim become due or within such further period as the Employees' Insurance Court may allow on grounds which appear to it to be reasonable.

(b) the cause of action in respect of a claim by the Corporation for recovering contributions (including interest and damages) from the principal employer shall be deemed to have arisen on the date on which such claim is made by the Corporation for the first time.

Provided that no claim shall be made by the Corporation after five years of the period to which the claim relates;

- (c) the cause of action in respect of a claim by the principal employer for recovering contributions from an immediate employer shall not be deemed to arise till the date by which the evidence of contributions having been paid is due to be received by the Corporation under the regulations.
- (2) Every such application shall be in such form and shall contain such particulars and shall be accompanied by such fee, if any, as may be prescribed by rules made by the State Government in consultation with the Corporation [Explanation to Section 77 (2)].

[C] Appearance by legal practitioners, etc.

Any application, appearance or act required to be made or done by any person to or before an Employees' Insurance Court (other than appearance of a person required for the purpose of his examination as witness) may be made or done by a legal practitioner or by an officer of a registered trade union authorised in writing by such person or with the permission of the court, by any other person so authorised [Section 79].

[D] Reference to High Court

An Employees' Insurance Court may submit any question of law for the decisions of the High Court and if it does so, shall decide the question pending before it in accordance with such decisions [Section 81].

[E] Appeal

- (1) Save as expressly provided in this section, no appeal shall lie from an order of an Employees' Insurance Court [Section 82 (1)].
- (2) An appeal shall lie to the High Court from an order of an Employees' Insurance Court if it involves a substantial question of law [Section 82 (2)].
- (3) The period of limitation for an appeal under this section shall be sixty days [Section 82 (3)].
- (4) The provisions of Sections 5 and 12 of the Limitation Act, 1963 (36 of 1963) shall apply to appeals under this section [Section 82 (4)].

[F] Appeal in respect of determination of disablement questions

A disablement question is to be determined first by a medical board [Section 54]. An appeal against his determination lies to the medical appeal tribunal or the Employees' Insurance Court directly [Section 54-A]. The relevant provisions in this respect have been done in Section 75 (2-A) which have been already given under the heading "Matters to be decided by Employees' Insurance Court".

[G] Stay of payment pending appeal

Where the Corporation has presented an appeal against an order of the Employees Insurance Court, that Court may, and if so directed the High Court, shall, pending the decision of the appeal, withhold the payment of any sum directed to be paid by the order appealed against [Section 83].

2.10 Penalties

In Chapter VII of the Employees' State Insurance Act of 1948, provisions have been made in Sections 84 to 86 regarding the penalties for certain offences. These provisions are as under:

2.10.1 Punishment for False Statement

Whoever, for the purpose of causing any increase in payment or benefit under this Act, or for the purpose of causing any payment or benefit to be made where no payment or benefit is authorised by or under this Act, or for the purpose of avoiding any payment to be made by himself under this Act or enabling any other person to avoid any such payment, knowingly makes or causes to be made any false statement or false representation, shall be punishable with imprisonment for a term which may extend to six months, or with fine not exceeding two thousand rupees or with both [Section 84].

Provided that where an insured person is convicted under this section, he shall be entitled for any cash benefit under this Act for such period as may be prescribed by the Central Government [Proviso to Section 84].

Bar on grant of cash benefits:

Where an insured person is convicted under Section 84 of the Act, he shall not be entitled to any cash benefit admissible under the Act for a period of three months for the first conviction and six months for each subsequent conviction from the date of receipt of the judgement from the Court in the concerned office of the Corporation [Rule 62] of the Employees' State Insurance Court (Central) Rules of 1950.

2.10.2 Punishment for Failure to Pay Contributions

If any person –
(a) fails to pay any contribution which under this Act he is liable to pay, or
(b) deducts or attempts to deduct from the wages of an employee the whole or any part of the employer's contribution, or
(c) in contravention of Section 72 reduces the wages or any privileges or benefits admissible to an employee, or
(d) in contravention of Section 73 or any regulation dismisses, discharges, reduces or otherwise punishes an employee; or
(e) fails or refuses to submit any return required by the regulations, or makes a false return, or
(f) obstructs any Inspector or other official of the Corporation in the discharge of his duties; or
(g) is guilty of any contravention of or non-compliance with any of the requirements of this Act or the rules or regulations in respect of which no special penalty is provided,
he shall be punishable –
(i) where he commits an offence under clause (a), with imprisonment for a term which may extend to three years but –
(a) which shall not be less than one year, in case of failure to pay the employee's contribution which has been deducted by him from the employee's wages and shall also be liable to fine of ten thousand rupees;

(b) which shall not be less than six months, in any other case, and shall also be liable to fine of five thousand rupees;

Provided that the Court may, for any adequate and special reasons to be recorded in the judgement, impose a sentence of imprisonment for a lesser term;

(ii) where he commits an offence under any of the clauses (b) to (g) (both inclusive), with imprisonment for term which may extend to one year or with fine which may extend to four thousand rupees or with both [Section 85].

2.10.3 Enhanced Punishment in certain cases after Previous Conviction

Whoever, having been convicted by a Court of an offence punishable under this Act, commits the same offence shall, for every subsequent offence, be punishable with imprisonment for a term which may extend to two years and with a fine of five thousand rupees [Section 85-A].

It is provided that where such subsequent offence is for failure by the employer to pay any contribution, which under this Act he is liable to pay he shall for, every such subsequent offence, be punishable with imprisonment for a term which may extend to five years, but which shall not be less than two years and shall also be liable to a fine of twenty five thousand rupees [Proviso to Section 85-A].

2.10.4 Power to Recover Damages

(1) Where an employer fails to pay the amount due in respect of any contribution or any other amount payable under this Act, the Corporation may recover from the employer by way of penalty, such damages, not exceeding the amount of arrears as may be specified in the regulations [Section 85-B (1)].

It is provided that before recovering such damages, the employer shall be given a reasonable opportunity of being heard [Proviso 1 to Section 85-B (1)].

It is provided that the Corporation may reduce or waive the damages recoverable under this section in relation to an establishment which is a sick industrial company in respect of which a scheme for rehabilitation has been sanctioned by the Board for Industrial and Financial Reconstruction, established under Section 4 of the Sick Industrial Companies (Special Provisions) Act, 1985 (1 of 1986) subject to such terms and conditions as may be specified in regulations [Proviso 2 to Section 85-B (1)].

(2) Any damages recoverable under sub-section (1) may be recovered as an arrear of land revenue or under Section 54-I [Section 85-B (2)].

We have already considered the provisions of Sections 45-C to Section 45-I under the heading 'Contributions'.

2.10.5 Power of Court to make orders [Section 85-C]

(1) Where an employer is convicted of an offence for failure to pay any contribution payable under this Act, the Court may, in addition to awarding any punishment, by order, in writing, require him within a period specified in the order (which the Court if it thinks fit and an application in that behalf, from time to time, extend), to

pay the amount of contribution in respect of the offence was committed and to furnish the return relating to such contributions [Section 85-C (1)].

(2) Where an order is made under sub-section (1), the employer shall not be liable under this Act in respect of the continuation of the offence during the period or extended period, if any, allowed by the Court, but if, on the expiry of such period or extended period, as the case may be, the order of the Court has not been fully complied with, the employer shall be deemed to have committed a further offence and shall be punishable with imprisonment in respect thereof under Section 85 and shall also be liable to pay fine which may extend to one thousand rupees for every day after such expiry on which the order has not been complied with [Section 85-C (2)].

2.10.6 Prosecutions [Section 86]

(1) No prosecution under this Act shall be instituted except by or with the previous sanction of the Insurance Commissioner or of such other officer of the Corporation as may be authorised in this behalf by the Director General of the Corporation [Section 86 (1)].

(2) No Court inferior to that of a Metropolitan Magistrate or Judicial Magistrate of the First Class shall try any offence under this Act [Section 86 (2)].

(3) No Court shall take cognizance of any offence under this Act except on a complaint made in writing in respect thereof, [Section 86 (3)].

2.10.7 Offences by Companies [Section 86-A]

(1) If the person committing an offence under this Act is a company, every person, who at the time of the offence was committed was in charge of, and was responsible to, the company for the conduct of the business of the company, as well as the company, shall be deemed to be guilty of the offence and shall be liable to be proceeded against and punished accordingly [Section 86-A (1)].

It is provided that nothing contained in this sub-section shall render any person liable to any punishment, if he proves that the offence was committed without his knowledge or that he exercised all due diligence to prevent the commission of such offence [Proviso to Section 86-A (1)].

(2) Notwithstanding anything contained in sub-section (1), where an offence under this Act has been committed with the consent or connivance of, or is attributable to, any neglect on the part of, any director or manager, secretary or other officer of the company, such director, manager, secretary or other officer shall be deemed to be guilty of that offence and shall be liable to be proceeded against and punished accordingly [Section 86-A (2)].

Explanation:

For the purposes of this section –

(i) "company" means anybody corporate and includes a firm and other associations of individuals; and

(ii) "director" in relation to –
   (a) a company, other than a firm, means the managing director or a whole-time director;
   (b) a firm means a partner in the firm [Explanation to Section 86-A].

2.11 Miscellaneous Provisions of the Act

Chapter VIII contains Sections from 87 to 100 under the heading 'Miscellaneous'. The provisions of some of the Sections e.g. 87, 88, 89, 90, 91-B etc. we have already considered while discussing the topics related to them. The remaining important provisions are given below.

[I] Writing off of losses

Subject to the conditions as may be prescribed by the Central Government, where the Corporation is of opinion that the amount of contribution, interest and damages due to the Corporation is irrecoverable, the Corporation may sanction the writing off finally of the said amount [Section 91 (c)].

[II] Power of Central Government to give directions

(1) The Central Government may give directions to a State Government as to the carrying into execution of this Act in the State [Section 92 (1)].

(2) The Central Government may, from time to time, give such directions to the Corporation as it may think fit for the efficient administration of the Act, and if any such direction is given, the Corporation shall comply with such directions. [Section 92 (2)].

[III] Corporation officers and servants to be public servants

All officers and servants of the Corporation shall be deemed to be public servants within the meaning of Section 21 of the Indian Penal Code (45 to 1860) [Section 93].

[IV] Liability in case of transfer of establishment

Where an employer, in relation to a factory or establishment, transfers that factory or establishment in whole or in part, by sale, gift, lease or license or in any other manner whatsoever, the employer and the person to whom the factory or establishment is so transferred shall jointly and severally be liable to pay the amount due in respect of any contribution or any other amount payable under this Act in respect of the periods up to the date of such transfer [Section 93-A].

It is provided that the liability of the transferee shall be limited to the value of the assets obtained by him by such transfer [Proviso to Section 93-A].

[V] Contributions, etc. due to Corporation to have priority over other debts

There shall be deemed to be included among the debts which, under Section 49 of the Presidency Towers Insolvency Act, 1909 (3 of 1909) or under Section 61 of the Provincial Insolvency Act, 1920 (5 of 1920) or under any law relating to insolvency in force in the territories which, immediately before the 1st November, 1956, were comprised in a Part B State or under Section 530 of the Companies Act 1956 (1 of 1956) are in the distribution of the property of the insolvent or in the distribution of the assets of a company being wound up, to be paid in priority to all other debts, the amount due in respect of any contribution or any other amount payable under this Act the liability wherefor accrued before the date of the order of adjudication of the insolvent or the date of the winding up, as the case may be [Section 94].

[VI] Delegation of powers

The Corporation, and, subject to any regulations made by the Corporation in this behalf, the Standing Committee may direct that all or any of the powers and functions which may be exercised or performed by the Corporation or the Standing Committee, as the case may be, may, in relation to such matters and subject to such conditions, if any, as may be specified, be also exercisable by any officer or authority subordinate to the Corporation [Section 94-A].

[VII] Power of the Central Government to make rules

(1) The Central Government may; after consultation with the Corporation and subject to the condition of previous publication, make rules not inconsistent with this Act for the purpose of giving effect to the provisions thereof. [Section 95 (1)].

(2) In particular and without prejudice to the generality of the foregoing power, such rules may provide for all or any of the following matters, namely:

(a) the limit of wages beyond which a person shall not be deemed to be an employee;

(ab) the limit of maximum monthly salary for the purpose of sub-section (1) of Section 17;

(ac) the manner in which appointments and elections of members of the Corporation, the Standing Committee and the Medical Benefit Council shall be made;

(b) the quorum at meetings of the Corporation, the Standing Committee and the Medical Benefit Council Fund the minimum number of meetings of those bodies to be held in a year;

(c) the records to be kept of take transaction of business by the Corporation, the Standing Committee and the Medical Benefit Council;

(d) the powers and duties of the Director General and the Financial Commissioner and the conditions of their service;

(e) the powers and duties of the Medical Benefit Council;

(ea) the types of expenses which may be termed as administrative expenses, the percentage of income of the Corporation which may be spent for such expenses;

(eb) the rates of contributions and limits of wages below which employees are not liable to pay contribution;

(ec) the manner of calculation of the average daily wage;

(ed) the manner of certifying the certificate to recover amount by the Recovery Officer;

(ee) the amount of funeral expenses;

(ef) the qualifications, conditions, rates and period of sickness benefit, maternity benefit, disablement benefit an dependant's benefit;

(eg) the conditions for grant of medical benefits for insured person, who cease to be in insurable employment on account of permanent disablement;

(eh) the conditions for grant of medical benefits for persons who have attained the age of superannuation;

(ei) the manner in which and the time within which appeals may be filed to medical appeal tribunals or Employees' Insurance Courts;

(f) the procedure to be adopted in the execution of contracts;

(g) the acquisition, holding and disposal of property by the Corporation;

(b) the raising and repayment of loans;

(i) the investment of the funds of the Corporation and of any provident or other benefit fund and their transfer or realisation;

(j) the basis on which the periodical valuation of the assets and liabilities of the Corporation shall be made;

(k) the bank or banks in which the funds of the Corporation may be deposited, the procedure to be followed in regard to the crediting of moneys accruing or payable to the Corporation and the manner in which any sums, may be paid out of the Corporation funds and the officers by whom such payment may be authorised;

(l) the accounts to be maintained by the Corporation and the forms in which such accounts shall be kept and the times at which such accounts shall be audited;

(m) the publication of the accounts of the Corporation and the report of auditors, the action to be taken on the audit report, the powers of auditors to disallow and surcharge items of expenditure and the recovery of sums so disallowed or surcharged;

(n) the preparation of budget estimates and supplementary estimates and the manner in which such estimates shall be sanctioned and published;

(o) the establishment and maintenance of provident or other benefit fund for officers and servants of the Corporation;

(oa) the period of non-entitlement for cash benefit in case of conviction of an insured person;

(p) any matter which is required or allowed by this Act to be prescribed by the Central Government [Section 95 (2)].

(2-A) The power to make rules conferred by this section shall include the power to give retrospective effect, from a date not earlier than the date of commencement of this Act, to the rules or any of them but no retrospective effect shall be given to any rules so as to prejudicially affect the interest of any person other than the Corporation to whom such rule may be applicable [Section 95 (2-A)].

(3) Rules made under this section shall be published in the Official Gazette and thereupon shall have effect as if enacted in this Act [Section 95 (3)].

(4) Every rule made under this section shall be laid, as soon as may be after it is made, before each House of Parliament while it is in session for a total period of thirty days which may be comprised in one session or in two or more successive sessions, and if, before the expiry of the session immediately following the session or the successive sessions aforesaid, both Houses agree in making any modification in the rule or both Houses agree that the rule should not be made, the rule shall thereafter have effect only in such modified form or be of no effect, as the case may be so however, that any such modification or annulment shall be without prejudice to the validity of anything previously done under that rule [Section 95 (4)].

[VIII] Power to remove difficulties

(1) If any difficulty arises in giving effect to the provisions of this Act the Central Government may, by order published in the Official Gazette, make such provisions or give such directions, not inconsistent with the provisions of this Act, as appears to it to be necessary or expedient for removing the difficulty. [Section 99-A (1)].

(2) Any order made under this section shall have effect notwithstanding anything inconsistent therewith in any rules or regulations made under this Act [Section 99-A (2)].

[IX] Power of State Government to make rules

(1) The State Government may after consultation with the Corporation and subject to the condition of previous publication, make rules not inconsistent with this Act in regard to all or any of the following manners, namely:

(a) the constitution of Employees' Insurance Courts, the qualifications of persons who may be appointed Judges thereof, and the conditions of service of such Judges;

(b) the procedure to be followed in proceedings before such Courts and the execution of orders made by such Courts;

(c) the fee payable in respect of applications made to the Employees' Insurance Court, the costs incidental to the proceedings in such Court, the form in which applications should be made to it and the particulars to be specified in such applications;

(d) the establishment of hospitals, dispensaries and other institutions, the allotment of insured persons or their families to any such hospital, dispensary or other institution;

(e) the scale of medical benefit which shall be provided at any hospital, clinic, dispensary or institution, the keeping of medical records and the furnishing of statistical returns;

(f) the nature and extent of the staff, equipment and medicines that shall be provided at such hospitals, dispensaries and institutions;

(g) the conditions of service of the staff employed at such hospitals, dispensaries and institutions; and

(h) any other matter which is required or allowed by this Act to be prescribed by the State Government [Section 96 (1)].

(2) Rules made under this section shall be published in the Official Gazette and thereupon shall have effect as if enacted in this Act [Section 96 (2)].

(3) Every rule made under this section shall be laid as soon as may be after it is made, before each House of the State Legislature where it consists of two Houses, or, where such Legislature consists of one House, before that House [Section 96 (3)].

[X] Power of Corporation to make regulations

(1) The Corporation may, subject to the condition to previous publication, make regulations, not inconsistent with this Act and the rules made thereunder, for the administration of the affairs of the Corporation and for carrying into effect the provisions of this Act [Section 97 (1)].

(2) In particular and without prejudice to the generality of the foregoing power, such regulations may provide for all or any of the following matters namely:

(i) the time and place of meetings of the Corporation, the Standing Committee and the Medical Benefit Council and the procedure to be followed at such meetings;

(i-a) the time within which and the manner in which a factory or establishment shall be registered;

(ii) the matters which shall be referred by the Standing Committee to the Corporation for decision;

(iii) the manner in which any contribution payable under this Act shall be assessed and collected

(iii-a) the rate of interest higher than twelve per cent on delayed payment of contributions;

(iv) reckoning of wages for the purpose of fixing the contribution payable under this Act;

(iv-a) the register of employees to be maintained by the immediate employer;

(iv-b) the entitlement of sickness benefit or disablement benefit for temporary disablement on any day on which person works or remains on leave or on holiday and in respect of which he receives wages or for any day on which he remains on strike;
(v) the certification of sickness and eligibility for any cash benefit;
(vi) the method of determining whether an insured person is suffering from one or more of the diseases specified in the Third Schedule;
(vii) the assessing of the money value of any benefit which is not a cash benefit;
(viii) the time within which and the form and manner in which any claim for
(xi) the method of calculating the amount of cash benefit payable and the circumstances in which and the extent to which commutation of disablement and dependants' benefits, may be allowed and the method of calculating the commutation value;
(xii) the notice of pregnancy or of confinement and notice and proof of sickness;
(xii-a) specifying the authority competent to give certificate of eligibility for maternity benefit;
(xii-b) the manner of nomination by an insured woman for payment of maternity benefit in case of her or her child's death;
(xii-c) the production of proof in support of claim for maternity benefit, or additional maternity benefit;
(xiii) the conditions under which any benefit may be suspended;
(xiv) the conditions to be observed by a person when in receipt of any benefit and the periodical medical examination of such persons;
(xvi) the appointment of medical practitioners for the purposes of this Act, the duties of such practitioners and the form of medical certificates;
(xvi-a) the qualifications and experience which a person should possess for giving certificate of sickness;
(xvi-b) the constitution of medical boards and medical appeal tribunals;
(xvii) the penalties for breach of regulations by fine (not exceeding two days' wages for a first breach and not exceeding three days' wages for any subsequent breach) which may be imposed on employees;
(xvii-a) the amount of damages to be recovered as penalty;
(xvii-b) the terms and conditions for reduction or waiver of damages in relation to a sick industrial company;
(xviii) the circumstances in which and the conditions subject to which any regulation may be relaxed, the extent of such relaxation, and the authority by whom such relaxation may be granted;
(xix) the returns to be submitted and the registers or records to be maintained by the principal and immediate employers. The forms of such returns, registers or records, and the times at which such returns should be submitted and the particulars which such returns, registers and records should contain;

(xx) the duties and powers of Inspectors and other officers and servants of the Corporation;

(xxi) the method of recruitment, pay and allowances, discipline; superannuation benefits and other conditions of service of the officers and servants of the Corporation other than the Director General and Financial Commissioner;

(xxii) the procedure to be followed in remitting contributions to the Corporation; and

(xxiii) any matter in respect of which regulations are required or permitted to be made by this Act [Section 97 (2)].

(2-A) The condition of previous publication shall not apply to any regulations of the nature specified in clause (xxi) of sub-section (2) [Section 97 (2-A).

(3) Regulations made by the Corporation shall be published in the Gazette of India and thereupon shall have effects as if enacted in this Act [Section 97 (3)].

(4) Every regulation shall, as soon as may be, after it is made by the Corporation, be forwarded to the Central Government and that Government shall cause a copy of the same to be laid before each House of Parliament, while it is in session for a total period of thirty days, which may be comprised in one session or in two or more successive sessions, and if, before the expiry of the session immediately following the session or the successive sessions aforesaid, both Houses agree in making any modification in the regulation or both Houses agree that the regulation should not be made, the regulation shall thereafter have effect only in such modified form or be of no effect, as the case may be, so, however, that any such modification of annulment shall be without prejudice to the validity of anything previously done under that regulation [Section 97 (4)].

Questions For Discussion

1. Explain the main object and scope of the Employees' State Insurance Act, of 1948.
2. Define and explain the following terms as used in the Employees' State Insurance Act, 1948.
   (a) Appropriate Government,
   (b) Dependent,
   (c) Employment Injury,
   (d) Employee
   (e) Exempted Employee,
   (f) Family,
   (g) Factory,
   (h) Seasonal Factory,
   (i) Immediate Employer,
   (j) Principal Employer,
   (k) Wages,
   (l) An Insurable workman
3. Explain the constitution of the E.S.I Corporation. Who are the principal officers of the Corporation?
4. Explain the powers and duties of the E.S.I. Corporation.

5. Explain the constitution, powers and duties of the Standing Committee.
6. Explain the constitution, powers and duties of the Medical Benefit Council.
7. What is the effect of suppression of the E.S.I. Corporation or the Standing Committee.
8. Give an outline of the composition and functions of the E.S.I. Corporation.
9. What is the term of the office of the members of the E.S.I. Corporation?
10. How is the Medical Benefit Council constituted?
11. What is "Employees' State Insurance Fund"? What are the purposes for which this fund may be expended?
12. State various purposes of the 'Employees' Insurance Fund'.
13. What are the different types of benefits provided by the Employees' State Insurance Act, 1948?
14. Is the right to receive payment of any benefit under this Act transferable or assignable?
15. Are any of the benefits payable under this Act liable to attachment in execution of any decree of a Court?
16. State the rules as to the employers' and employees' contribution as provided in this Act.
17. Explain the manner in which the contributions have been made payable and recoverable under this Act.
18. How are the Inspectors appointed under this Act? What are their functions and duties?
19. What do you mean by the term 'Sickness'? When is a person eligible for a sickness benefit?
20. When will a person become eligible for sickness benefit under this Act?
21. What is 'Maternity Benefit'? Under what circumstances is an insured woman entitled to the maternity benefit under this Act?
22. What is a disablement benefit? Who is entitled to receive periodical payment in respect of disablement benefit under this Act?
23. Who are entitled to get dependant's benefit in case of death arising out of employment injury?
24. If the injured employee dies, are his dependants entitled to benefits?
25. To whom is disablement benefit payable under this Act?
26. Explain the nature of medical benefit? State the provisions of this Act relating to medical benefits.

27. Explain the provisions of this Act relating to the benefit in respect of funeral expenses.
28. What are the medical and maternity benefits to which the insured persons are entitled under this Act?
29. What are the different kinds of benefits to which insured persons are entitled under this Act?
30. Can an insured woman be entitled to sickness benefit and maternity benefit together for the same period?
31. What are the benefits available under Section 46 of this Act?
32. Explain the important duties of an employer under this Act.
33. What is meant by total permanent disablement as per E.S.I. Act of 1948?
34. What are the provisions in regard to E.S.I. Corporation's rights where the principal employer fails or neglects to pay any contribution?
35. Discuss the powers of Employee's Insurance Court under this Act. What matters can this court decide?
36. Describe the benefits available to an employee in case of sickness and disablement under this Act.
37. Enumerate the matters to be decided by the Employees' Insurance Court.
38. Explain the conditions to be observed by the recipients of sickness or disablement benefit.
39. Discuss the provisions of this Act relating to sickness and maternity benefits.
40. How is the E.S.I. Corporation constituted?
41. State the circumstances under which the E.S.I. Corporation can claim from the owner of the factory the amount of extra expenditure incurred by the E.S.I. Corporation as sickness benefit under this Act.
42. What is meant by occupational disease as per this Act?
43. Who is an insured person according to this Act?
44. What are the penalties prescribed by this Act for contravention of the provisions of the Act or the Rules made thereunder?
45. Explain the provisions relating to punishment for false statement.
46. State and explain the welfare measures under Factory Act.

Chapter 3...

The Industrial Disputes Act, 1947

Contents ...

3.1 Objects of the Act
3.2 Application of the Act
3.3 Definitions
3.4 Machinery for Settlement of Industrial Disputes
3.5 Filling of Vacancies and Finality of Orders [Section 8]
3.6 Notice of Change [Section 9-A and 9-B]
3.7 Reference of Certain Individual Disputes to Grievance Settlement Authorities [Section 9-C]
3.8 Reference of Disputes to Board, Courts etc. [Section 10]
3.9 Procedure and Powers of the Authorities [Section 11]
3.10 Award and Settlement [Sections 16 to 21]
3.11 Strikes and Lock-outs [Sections 22 to 25]
3.12 Lay-off and Retrenchment
3.13 Closure of an Industrial Undertaking [Section 25 FFA]
3.14 Special Provisions relating to Lay-off, Retrenchment and Closure in certain Establishments
3.15 Offences and Penalties
3.16 Conditions of Service to Remain Unchanged
3.17 Recovery of Money Due from an Employer
3.18 Representation of Parties
3.19 Protection given to a Person or Persons under this Act
3.20 Powers given to an Appropriate Government
• Questions for Discussion
• Task for Practicals

The First World War broke out in 1914 and lasted for about four years. At the close of the War, there was a great outbreak of industrial unrest which led to the passing of the **first Industrial Trade Disputes Act**. This Act was known as the **Trade Disputes Act, 1929**. Chapter 3 and Chapter 4 of this Act were related to the establishment of tribunals for investigation and settlement of Trade Disputes. During Second World War, several emergency measures were introduced by the Central Government. In 1942, Rule 81 A was added with a view to restrain strikes and lock-outs. This Rule 81 A gave power to the Central Government to make orders prohibiting strikes, lock-outs etc. with regard to any trade disputes unless reasonable notice was given.

At the close of the year 1942, the Government promulagated an order under Rule 81-A making fourteen days previous notice essential for strikes or lock-outs. Then later on the Industrial Disputes Act, 1947 was passed which embodies important provisions of the Trade Disputes Act 1929 and also important principles of Rule 81 A.

The Industrial Disputes Act of 1947 was amended several times. The Industrial Disputes (Amendment) Act of 1982 provided for extensive changes. It had recast many terms used in the main Act, e.g. Workman, Industry, Industrial Establishment etc. The rules regarding closure, lay off, reinstatement, retrenchment etc. were also altered, Moreover, certain new concepts as well as rules had been introduced, e.g. a time limit for adjudication of disputes, a model grievances redressal procedure etc. The latest amendment a model grievances redressal procedure was made in August 1996. This Act i.e. The Industrial Disputes (Amendment) Act, 1996 received the assent of the President of India on 16th August, 1996.

3.1 Objects of the Act

The Industrial Disputes Act, 1947 can be described as a milestone in the historical development of Industrial Law in India. It is one of the self-contained Acts. It provides the machinery and procedure for the investigation and settlement of industrial disputes. The Act is mainly passed,

(a) To secure and maintain industrial peace by preventing and settling industrial disputes between the employers and workmen, or employers and employees.

(b) To promote the measures for securing amity and good relations between employers and workmen through internal works committees.

(c) To promote good relations through an external machinery of conciliation, Courts of Inquiry, Labour Courts, Industrial Tribunals and National Tribunals.

(d) To ameliorate the condition of workmen by redressal of grievances of workmen through a statutory machinery.

(e) To provide for job security to the workmen employed in industries.

(f) To prevent illegal strikes and lock-outs.

(g) To encourage collective bargaining.

1.2 Application of the Act

The law relating to industrial relations in India is contained in the Industrial Disputes Act of 1947 and several local Acts have been passed in different states a e.g. in Punjab in Rajasthan, in Maharashtra etc. The Industrial Disputes Act, of 1947 is a Central Act which came which into force on the first day of April, 1947 [Section 1 (3)]. This Act extends to the whole of India [Section 1 (2)] including the state of Jammu and Kashmir. It is applicable to all existing industries whether they are carried on by private owners or by the Government. In this chapter, we shall study various definitions given in this Act, nature of the machinery for settlement of disputes, provisions related strikes, lock-outs etc.

3.2.1 Important Features of the Industrial Disputes Act, 1947

From the provisions of the Act, we come to know certain important features of the Act which are as follows:

(a) Application of the Act:

As already made clear the law relating to industrial relations in India is contained in the Industrial Disputes Act of 1947 and several local Acts have been passed in different states, e.g. in Punjab in Rajasthan, in Maharashtra etc. The Industrial Disputes Act, of 1947 is a Central Act that came into force on the first day of April, 1947 [Section 1 (3)]. This Act extends to the whole of India [Section 1 (2)] including the state of Jammu and Kashmir. It is applicable to all existing industries. All the employees of the 'Industry' [Section 2 (j)], who are covered according to the definition of 'Workman' [Section 2 (s)] as given in the Act, are entitled to take the benefit of this Act.

(b) Meaning of 'Industrial Dispute':

In the Act, the definition and meaning of 'Industrial Dispute' is given in Section 2 (k). From that definition, we come to know as to which dispute can be called as industrial dispute.

(c) Provision of comprehensive machinery for the purpose of investigation and settlement of industrial disputes:

In the preamble of the Industrial Disputes Act of 1947, it is stated that, "*An Act to make provisions for the investigation and settlement of industrial disputes and for certain other purposes*". Thus, the Act intends the prevention and settlement of industrial disputes by making necessary provisions and for that purpose, various authorities are constituted under the Act with sufficient powers to bring about a settlement between the concerned parties. These authorities are both internal as well as external.

Voluntary settlement and conciliation, adjudication and arbitration are the three modes which have been provided for settlement of disputes under the Industrial Disputes Act of 1947. Works Committees, Conciliation Officers, Boards of Conciliation and Courts of Inquiry are the authorities under the Act which make use of conciliation as a method of settlement of industrial disputes. These authorities can only help to promote settlement of industrial disputes or inquire into them, but they cannot make any awards which are binding on the concerned parties.

Adjudication authorities are labour courts, Industrial Tribunals and National Tribunal.

(d) Speedy disposal of industrial disputes:

Provisions have been made in the Act regarding the time period within which the Conciliation Officers and the Board of Conciliation must send the reports of their efforts to bring about conciliation between the concerned parties involved in the industrial disputes. The time period is also specified in the provisions of the Act within which the Labour Courts, Industrial Tribunals and the national Industrial Tribunal should send their award after the adjudication of industrial disputes. Thus, efforts have been made by making the provisions in the Act for speedy disposal of industrial disputes.

(e) Provisions relating to strikes and lock-outs:

Strikes and lock-outs are the weapons in the hands of workmen and employers respectively to compel each other to agree to their demand or demands. The provisions relating to strikes and lock-outs have been made in Sections from 22 to 25. The Act prohibits the declaration of strike and lock-out with respect to any matter connected with an industrial disputes already pending for disposal before any of the authorities under this Act. The Act also declares a strike or lock-out illegal if it is declared by employees working in a public utility service without giving a prior notice in accordance with the provisions of this Act. Thus, it is one of the important features of the Act wherein strikes and lock-outs are prohibited under certain conditions which have been made clear in the provisions of the Act.

(f) Provisions relating to lay-off and retrenchment:

In Chapter V-A, provisions related to lay-off and retrenchment have been made. The Act lays down special provisions of lay-off, retrenchment, transfer, closure etc. of an industrial establishment for the industrial establishments which are not seasonal in their character and in which not less than one hundred workmen were employed on an average per working day for the preceding twelve months.

(g) Provisions relating to compensation to workmen in case of lay-off, retrenchment, transfer of closure of an industrial establishment:

We can find the procedure for retrenchment in the provisions of Section 25-G of the Act and re-employment of retrenched workman in Section 25-H. The Act also provides for the right of the workmen to claim compensation for lay-off, retrenchment, transfer or closure of the industrial establishment subject to certain conditions. Thus, those provisions enable the workmen to face and to overcome the economic hardships arising due to non-employment on account of their retrenchment or lay-off or due to transfer or closure of the industrial establishment wherein they are employed. These provisions are important from the viewpoint of protecting the interests of all workmen.

(h) Provisions relating to penalties for various offences:

Provisions have been made in various sections of the Act relating to the penalties for offences, e.g. penalty for closure, for committing unfair labour practices, for illegal strikes and lock-outs etc.

(i) The Act helps to maintain good industrial relations:

Maintenance of good industrial relations is important for healthy industrial and economic development. Industrial relations do not constitute a simple relationship, but they are a set of functional, inter-dependent complexities involving various factors or various variables such as economic, political, social, psychological, legal factors or variables. From this point of view and in order to provide legal, social and economic justice, various Acts relating to labour have been passed. The Industrial Disputes Act of 1947 is one of such Acts which helps to solve or to settle industrial disputes. It becomes crucial to aid all the objects of the Act which have been already stated.

3.3 Definitions

Appropriate Government [Section 2 (a)]

"Appropriate Government" means –

1. In relation to any industrial dispute that involves any industry carried on by or under the authority of the Central Government or by a railway company or concerning any

such industry as may be specified in this behalf by the Central Government or in relation to an industrial dispute concerning a Dock Labour Board established under Section 5-A of the Dock Workers (Regulation of Employment) Act, 1948 (9 of 1948), or the Industrial Finance Corporation of India established under Section 3 of the Industrial Finance Corporation Act 1948, or the Employees State Insurance Corporation established under Section 3 of the Employee's State Insurance Act, 1948, or the Board of Trustees constituted under Section 3-A of the Coal Mines Provident Fund and Miscellaneous Provisions Act 1948, or the Central Board of Trustees and the State Boards of Trustees constituted under Section 5-A and Section 5-B, respectively, of the Employees Provident Fund and Miscellaneous Provisions Act, 1952, or the Life Insurance Corporation of India established under Section 3 of the Life Insurance Corporation Act, 1956, or the Oil and Natural Gas Corporation Limited recognised under the Companies Act, 1956 and Natural Gas Commission established under Section 3 of the Oil and Natural Gas, or the Deposit Insurance and Credit Guarantee Corporation established under Section 3 of the Deposit Insurance and Credit Guarantee Corporation Act, 1961 (47 of 1961), or the Central Warehousing Corporations Act, 1962 (58 of 1962), or the Unit Trust of India established under Section 3 of the Unit Trust of India Act, 1963 (52 or 1963), or the Food Corporation of India established under Section 3, or a Board of Management established for two or more contiguous States under Section 16, of the Food Corporations Act 1964 (37 of 1964), or the Airports Authority of India constituted under Section 3 of the Airports Authority of India Act, 1994 (43 of 1994), or a Regional Rural Bank established under Section 8 of the Regional Rural Banks Act, 1976 (21 of 1976), or the Export Credit and Guarantee Corporation Limited or the Industrial Reconstruction Corporation of India Limited; Rural Bank established under Section 3 of the Regional Rural Banks Act, 1976 (21 of 1976), or the Banking Service Commission established under Section 3 of the Banking Service Commission Act, 1975 (42 of 1975), a banking or an Insurance Company, a mine, an oilfield, a Cantonment Board or a major port, the Central Government; and

2. In relation to any other industrial dispute, the State Government;

The definition of appropriate Government has a great significance and relevance under this Act. It should be remembered that the definition of appropriate Government denotes that wheresoever an industrial dispute between an establishment and workmen of such establishment may arise, the Government having jurisdiction over that area is competent to make a reference. Industrial disputes relate to different industries. Some industries are controlled by the Central Government while some industries are controlled by State Governments. The appropriate Government of that industry which is controlled by the Central Government, as given in the definition [Section 2 (a)] above, is the Central Government while in relation to any other dispute not falling within the classification of Government list, is the concerned State Government.

Arbitrator [Section 2 (aa)]:

In the Industrial Disputes Act of 1947, the definition of 'Arbitrator' is given in Section 2 (act) and it is only stated that **'Arbitrator'** includes an umpire. However, provisions relating to appointment of an umpire and to voluntary reference of dispute to arbitration have been made in Section 10-A which are as follows.

1. **Time of making voluntary reference of dispute to arbitration and who can make such reference:** Where any industrial dispute exists or is apprehended and the employer and the workmen agree to refer the dispute to arbitration, they may, at any time before the dispute have been referred under Section 10 to a Labour Court or Tribunal or National Tribunal, by a written agreement, but save as aforesaid refer the dispute to arbitration [Section 10 A (1)].

   Thus, the reference to arbitration must be made before the dispute has been referred to any authority under Section 10. Such reference to arbitration can be made by the employer and the workmen on the agreement amongst themselves where any industrial dispute exists or is apprehended.

2. **To whom arbitration reference can be made:** Section 10-A (1) makes it clear that voluntary reference of dispute to arbitration shall be made to such person or persons including the Presiding Officer of a Labour Court, Industrial Tribunal or National Tribunal as an arbitrator or arbitrators as may be specified in the arbitration agreement.

3. **Appointment of an Umpire:** The parties to the dispute can select any person as an arbitrator or persons as arbitrators. But where an arbitrator agreement provides for a reference of the dispute to an even number of arbitrators, the agreement shall provide for the appointment of another person as an umpire. The umpire thus appointed shall enter upon the reference, if the arbitrators are equally divided in their opinion, and the award of the umpire shall prevail and shall be deemed to be the arbitration award for the purpose of this Act [Section 10-A (1-A)].

4. **Form of arbitration agreement:** An arbitration agreement referred to in Section 10 A (1) shall be in such form and shall be signed by the parties there in such a manner as may be prescribed [Section 10 A (2)].

5. **Provisions relating to forward a copy of the arbitration agreement to the appropriate Government and the conciliation officer:** Section 10-A (3) states that, "A copy of the arbitration agreement shall be forwarded to the appropriate Government and the conciliation officer and the appropriate Government shall, within one month from the date of the receipt of such copy, publish the same in the Official Gazette".

6. **Opportunity to employers and workmen who are not parties to the arbitration agreement but are concerned in the dispute to represent their case:** Where an industrial dispute has been referred to arbitration and the appropriate Government is satisfied that the persons making the reference represent the majority of each party, the appropriate Government may, within one month, issue a notification in such manner as may be prescribed, and when any such notification is issued, the employers and workmen who are not parties to the

arbitration agreement but are concerned in the dispute, shall be given an opportunity of representing their case before the arbitrator or arbitrators [Section 10-A (3-A)].

7. **Duty of the arbitrators:** It is the duty of the arbitrator or arbitrators to investigate the dispute and then to submit the arbitration award duly signed to the appropriate Government. Section 10-A (4) lays down that, "The arbitrator or arbitrators shall investigate the dispute and submit to the appropriate Government the arbitration award signed by the arbitrator or arbitrators, as the case may be".

8. **Prohibition of continuance of strike or lock-out:** When a dispute is referred to arbitration, the appropriate Government may prohibit the continuance of any strike or lock-out by issuing an order. Section 10-A (4-A) states that, "where an industrial disputes has been referred to arbitration and notification has been issued under Section 10-A (3-A), the appropriate Government may, by order, prohibit the continuance of any strike or lock-out in connection with such dispute which may be in existence on the date of the reference".

9. **Arbitration Act of 1940 not to apply:** According to Section 10-A (5), "Nothing in the Arbitration Act, 1940 (10 of 1940) shall apply to arbitrations under this section". Thus, when a dispute is referred to arbitration under Section 10-A, the provisions of the Arbitration Act of 1940 do not apply to an arbitration under Section 10-A of the Industrial Disputes Act of 1947.

Average Pay [Section 2 (a a a)]:

"Average pay" means the average of the wages payable to a workman;

(i) in the case of monthly paid workman, in the three complete calendar months;

(ii) in the case of weekly paid workman, in the four complete weeks;

(iii) in the case of daily paid workman, the twelve full working days, preceding the date on which the average pay becomes payable if the workman had worked for three complete calendar months or four complete weeks or twelve full working days, as the case may be, and where such calculation cannot be made, the average pay shall be calculated at the average of the wages payable to a workman during the period he actually worked.

From the above definition, it becomes clear that this Section 2 (aaa) lays down the basis as to how the average pay of a workman is to be calculated.

When the average pay cannot be calculated on the above mentioned basis, the average is to be calculated as the average of wages payable to a workman during the period he actually worked. While calculating the average wages to a daily paid workman, weekly or other holidays should be excluded.

Muster Roll:

Muster roll simply means official list. Section 25 D of the Industrial Disputes Act of 1947 provides that notwithstanding that workmen in any industrial establishment have been laid off, it is the duty of every employer to maintain for the purposes of Sections 25-A to 25-J, a muster roll and also to provide for the making of entries properly therein by workmen who may present themselves for work at the establishment at the appointed time during normal working hours. Thus, muster roll proves to be very useful for calculating the average pay.

Award [Section 2 (b)]:

"Award" means an interim or a final determination of any industrial dispute or of any question relating thereto by and Labour Court, Industrial Tribunal or National Industrial Tribunal and includes an arbitration award made under Section 10-A.

From the above mentioned definition of award, it becomes clear that the award is of the following two kinds or types.

(a) Interim or a final determination of industrial dispute or of any other question relating thereto by any Labour Court, Industrial Tribunal or National Tribunal, and

(b) An arbitration award made under Section 10-A. The important provisions relating to award have been made in Section 16, 17, 17-A.

The following important points should be noted so far as 'award' is concerned.

1. Subject to the provisions of Section 17-A, the award published under Section 17 (1) is final and cannot be called in question by any Court in any manner whatsoever [Section 17 (2)].
2. The report of a Board or Court must be in writing and must be signed by all its members. However, a member may record a minute of dissent [Section 16 (1)].
3. The award of a Labour Court, Tribunal or National Tribunal must be signed by its Presiding Officer [Section 16 (2)].
4. Every such award must be published by the appropriate Government within *Thirty Days* from its receipt [Section 17 (1)].
5. An arbitrator functioning under Section 10-A of the Industrial Disputes Act of 1947 is a statutory tribunal. If in its award, there is any apparent error of law, it can be set aside [Rohtas Industries Limited V. Rohtas Industries Staff Union and Others - AIR (1976) Supreme Court - 425].

Banking Company [Section 2 (b b)]:

"Banking Company" means a banking company as defined in Section 5 of the Banking Companies Act, 1949 (X of 1949), having branches or other establishments in more than one State, and The Export and Import Bank of India, includes the Industrial Reconstruction Bank of India, the Reserve Bank of India, the State Bank of India, a corresponding new bank constituted under Section 3 of the Banking Companies (Acquisition and Transfer of Undertaking) Act, 1970 (5 to 1970), a corresponding new bank constituted under Section 3 of the Banking Companies (Acquisition and Transfer of Undertakings) Act, 1980 (40 to 1980), and any subsidiary bank as defined in the State Bank of India (Subsidiary Banks) Act, 1959 (38 of 1959);

Board [Section 2 (c)]:

"Board" means a Board of conciliation constituted under this Act.

Section 5 of the Industrial Disputes Act of 1947 provides for the constitution of a Board of Conciliation.

The Appropriate Government may as occasion arises, by notification in the Official Gazette, constitute a Board of Conciliation for promoting the settlement of any industrial dispute. Thus, the settlement of an industrial dispute is the main purpose behind the constitution of a Board of Conciliation. A Board of conciliation consists of a chairman and two or four members as the appropriate Government thinks fit. The chairman of a Board of Conciliation shall be an independent person. The definition of 'Independent Person' according to Section 2 (i) of the Act is given below. The other members of a Board of Conciliation are appointed in equal numbers to represent the two parties to the dispute. Each party is to recommend the names of their representatives. But, if they do not recommend the names of their representatives, the appropriate Government selects such members.

Provisions relating to the constitution, duties at of Board of conciliation have been done in Section 5 and 13 of the Act which we shall consider later.

Independent Person [Section 2 (i)]:

A person shall be deemed to be "independent" for the purpose of his appointment as the Chairman or other member of a Board, Court or Tribunal, if he is unconnected with the industrial dispute referred to such Board, Court or Tribunal or with any industry directly affected by such dispute:

Provided that no person shall cease to be independent by reason only of the fact that he is a shareholder of an incorporated company which is connected with, or likely to be affected by such industrial dispute; but in such a case, he shall disclose to the appropriate Government the nature and extent of the shares held by him in such company;

Closure [Section 2 (c c)]:

"Closure" means the permanent closing down of the place of employment or part thereof.

The definition of the term 'closure' is given in the State Acts of Maharashtra and Madhya Pradesh which is as follows.

"Closure means the closing of any place or a part of a place of employment or the total or partial suspension of work by an employer or the total partial refusal by an employer to continue to employ persons employed by him whether such closing, suspension or refusal is or is not in consequence of an industrial dispute".

Closure of an undertaking means closing of industrial activity and as a result, workmen employed in such undertaking are rendered jobless. When an undertaking is closed, compensation is required to be paid to the workmen working in such undertaking. Provisions have been made in Section 25 - FFF of the Industrial Disputes Act of 1947 regarding the compensation to be paid to workmen in case of closing down of undertaking.

Conciliation Officer [Section 2 (d):

"Conciliation Officer" means Conciliation Officer appointed under this Act.

The appropriate Government appoints such number of persons as it thinks fit to be conciliation officers by notification in the Official Gazette. A conciliation officer can be appointed for a specified area or specified industries in a specified area or for one or more specified industries and either permanently or for a limited period. Such conciliation officers are charged with the duty of mediating in and promoting the settlement of industrial disputes.

The conciliation officers thus appointed are the public servants within the meaning of Section 21 of the Indian Penal Code of 1960. Provisions relating to the appointment and duties of the conciliation officers have been made in Sections 4 and 12 respectively.

Conciliation Proceeding [Section 2 (e)]:

"Conciliation Proceeding" means any proceeding held by a conciliation officer of Board under this Act.

Controlled Industry [Section 2 (e e)]:

"Controlled Industry" means any industry the control of which by the Union has been declared by the Central Act to be expedient in the public interest.

Here it must be remembered that only when the declaration is made by the Central Act that the control of industry by the Union is necessary or suitable in the public interest then an industry is called a controlled industry.

Court [Section 2 (f)]:

"Court" means a court of enquiry constituted under this Act.

Section 6 of the Act empowers the Appropriate Government to appoint a Court of Inquiry for enquiring into any matter appearing to be connected with a relevant to an industrial dispute. A court may consist of one independent person or of such number of independent persons as the Appropriate Government may think fit and where a court consists of two or more members, one of them is appointed as the chairman. All members of the Court of Inquiry are deemed to be public servants within the meaning of Section 21 of the Indian Penal Code.

Employer [Section 2 (g)]:

"Employer" means

(i) In relation to an industry carried on by or under the authority of any department of the Central Government or a State Government, the authority prescribed in this behalf, or where no authority is prescribed, the head of the department;

(ii) In relation to an industry carried on by or on behalf of a local authority, the chief executive officer of that authority;

This definition of an employer is not exhaustive. But it must also be noted that it does not limit its sphere merely to businesses run by the Government or local authority. The Act applies to all industries carried on either by an individual or an association.

In many states the term 'employer' has been extended. For example, the Rajasthan as well as the Uttar Pradesh Industrial Disputes Act adds following two clauses after sub-clause (ii) in clause (g) which is reproduced above.

(iii) An association of a group of employees;

(iv) Where the owner of an industry in the course of or for the purpose of conducting the industry contracts with any person for the execution by or under such person of the whole or any part of any work which is ordinarily a part of the industry, the owner of such industry.

The Maharashtra Industrial Relations Act also adds the phrase "Any agent of the employer". The agent of the employer includes general manager, director and the occupier of a factory.

Executive [Section 2 (g g)]:

"Executive" in relation to a trade union, means the body by whatever name called, to which the management of the affairs of the trade union is entrusted.

Industry [Section 2 (J)]:

"Industry" means any systematic activity carried on by co-operation between an employer and his workmen (whether such workmen are employed by such employer directly or by or through any agency, including a contractor) for the production, supply or distribution of goods or services with a view to satisfy human wants to wishes (not being wants or wishes which are merely spiritual or religious in nature), whether or not –

(i) Any capital has been invested for the purpose of carrying on such activity; or

(ii) Such activity is carried on with a motive to make any gain or profit, and includes –

  (a) Any activity of the Dock Labour Board established under Section 5-A of the Dock Workers (Regulation of Employment) Act, 1948 (9 to 1948);

  (b) Any activity relating to the promotion of sales or business or both carried on by an establishment, but does not include -

1. Any agricultural operation except where such agricultural operation is carried on in an integrated manner with any other activity (being any such activity as is referred to in the foregoing provisions of this clause) and such other activity is the predominant one.

Explanation:

For the purposes of this sub-clause, "agricultural operation" does not include any activity carried on in a plantation as defined as clause (f) of Section 2 of the Plantations Labour Act 1951(69 of 1951); or

2. Hospitals or dispensaries; or

3. Educational, scientific, research or training institutions; or

4. Institutions owned or managed by organisations wholly or substantially engaged in any charitable, social or philanthropic service; or

5. Khadi or village industries; or

6. Any activity of the Government relatable to the sovereign functions of the Government including all the activities carried on by the departments of the Central Government dealing with defence research, atomic energy and space; or

7. Any domestic service; or

8. Any activity, being a profession practised by an individual or body of individuals, if the number of persons employed by the individual or body of individuals in relation to such profession is less than ten; or

9. Any activity, being an activity carried on by a co-operative society or a club or any other like body of individuals, if the number of persons employed by the co-operative society, club or other like body of individuals in relation to such activity is less than ten.

From this definition of an industry it becomes clear that an industry means –

(a) Any systematic activity which is carried on by co-operation between an employer and his workmen.

(b) Such activity is carried on for the production, supply or distribution of goods and/or services with a view to satisfy human wants. Such wants must be material and not merely spiritual or religious in nature.

(c) Whether capital for carrying on such activity is invested or not is immaterial.

(d) Such industry may be carried on for profit or gain or there may be an absence of profit motive.

(e) Such industry may be the venture in the private, public, joint or in any other sector.

The definition of 'industry' in the Industrial Disputes Act, 1947 is very comprehensive. There are two parts of the definition of 'Industry'. One part defines 'Industry' from the standpoint of an employer while the other part considers the standpoint of an employee. If an activity falls under either part of the definition, it will be an industry. This can be considered as the test for determining an industry.

Industrial Dispute (Section 2 (k):

"Industrial dispute" means any dispute or difference between employers and employers or between employers and workmen, or between workmen and workmen, which is connected with the employment or non-employment or the terms of employment or with the conditions of labour, of any person.

For any dispute to be called as an industrial dispute, it should satisfy the following essentials –

(a) There must be a difference or dispute (i) between employers and employers (ii) between workmen and workmen or (iii) between workmen and employers.

(b) A workman concerned with the dispute should not be employed in any administrative or managerial capacity.

(c) Industrial dispute must pertain to an industrial matter or

(d) It may be connected with the employment or non-employment or the terms of employment.

(e) Industrial dispute may be concerned with the condition of labour of any person.

Industrial dispute implies a real and substantial difference having some element of persistency and continuity till resolved and if not adjusted it is likely to endanger the industrial peace of the undertaking.

Here in this section, an industrial dispute means a dispute relating to an existing industry.

When a demand is made by one party and it is refused by the other party, it naturally gives rise to a dispute. Such demand can be oral or in writing. Any request contained in a letter from workmen may amount to a demand. If such request is not complied with, a dispute may arise. A demand can be made by a group of workmen or it can be made by a trade union on behalf of its members. A dispute with an individual workman may lead to an industrial dispute, if the workman is supported by his fellow workmen or his trade union.

Industrial disputes may be collective disputes or individual disputes.

Collective Disputes:

When disputes are supported by a large number of workmen, they are called collective disputes. However, there is no rigid rule laid down regarding the number of workmen whose association converts an individual dispute into a collective dispute. It is obvious that the number of workmen depends upon the facts of the case as well as the nature of the dispute.

A collective dispute may relate to any of the following matters.

(i) Hours of work, leave with pay, holidays.

(ii) Wages, bonus, gratuity, profit sharing, compensatory and other allowances.

(iii) Rules of discipline, retrenchment of workers, rationalisation, closure of establishment etc.

Individual Dispute:

Dismissal, discharge etc. of an individual workman are the causes which give rise to an individual industrial dispute. Section 2-A of the Industrial Disputes Act of 1947 throws light in the nature of individual disputes. Section 2-A is as follows –

Where any employer discharges, dismisses, retrenches or otherwise terminates the services of an individual workman, any dispute or difference between that workman and his employer connected with or arising out of, such discharge, dismissal, retrenchment or termination shall be deemed to be an industrial dispute notwithstanding that no other workman nor any union of workmen is a party to the dispute.

A few cases given below make the nature of industrial dispute more clear.

1. The term 'Industry' does not include the case of an individual who carries on his profession dependent upon his own intellectual skill. From this point of view, the calling of a solicitor is not an industry so long as a solicitor carries on the normal avocation of a solicitor. However, the calling of a solicitor may become an industry under certain circumstances, e.g. if he carries on an investment business. Hence, a dispute between a firm of solicitors and its employees is not an industrial dispute so long as it carries on only the normal avocation [Brijmohan Bagaria V.N.C. Chatterjee case, (1958) 62 C.W.N. 473].

2. An union of workmen wrote a letter to its employers, requesting to pay additional bonus. The request by the union of workers was refused. It was held that the industrial dispute arose from the refusal [Shri Minakshi Mills V. State of Madras case, AIR (1951) Mad. 974].

3. A dispute centred around a verbal assurance that the business would not be transferred at least for some years, the transfer cannot be the subject-matter of an industrial dispute [Express Newspapers Pvt Ltd. V. Workmen case. AIR 1963 SC 569].

4. A dispute between a line-operator and his management was espoused by a trade union of another organisation. As that was the 'foreign' union, it was held that it was not an industrial dispute [Newspapers Ltd., Allahabad V. State Industrial Tribunal U.P. case (1960) S.C. 1328].

5. Any claim for compensation for loss of business cannot be the subject-matter of an industrial dispute [Rohtas Industries Ltd. V. Staff Union case, A.I.R. 1976-SC-425].

6. A dispute becomes an industrial dispute even where it is sponsored by an unregistered union and where the dispute is raised by only some of the workmen [State of Bihar V. Kripa Shankar Jaiswal case - A.I.R. 1961-SC-304].

7. Two employees of a municipality were dismissed on certain charges and as a result, there arose a dispute between the municipality and the workmen employed by it. In that case, it was held that the dispute was an industrial dispute. In the term 'industry' the work 'undertaking' is used and a municipality is an undertaking which supplies light, water etc. for payment. [D.N. Banerjee V.P.R. Mukharjee case-1953-S.C.A. 303].

Industrial Establishment or Undertaking [Section 2 (ka)]:

"Industrial establishment or undertaking" means an establishment or undertaking in which any industry is carried on;

Provided that where several activities are carried on in an establishment or undertaking or undertakings and only one or some of such activities is or are an industry or industries, then –

(a) If any unit of such establishment or undertaking carrying on any activity, being an industry, is severable from the other unit or units of such establishment or undertaking such unit shall be deemed to be a separate industrial establishment or undertaking;

(b) If the predominant activity or each of the predominant activities carried on in such establishment or undertaking or any unit thereof is an industry and the other activity or each of the other activities carried on in such establishment or undertaking or unit thereof is not severable from and is, for the purpose of carrying on, or aiding the carrying on of, such predominant activity or activities, the entire establishment or undertaking or, as the case may be, unit thereof shall be deemed to be an industrial establishment or undertaking.

Insurance Company [Section 2 (kk)]:

'Insurance Company" means an insurance company as defined in Section 2 of the Insurance Act, 1938, having branches or other establishments in more than one state.

Khadi (Section 2 (kka)]:

"Khadi" has the meaning assigned to it in clause (b) of Section 2 of the Khadi and Village Industries Commission Act, 1956.

Labour Court [Section 2 (kkb)]:

Labour Court means a Labour Court constituted under Section 7.

According to Section 7 of this Act, the appropriate Government may constitute one or more Labour Courts for the adjudication of industrial disputes relating to any matter specified in the Second Schedule. The appropriate Government may also entrust certain other functions to Labour Courts. A Labour Court consists of one person only who is appointed by the appropriate Government [Section 7 (2)].

Provisions relating to jurisdiction, duties, qualifications, disqualifications etc. have been made in Section 7 of the Industrial Disputes Act. 1947.

Lay-off [Section 2 (kkk)]:

"Lay-off " (with its grammatical variations and cognate expressions) means *the failure, refusal or inability of an employer on account of shortage of coal, power or raw materials or the accumulation of stock or the break down of machinery or natural calamity or of any other connected reason to give employment to a workman whose name is borne on the muster-rolls of his industrial establishment and who has not been retrenched.*

Explanation:

Every workman whose name is borne on the muster-rolls of the industrial establishment and who presents himself for work at the establishment at the time appointed for the purpose during normal working hours on any day and is not given employment by the employer within two hours of his so presenting himself shall be deemed to have been laid-off for that day within the meaning of this clause;

Provided that if the workman, instead of being given employment at the commencement of any shift for any day is asked to present himself for the purpose during the second half of the shift for the day and is given employment then, he shall be deemed to have been laid-off only for one-half of that day;

Provided further that if he is not given any such employment even after so presenting himself, he shall not be deemed to have been laid-off for the second half of the shift for the day and shall be entitled to full basic wages and dearness allowance for that part of the day;

Thus, lay-off means to discontinue work or activity; to dismiss or discharge temporarily. In other words, it means the failure, refusal or inability on the part of an employer to provide an employment to a workman whose name is borne on the muster-rolls of the industrial establishment and who is not retrenched.

The refusal, failure or inability to provide an employment may be due to –

(a) Shortage of fuel, coal, power, raw materials, or
(b) Break down of machinery, or
(c) The accumulation of stocks, or
(d) Natural calamity or
(e) Any other connected reason.

A workman is deemed to have been laid off for any day if he remains present for work at the industrial establishment at the appointed time for the purpose and during the normal working hours on that day and if he is not given employment within two hours of his so presenting himself.

If the workman, instead of being given employment at the beginning of any shift for any day, is asked to remain present for the purpose during the second half of the shift for the day and is given employment then, such worker is deemed to have been laid-off only for one half of the day [Proviso to Section 2 (k k k)].

If the workman is not given any such employment even after so remaining present, he is not deemed to have been laid off for the second half of the shift for the day and such workman is entitled to full basic wages and dearness allowance for that part of the day. [Proviso to Section 2 (kkk)] .

Lock-out [Section 2 (L)]:

"Lock-out" means *the temporary closing of a place of employment or the suspension of work, or the refusal by an employer to continue to employ any number of persons employed by him.*

From the above mentioned definition of Lock-out, it becomes clear that in lock-out the employer refuses to continue to employ the workmen appointed by him but the business activity is not closed down or stopped or intended to be closed down. Lock-out means (1) temporary closing of a place of employment or (2) the suspension of work, or (3) the refusal by an employer to continue to employ any number of workmen employed by him. Lock-out is the antithesis of a strike.

A strike is a weapon available to workmen for enforcing their demands while lock-out is a weapon available to an employer to persuade the workmen to see his point of view and to accept his demand. Lock-out is also a coercive process.

The liability of an employer in the case of lock-out depends upon whether the lock-out is justified and legal or not. In one case where the manager was attacked and the staff were also threatened, the lock out declared was justified.

Lock-out does not include a discharge. When an industrial establishment closes down its activities or business, terminates its workmen, such act of the industrial establishment cannot be regarded as lock-out. Even mere refusal by an employer to allow late comers on any days to work on that day does not amount to a lock-out.

Lock-out is really a collective dispute which must be either antecedent to or simultaneous with the refusal to provide employment or work.

Characteristics of Lock-out:

The important characteristics of lock-out are as follows:

1. Lock-out is an act of management. It is generally intended to put some pressure on the workers in order to make them agree to the terms of work of their employer.
2. Mere suspension of work (e.g. on account of shortage of raw materials, coal, supply of water etc.) is not lock-out.
3. Lock-out indicates the temporary closure of the place of business and not the closure of the business itself.
4. Lock-out is generally caused by strike, fear of disorder, fear of destruction of the properties of the firm, company etc. Most of these causes are the results of industrial disputes.
5. Lock-out indicates the temporary closing of a place of employment, or the suspension of work or the refusal by an employer to continue to employ any number of persons employed by him.

Major Port [Section 2 (1a)]:

"Major port" means a major-port as defined in clause (8) of Section - 3 of the Indian Ports Act, 1908.

Mine [Section 2 (1b)]:

"Mine" means a mine as defined in clause J of Section 2 (1) of the Mines Act, 1952.

National Tribunal [Section 2 (11)]:

"National Tribunal" means a National Industrial Tribunal Constituted under Section 7-B.

The Central Government is authorised under this Act to constitute one or more National Industrial Tribunals for the adjudication of industrial disputes, which involve questions of national importance or such disputes in which the industrial establishments situated in more than one state are interested or affected by such disputes. A National Tribunal consists of one person only and such person is appointed by the Central Government. Certain functions or duties are entrusted to National Tribunal as the Government may think fit.

Office-bearer [Section 2 (111)]:

"Office-bearer" in relation to a trade union includes any member of the executive thereof, but does not include an auditor.

Prescribed [Section 2 (m)]:

"Prescribed" means prescribed by rules made under this Act.

Public Utility Service [Section 2 (n)]:

Public utility service "means"

1. Any railway service or any transport service for the carriage of passengers or goods by air;
    (a) Any service in, or in connection with the working of, any major port of dock;
2. Any section of an industrial establishment on the working of which the safety of the establishment or the workmen employed therein depends;
3. Any postal, telegraph or telephone service;
4. Any industry which supplies power, light or water to the public;
5. Any system of public conservancy or sanitation;
6. Any industry specified in the First Schedule which the appropriate Government may, if satisfied that public emergency or public interest so requires, by notification in the Official Gazette, declare to be public utility service for the purposes of this act, for such period as may be specified in the notification.

Provided that the period so specified shall not, in the first instance, exceed six months but may by a like notification, be extended from time to time, by any period not exceeding six months, at any one time, if in the opinion of the appropriate Government public emergency of public interest requires such extension;

The First Schedule:

The industries which may be declared to be public utility services under Section 2 (n) (vi) are given below.

1. Transport, other than railways, for the carriage of pasengers or goods by land or water.
2. Banking.
3. Cement.
4. Coal.
5. Cotton textiles.

6. Food stuffs.
7. Iron and steel.
8. Defence establishments.
9. Service in hospitals and dispensaries.
10. Fire brigade service.
11. India Government Mints.
12. India Security Press.
13. Copper mining.
14. Lead mining.
15. Zinc mining.
16. Iron ore mining.
17. Service in any oil field.
18. Service in Uranium industry.
19. Pyrites mining industry.
20. Security paper mill (Hoshingabad).
21. Service in Bank note press (Dewas).
22. Phosphorite mining.
23. Magnesite mining.
24. Currency note press.
25. Manufacture of production of mineral oil (crude oil), motor and aviation spirit, diesel oil, kerosence oil, fuel oil, diverse hydrocarbon oils and their blends including synthetic fuels, lubricating oils and the like.
26. Service in the International Airports Authority of India.
27. Industrial establishments manufacturing or producing Nuclear Fuel and Components, Heavy Water and Allied Chemicals and Atomic Energy.

The appropriate Government may declare any industry specified in the First Schedule reproduced above to be a public utility service for the purpose of this Act if it is satisfied that the public emergency or interest so demands. Of course an appropriate Government may declare any industry in the first schedule as the public utility service for such period as may be specified in the notification but in the first instance such period may not exceed six months.

Railway Company [Section 2 (0)]:

"Railway Company" means railway company as defined in Section 3 of the Indian Railways Act, 1890.

Retrenchment [Section 2 (00)]:

"Retrenchment" means the termination by the employer of the service of a workman for any reason whatsoever, otherwise than as punishment inflicted by way of disciplinary action, but does not include –

(a) Voluntary retirement of the workman; or

(b) Retirement of the workmen on reaching the age of superannuation if the contract of the employment between the employer and the workman concerned contains a stipulation in that behalf; or
  (i) Termination of the service of the workmen as a result of the non-renewal of the contract of employment between the employer and the workmen concerned on its expiry or of such contract terminated under a stipulation in that behalf contained therein, or;
(c) Termination of the service of a workman on the ground of continued ill health.

The word or the term 'retrenchment' as used in this Act means the termination by the employer of the services of a workman for any reason whatsoever, otherwise than a punishment inflicted by way of disciplinary action. Retrenchment does not include -

(a) Voluntary retirement (b) termination of services on the ground of ill health (c) termination on the ground of non-renewal of service contract (d) retirement on reaching the age of superannuation.

Retrenchment simply means "to end, conclude or cease", the business may be continued but a portion of the staff is discharged as surplus age. The termination of services of all workmen as a result of the closure of business cannot be described as retrenchment.

Automatic termination of service on efflux of contractual period amounts to retrenchment. Termination of service on the ground of reduction in the volume of business also amounts to retrenchment. Thus, retrenchment includes all kinds of termination of services by an employer for any reason whatsoever except those not expressly included in section 25 F, 25 FF and 25 FFF. Even discharge of a workman as the ground of his failure to pass confirmation test also amounts to retrenchment.

Settlement [Section 2 (p)]:

"Settlement" means *a settlement arrived at in the course of conciliation proceeding and includes a written agreement between the employer and workmen arrived at otherwise than in the course of conciliation proceeding where such agreement has been signed by the parties thereto in such manner as may be prescribed and a copy thereof has been sent to an officer authorised in this behalf by the appropriate Government and Conciliation Officer.*

A settlement must settle the dispute in question. Where parties to a dispute agree to refer the dispute to arbitration, such an agreement is not a settlement as the dispute continues to subsist even after the agreement. Therefore an arbitration agreement is not a settlement. In one case, it was held that where there was no settlement of the dispute or any part thereof and as the dispute continued to subsist after the arbitration agreement, it was not settlement under Section 2 (p) of the Industrial Disputes Act, 1947.

A written agreement, between the employer and the workmen arrived at otherwise than in the course of the conciliation proceedings must satisfy that the agreement is signed by the parties thereto in the prescribed manner and a copy of such agreement is sent to the authorities indicated in Section 2 (p). Memorandum of settlement signed by the office-bearers of trade union without being authorised to enter into any agreement with the management or the employer does not amount to settlement.

Strike [Section 2 (q)]:

"Strike" means a cessation of work by a body of persons employed in any industry acting in combination, or a concerted refusal, or a refusal under a common understanding, of any number of persons who are or have been so employed to continue to work or to accept employment.

From the above mentioned definition of strike, it becomes clear that strike is nothing but –

(a) Cessation or stopping of work by workmen employed or

(b) A concerted refusal of any number of workmen employed, or

(c) A refusal under a common understanding of any number of workmen employed to continue to work. But merely remaining absent from work does not amount to taking part in the strike. Duration of strike is immaterial. Stoppage and/or refusal to work even for a few minutes may amount to strike if there is concert and combination of the workmen in stopping and refusing to start the work.

A strike, if it is not illegal, does not put an end to the relationship between employee and employer. It is a recognised weapon in the hands of workmen for fighting against the employer for the injustice made. It is really a necessary safety valve in the industrial relations. This weapon should be used as a last resort when all other avenues for settling the industrial disputes as provided for in this Act have proved to be futile. Strikes are not banned in public utility services.

The following important points may be noted so far as a strike is concerned.

1. A strike is a weapon which is used by employees, or workmen acting together to force their employer to agree to the demands made by them.
2. A strike implies a stoppage of work by a number of employees acting together. But mere absence from work on personal ground does not amount to cessation or stoppage or refusal of work. There should be premeditation or plan to cease or to refuse to work in a body of workmen.
3. The duration of the stoppage or cessation of work is immaterial. If the workmen acting together cease their work even for an hour or a part thereof, it can be called a strike.
4. When workmen go on strike against the provisions of the Industrial Disputes Act of 1947, such strike is considered as illegal.
5. Even a partial refusal of work by a body of workmen may constitute a strike.
6. A strike can also be a 'Stay-in strike' or 'Go-slow' strike. When workmen stay inside the factory but they do not work, the stay-in striker happens. Stay-in strike is also known as 'pen-down strike' or 'sit-down strike'. In 'Go-slow strike', there is a deliberate delay in production by workmen. It leads to delay in production and thereby the production is reduced. However, the workmen are entitled to get full wages.

7. In certain industries, overtime work is considered essential and it is a legal obligation. While in certain industries, overtime work is done habitually and is customary. Refusal of overtime work is considered to be against the conditions of service. If over-time work is refused, it may be considered as a strike.

Trade Union [Section 2 (gg)]:

'Trade Union' means a trade union registered under the Trade Union Act, 1926,

According to Section 2 (h) of the Trade Union Act, 1926, a trade union means any combination formed primarily for the purpose of regulating the relations between workmen and employers or between workmen and workmen or between employers and employers for imposing restrictive conditions on the conduct of any trade or business and includes any federation of two or more trade unions.

Tribunal [Section 2 (r)]:

"Tribunal" means an Industrial Tribunal constituted under Section 7-A and includes an Industrial Tribunal constituted before the 10th March 1975, under this Act.

Industrial Disputes Act, 1947 provides for the constitution of one or more Industrial Tribunals. The appropriate Government may constitute one or more Industrial Tribunals for the adjudication of industrial disputes relating to any matter specified in the second schedule or the Third Schedule appended to this Act. The Second and the Third Schedules are reproduced below.

Second Schedule:

1. The propriety of legality of an order passed by an employer under the standing order.
2. The application and interpretation of standing orders.
3. Discharge or dismissal of workmen including reinstatement of, or grant of relief to, workmen wrongfully dismissed.
4. Withdrawal of any customary concession or privilege.
5. Illegality or otherwise of strike or lock-out, and
6. All matters other than those specified in the Third Schedule.

It must be remembered that all the matters included in the Second Schedule are within the Jurisdiction of the Labour courts but they also can be referred to the Industrial Tribunal if necessary.

Third Schedule:

Matters within the jurisdiction of an Industrial Tribunal;

1. Wages including the period and mode of payment;
2. Compensatory and other allowances;
3. House of work and rest intervals;

4. Leave with wages and holidays;
5. Bonus, profit-sharing, provident fund, gratuity;
6. Shift working otherwise than in accordance with standing orders;
7. Classification of discipline;
8. Rules of discipline;
9. Rationalisation;
10. Retrenchment of workmen and closure of establishment; and
11. Any other matter that may be prescribed.

An Industrial Tribunal consists of one person only and such person is appointed by the appropriate Government.

Unfair labour Practice [Section 2 (r a)]:

'Unfair Labour Practice' means any of the Fifth Schedule.

The Industrial Disputes Act, 1947 was amended many times. In 1982 it was amended and that amendment introduced Section 25-T. This section prohibits any employer or workman or any trade union from committing any unfair labour practice as defined in Section 2 (r a) and any person who commits any unfair labour practice is punishable with imprisonment for a term which may be extended to six months or with fine which may be extended upto one thousand rupees or with both [Section 25-U].

The fifth schedule is reproduced below.

The Fifth Schedule:

Unfair Labour Practices

I. On the part of employers and trade unions of employees.

1. To interfere with, restrain from or coerce, workmen in the exercise of their right to organise, form, join or assist a trade union or to engage in concerted activities for the purposes of collective bargaining or other mutual aid or protection, that is to say –

    (a) Threatening workmen with discharge or dismissal, if they join a trade union;

    (b) Threatening a lock-out or closure, if a trade union is organised;

    (c) Granting wage increase to workmen at crucial periods of trade union organisation, with a view to undermining the efforts of the trade union at organisation.

2. To dominate, interfere with or contribute support, financial or otherwise, to any trade union, that is to say –

    (a) An employer taking an active interest in organising a trade union of his workmen; and

(b) An employer showing partiality or granting favour to one of several trade unions attempting to organise his workmen or to its members, where such a trade union is not a recognised union.

3. To establish employer sponsored trade unions of workmen.

4. To encourage or discourage membership in any trade union by discriminating against any workman, that is to say.

   (a) Discharging or punishing a workman, because he urged other workmen to join or organise a trade union;

   (b) Discharging or punishing a workman for taking part in any strike (not being a strike which is deemed to be an illegal strike under this Act).

   (c) Changing seniority rating of workmen because of trade union activities.

   (d) Refusing to promote workmen to higher posts on account of their union activities.

   (e) Giving unmerited promotions to certain workmen with a view to creating discord amongst other workmen, or to undermine the strength of their trade union;

   (f) Discharging officer-bearers or active members of the trade union on account of their trade union activities.

5. To discharge or dismiss workmen –

   (a) By way of victimisation;

   (b) Not in good faith, but in the colourable exercise of the employer's rights;

   (c) By falsely implicating a workman in a criminal case on false evidence or on concocted evidence;

   (d) For patently false reasons;

   (e) On untrue or trumped up allegations of absence without leave;

   (f) In utter disregard of the principles of natural justice in the conduct of domestic enquiry or with undue haste;

   (g) For misconduct of a minor or technical character, without having any regard to the nature of the particular misconduct or the past record or service of the workman, thereby leading to a disproportionate punishment.

6. To abolish the work of a regular nature being done by workmen and to give such work to contractors as a measure of breaking a strike.

7. To transfer a workman *mala fide* from one place to another place, under the guise of following management policy.

8. To insist upon individual workmen, who are on a legal strike to sign a good conduct bond, as a pre-condition to allowing them to resume work.

9. To show favouritism or partiality to one set of workers regardless of merit.
10. To employ workmen as **'badlis'**, casuals or temporaries and to continue them as such for years, with the object of depriving them of the status and privileges of permanent workmen.
11. To discharge or discriminate against any workman for filing charges or testifying against an employer in any enquiry or proceeding relating to any industrial dispute.
12. To recruit workmen during a strike which is not an illegal strike.
13. Failure to implement award, settlement or agreement.
14. To indulge in acts of force or violence.
15. To refuse to bargain collectively, in good faith with the recognised trade unions.
16. Proposing or continuing a lock-out deemed to be illegal under this Act.

II. On the part of workmen and trade unions of workmen.
1. To advise or actively support or instigate any strike deemed to be illegal under this Act.
2. To coerce workmen in the exercise of the right to self organisation or to join a trade union or refrain from joining any trade union, that is to say –
   (a) For a trade union or its members to picketing in such a manner that non-striking workmen are physically debarred from entering the work places;
   (b) To indulge in acts of force or violence or to hold out threats of intimidation in connection with a strike against non-striking workmen or against managerial staff.
3. For a recognised union to refuse to bargain collectively in good faith with the employer.
4. To indulge in coercive activities against certification of a bargaining representative.
5. To stage, encourage or instigate such forms of coercive actions as willful 'go slow', squatting on the work premises after working hours or 'gherao' of any of the members of the managerial or other staff.
6. To stage demonstrations at the residence of the employers or the managerial staff members.
7. To incite or indulge in willful damage to employer's property connected with the industry.
8. To indulge in acts of force or violence or to hold out threats of intimidation against any workman with a view to prevent him from attending work.

Village Industries [Section 2 (r b)]:

"Village Industries" has the same meaning assigned to it in clause (h) of Section 2 of the Khadi and Village Industries Commission Act, 1956.

Wages [Section 2 (r r)]:

"Wages" means all remuneration capable of being expressed in terms of money, which would, if the terms of employment, express or implied, were fulfilled, be payable to a workman, in respect of his employment or of work done in such employment, and includes –

(i) Such allowances (including dearness allowance) as the workman is for the time being entitled to;
(ii) Such value of any house accommodation, or of supply of light, water, medical attendance or other amenity of any service or of any concessional supply of foodgrains of other articles;
(iii) Any travelling concession;
(iv) Any commission payable on the promotion of sales or business or both; but does not include -
 (a) Any bonus;
 (b) Any contribution paid or payable by the employer to any pension fund or provident fund or for the benefit of the workman under any law for the time being in force;
 (c) Any gratuity payable on the termination of his service;
(v) Any commission payable on the promotion sales or business or both.

In the above mentioned definition of 'wages', two terms i.e. bonus and gratuity are used. Let us make clear the meaning of these two terms.

Gratuity:

The term 'Gratuity' is not defined anywhere in the Industrial Disputes Act of 1947. But, so far as gratuity is concerned, the payment of Gratuity Act, 1972 was passed and is amended from time to time. This Act has made provisions for a scheme for the payment of gratuity to employees covered by the Act. Gratuity is a sum of money, a lumpsum, payable to an employee by his employer at the time of superannuation or retirement or resignation i.e. at the end of service or on his death provided he has completed five years of his service. Thus, the gratuity is payable to the employees by their employers according to the provisions of the Payment of Gratuity Act of 1972. Provisions have been made in this Act in respect of gratuity payable on termination of employment, rate of gratuity, maximum gratuity etc.

Bonus:

Bonus is an extra payment made to workmen by their employer in addition to their wages, allowances and usual fringe benefits. The Payment of Bonus Act of 1965 has made various provisions so far as payment of bonus is concerned. The payment of bonus to the workmen to whom the Payment of Bonus Act is applicable does not depend on the profit of their employers or their will. According to the provisions of the Payment of Bonus Act, the bonus is required to be paid to the employers.

Workman [Section 2 (s)]:

"Workman" means any person (including an apprentice) employed in any industry to do any manual, unskilled, skilled, technical, operations, clerical or supervisory work for hire or reward, whether the terms of employment, be express or implied, and for the purposes of any proceeding under this act in relation to an industrial dispute, includes any such person who has been dismissed, discharged or retrenched in connection with, or as a consequence

of, that dispute, or whose dismissal discharge, or retrenchment has led to that dispute, but does not include any such person –
1. Who is subject to the Air Force Act of 1950 or the Army Act of 1950 or the Navy Act 1957; or
2. Who is employed in the Police Service or as an officer or other employee of a prison; or
3. Who is employed mainly in a managerial or administrative capacity; or
4. Who, being employed in a supervisory capacity, draws wages exceeding one thousand and six hundred rupees per month or exercises, either by the nature of the duties attached to the office or by reason of the powers vested in him, functions mainly of a managerial nature.

The following test can be applied for the person to be considered a workman under Section 2 (s) of this Act.

If the person is employed by an industry, no matter where he is employed, shall be a workman. Thus, the definition of a workman presupposes the relationship of master and servant or employer and employee. This relationship of master and servant or employer and employee exists between them as a result of an agreement between them. Such agreement can be express or implied. By entering into such agreement, a workman remains under the supervision, control and direction of his master. An employee is said to be under the control, direction and supervision of the employer if such an employee has to follow the orders of the employer –
1. Regarding the work entrusted to him and the details of work and
2. The manner in which the work shall be executed or done or completed.

From this point of view, the following persons are deemed to be workmen.
1. Salesmen receiving wages but not commission.
2. Employees of municipalities.
3. Transport engineers, Blending supervisors etc.
4. A time-keeper, a guard, malis employed for looking after gardens attached with officers bungalows, factories etc.
5. An auditor doing clerical work.
6. An employee occasionally doing supervisory work.
7. Accountants who are merely clerks with supervisory duties.
8. Assistant medical officers doing technical work.
9. Development officers of Life Insurance Corporation.
10. Retrenched workmen.

Thus, when the employee is employed to do manual or clerical work; skilled or unskilled work; technical or non-technical work, he is considered as a workman even if he is employed in a supervisory capacity, unless his wages exceeds ₹ 1600/- or his duties are mainly of managerial nature. In different cases, the following persons were held not to be workmen.
   (a) Persons authorised to assign duties and distribute works in various banks.

(b) Employees working in the head office of a managing agency which manages several concerns.

(c) Head clerk in the State Transport Authority.

(d) Casual and temporary workers after finishing their jobs.

(e) The staff members of seasonal factories, who are not permanent, are not workmen during off-season.

(f) Sales representatives, medical representatives who gets only commission are not workmen.

(g) Persons holding supervisory and managerial posts.

(h) Maintenance Engineers, performing supervisory work and authorised to make temporary appointments, grant leave, etc.

(i) Apprentices governed by Apprentices Act 1961.

(j) Blending supervisors and fuelling superintendents.

Important tests for determining "workmen":

Some of the important tests or conditions in determining 'Workman' are as follows:

1. There should be a relationship between an employer and an employee or a master and a servant. The question whether the relationship between these parties is one as between an employer and the employees or between a master and his servant is purely a question of fact depending upon the circumstances in each case.

2. The relationship between an employer and an employee arises between two persons by agreement between two persons by agreement between them. Such agreement can be expressed or implied [Chintamani Rao and others Vs. State of Madhya Pradesh case, AIR (1953) Supreme Court 388].

3. An employee must be under the control and supervision of his employer. It is not necessary that an employee should be under exclusive control of his employer and should work for the whole time.

   An employee is said to be under the control of his employer if he is bound to follow the orders of the employer regarding (i) the work he has to do (ii) the details or work and (iii) the manner of doing the work.

4. Supervision work is not a decisive factor. Supervision work can be carried on by a workman occasionally.

5. Even a supervisor is a workman if he draws monthly wages less than one thousand and six hundred rupees.

6. Payment to a workman for his work as a remuneration or reward may be in any manner. It can be (i) time wages, (ii) at piece rates, or (iii) a commission on production or sale.

In the following cases, persons were held to be workmen.

(a) **Manager of a hotel:** A manager of a hotel who had to write ledgers, file correspondence, enter cash books, keep accounts etc. was held to be a workman in Indian Iron and Steel Company Limited V. Workmen case [AIR 1958 SC 130].

(b) **Malis as workmen:** A mali is an employee and his work is to maintain the gardens. mali who are employed by their employers for looking after the gardens attached to the bungalows which are owned by their employers and even allotted to the officers for residence are 'workmen. Their work cannot be characterised as remote, indirect or far fetched. Mali employed by the J.K. Spinning and Weaving Mills company limited for looking after gardens attached with 'Officers' bungalows which were situated in the Mill's colony were held as workmen in the case of J.K. Spinning and Weaving Company Ltd. V. Badri Mali [AIR - 1964 - SC 737].

(c) **Tailors undertaking jobs or Piece rated tailors:** It is not necessary that an employee should be under the exclusive control of his employer and he must do his work in the shop or at other such place. He can be employed by more than one employer. Many times, tailors attend the shop regularly for work and different rates are also fixed for their work according to their skill and the nature of work. There may not be any obligation to do their work at their own places. Still there is relationship of an employer and an employee between the shop-keeper and the tailors [Silver Jubilee Tailoring House V. Chief Inspector of Shop and Establishments - AIR 1974 - SC 37]. In Shining Tailor V. Industrial Tribunal II, U.P. Lucknow and others case [AIR (1984) Supreme Court 23], piece rated tailors working in the large tailoring establishment were held as workmen.

(d) **Senior clerk of a bank doing some supervisory work:** In banks, there are accountants who are officers and also accountants who are only senior clerks with some supervisory duties. The accountants doing only clerical duties and going by the designation as accountants are workmen [South India Bank Ltd. V.A.R. Chacko case A.I.R. 1964 - SC 1522].

(e) **The bus or car drivers:** We find that many factories provide transport facilities to their employees and for that purpose, bus drivers are employed. Those drivers look after the buses. They are held as workmen. But a car driver was engaged by a manager of a bank for which he was given certain allowance. The car driver was not held as a workman though the car was maintained at the expenses of the bank, as the control and direction of the driver did not rest with the bank [Punjab National Bank V. Gulam Dastgir. 1978-2 SCC 358].

(f) **Employee occasionally doing supervisory work:** When the main work entrusted to an employee is of clerical nature and occasionally some supervisory duties are carried on incidentally or as a small fraction of work done by him does not convert his employment as a clerk into one in supervisory capacity. The mere designation as a supervisor or a manager cannot be decisive of the nature of employment. He is just a workman [Anand Bazar Patrika Pvt. Ltd. V. Workmen. 1970 - 3 SCC 248].

3.4 Machinery for Settlement of Industrial Disputes

In the preamble of the Industrial Disputes Act of 1947, it is stated that, "An Act to make provisions for the investigation and settlement of industrial disputes and for certain other purposes". Thus, the Act intends the prevention and settlement of industrial disputes by making necessary provisions and for that purpose, various authorities are constituted under the Act with sufficient powers to bring about settlement between the concerned parties. These authorities are both internal as well as external.

Voluntary settlement and conciliation, adjudication and arbitration are the three modes which have been provided for settlement of disputes under the Industrial Disputes Act of 1947. Works Committees, Conciliation Officers, Boards of Conciliation and Courts of Inquiry are the authorities under the Act which make use of conciliation as a method of settlement of industrial disputes. These authorities can only help to promote settlement of industrial disputes or inquire into them, but they cannot make any awards which are binding on the concerned parties.

Adjudication authorities are labour courts, Industrial Tribunals and National Tribunal.

Provisions relating to voluntary reference of dispute to arbitration have been made in Section 10-A which we have already studied while considering the definition of an arbitrator.

3.4.1 Conciliation Machinery

(A) Works Committees [Section 3]:

A works committee is a forum provided under the Act for explaining the difficulties of the parties concerned with the disputes. It endeavours to maintain cordial relationship even though there are disputes or differences between the parties to the disputes. The success of work committees mainly depends on the efforts and co-operation of both the parties to the disputes.

Section 3 (1) of this Act provides for a Works Committee. According to this section, in the case of any industrial establishment in which one hundred or more workmen are employed or have been employed on any day in the preceding twelve months, the appropriate Government may by general or special order require the employer to constitute in the prescribed manner a Works Committee consisting of representatives of employers and workmen engaged in the establishment. However the number of representatives of workmen on the committee shall not be less than the number of representatives of the employer. The representatives of the workmen shall be chosen in the prescribed manner from among the workmen engaged in the establishment and in consultation with their trade union, if any, registered under the Indian Trade Unions Act, 1926. Section 3 (2) further provides that it shall be the duty of the Works Committee to promote measures for securing and preserving amity and good relations between the employer and workmen and, to that end to comment upon matters of their common interest or concern and endeavour to compose any material difference of opinion in respect of such matters.

Industrial Disputes Act 1947 promotes the settlement of industrial disputes firstly by voluntary negotiations. The Works Committees are the prominent effort towards that goal. Works Committees are joint committees having equal number of representatives of employers and workmen. The constitution of Works Committee is a must in an industrial establishment wherein one hundred or more workmen are employed on any day in the preceding twelve months. Works Committee is an internal media for settlement of Industrial Disputes Act within the industry.

Sub-Section 2 of Section 3 of this Act enumerates the duties or functions of a Works Committee which are as follows –
- (a) To remove the disparities between employers and workmen;
- (b) To promote measures for securing and preserving amity and friendly and good relations between the employers and workmen;
- (c) To that end, to comment upon all matters of their common interest or concern;
- (d) To make efforts to compose any material difference of opinion in respect of various matters. These matters include many aspects such as welfare of workers, provision and supervision of various recreational facilities, training of workmen and their wages, bonus, gratuity, working conditions including discipline, promotions, transfers etc. Thus, it seems that there is no subject concerning the relation between the employers and workmen which the Works Committee is precluded from considering. However the following points must be remembered in this connection.

1. Findings of the Works Committee are advisory or recommendatory and not mandatory. It cannot decide and pass final judgement. Its duty is only to comment because it is mainly a negotiating organ. It is the function of the Works Committee to promote measures for harmonious and friendly and good relations between the employers and workmen.
2. Works Committees are not intended to supersede or supplement the trade unions for the purpose of collective bargaining. They are not authorised to consider real changes or substantial changes in the service conditions. They are not a substitute of trade unions.

(B) Conciliation Officers [Section 4]:

Section 4 of the Industrial Disputes Act, 1947 provides for conciliation officer. According to Section 4 (1), the Appropriate Government, by notification in the Official Gazette, may appoint such number of persons as it thinks fit, to be conciliation officers, charged with the duty of mediating in and promoting the settlement of industrial disputes. Section 4 (2) further states that a Conciliation Officer may be appointed for a specified area or for specified industries in a specified area or for one or more specified industries and either permanently or for a limited period. Thus, Section 4 makes it clear that a Conciliation Officer may be appointed by the appropriate Government –
- (a) Either permanently or for a limited period;
- (b) For a specified area or for a specified industry in a specified area; or
- (c) For one or more specified industries.

The appropriate Government appoints such number of Conciliation officers as it thinks fit.

The Conciliation Officers thus appointed are the public servants within the meaning of Section 21 of Indian Penal Code 1960 [Section 11(6) of Industrial Disputes Act 1947].

Duties of the Conciliation Officers [Section 12]:

The main duties of the conciliation officers consist of mediating in and promoting the settlement of industrial disputes.

According to Section 12 of this Act, following are the duties of the Conciliation Officers.

(a) **To hold conciliation proceedings:**

Where any industrial dispute exists or is apprehended, the Conciliation Officer may, or where the dispute relates to a public utility service and a notice of strike or lock-out under Section 22 of this Act has been given, shall hold conciliation proceedings in the prescribed manner. [Section 12 (1)].

Thus, it is obligatory on the Conciliation Officers to hold conciliation proceedings in public utility services where –

1. An industrial dispute exists, or
2. An industrial dispute is apprehended; or
3. Where notice of a strike or a lock-out is given under Section 22 of this Act.

(b) **Investigation of an industrial dispute:**

For the purpose of bringing about a settlement of the dispute without delay, the Conciliation Officer shall investigate the dispute and all matters affecting the merits and the right settlement of the dispute, and may do all such things as he thinks fit for the purpose of inducting the parties to come to a fair and amicable settlement of the dispute [Section 12 (2)]. Thus, it is expected that the Conciliation Officers should take necessary steps to conduct conciliation proceedings expeditiously and a discretion is vested in the Conciliation Officers to conduct these proceedings in such a manner as they think proper.

(c) **Memorandum of settlement:**

If the settlement of the dispute or of any of the matters in dispute is arrived at in the course of the conciliation proceedings, the Conciliation Officer shall send a report thereof to the appropriate Government or an officer authorised in this behalf by the appropriate Government together with a memorandum of the settlement signed by the parties to the dispute [Section 12 (3)].

(d) **Submission of report with facts to the Appropriate Government:**

If no settlement is arrived at, the conciliation officer, as soon as practicable after the close of the investigation, shall send to the Appropriate Government a full report setting forth the steps taken by him for ascertaining the facts and circumstances relating to the dispute and, for bringing about a settlement thereof, together with a full statement of such facts and circumstances, and the reason on account of which in his opinion a settlement could not be arrived at [Section 12 (4)].

(e) Reference to a Board, Labour Court, Tribunal or National Tribunal:

On a consideration of the report referred to in sub-section 4 of Section 12, if the Appropriate Government is satisfied that there is a case for reference to a Board, Labour Court; Tribunal or National Tribunal, it may make such reference. Where the appropriate Government does not make such reference, it shall record and communicate to the parties concerned its reasons therefore [Section 12 (5)].

(f) Submission of report within fourteen days:

A report under this section shall be submitted within fourteen days of the commencement of the conciliation proceedings or within such shorter period as may be fixed by the Appropriate Government [Section 12 (6)] Provided that subject to the approval of the Conciliation Officer the time for the submission of the report may be extended by such period as may be agreed upon in writing by all the parties to the dispute [Proviso to Section 12 (6)].

When conciliation proceedings are started under Section 12 (1), the further procedure enjoined by this Act is required to be followed. When any settlement is not arrived at during the conciliation proceedings, the appropriate Government has to proceed under Section 12 (5) either to make a reference to a Board, Labour Court, Tribunal or National Tribunal as the case may be or to record and communicate to the parties concerned the reasons for not making a reference.

If the refusal of the Appropriate Government to make a reference is based on extraneous or irrelevant grounds and if the appeal is made, the court may direct the Appropriate Government to reconsider its decision on relevant grounds. Thus, a writ of mandamus can be issued directing the Appropriate Government to discharge the duty cast on it under sub-section 5 of Section 12.

The Government has a right to go into *prima facie* merits of the dispute for deciding whether to refer the dispute or not. The High Court under Article 226 cannot sit in appeal over the order of the Government refusing to make a reference. [Bombay Union of Journalists V. State of Bombay (1964)]. But if a party can show that the refusal to refer a dispute is not based on bonafide grounds or based on a consideration of wholly irrelevant facts, a writ of mandamus would lie. [Hochtief Gammon V. State of Orissa (1975)].

Powers of a Conciliation Officer:

Powers of conciliation officers are embodied in Section 11 (Chapter IV) of the Industrial Disputes Act of 1947. These powers are as follows.

(a) A conciliation officer shall follow such procedure as he may think fit, subject to rules that may be made in this behalf. Generally he calls all the concerned parties and they discuss the dispute sitting around a table [Section 11 (1)].

(b) A conciliation officer may for the purpose of inquiry into any existing or apprehended industrial dispute, after giving a reasonable notice, enter the premises occupied by any establishment to which the dispute relates. [Section 11 (2)].

(c) A conciliation officer may enforce the attendance of any person for the purpose of examination of such person or call for and inspect any document which he has ground for considering to be relevant to the industrial dispute or to be necessary for the purpose of verifying the implementation of any award or carrying out any other duty imposed on him under this Act [Section 11(4)].

(d) The conciliation officer has the same powers for the purposes mentioned above as are vested under the Code of Civil Procedure of 1908 in respect of enforcing the attendance of any person and examining him or of compelling the production of documents [Section 11 (4)].

All conciliation officers appointed under this Act are deemed to be public servants within the meaning of Section 21 of the Indian Penal Code (45 of 1860).

Commencement and conclusion of Conciliation Proceedings:

According to Section 20 (1), a conciliation proceeding shall be deemed to have commenced on the date on which a notice of strike or lock-out under Section 22 is received by the conciliation officer. It is deemed to have concluded –

(a) Where a settlement is arrived at, when a memorandum of settlement is signed by the parties to the dispute, or

(b) Where no settlement is arrived at, when the report of the conciliation office by the appropriate Government [Section 20 (2)].

(C) Board of Conciliation [Section 5]:

Section 5 of the Industrial Disputes Act 1947 provides for the constitution of a Board of Conciliation, Section 5 is reproduced below –

The Appropriate Government may as occasion arises, by notification in the Official Gazette, constitute a Board of Conciliation for promoting the settlement of any industrial dispute [Section 5 (1)].

A Board shall consist of a chairman and two or four other members as the Appropriate Government thinks fit [Section 5 (2)].

The chairman shall be an independent person and the other members shall be persons appointed in equal numbers to represent the parties to the dispute and any person appointed to represent a party shall be appointed on the recommendation of the party [Section 5 (3)]: Provided that if any party fails to make a recommendations as aforesaid within the prescribed time the Appropriate Government shall appoint such person as it thinks fit to represent that party [Proviso to Section 5 (3)].

Validity of sitting of a Board of Conciliation:

A Board having the prescribed quorum may act, notwithstanding the absence of the Chairman or any of its members or any vacancy in its number [Section 5 (4)]: Provided that if the appropriate Government notifies the Board that the services of the Chairman or of any other member have ceased to be available, the Board shall not act until a new chairman or member, as the case may be, has been appointed [Proviso to Section 5 (4)].

Quorum of the Board of Conciliation:

The quorum necessary to constitute a sitting of a Board of conciliation is as follows –

1. Where the number of members is three …… Quarum 2 members.
2. Where the number of members is five …… Quarum 3 members.

Reference of Disputes to a Board of Conciliation:

Where the appropriate Government is of the opinion that any industrial dispute exists or is apprehended, it may at any time, by order in writing refer the dispute to a Board of Conciliation for promoting a settlement thereof [Section 10 (1)].

Where the parties to an industrial dispute act apply in the prescribed manner, whether jointly or separately, for a reference of the dispute to a Board of Conciliation, the appropriate Government if satisfied that the persons applying represent the majority of such party, shall make reference accordingly [Section 10 (2)].

Duties of a Board of Conciliation:

Thus, a Board of Conciliation is a body of persons appointed by the Appropriate Government by notification in the Official Gazette for the purpose of promoting the settlement of an industrial dispute. Section 13 of this Act provides for the following duties of the Board of Conciliation.

   (a) **Efforts to bring about a settlement:** Where a dispute has been referred to a Board of conciliation under this Act, it shall be the duty of the Board to endeavour for bringing about a settlement of the same and for this purpose the Board shall in such manner as it thinks fit and without delay, investigate the dispute and all matters affecting the merits and the right settlement thereof and may do all such things as it thinks fit for the purpose of inducing the parties to come to a fair and amicable settlement of the dispute [Section 13 (1)].

   (b) **Submission of the memorandum of settlement:** If a settlement of the dispute or any of the matters in dispute is arrived at in the course of the conciliation proceedings, the Board shall send a report thereof to the appropriate Government together with a memorandum of the settlement signed by the parties to the dispute [Section 13 (2)].

   (c) **Submission of report with facts, circumstances etc.:** If no settlement is arrived at, the Board shall, as soon as practicable after the close of the investigation, send to the appropriate Government a full report setting forth proceedings and steps taken by the Board for ascertaining the facts and circumstances relating to the disputes and for bringing about a settlement thereof, together with full statement of such facts and circumstances, its findings thereon, the reasons on account of which, in its opinion, a settlement could not be arrived at and its recommendations for determination of the dispute [Section 13 (3)].

   (d) **Communication to the parties:** If on the receipt of a report under sub-section 13 (3) in respect of a dispute relating to public utility service, the appropriate Government does not make a reference to a Labour Court, Tribunal or National Tribunal under Section 10, it shall record and communicate to the parties concerned its reasons therefor [Section 13 (4)].

(e) Submission of reports within two months: The Board of conciliation shall submit its report under this section within two months of the date on which the dispute was referred to it or within such shorter period as may be fixed by the appropriate Government [Section 13 (5)].

Provided that the Appropriate Government may, from time to time extend the time for the submission of the report by such further periods not exceeding two months in the aggregate. It is further provided that the time for submission of the report may be extended by such period as may be agreed on in writing by all parties to dispute.

Form of Report and Publication of Report:

The report of a Board of conciliation must be in writing and is required to be signed by all members of the Board. However, any member can submit a dissenting report. Every report together with the minute of dissent is required to be published by the appropriate Government within thirty days from its receipt [Section 16 (1) and Section 17 (1)].

Powers of a Board of Conciliation:

Provisions have been made relating to the powers of the Boards of Conciliation in Section 11 which are as follows.

(a) A conciliation officer or a member of a Board of Conciliation may for the purpose of inquiry into any existing or apprehended industrial dispute enter the premises occupied by any establishment to which the dispute relates after giving a reasonable notice [Section 11(2)].

(b) According to Section 11(3) every Board of Conciliation shall have the same powers as are vested in a Civil Court under the Code of Civil Procedure of 1908, when trying a suit, in respect of the following matters, namely –

   (i) Enforcing the attendance of any person and examining him on oath.
   (ii) Compelling the production of documents and material objects.
   (iii) Issuing commissions for the examination of witnesses.
   (iv) In respect of such matters as may be prescribed.
   (v) Every inquiry or investigation by a Board of Conciliation shall be deemed to be a judicial proceeding within the meaning of Sections 193 and 228 of the Indian Penal Code of 1860.

All members of a Board of Conciliation are public servants:

It is made clear in the provisions of Section 11 (6) that all members of a Board of Conciliation are deemed to be public servants within the meaning of Section 21 of the Indian Penal Code of 1860.

Procedure to be followed by a Board of Conciliation:

Subject to any rules that may be made in this behalf, a Board of Conciliation shall follow such procedure as it may think fit [Section 11 (1)].

Commencement and Conclusion of Proceeding:

A conciliation proceeding is deemed to commence on the date of order referring the dispute to the Board conciliation [Section 20 (1)] and it is deemed to have concluded (a) when a memorandum of the settlement is signed by the parties to the dispute or (b) when the report of the Board of conciliation is published [Section 20 (2)].

Finality of the Governments order:

It is made clear in Section 9 (1) that no order of the appropriate Government or of the Central Government appointing any person as the chairman or any other member of a Board at conciliation shall be called in question in any manner, and no act or proceeding before any Board of conciliation shall be called in question in any manner on the ground merely of the existence of any vacancy in, or defect in the constitution of such Board of condition.

(D) Courts of Inquiry [Section 6]:

Where conciliation officers do not become successful, a Board of conciliation takes over. The functions of such Board of Conciliation are the same as those of conciliation officers. The purpose of constituting the Boards of Conciliation is also to bring about the settlement of industrial disputes. The next step in the process of settlement of industrial dispute under this Act is adjudication for which various provisions are made in Sections 6, 7, 7-A and 7-B of the Act. Now let us study one important aspect of adjudication first i.e. Courts of Inquiry.

Composition and Appointment of Members of a Court of Inquiry:

Provisions relating to composition and appointment of members of a Inquiry have been made in Section 6 of this Act which are as follows –

The appropriate Government may as occasion arises, by notification in the Official Gazette, constitute a Court of Inquiry for enquiring into any matter appearing to be concerned with or relevant to an industrial dispute [Section 6 (1)].

A court may consist of one independent person or of such number of independent persons as the appropriate Government may think fit and where a Court consists of two or more members, one of them shall be appointed as the Chairman [Section 6 (2)].

Quorum of a Court of Inquiry:

According to the Rule 14 of the Industrial Disputes (Central) Rules of 1957, the quorum necessary to constitute a sitting of a Court of Inquiry shall be as follows –

(a) Where the number of members is not more than Two ... Quorum One.

(b) Where the number of members is more than two but less than five ... Quorum Two.

(c) Where the number of members is five or more ... Quorum Three.

Validity of sitting of a Court of Inquiry:

A Court, having the prescribed quorum, may act, notwithstanding the absence of the Chairman or any of its members of any vacancy in its number [Section 6 (3)].

Provided that, if the Appropriate Government notifies the Court that the services of the chairman have ceased to be available, the court shall not act until a new chairman has been appointed. [Proviso to Section 6 (3)].

Duties of a Court of Inquiry:

The powers, duties etc. of various authorities concerned with investigation and settlement of industrial disputes are narrated in Sections 11, 14 and also in Sections 16 to 21 of Chapter IV of the Industrial Disputes Act 1947.

The relevant portion of these sections is reproduced below.

(a) **Appointment of Assessor or Assessors:** A Court of Inquiry may, if it so thinks fit, appoint one or more persons having special knowledge of the matter under consideration as assessor or assessors to advise it in the proceedings before it. [Section 11 (5)].

(b) **Holding of an enquiry and submission of report:** A court shall inquire into the matters referred to it and report thereon to the appropriate Government ordinarily within a period of six months from the commencement of its inquiry [Section 14].

(c) **Report in writing:** The report of a Court of Inquiry shall be in writing and shall be signed by all the members of the Board or Court as the case may be [Section 16 (1)]. Provided that nothing in this section shall be deemed to prevent any member of the Court from recording any minute of dissent from a report or from any recommendation made therein [Proviso to Section 16 (1)].

Publication of a report of a Court of Inquiry:

Every report of a Court of Inquiry together with any minute of dissent recorded therewith shall, within a period of thirty days from the date of its receipt by the appropriate Government, be published in such a manner as the appropriate Government thinks fit [Section 17 (1)].

Procedure to be followed by a Court of Inquiry:

Subject to any rules that may be made in this behalf, a Court of Inquiry shall follow such procedure as it may think fit [Section 11 (1)].

Reference of a Industrial Dispute to a Court of Inquiry:

Where the appropriate Government is of the opinion that any industrial dispute exists or is apprehended, it may at any time, by order in writing refer any matter appearing to be connected with or relevant to the dispute to a Court of Inquiry for Inquiry [Section 10 (1)]. In Section 10 (2), it is further stated that where the parties to an industrial dispute apply in the prescribed manner, whether jointly or separately, for a reference of the dispute to a Court of Inquiry, the appropriate Government if satisfied that the persons applying represent the majority of each party, shall make the reference accordingly.

Powers of a Court of Inquiry:

Powers of a Court of Inquiry are given in Section 11 (Chapter IV) of the Industrial Disputes Act of 1947. These powers are enumerated below.

1. Any member of a Court of Inquiry may for the purpose of inquiry into any existing or apprehended industrial dispute, after giving a reasonable notice, enter the premises occupied by any establishment to which the dispute relates [Section 11 (2)].
2. According to Section 11 (3) every Court of Inquiry shall have the same powers as are vested in a Civil Court under the Code of Civil procedure of 1908, when trying a suit, in respect of the following matters, namely,
    (a) Enforcing the attendance of any person and examining him on oath;
    (b) Compelling the production of documents and material objects;
    (c) Issuing commissions for the examination of witness;
    (d) In respect of such other matters as may be prescribed.

Every inquiry or investigation by a Court of Inquiry is deemed to be a judicial proceeding within the meaning of Sections 193 and 228 of the Indian Penal Code of 1860. Every Court of Inquiry is deemed to be Civil Court for the purpose of Sections 345, 346 and 348 of the Code of Criminal Procedure, 1973.

3. A Court of Inquiry has the power, if it thinks fit, to appoint one or more persons having special knowledge of the matter under consideration as an assessor or assessors to advice it in the proceeding before it [Section 11 (5)].

All members of a court of Inquiry are public servants:

All members of a Court of Inquiry are deemed to be public servants within the meaning of Section 21 of the Indian Penal Code of 1860 [Section 11 (6)].

Finality of orders constituting a Court of Inquiry:

No order for the appropriate Government or of the Central Government, as the case may be appointing any person as the Chairman or any other member of a Court of Inquiry shall be called in question in any manner, and no act or proceeding before any Court of Inquiry shall be called in question in any manner on the ground merely of the existence of any vacancy in, or defect in the constitution of such Court of Inquiry [Section 9 (1)].

3.4.2 Adjudication Machinery

Labour courts, Industrial Tribunals and National Tribunals are adjudication authorities constituted under the Industrial Disputes Act of 1947 for settlement of industrial disputes and bringing about industrial peace. Let us now consider the provisions of the Act relating to appointments, constitution, qualifications, duties and powers etc. of these authorities.

(E) Labour Courts [Section 7]:

The ultimate legal remedy for settling an unresolved industrial dispute is its reference to adjudication by the appropriate Government. The Industrial Disputes Act, 1947 empowers the appropriate Government to Constitute Labour Courts, Industrial Tribunals or National Tribunal to adjudicate Industrial Disputes [Section 7, 7-A, 7-B].

According to Section 7 of the Industrial Disputes Act 1947, the appropriate Government may, by notification in the Official Gazette, constitute one or more Labour Courts for the adjudication of industrial disputes relating to any matter specified in the second schedule (which is given below) and for performing such other functions as may be assigned to them under this Act [Section 7 (l)]. A Labour Court shall consist of one person only to be appointed by the appropriate Government [Section 7 (2)].

Jurisdication of Labour Courts:

The second Schedule to the Industrial Disputes Act 1947 specifies various matters within the jurisdiction of Labour Court.

Second Schedule:

Matters within the Jurisdication of the Labour Courts.
1. The propriety of legality of an order passed by an employer under the standing orders;
2. The application and interpretation of standing orders.
3. Discharge or dismissal of workmen including reinstatement of, or grant of relief to, workmen wrongfully dismissed.
4. Withdrawal of any customary concession or privilege;
5. Illegality or otherwise of strike or lock-out, and
6. All matters other than those specified in the third schedule.

Qualifications and disqualifications of a person to be appointed as a presiding officer of a Labour Court:

Section 7 (3) of this act prescribes the qualifications of persons to be appointed as the presiding officers. According to Section 7 (3), a person shall not be qualified for appointment as the Presiding Officer of a Labour Court, unless –
  (i) he is or has been a Judge of a High Court; or
  (ii) he has been a District Judge or an Additional District Judge for a period of not less than three years; or
  (iii) he has held any judicial office in India for not less than seven years; or
  (iv) he has been the Presiding Officer of a Labour Court constituted under any Provincial Act or State Act for not less than five years.

Disqualifications to become presiding officer of a Labour Court:

Section 7-C provides that no person shall be appointed to, or continue in, the office of the presiding officer of a Labour Court; Tribunal or National Tribunal, if –
  (a) He is not an independent person; or
  (b) He has attained the age of sixty-five years.

Duties of a Labour Court:

Duties of a Labour Court are as follows.
  (a) To Adjudicate: It is the duty of a Labour Court to adjudicate upon the industrial disputes relating to any matter specified in the Second Schedule which is already given above and to perform all such other functions as may be assigned to it under this Act [Section 7 (1)].

(b) To hold proceedings and submission of Awards: Where an industrial dispute has been referred to a Labour Court for adjudication, it shall hold its proceedings expeditiously and shall, within the period specified in the order referring such industrial dispute or the further period extended under the second proviso to sub-section 2 A of Section 10, submit its award to the appropriate Government [Section 15].

Powers of a Labour Court:

The important powers of a Labour Court are as follows:

1. **Power to enter the premises:** The Presiding Officer of a Labour Court may for the purpose of inquiry into any exciting or apprehended industrial dispute enter the premises occupied by any establishment to which the dispute relate, after giving a reasonable notice [Section 11(2)].

2. **Powers of the Civil Court:** According to Section 11 (3), every Labour Court shall have the same powers as are vested in a Civil Court under the Code of Civil Procedure, of 1908, when trying a suit, in respect of the following matters, namely –
   (i) Enforcing the attendance of any person and examining him on oath.
   (ii) Compelling the production of documents and material objects.
   (iii) Issuing commissions for the examination of witnesses.
   (iv) In respect of such matters as may be prescribed.

3. **Powers in respect of Judicial Proceedings:** Every inquiry or investigation by a Labour Court shall be deemed to be a judicial proceeding within the meaning of Sections 193 and 228 of the Indian Penal Code of 1860 [Section (3) (d)].

4. **Power of appointing an assessor or assessors:** A Labour Court, if it so thinks fit, may appoint one or more persons having special knowledge of the matter under consideration as assessor or assessors to advice it in the proceeding before it [Section 11 (5)].

5. **Some Powers of a Civil Court and Status of Civil Court:** Every Labour Court is deemed to be a Civil Court for the purposes of Sections 345, 346, and 348 of the Code of Criminal Procedure of 1973 (2 of 1974). [Section 11 (8)].

6. **Power to set aside the order of discharge dismissal of workman and to direct reinstatement:** Where an industrial dispute relating to the discharge or dismissal of a workman has been referred a Labour Court for adjudication and, in the course of adjudication proceedings, the Labour Court is satisfied that the order of discharge or dismissal was not justified, it may by its award, set aside the order of discharge or dismissal and direct re-instatement of the workman on such terms and conditions, if any, as it thinks fit or give such other relief to the workman including the award of any lesser punishment in lieu of discharge or dismissal as

the circumstances of the case may require [Section 11-A]. It is also provided that in any proceeding under Section 11-A, the Labour Court shall rely only on the materials on record and shall not take any fresh evidence in relation to the matter [Proviso to Section 11-A].

7. **Power of a Labour Court to allow costs:** It is stated in Section 11 (7) that, "Subject to any rules made under this Act, the costs of, and incidental to, any proceeding before a Labour Court, the Labour Court shall have full power to determine by and to whom and to what extent and subject to what conditions, if any, such costs are to be paid, and to give all necessary directions for the purposes aforesaid and such costs may, an application made to the appropriate Government by the person entitled, to be recovered by that Government in the same manner as an arrear of land revenue".

Thus, Section 11 (7) empowers a Labour court to determine the costs of any proceedings before it and also to determine by whom and to what extent and subject to what conditions, if any, such costs are to be paid. A Labour Court is also empowered to give all necessary directions for the purposes aforesaid.

The Presiding of a Labour Court is a Public Servant:

It is made clear in the Provisions of Section 11 (6) that the Presiding Officer of a Labour Court is deemed to be public servants within the meaning of Section 21 of the Indian Penal Code of 1860.

Procedure to be followed by a Labour Court:

Subject to any rules that may be made in this behalf, a labour court shall follow such procedure as it may think fit [Section 11 (1)].

Finality of the orders of the Government constituting a Labour Court:

No order of the appropriate Government appointing any person as the presiding officer of a Labour Court shall be called in question in any manner, and no act or proceeding before any Labour Court shall be called in question in any manner on the ground merely of the existence of any vacancy in, or defect in the constitution of such Labour Court [Section 9 (1)].

Filling of a vacancy in the office of Presiding Officer of a Labour Court:

If, for any reason a vacancy (other than a temporary vacancy) occurs in the office of the Presiding Officer of a Labour Court, the appropriate Government shall appoint another person in accordance with the provisions of this Act to fill the vacancy, and the proceeding may be continued before the Labour Court from the stage at which the vacancy is filled [Section 8].

Reference of disputes to a Labour Court:

1. Where the appropriate Government is of the opinion that any industrial dispute exists or is apprehended, it may at any time, by order in writing refer the dispute or any matter to be connected with, or relevant to the dispute, if it relates to the matter specified in the second schedule, to a Labour Court for adjudication [Section 10 (1) (c)].

2. Where the dispute relates to any matter specified in the Third Schedule and is not likely to affect more than one hundred workmen, the appropriate Government may, if it so thinks fit, make the reference to a Labour Court under Section 10 (1) (c) which is reproduced above [Proviso to Section 10 (1)].
3. Where the dispute in relation to which the Central Government is the appropriate Government, it shall be competent for that Government to refer the dispute to a Labour Court constituted by the State Government [Proviso to Section 10 (1)].
4. Where the parties to an industrial dispute apply in the prescribed manner, whether jointly or separately, for a reference of the dispute to a Labour Court, the appropriate Government, if satisfied that the persons applying represent the majority of each party, shall make the reference accordingly [Section 10 (2)].

Points of Reference and Jurisdication:

Where in an order referring an industrial dispute to a Labour Court or in a subsequent order, the appropriate Government has specified the points of dispute for adjudication, the Labour Court shall continue its adjudication (Jurisdiction) to those points and matters incidental thereto [Section 10 (4)].

Prohibition of any strike or Lock-out:

Section 10 (3) states that, "Where an industrial dispute has been referred to a Labour Court under this section, the appropriate Government may by order prohibit the continuance of any strike or lock-out in connection with such dispute which may be in existence on the date of reference".

Order of inclusion of either an industrial establishment or a group or class of establishment:

Where a dispute concerning any establishment or establishments has been, or is to be referred to a Labour Court under Section 10 and the appropriate Government is of the opinion, whether on an application made to it in this behalf or otherwise, that the dispute is of such nature that any other establishment group or class of establishments of a similar nature is likely to be interested in, or affected by, such dispute, the appropriate Government may, at any time of making the reference or at any time thereafter but before the submission of award, include in that reference such establishment, group or class of establishments, whether or not at the time of such inclusion any dispute exists or is apprehended in that establishment, group or class of establishments [Section 10 (5)].

Forms of Award:

The award of a Labour Court must be in writing and it must be signed by its Presiding Officer [Section 16 (2)].

Publication of Award:

According to the Provisions of Section 17 (1), every award of a Labour Court must be published within a period of thirty days from the date of its receipt by the appropriate Government and it must be published in such a manner as the appropriate Government thinks fit.

It is stated in Section 17 (2) that, "Subject to the Provisions of Section 17-A, the award published under Section 17 (1) shall be final and shall not be called in question by any Court in any manner whatsoever".

Period for submitting of an award:

An order referring an industrial dispute to a Labour Court under Section 10 shall specify the period within which such Labour Court shall submit its award on such dispute to the appropriate Government [Section 10 (2-A)].

Where such industrial dispute is connected with an individual workman, no such period shall exceed three months [Proviso to Section 10 (2-A)]. But where the parties to an industrial dispute apply in the prescribed manner, whether jointly or separately, to the Labour Court for extension of such period or for any other reason, and the Presiding Officer of such Labour court considers it necessary or expedient to extend such period, he may for reasons to be recorded in writing extend such period by such further period as he may think fit [Proviso to Section 10 (2-A)].

In computing any period specified in this section the period, if any, for which the proceedings before the Labour Court had been stayed by any injunction or order of a Civil Court shall be excluded [Proviso to Section 10 (2-A)].

It is also further provided in Section 10 (2-A) that no proceedings before the Labour Court shall lapse merely on the ground that any period specified under this sub-section had expired without such proceeding being completed.

On the death of parties, proceedings do not lapse:

Provisions have been made in the Section 10 (8) of the Act relating to the proceedings pending on the death of the parties to the dispute. Section 10 (8) lays down that, "No proceedings pending before a Labour Court in relation to an industrial dispute shall lapse merely by reason of the death of any of the parties to the dispute being a workman, and such labour court shall complete such proceedings and submit its award to the appropriate Government.

(F) Industrial Tribunals [Section 7-A]:

Constitution and Jurisdiction: Section 7-A of the Industrial Disputes Act 1947 provides for the constitution of one or more Industrial Tribunals. According to Section 7 A (1), the appropriate Government, by notification in the Official Gazette, may constitute one or more Industrial Tribunals for the adjudication of industrial disputes relating to any matter whether specified in the Second Schedule (which is already given elsewhere) or the third schedule and for performing such other functions as may be assigned to them under this Act. The Third Schedule appended to this Act is reproduced as follows.

The Third Schedule:

Matters within the Jurisdiction of Industrial Tribunals.
1. Wages including the period and mode of payment;
2. Compensatory and other allowances;
3. Hours of Work and rest intervals;
4. Leave with wages and holidays;

5. Bonus, profit-sharing, provident fund and gratuity;
6. Shift working otherwise than in accordance with standing orders;
7. Classification of discipline;
8. Rules of discipline;
9. Rationalisation;
10. Retrenchment of workmen and closure of establishment, and
11. Any other matter that may be prescribed.

A Tribunal shall consist of one person only to be appointed by the appropriate Government [Section 7-A (2)].

Qualifications and disqualifications of Presiding Officer of a Tribunal:

A person shall not be qualified for appointment as the Presiding Officer of a Tribunal unless –

(i) He is or has been, a Judge of a High Court; or

(ii) He has been a District Judge or an Additional District Judge for a period of not less than three years. [Section 7-A (3)].

Disqualification of Presiding Officer of a Tribunal:

No person shall be appointed to, or continue in the office of the presiding officer of a Tribunal, if

(a) He is not an independent person; or

(b) He has attained the age of sixty-five years [Section 7-C].

Appointment of Assessors:

The appropriate Government may, if it thinks fit, appoint two persons as assessors, to advise the Tribunal in the proceedings before it [Section 7-A (4)].

Duties of Industrial Tribunals:

Section 15 of this Act describes the duties of Tribunals and accordingly, "Where an industrial dispute has been referred to a Tribunal for adjudication, it shall hold its proceedings expeditiously and shall within the period specified in the order referring such industrial dispute or the further period extended under the second proviso to sub-section 2 (A) of Section 10, submit its award to the appropriate Government.

Powers of an Industrial Tribunal:

Powers of an Industrial Tribunal are given in Section 11 (Chapter IV) of the Industrial Disputes Act of 1947. These powers are enumerated below.

1. The Presiding Officer of a Tribunal may for the purpose of inquiry into any existing or apprehended industrial dispute, after giving a reasonable notice, enter the premises occupied by any establishment to which the dispute relates [Section 11 (2)].

2. Every Tribunal shall have the same powers as are vested in a Civil Court under the Code of Civil Procedure of 1908, when trying a suit, in respect of following matters namely,
   (a) Enforcing the attendance at any person and examining him on oath;
   (b) Compelling the production of documents and material objects;
   (c) Issuing commissions for the examination of witness;
   (d) In respect of such other matters as may be prescribed.

Every inquiry or investigation by a Tribunal is deemed to be a judical proceeding within the meaning of Sections 193 and 228 of the Indian Penal Code of 1860. Every court of inquiry is deemed to be Civil Court for the purpose of Sections 345, 346 and 348 of the Code of Criminal Procedure, 1973.

3. **Power of appointing an assessor or assessors:** A Tribunal if it so thinks fit, may appoint one or more persons having special knowledge of the matter under consideration as an assessor or assessors to advice it in the proceeding before it [Section 11 (5)].

4. **Some Powers of a Civil Court and status of Civil Court:** Every Tribunal is deemed to be Civil Court for the purposes of Sections 345, 346 and 348 of the Code of Criminal Procedure of 1973 (2 of 1974). [Section 11 (8)].

5. **Power to give relief in case discharge dismissal of workman and to direct reinstatement:** Where an industrial dispute relating to the discharge or dismissal of a workman has been referred a Tribunal for adjudication and, in the course of adjudication proceedings the Tribunal is satisfied that the order of discharge or dismissal was not justified it may by its award set aside the order of discharge or dismissal and direct re-instatement of the workman on such terms and conditions if any, as it thinks fit, or give such other relief to the workman including the award of any lesser punishment in lieu of discharge or dismissal as the circumstances of the case may require [Section 11-A]. It is also provided that in any proceeding under Section 11-A the Tribunal shall rely only on the materials on record and shall not take any fresh evidences in relation to the matter [Proviso to Section 11-A].

6. **Power of an industrial tribunal to allow costs:** It is stated in Section 11 (7) that, 'Subject to any rules made under this act, the costs of, and incidental to, any proceeding before an Industrial Tribunal shall have full power to determine by and to whom and to what extent and subject to what conditions if any, such costs are to be paid, and to give all necessary directions for the purposes aforesaid and such costs may, on application made to the appropriate Government by the person entitled, to be recovered by that Government in the same manner as an arrear of land revenue.

Thus, Section 11 (7) empowers an Industrial Tribunal to determine the costs of any proceedings before it and also to determine by whom and to what extent and subject to what conditions if any, such costs are to be paid. An Industrial Tribunal is also empowered to give all necessary directions for the purposes aforesaid.

The Presiding Officer of a Tribunal is a Public Servant:

It is made clear in the provisions of Section 11 (6) that the presiding officer of a Tribunal is deemed to be the public servant within the meaning of Section 21 of the Indian Penal Code of 1860.

Procedure to be followed by a Tribunal:

Subject to any rules that may be made in this behalf, a Tribunal shall follow such procedure as it may think fit [Section 11 (1)].

Finality of the orders of the Government:

No order of the Appropriate Government appointing any person as the Presiding Officer of a Tribunal shall be called in question in any manner and no act or proceeding before any Tribunal shall be called in question in any manner on the ground merely of the existence of any vacancy in or defect in the constitution of such Tribunal [Section 9 (1)].

Filling of a vacancy in the Office of Presiding Officer of a Tribunal:

If, for any reason a vacancy (other than a temporary absence) occurs in the office of the Presiding Officer of a Tribunal the appropriate Government shall appoint another person in accordance with the provisions of this Act to fill the vacancy; and the proceeding may be continued before the Tribunal from the stage at which the vacancy is filled [Section 8].

Reference of disputes to a Tribunal:

1. Where the appropriate Government is of the opinion that any industrial dispute exists or is apprehended, it may at any time, by order in writing refer the dispute or any matter to be connected with, or relevant to the dispute, if it relates to the matter specified in the Second schedule or the Third schedule to a Tribunal for adjudication [Section 10 (1) (c)]. The Third schedule is already reproduced elsewhere.
2. Where the dispute in relation to which the Central Government is the appropriate Government it shall be competent for that Government to refer the dispute to an Industrial Tribunal constituted by the State Government [Proviso to section 10 (1)].
3. Where the parties to an industrial dispute apply in the prescribed manner, whether jointly or separately for a reference of the dispute to a Tribunal the appropriate Government, if satisfied that the persons applying represent the majority of each party, shall make the reference accordingly [Section 10 (2)].

Points of Reference and Jurisdiction:

Where in an order referring an industrial dispute to a Tribunal or in a subsequent order the appropriate Government has specified the points of dispute for adjudication the Tribunal shall continue its adjudication (Jurisdiction) to those points and matters incidental thereto [Section 10 (4)].

Prohibition of any strike or Lock-out:

Section 10 (3) states that, "where an industrial dispute has been referred to a Tribunal under this section, the appropriate Government may by order prohibit the continuance of any strike or lock-out in connection with such dispute which may be in existence on the date of reference.

Order of inclusion of either an industrial establishment or a group or class of establishment:

Where a dispute concerning any establishment or establishments has been or is to be referred to an Industrial Tribunal under Section 10 and the appropriate Government is of the opinion, whether on an application made to it in this behalf or otherwise, that the dispute is of such nature that any other establishment, group or class of establishments of a similar nature is likely to be interested in, or affected by, such dispute, the appropriate Government may, at any time of making the reference or at any time thereafter but before the submission of award, include in that reference such establishment, group or class of establishments, whether or not at the time of such inclusion any dispute exists or is apprehended in that establishment group or class of establishments [Section 10 (5)].

Form of Award:

The award of a Tribunal must be in writing and it must be signed by its Presiding Officer [Section 16 (2)].

Publication of Award:

According to the provisions of Section 17 (1), every award of a Tribunal must be published within a period of thirty days from the date of its receipt by the appropriate Government and it must be published in such manner as the appropriate Government thinks fit.

It is stated in Section 17 (2) that, "Subject to the provisions of Section 17-A, the award published under Section 17 (1) shall be final and shall not be called in question by any court in any manner whatsoever".

Period for submitting of an award:

An order referring an industrial dispute to an Industrial Tribunal under Section 10 shall specify the period within which such Tribunal shall submit its award on such dispute to the appropriate Government [Section 10 (2-A)].

Where such industrial dispute is connected with an individual workman, no such period shall exceed three months [Proviso to section 10 (2-A)]. But where the parties to an industrial dispute apply in the prescribed manner, whether jointly or separately, to the Industrial Tribunal for extension of such period or for any other reason, and the Presiding Officer of such Tribunal considers it necessary or expedient to extend such period, he may for reasons to be recorded in writing, extend such period by such further period as he may think fit [Proviso to Section 10 (2-A)].

In computing any period specified in this section the period, if any, for which the proceedings before the Tribunal had been stayed by any injunction or order of a Civil Court shall be excluded [Proviso to Section 10 (2-A)].

It is also further provided in Section 10 (2-A) that no proceedings before the Tribunal shall lapse merely on the ground that any period specified under this sub section had expired without such proceeding being completed.

On the death of parties, proceedings do not lapse:

Provisions have been made in Section 10 (8) of the Act relating to the proceedings pending on the death of the parties to the dispute. Section 10 (8) lays down that, "No proceedings pending before a Tribunal in relation to an industrial dispute shall lapse merely by reason of the death of any of the parties to the dispute being a workman, and such Tribunal shall complete such proceedings and submit its award to the appropriate Government.

(G) National Industrial Tribunal [Section 7-B]:

Constitution of National Tribunal, its composition and appointment of presiding officer:

The Central Government, by notification in the Official Gazette, may constitute one or more National Industrial Tribunals for the adjudication of industrial disputes which, in the opinion of the Central Government, involve questions of national importance or are of such a nature that industrial establishments situated in more than one state are likely to be interested in, or affected by, such disputes [Section 7-B (1)].

A National Tribunal shall consist of one person only to be appointed by the Central Government [Section 7-B (2)].

Qualifications and disqualifications of a presiding officer of National Industrial Tribunal [Section 7-B (3) and 7-C]:

Qualifications and disqualifications: A person shall not be qualified for the appointment as the presiding officer of National Tribunal unless he is or has been a judge of a High Court [Section 7-B (3)].

No person shall be appointed to, or continue in, the office of the presiding officer of a National Tribunal if –

(a) He is not an independent person; or

(b) He has attained at the age of sixty-five years [Section 7-C].

Appointment of Assessors [Section 7-B (4)]:

Assessors: The Central Government may, if it thinks fit, appoint two persons as assessors to advice the National Industrial Tribunal in the proceedings before it [Section 7-B (4)].

Duties of a National Tribunal:

(a) **Proceedings and Award:** Where an industrial dispute has been referred to a National Tribunal for adjudication, it shall hold its proceedings expeditiously and shall within the period specified in the order referring such industrial dispute or the further period extended under the second proviso to sub-section 2 (A) of Section 10, submit its award to the appropriate Government [Section 15].

(b) Disputes of National Importance: The National Tribunals are to adjudicate industrial disputes which, in the opinion of the Central Government.

  (i) Involve various questions of national importance; or/and

  (ii) Are of such a nature that industrial establishments situated in more than one state are likely to be interested in, or affected by, such industrial disputes.

Powers of a National Tribunal:

Powers of a National Tribunal are given in Section 11 (Chapter IV) of the Industrial Disputes Act of 1947. These powers are enumerated below.

1. The presiding officer of a National Tribunal may for the purpose of inquiry into any existing or apprehended industrial dispute, after giving reasonable notice, enter the premises occupied by any establishment to which the dispute relates. [Section 11 (2)].

2. According to Section 11 (3) every National Tribunal shall have the same powers as are vested in a civil court under the code of civil procedure of 1908, when trying a suit, in respect of the following matters, namely,

   (a) Enforcing the attendance of any person and examining him on oath;

   (b) Completing the production of documents and material objects;

   (c) Issuing commissions for the examination of witness;

   (d) In respect of such other matters as may be prescribed.

Every inquiry or investigation by a National Tribunal is deemed to be a judicial proceedings within the meaning of Sections 193 and 228 of the Indian Penal Code of 1860. Every National Tribunal is deemed to be Civil Court for the purpose of sections 345 (1), 346 and 348 of the code of criminal procedure, 1973.

3. **Power of appointing an assessor or assessors:** A National Tribunal if it so thinks fit, may appoint one or more persons having special knowledge of the matter under consideration as an assessor or assessors to advice it in the proceeding before it [Section 11 (5)].

4. **Some powers of a Civil Court and Status of Civil Court:** Every National Tribunal is deemed to be a Civil Court of the purposes of Section 345 (1), 346 and 348 of the code of Criminal Procedure of 1973 (2 of 1974) [Section 11 (8)].

5. **Power to set aside the order of discharge, dismissal of workman and to direct reinstatement:** Where an industrial dispute relating to the discharge or dismissal of a workman has been referred a National Tribunal for adjudication and in the course of adjudication proceeding, the National Tribunal is satisfied that the order of discharge or dismissal was not justified, it may by its award set aside the order of discharge or dismissal and direct re-instatement of the workman on such terms and conditions if any, as it thinks fit, or give such other relief to the workman including the award of any lesser punishment in

lieu of discharge or dismissal as the circumstances of the case may require [Section 11-A]. It is also provided that in any proceeding under Section 11-A the National Tribunal shall rely only on the materials on record and shall not take any fresh evidence in relation to the matter [Proviso to Section 11-A].

6. Power of a National Tribunal to allow costs: It is stated in Section 11 (7) that, "Subject to any rules made under this Act, the costs of, and incidental to, any proceeding before a National Tribunal the National Tribunal shall have full power to determine by and to when and to what extent and subject to what conditions, if any, such costs are to be paid, and to give all necessary directions for the purposes aforesaid and such costs may, on application made to the appropriate Government by the person entitled, to be recovered by that Government in the same manner as an arrear of land revenue".

Thus, Section 11 (7) empowers a National Tribunal to determine the costs of any proceedings before it and also to determine by whom and to what extent and subject to what conditions, if any, such costs are to be paid. A National Tribunal is also empowered to give all necessary directions for the purposes aforesaid.

The Presiding Officer of a National Tribunal is a public servant:

It is made clear in the Provisions of Section 11(6) that the presiding officer of a National Tribunal is deemed to be public servant within the meaning of Section 21 of the Indian Penal Code of 1860.

Procedure to be followed by a National Tribunal:

Subject to any rules that may be made in this behalf a National Tribunal shall follow such procedure as it may think fit [Section 11 (1)].

Finality of the order of the Government:

No order of the appropriate Government appointing any person as the Presiding Officer of a National Tribunal shall be called in question in any manner and no act or proceeding before any National Tribunal shall be called in question in any manner on the ground merely of the existence of any vacancy in, or defect in the constitution of such Labour Court [Section 9 (1)].

Fitting of a vacancy in the office of presiding officer of a National Tribunal:

If, for any reason a vacancy (other than a temporary vacancy) occurs in the office of the presiding officer of a National Tribunal the appropriate Government shall appoint another person in accordance with the provisions of this Act to fill the vacancy and the proceeding may be continued before the National Tribunal from the stage at which the vacancy is filled [Section 8].

Reference of disputes to National Tribunal:

1. Where the Central Government is of the opinion that any industrial dispute exists or is apprehended and
    (a) The dispute involves any question of national importance or;
    (b) That is of such a nature that industrial establishments situated in more than one state are likely to be interested in, or affected by such dispute, and

(c) That the dispute should be adjudicated by a National Tribunal, then –

The Central Government may, whether or not it is the appropriate Government in relation to that dispute, at any time, by order in writing, refer the dispute or any matter appearing to be connected with, or relevant to the dispute whether it relates to any matter specified in the Second Schedule or the Third Schedule [These schedules are already reproduced elsewhere], to a National Tribunal for adjudication [Section 10 (1-A)].

2. Where the parties to an industrial dispute apply in the prescribed manner, whether jointly or separately, for a reference of the dispute to a National Tribunal the appropriate Government, if satisfied that the persons applying represent the majority of each party, shall make the reference accordingly [Section 10 (2)].

Points of Reference and Jurisdiction:

Where in an order referring an industrial dispute to a National Tribunal or in a subsequent order the appropriate Government has specified the points of dispute for adjudication, the National Tribunal shall continue its adjudication (Jurisdiction) to those points and matters incidental thereto [Section 10 (4)].

Prohibition of any strike or Lock-out:

Section 10 (3) states that, "Where an industrial dispute has been referred to a National Tribunal under this section, the appropriate Government may by order prohibit the continuance of any strike or lock-out in connection with such dispute which may be in existence on the date of reference.

Order of inclusion of either an industrial establishment or a group or class of establishment:

Where a dispute concerning any establishment or establishments has been, or is to be referred to a National Tribunal under Section 10 and the appropriate Government is of the opinion, whether on an application made to it in this behalf or otherwise, that the dispute is of such nature that any other establishment group or class of establishments of a similar nature is likely to be interested in or affected by, such dispute, the appropriate Government may, at any time of making the reference or at any time thereafter but before the submission of the award, include in that reference such establishment, group or class of establishments, whether or not at the time of such inclusion any dispute exists or is apprehended in that establishment, group or class of establishments [Section 10 (5)].

Form of Award:

The award of a National Tribunal must be in writing and it must be signed by its Presiding Officer [Section 16 (2)].

Publication of Award:

According to the Provisions of Section 17 (1), every award of a National Tribunal must be published within a period of thirty days from the date of its receipt by the appropriate Government and it must be published in such manner as the appropriate Government thinks fit.

It is stated in Section 17 (2) that, 'Subject to the provisions of Section 17-A, the award published under Section 17 (1) shall be final and shall not be called in question by any court in any manner whatsoever'.

Period for submitting of an award:

An order referring an industrial dispute to the National Tribunal under Section 10 shall specify the period within which such National Tribunal shall submit its award on such dispute to the appropriate Government [Section 10 (2-A)].

Where such industrial dispute is connected with an individual workman, no such period shall exceed three months [Proviso to section 10 (2-A)]. But where the parties to an industrial dispute apply in the prescribed manner, whether jointly or separately, to the National Tribunal for extension of such period or for any other reason, and the Presiding Officer of such National Tribunal considers it necessary or expedient to extend such period, he may for reasons to be recorded in writing extend such period by such further period as he may think fit [Proviso to Section 10 (2-A)].

In computing any period specified in this section the period, if any, for which the proceedings before the National Tribunal had been stayed by any injunction or order of a Civil Court shall be excluded [Proviso to Section 10 (2-A)].

It is also further provided in Section 10 (2-A) that no proceedings before the National Tribunal shall lapse merely on the ground that any period specified under this sub-section had expired without such proceeding being completed.

On the death of Parties, Proceedings do not lapse:

Provisions have been made in Section 10 (8) of the Act relating to the proceedings pending on the death of the parties to the dispute. Section 10 (8) lays down that, "No proceedings pending before National Tribunal in relation to an industrial dispute shall lapse merely by reason on the death of any of the parties to the dispute being a workman, and such National Tribunal shall complete such proceedings and submit its award to the appropriate Government.

Barring of the other authorities under this Act for adjudication of an industrial dispute pending before the National Tribunal:

Where any reference has been made under Section 10 (1-A) to a National Tribunal [Please see the provisions of Section 10 (1-A)] given under the heading "Reference disputes to National Tribunal"] then notwithstanding anything contained in this Act, no Labour Court or Tribunal shall have jurisdiction to adjudicate upon any matter which is under adjudication before the National Tribunal, and accordingly –

(a) If the matter under adjudication before the National Tribunal is pending in a proceeding before a Labour Court or the Tribunal the proceeding before the Labour Court or the Tribunal, as the case may be, in so far as it relates to such matter shall be deemed to have been quashed on such reference to the National Tribunal; and

(b) It shall not be lawful for the appropriate Government to refer the matter under adjudication before the National Tribunal to any Labour Court or Tribunal for adjudication during the pendency of the proceeding in relation to such matter before the National Tribunal.

In this sub-section, which is mentioned above 'Labour Court' or 'Tribunal' includes any court or Tribunal or any other authority constituted under any law relating to investigation and settlement of industrial disputes in force in any state [Explanation to Section 10 (6)].

(H) Voluntary Reference to Arbitration:

Section 10-A of the Industrial Disputes Act of 1947 provides for the voluntary reference of disputes to arbitration. Where any industrial dispute exists or is apprehended and the employer and the workmen agree to refer the dispute to arbitration, they may do so by an agreement in writing in the form prescribed by the rules and signed in the manner laid down in the rules. However, the reference to the arbitration must be made before the dispute has been referred to any authority under Section 10. The definition of 'Arbitrator' and provisions relating to voluntary reference of a dispute arbitration are discussed below.

Definition of 'Arbitrator and Provisions relating to voluntary reference of a dispute to arbitration:

Arbitrator [Section 2 (a a)]:

In the Industrial Disputes Act of 1947, the definition of 'Arbitrator' is given in Section (aa) and it is only stated that **'Arbitrator' includes an umpire**. However, provisions relating appointment at an umpire and to voluntary reference of dispute to arbitration have been made in Section 10-A which are as follows:

1. Time to making voluntary reference of dispute to arbitration and who can make such reference: Where any industrial dispute exists or is apprehended and the employer and the workmen agree to refer the dispute to arbitration, they may, at any time before the dispute has been referred under section 10 to a Labour Court or Tribunal or National Tribunal, by a written agreement, but save as aforesaid refer the dispute to arbitration [Section 10-A (1)].

Thus, the reference to arbitration must be made before the dispute has been referred to any authority under section 10. Such reference to arbitration can be made by the employer and the workmen on the agreement amongst themselves where any industrial dispute exists or is apprehended.

2. To whom arbitration reference can be made: Section 10-A (1) makes it clear that voluntary reference of dispute to arbitration shall be made to such person or persons including the Presiding Officer of a Labour Court, Industrial Tribunal or National Tribunal as an arbitrator or arbitrators as may be specified in the arbitration agreement.

3. Appointment of an Umpire: The parties to the dispute can select any person as an arbitrator or person as arbitrators. But where an arbitrator agreement provides for a reference of the dispute to an even number of arbitrators, that agreement shall provide for the appointment of another person as an umpire. The umpire thus appointed shall enter upon the reference if the arbitrators are equally divided in their opinion, and the award of the umpire shall prevail and shall be deemed to be the arbitration award for the purposes of this Act [Section 10-A (1-A)].

4. Form of arbitration agreement: An arbitration agreement referred to in Section 10-A (1) shall be in such form and shall be signed by the parties thereto in such manner as may be prescribed [Section 10-A (2)].

5. Provisions relating to forward a copy of the arbitration agreement to the appropriate Government and the conciliation officer: Section 10-A (3) states that, "A copy of the arbitration agreement shall be forwarded to the appropriate Government and the conciliation officer and the appropriate Government shall, within one month from the date of the receipt of such copy, publish the same in the Official Gazette.

6. Opportunity to employers and workmen who are not parties to the arbitration agreement but are concerned in the dispute to represent their case: Where an industrial dispute has been referred to arbitration and the appropriate Government is satisfied that the persons making the reference represent the majority of each party, the appropriate Government may, within one month, issue a notification in such manner as may be prescribed, and when any such notification is issued, the employers and workmen who are not parties to the arbitration agreement but are concerned in the dispute, shall be given an opportunity of representing their case before the arbitrator or arbitrators [Section 10-A (3-A)].

7. Duty of the arbitrators: It is the duty of the arbitrator or arbitrators to investigate the dispute and then to submit the arbitration award duly signed to the appropriate Government. Section 10 - A (4) lays down that, "The arbitrator or arbitrators shall investigate the dispute and submit to the appropriate Government the arbitration award signed by the arbitrator or arbitrators, as the case may be".

8. Prohibition of continuance of strike or lock-out: When a dispute is referred to arbitration, the appropriate Government may prohibit the continuance of any strike or lock-out by issuing an order. Section 10 - A [4 - A] states that, "where an industrial dispute has been referred to arbitration and notification has been issued under Section 10-A (3-A), the appropriate Government may, by order, prohibit the continuance of any strike or lock-out in connection with such dispute which may be in existence on the date of the reference".

9. Arbitration Act of 1940 not to apply: According to Section 10-A (5), "Nothing in the Arbitration Act, 1940 (10 of 1940) shall apply to arbitrations under this section". Thus, when a dispute is referred to arbitration under Section 10-A, the provisions of the Arbitration Act of 1940 do not apply to an arbitration under Section 10-A of the Industrial Disputes Act of 1947.

3.5 Filling of Vacancies and Finality of Orders [Section 8]

According to Section 8 of this Act, if, for any reason a vacancy (other than temporary absence) occurs in the office of the Presiding Officer of a Labour Court, Tribunal or National Tribunal or in the office of the Chairman or any other members of a Board or Court, then in the case of a National Tribunal, the Central Government, and in any other case, the Appropriate Government, shall appoint another person in accordance with the provisions of this act to fill the vacancy, and the proceeding may be continued before the Labour Court Tribunal, National Tribunal, Board or Court, as the case may be, from the stage at which vacancy is filled.

Finality of orders constituting boards etc. [Section 9]:

No order of the appropriate Government or of the Central Government appointing any person as the Chairman or any other member of a Board or of a Court or as the Presiding Officer of a Labour Court, Tribunal or National Tribunal shall be called in question in any manner; and no act or proceeding before any Board or Court shall be called in question in any manner on the ground merely of the existence of any vacancy in, or defect in the constitution of, such Board or Court [Section 9 (1).

No settlement arrived at in the course of a conciliation proceeding shall be invalid by reason only of the fact that such settlement was arrived at after expiry of the period referred to in sub-section (6) of Section 12 or sub-section (5) of Section 13, as the case may be [Section 9 (2)]. (Sections 12 and 13 are already explained in this chapter).

Where the report of any settlement arrived at in the course of conciliation before a Board is signed by the Chairman and all the other members of the Board, no such settlement shall be invalid by reason only of the casual or unforeseen absence of any of the members including Chairman of the Board, during any state of the proceeding [Section 9 (3)].

3.6 Notice of Change [Section 9-A and 9-B]

In Chapter II-A [Section 9-A and 9-B) of this Act, provisions have been made relating to the notice of change.

According to Section 9-A, no employer, who proposes to affect any change in the conditions of service applicable to any workmen *in respect of any matter specified in the Fourth Schedule*, shall affect such change –

(a) Without giving to the workmen likely to be affected by such change a notice in the prescribed manner of the nature of the change proposed to be effected; or

(b) Within twenty-one days of giving such notice.

Provided that no notice shall be required for affecting such change (a) where the change is affected in pursuance of settlement of award and (b) where the workmen likely to be affected by the change are persons to whom the Fundamental and Supplementary Rules, Civil Services Rules, Revised Leave Rules etc. are applicable.

The conditions of service for change of which notice is required to be given are mentioned in the Fourth Schedule given below:

The Fourth Schedule:

Conditions of service for change of which notice is to be given –

1. Wages including the period and mode of payment.
2. Contribution pair or payable, by the employer to any provident fund or pension fund or for the benefit of the workmen under any law for the time being in force;
3. Compensatory and other allowances;
4. Hours of work and intervals;
5. Leave with wages and holidays;
6. Starting, alteration or discontinuance of shift working otherwise than, in accordance with standing orders;
7. Classification by grades;
8. Withdrawal of any customary concession or privilege or change in usages;
9. Introduction of new rules of discipline, or alteration of existing rules; except in so far as they are provided in standing orders;
10. Rationalisation, standardisation or improvement of plant or technique which is likely to lead to retrenchment of workmen;
11. Any increase or reduction (other than casual) in the number of persons employed or to be employed in any occupation or process of department or shift not occasioned by circumstances over which the employer has no control.

No notice is required for certain changes:

No notice is required to be given to an employer, who proposes to effect any change in the conditions of service applicable to any workmen in respect to any matter specified in the Fourth Schedule where the change in affected in pursuance of any settlement of award and where the workmen likely to be affected by the change are persons to whom the Fundamental and Supplementary Rules, Civil Services Rules, Revised Leave Rules etc. are applicable.

Power of Government to Exempt [Section 9-B]:

Where the appropriate Government is of the opinion that the application of the provisions of section 9-A to any class of industrial establishments or to any class of workmen in any industrial establishment affects the employees in relation thereto so prejudicially, that such application may cause serious repercussion on the industry concerned and that public interest so requires, the appropriate Government may, by notification in the Official Gazette, direct the provisions of the said section *shall not apply, or shall subject to such conditions as may be specified in the notification*, to that class of industrial establishment or to that class of workmen employed in any industrial establishment.

3.7 Reference to Certain Individual Disputes to Grievance Settlement Authorities [Section 9-C]

Section 9-C of this Act provides for setting up of Grievance Settlement Authorities and reference of certain individual disputes to such authorities. The employer in relation to every industrial establishment in which fifty or more workmen are employed or have been employed on any day in the preceding twelve months, shall provide for, in accordance with rules made in that behalf under this Act, a Grievance Settlement Authority for the settlement of industrial disputes connected with an individual workman employed in the establishment [Section 9-C (1)].

Where an industrial dispute connected with an individual workman arises in an establishment referred to in sub-section (1) above, a workman or any trade union of workmen of which such workman is a member, refer, in such manner as may be prescribed, such dispute to the Grievance settlement Authority provided for by the employer under that sub-section for settlement of disputes [Section 9-C (2)].

The Grievance Settlement Authority referred to in Section 9-C (1) shall follow such procedure and complete its proceedings within such period as may be prescribed [Section 9-C (3)].

No reference shall be made under Chapter III with respect to any dispute referred to in this section unless such dispute has been referred to the Grievance Settlement Authority concerned and the decision of that authority is not acceptable to any of the parties to the disputes. [Section 9-C (4)].

3.8 Reference of Disputes to Board, Courts, Etc. [Section 10]

In Chapter III of this Act, provisions have been made for reference of disputes to various authorities. These provisions are as under.

Where the appropriate Government is of the opinion that any industrial dispute exists or is apprehended, it may at any time, by order in writing –

(a) Refer the dispute to a Board for promoting a settlement thereof, or
(b) Refer any matter appearing to be connected with or relevant to the dispute, to a Court of inquiry; or
(c) Refer any dispute or any matter appearing to be connected with or relevant to, the dispute, if it relates to any matter specified in the Second Schedule (which is already reproduced elsewhere in this chapter), to a Labour Court for adjudication; or
(d) Refer the dispute or any matter appearing to be connected with, or relevant to, the dispute, whether it relates to any matter specified in the Second Schedule or the Third Schedule to a Tribunal for adjudication [Section 10 (1)].

Provided that where the dispute relates to any matter specified in the Third Schedule and is not likely to affect more than one hundred workmen, the appropriate Government may, if it thinks fit, make the reference to a Labour Court under clause C of Section 10 (1). [Proviso to Section 10 (1)].

Provided further that where the dispute relates to a public utility service and a notice under Section 22 has been given, the appropriate Government shall, unless it considers that the notice has been frivolously or vexatiously given or that it would be inexpedient so to do; make reference under this subsection notwithstanding that any other proceeding under this Act in respect of the dispute may have commenced [Proviso to Section 10 (1)].

Provided also that where the dispute in relation to which the Central Government is the appropriate Government, it shall be competent for that Government to refer the dispute to a Labour Court or an Industrial Tribunal, as the case may be, constituted by the State Government [Proviso to Section 10 (1)].

Where the Central Government is of the opinion that any industrial dispute exists or is apprehended and the dispute involves any question of national importance or is of such a nature that industrial establishments situated in more than one state are likely to be interested in or affected by such dispute and that dispute should be adjudicated by a National Tribunal, then the Central Government may, whether or not it is the appropriate Government in relation to that dispute at any time, by order in writing, refer the dispute or any matter appearing to be connected with, or relevant to the dispute, whether it relates to any matter specified in the Second Schedule, to a National Tribunal for adjudication [Section 10 (1-A)].

Where the parties to any industrial dispute apply in the prescribed manner whether jointly or separately, for a reference of the dispute to a board, Court, Labour Court, Tribunal or National Tribunal, the appropriate Government, if satisfied that the persons applying represent the majority of each party, shall make the reference accordingly [Section 10 (2)].

An order referring an industrial dispute to a Labour Court, National Tribunal or Tribunal under this section shall specify the period within which such Labour Court, Tribunal or National Tribunal shall submit its award on such dispute to the appropriate Government [Section 10 (2-A)].

Provided that where such industrial dispute is connected with an industrial workman, no such period shall exceed three months.

Provided further that where the parties to an industrial dispute apply in the prescribed manner, whether jointly or separately, to the Labour Court, Tribunal or National Tribunal for extension of such period or for any other reason, and the Presiding Officer of such Labour Court, Tribunal or National Tribunal considers it necessary or expedient to extend such period, he may for reasons to be recorded in writing, extend such period by such further period as he may think fit.

Provided also that in computing any period specified in this sub-section, the period, if any, for which the proceedings before the Labour Court, Tribunal or National Tribunal had been stayed by any injuction or order of a Civil Court shall be excluded.

Provided also that no proceedings before a Labour Court, Tribunal or National Tribunal shall lapse merely on the ground that any period specified under this sub-section had expired without such proceedings before completed.

Where an industrial dispute has been referred to a Board, Labour Court, Tribunal or National Tribunal under this section the appropriate Government may by order prohibit the continuance of any strike or lock-out in connection with such dispute which may be existence on the date of reference [Section 10 (3)].

Wherein an order referring an industrial dispute to a Labour Court, Tribunal or National Tribunal under this section or in a subsequent order, the appropriate Government has specified the points of disputes for adjudication, the Labour Court, or the Tribunal or the National Tribunal, as the case may be, shall confine its adjudication to those points and matters incidental thereto [Section 10 (4)].

Where a dispute concerning any establishment or establishments has been, or is to be, referred to a Labour Court, Tribunal, or National Tribunal under this Section and the appropriate Government is of opinion, whether on an application made to it in this behalf or otherwise, that the dispute is of such a nature that any other establishment, group or class of establishments of a similar nature is likely to be interested in, or affected by such dispute, the appropriate Government may, at the time of making the reference or at any time thereafter but before the submission of the award, include in that reference such establishment, group or class of establishments, whether or not at the time of such inclusion any dispute exists or is apprehended in that establishment, group or class of establishments. [Section 10 (5)].

Where any reference has been made to a National Tribunal under Section 10 (1-A), then, notwithsanding anything contained in this Act, no Labour Court or Tribunal shall have jurisdiction upon any matter which is under adjudication before the National Tribunal. [Section 10 (6)].

Where any industrial dispute, in relation to which the Central Government is not the appropriate Government, is referred to a National Tribunal, then notwithstanding anything contained in this Act, any reference in Sections 15, 17, 19, 33-A, 33-B and 36-A to the appropriate Government in relation to such dispute shall be construed as a reference to the Central Government, but, save as aforesaid and as otherwise expressly provided in this Act, any reference in any other provision of this Act to the appropriate Government in relation to that dispute shall mean a reference to the State Government [Section 10 (7)].

No proceedings pending before a Labour Court, Tribunal or National Tribunal in relation to an industrial dispute shall lapse merely because of the death of day of the parties to the dispute being a workman and such Labour Court, Tribunal or National Tribunal shall complete such proceedings and submit its award to the appropriate Government [Section 10 (8)].

3.9 Procedure and Powers of the Authorities [Section 11]

We have already considered the duties of various authorities appointed by the Appropriate or Central Government under this Act. The procedure to be followed and powers given to the authorities are also explained in Chapter IV of this Act.

Let us consider them briefly. Section 11 of this Act provides for the procedure and powers of Conciliation Officers, Boards, Courts and Tribunals.

Section 11: Procedure and Powers of Conciliation Officers, Boards, Courts and Tribunals:

1. Subject to any rules that may be made in this behalf, an arbitrator, a Board, Court, Tribunal or National Tribunal shall follow such procedure as the arbitrator or other authority concerned may think fit.

2. A Conciliation Officer or a member of a Board or Court or the Presiding Officer of a Labour Court, Tribunal or National Tribunal may, for the purpose of inquiry into any existing or apprehended industrial dispute, after giving reasonable notice, enter the premises occupied by the establishment to which the disputes relate.

3. Every Board, Court, Labour Tribunal and National Tribunal shall have the same powers as are vested in a Civil Court under the Code of Civil Procedure, 1908, when trying a suit in respect of the following matters, namely:

    (a) Enforcing the attendance of any person and examining him on oath;

    (b) Compelling the production of documents and material objects;

    (c) Issuing commission for the examination of witnesses;

    (d) In respect of such other matters as may be prescribed, and every inquiry or investigation by a Board, Court, Labour Court, Tribunal and National Tribunal shall be deemed to be a judicial proceeding, within the meaning of sections 193 and 228 of the Indian Penal Code.

4. A Conciliation Officer may enforce the attendance of any person for the purpose of examination of such person or call for and inspect any document which he has ground for considering to be relevant to the industrial dispute or to be necessary for the purpose of verifying the implementation of any award or carrying out any other duty imposed on him under this Act, and for the aforesaid purposes Conciliation Officer shall have the same powers as are vested in a Civil Court under the Code of Civil Procedure, 1908 in respect of enforcing the attendance of any person and examining him or of compelling the production of documents.

5. A Court, Labour Court, Tribunal or National Tribunal may, if it so thinks fit, appoint one or more persons having special knowledge of the matter under consideration as assessor or assessors to advise it in the proceeding before it.

6. All Conciliation Officers, members of a Board or Court and the Presiding Officers of a Labour Court, Tribunal or National Tribunal shall be deemed to be public servants within the meaning of Section 21 of the Indian Penal Code.

7. Subject to any rules made under this Act, the costs of, and incidental to any proceeding before a Labour Court, Tribunal or National Tribunal shall be in the

discretion of that Labour Court, Tribunal or National Tribunal and the Labour Court, Tribunal or National Tribunal, as the case may be, shall have full power to determine by and to when and to what extent and subject to what conditions, if any, such costs are to be paid, and to give all necessary directions for the purposes aforesaid and such costs may, on application made to the appropriate Government by the person entitled, be recovered by the Government in the same manner as an arrear of land revenue.

8. Every Labour Court, Tribunal or National Tribunal shall be deemed to be a Civil Court for the purposes of [sections 345, 346 and 348 of the Code of Criminal Procedure 1973].

Section 11-A makes clear the powers of Labour Courts, Tribunals and National Tribunals to give appropriate relief in case of discharge or dismissal of workmen. Section 11-A is as follows.

Section 11-A: Powers of Labour Courts, Tribunal and National Tribunals to give appropriate relief in case of discharge or dismissal of workmen:

Where an industrial dispute relating to the discharge or dismissal of a workman has been referred to a Labour Court, Tribunal or National Tribunal for adjudication and, in the course of the adjudication proceedings, the Labour Court, Tribunal or National Tribunal, as the case may be, is satisfied that the order of discharge or dismissal was not justified, it may, by its award, set aside the order of discharge or dismissal and direct reinstatement of the workman on such terms and conditions, if any, as it thinks fit, or give such other relief to the workman including the award of any lesser punishment in lieu of discharge or dismissal as the circumstances of the case may require:

Provided that in any proceeding under this section the Labour Court, Tribunal or National Tribunal, as the case may be, shall rely only on the materials on record and shall not take any fresh evidence in relation to the matter.

3.10 Award and Settlement [Sections 16 To 21]

3.10.1 Meaning of 'Award' and 'Settlement'

Award, so far the Industrial Disputes Act of 1947 is concerned, means an interim or a final determination of any industrial dispute or of any question relating thereto by any Labour Court, Tribunal or National Tribunal, as the case may be, and it includes an arbitration award made under Section 10 A of the said Act. While settlement implies a settlement arrived at in the course of conciliation proceedings and it includes a written agreement between the employer and workmen arrived at otherwise than in the course of conciliation proceeding where such agreement has been signed by the parties thereto in such manner as may be prescribed and a copy thereof has been sent to an officer authorised in this behalf by the appropriate Government and the Conciliation Officer.

3.10.2 Form of Report or Award

According to Section 16 (1), the report or award of a Board or Court must be in writing and shall be signed by all the members, as the case may be. It is further provided that nothing in this Section 16 (1) shall be deemed to prevent any member of the Board or Court from recording any minute of dissent from a report or from any recommendation made therein [Proviso to Section 16 (1)].

The Award of a Labour Court or Tribunal or National Tribunal shall be in writing and shall be signed by its Presiding Office [Section 16 (2)].

3.10.3 Publication of Reports and Awards

According to Section 17 (1) every report of a Board or Court together with any minute of dissent recorded therewith, every arbitration award and every award of a Labour Court, Tribunal or National Tribunal must be published within a period of thirty days from the date of its receipts by the appropriate Government in such manner as, the appropriate Government thinks fit and proper. Further it is provided that subject to the provisions of Section 17 - A (which is reproduced below), the award published under Section 17 (1) shall be final and shall not be called in question by any Court in any manner whatsoever [Section 17 (2)]. This implies that the awards thus published cannot be challenged.

3.10.4 Commencement of the Award [Section 17-A]

Section 17-A (1) states that an award, including an arbitration award, shall become enforceable on the expiry of thirty days from the date of its publication as provided in Section 17 (1). However, if the appropriate Government is of the opinion, in any case of award where the award has been given by a Labour Court or Tribunal in relation to an industrial dispute to which it is a party Or if the Central Government is of the opinion, in any case where the award has been given by a National Tribunal, that it will be in expedient to give effect to the whole or any part of the award, the appropriate Government or the Central Government, as the case may be, may be notification in the Official Gazette, declare that the award shall not become enforceable on the expiry of the said period of thirty days.

Thus, this section 17-A empowers the Government not to make the award given by a Labour Court a Tribunal or a National Tribunal, as the case may be, enforceable in whole or in part, if the appropriate Government thinks that it will be in expedient to do so. The concerned Government however, has to do so by given proper notification in the Official Gazette. Then obviously such award or an arbitration cannot become enforceable on the expiry of the period of thirty days from the date of its receipt by the appropriate Government.

Section 17 A (2) makes it clear that "where any declaration has been made in relation to an award under the proviso to sub-section (1), the appropriate Government or the Central Government may, within ninety days from the date of publication of the award under Section 17, make an order rejecting or modifying the award, and shall, on the first available opportunity, lay the award together with a copy of the order before the Legislature of the State, if the order has been made by a State Government or before Parliament, if the order has been made by the Central Government.

Where any award as rejected to modified by an order made under sub-section (2) is laid before the Legislature of a State or before Parliament, such award shall become enforceable on the expiry of fifteen days from the date on which it is so laid; and where no order under sub-section (2) is made in pursuance of a declaration under the proviso to sub-section (1), the award shall become enforceable on the expiry of the period of ninety days referred to in sub-section (2) [Section 17 A (3)].

Section 17 A (4) provides that subject to the provisions of sub-section (1) and sub-section (3) regarding the enforceability of an award, the award shall come into operation with effect from such date as may be specified therein, but where no date is so specified, it shall come into operation on the date when the award becomes enforceable under Section 17 (1) or Section 17 A (3) as the case may be.

3.10.5 Provisions Relating to Full Wages to Workman Pending Proceedings in Higher Courts [Section 17-B]

Section 17-B makes provisions relating to full wages to a workman during the period of pendency of such proceedings because of the cause mentioned in this section in the High Court or in the Supreme Court. These provisions are stated below.

"Where in any case, a Labour Court, Tribunal or National Tribunal by its award directs reinstatement of any workman and the employer prefers any proceedings against such award in a High Court or the Supreme Court, the employer shall be liable to pay such workman, during the period of pendency of such proceedings in the High Court or the Supreme Court, full wages last drawn by him, inclusive of any maintenance allowance admissible to him under any rule if the workman had not been employed in any establishment during such period and an affidavit by such workman had been filed to that effect in such Court".

It is also provided that where it is proved to the satisfaction of the High Court or the Supreme Court that such workman had been employed and had been receiving adequate remuneration during any such period or part thereof, the Court shall order that no wages shall be payable under this section for such period or part, as the case may be [Proviso to Section 17-B].

3.10.6 Persons on whom Settlements and Awards are Binding

According to Section 18, settlements and awards are binding on the following persons.

I. A settlement arrived at by agreement between the employer and workman otherwise than in the course of conciliation proceeding shall be binding on the parties to the agreement [Section 18 (1)].

II. Subject to the provisions of sub-section (3) an arbitration award which has become enforceable shall be binding on the parties to the agreement who referred the dispute to arbitration. [Section 18 (2)].

III. A settlement arrived at in the course of conciliation proceedings under this Act or an arbitration award in a case where a notification has been issued under sub-section (3-A) of Section 10-A or an award of a Labour Court, Tribunal or National Tribunal which has become enforceable shall be binding on –
   (a) All parties to the industrial dispute;
   (b) All other parties summoned to appear in the proceedings as parties to the Dispute, unless the Board, [arbitrator] [Labour Court, Tribunal or National Tribunal], as the case may be, records the opinion that they were so summoned without proper cause;
   (c) Where a party referred to in clause (a) or clause (b) is an employer, his heirs, successors or assigns in respect of the establishment to which the dispute relates;
   (d) Where a party referred to in clause (a) or clause (b) is composed of workmen, all persons who were employed in the establishment or part of the establishment, as the case may be, to which the dispute relates on the date of the dispute and all persons who subsequently become employed in that establishment or part [Section 18 (3)].

It should be noted that the main object of the Industrial Dispute Act is the settlement of industrial disputes. It is not merely the enactment bearing on terms and conditions of service. From this point of view, an award or settlement continues to regulate the relationship between the parties until it is replaced by new one. Hence distinction between award and settlement from the view point of their legal force need not be made [Life Insurance Corporation of India V. D. J. Bahadur and Others (AIR-1980-Supreme Court - 2181]. It must also be remembered that every settlement is always an agreement or arrangement. However every agreement or arrangement cannot be a settlement in the eyes of law [India Tobacco Company V. Deputy Labour Commissioner (1971-75-C.W.N. 217].

3.10.7 Period of Operation of a Settlement and an Award

(A) Period of operation of settlement: Provisions of Section 19 (1) and (2) throw light on the period of operation of a settlement. Section 19 (1) makes it clear that if any settlement arrived at in the course of conciliation proceedings before a Conciliation Officer or a Board of Conciliation, as the case may be, it shall come into operation (i) on such date as is agreed upon by the parties to the dispute, and (ii) if no such date is agreed upon, on the date on which the memorandum of the settlement is signed by the parties to the dispute.

Section 19 (2) provides that such settlement, thus arrived at, shall be binding for such period as is agreed upon by the parties. However, if no such period is agreed upon, it shall be binding for a period of six months from the date on which the memorandum of settlement is signed by the parties to the dispute. Section 19 (2) further states that it shall continue to be binding on the parties after the expiry of the period aforesaid, until the expiry of two months from the date on which a notice in writing of an intention to terminate the settlement is given by one of the parties to the other party or parties to the settlement." Thus, a settlement continues to be binding until any one of the parties gives in writing a notice of termination of the settlement and the settlement ceases to be binding on the expiry of two months from such notice of termination given.

Any notice thus given under Section 19 (2) shall not be operative unless it is given by a party representing the majority of persons bound by the settlement [Section 19 (7)].

(B) Period of operation of an award: So far as the period of operation of an award is concerned, the following provisions have been made in Section 19 of the Industrial Disputes Act of 1947.

(a) Subject to other provisions of Section 19, an award shall remain in operation for a period of one year from the date on which the award becomes enforceable under Section 17-A. [Section 19 (3)]. We have already considered the provisions of Section 17-A.

(b) The appropriate Government has been authorised to reduce this period of one year and to fix such period as it thinks fit [Proviso 1 to Section 19].

(c) The appropriate Government has also been authorised, before the expiry of the said period of one year, to extend the period of operation by any period not exceeding one year at a time as it thinks proper. But the total period of operation of any award shall not exceed three years from the date on which it came into operation [Proviso 2 to Section 19 (3)].

(d) Section 19 (5) lays down that, "Nothing contained in Section 19 (3) shall apply to any award which by its nature, terms or other circumstances does not impose, after it has been given effect to, any continuing obligations on the parties bound by the award."

(e) Provisions have been made in Section 19 (4) relating to shortening of period of operation of award on a material change in the circumstances.
These provisions are as follows:

Where the appropriate Government considers that since award was made, there has been a material change in the circumstances on which it was based, the appropriate Government, either on its own motion or on the application of any party bound by the award, may refer the award or a part of it (i) to a Labour Court, if the award was that of a Labour Court, or (ii) to a Tribunal, if the award was that of a Tribunal or of a National Tribunal, for a decision whether the period of operation of the award should not, by reason of such change, be shortened. The decision given by Labour Court or the Tribunal in that respect, one such reference, shall be final.

(f) Section 19 (6) states that, "Notwithstanding the expiry of the period of operation under Section 19 (3), the award shall continue to be binding on the parties until a period of two months has elapsed from the date on which notice is given by any party bound by the award to the other party or parties intimating its intention to terminate the award". Thus, the award continues to be binding on the parties until the expiry of the period of two months from the date of notice of its termination by a party and then such award ceases to be binding on the expiry of two months from such notice.

(g) The notice thus given by any party under section 19 (6) shall not have any effect unless such notice is given by a party representing the majority of persons bound by the award [Section 19 (7)].

3.10.8 Penalty for Breach of Settlement or Award [Section 29]

Any person who commits a breach of term of any settlement or award, which is binding on such person under this Act, is punishable with imprisonment for a period which may extend to six months or with a fine or with both; and where the breach is a continuing one, with a further fine which may extend to two hundred rupees for every day during which the breach continues after the conviction for the first breach and the Court trying the offence, if it imposes a fine on the offender, may direct that the whole or any part of the fine realised from him shall be paid, by way of compensation, to any person who, in the opinion of the Court, has been injured by such breach.

3.10.9 Provisions Relating to Commencement and Conclusion of Conciliation Proceedings

(A) Provisions relating to commencement of conciliation proceedings:

According to Section 20 (1), a conciliation proceeding shall be deemed to have commenced on the date on which a notice of strike or lock-out under Section 22 is received by the conciliation officer or on the date of the order referring the dispute to a Board, as the case may be.

(B) Provisions relating to conclusion of conciliation proceeding:

Section 20 (2) states that, "A conciliation proceeding shall be deemed to have concluded –

(a) Where a settlement is arrived at, when a memorandum of settlement is signed by the parties to the dispute;

(b) Where no settlement is arrived, when the report of the conciliation officer is received by the appropriate Government or when the report of the Board is published under Section 17, as the case may be; or when a reference is made to a Court of Inquiry, Labour Court, Industrial Tribunal or National Tribunal under Section 10 during the pendency of conciliation proceedings.

(c) Provisions relating to Arbitration and Adjudication proceedings: Section 20 (3) makes it clear that any proceedings before an arbitrator under Section 10-A or before a Labour Court, Tribunal or National Tribunal shall be deemed to have commenced on the date of the reference of the dispute for arbitration or adjudication, as the case may be, and such proceedings shall be deemed to have concluded on the date on which the award becomes enforceable under Section 17-A.

3.10.10 Provisions Relating to Keeping Certain Matters Confidential

Section 21 lays down that, "There shall not be included in any report or award under this Act, any information obtained by a Conciliation Officer, Board, Court, Labour Court, Tribunal, National Tribunal or an arbitrator in the course of any investigation or inquiry as to a trade union or as to any individual business, whether carried on by a person, firm or a company, which is not available otherwise than through the evidence given before such officer, Board, Court, Labour Court, Tribunal, National Tribunal or arbitrator, as the case may be, if the trade union, person, firm or company in question has made a request in writing to the Conciliation Officer, Board, Court, Labour Court, Tribunal, National Tribunal or arbitrator, as the case may be, that such information shall be treated as confidential, nor shall such conciliation officer or any individual member of the Board, or Court or the presiding officer of the Labour Court, Tribunal or National Tribunal or the arbitrator or any person present at or concerned in the proceedings disclose any such information without the consent in writing of the secretary of the trade union or the person, firm or company in question, as the case may be". However, it is also provided that, "nothing contained in this section shall apply to a disclosure of any such information for the purposes of a prosecution under Section 193 of the Indian Penal Code of 1860". [Proviso to Section 21].

From the above mentioned provisions of Section 21 it becomes clear that any information of a confidential nature obtained from the evidence given and not otherwise available should not be included in the reports and awards under the Act, neither it should be disclosed in any other way; if the persons concerned i.e. the employer, the trade union or any other concerned party makes a request in writing to the concerned authority dealing with the matter to keep any information secret. Section 30 expressly provides that if any person who purposely or wilfully discloses any such information as is referred to in Section 21 of this Act in contravention of the provisions of that Section 21 is, on complaint made by or on behalf of the trade union or individual whose business is affected such person is punishable with imprisonment for a term which may extent to six months, or with a fine which may extend to one thousand rupees or with both.

3.10.11 Distinction between 'Settlement' and 'Award'

Settlement	Award
1. 'Settlement' means a settlement arrived at in the course of conciliation proceedings and it includes a written agreement between the employer and workmen arrived at otherwise than in the course of conciliation proceedings where such agreement has been signed by the parties thereto in such manner as may be prescribed and a copy thereof has been sent to an officer authorised in this behalf by the appropriate Government and the Conciliation Officer [Section 2 (p)].	1. 'Award' means an interim or a final determination of any industrial dispute or of any question relating thereto by any Labour Court, Industrial Tribunal or National Industrial Tribunal and includes an arbitration award made under Section 10-A [Section 2 (b).
2. Settlement is the result of a purely non-judicial agreement.	2. Award is of a judicial nature.
3. In settlement, voluntary process of the parties to the dispute is predominant.	3. In award, a quasi-judicial machinery is set in motion.
4. Works Committee, Conciliation Officers, Boards of Conciliation and Courts of Inquiry constitute the conciliation machinery for settlement of industrial disputes. They can only promote settlement of industrial disputes or inquire into them but cannot make any award which are binding on the parties.	4. Labour Courts, Industrial Tribunals and National Tribunals constitute the adjudication authorities under the Act.
5. Settlement implies amicable settlement and amicability of the concerned parties to the dispute is the primary consideration.	5. Award is not influenced by the parties to the dispute. Decision is given by an independent quasi-judicial body and is not influenced by the parties to the dispute.

3.11 Strikes and Lock-Outs [Sections 22 TO 25]

3.11.1 Strikes

Lock-outs and strikes are the weapons in the hands of employers and workmen respectively to compel one other to agree to their demand or demands.

Strike has been defined in Section 2 (g) of this Act which means cessation of work by a body of persons employed in any industry acting in combination or a concerted refusal or a refusal under a common understanding of any number who are or have been so employed to continue to work or to accept employment. Strike is a powerful weapon in the hands of employees for collective bargaining. The employees in a way compel the employers to sit across with them for settling their disputes in the form of collective bargaining by using this powerful weapon of strike. When all other methods to settle the industrial disputes fail, this weapon of strike is used as at resort. The right to go on strike has been given to the workmen, but this Act imposes certain restrictions on this right of workmen. The Act prohibits strikes under certain circumstances. The Act makes separate provisions for public utility service and private enterprises.

The following important points may be noted so far as a strike is concerned.

1. A strike is a weapon which is used by employees or workmen acting together to force their employer to agree to the demands made by them.
2. A strike implies a stoppage of work by a number of employees acting together. But mere absence from work on personal grounds does not amount to cessation or stoppage or refusal of work. There should be premeditation or plan to cease or to refuse to work in a body of workmen.
3. The duration or stoppage or cessation of work is immaterial. If the workmen acting together cease their work even for an hour or a part thereof, it can be called a strike.
4. When workmen go on strike against the provisions of this Act, such strike is considered illegal.
5. Even a partial refusal of work by a body of workmen may constitute a strike.
6. A strike can be a 'stay-in strike' or 'Go-slow strike'.
7. In certain industries, overtime work is considered essential and it is a legal obligation and in certain industries, overtime work is done habitually and is customary. Refusal of overtime work in such cases is considered as against the conditions of service. If overtime work is refused, then it may be considered as a strike.

From the definition and the important points mentioned above, we come to know that the following two factors must exist in a strike.

(a) The workmen must be absent from work either in a body or in a group. They must refuse to work when they are expected to do under legal or contractual obligation for their employer.

(b) The cessation or refusal to do the work is voiced either in concerted form of all workmen or in a group of workmen. Mere absence from duty or work on any personal ground does not amount to cessation or refusal of work. There must be predetermination or some plan to cease or refuse to do the work in a body of workmen.

In the following cases, cessation or refusal to do the work amounted to strike.

(a) In Model Mills Nagpur Ltd. V. Daram Das Case [AIR-1958-SC-311], in addition to two workers who were required to work on the machine, other seven workers stopped to do their work. It was held in the case that the cessation of work was under concert and it constituted a strike.

(b) In Buckingham and Carnatic Mills Company Limited V. Workmen Case [AIR 1953 - Supreme Court], where the workmen for common understanding participated in the non-permitted stoppage of work for two hours, it was held that the cessation of work amounted to a strike.

(c) When the workmen enter the premises of their employment and under common understanding refuse to take the tools, whatever they may be, and start their usual work, it amounts to a strike. In Punjab National Bank V. All India Punjab National Bank Employee's Federation Case [AIR 1960 Supreme Court 160], under common understanding, the employees of the bank entered the premises of the bank but refused to take their pens in hands and start their usual work. It was held that the action of the employees amounted to a strike.

However, where the management substitutes weekly rest day without giving any proper notice of such change, the refusal of work by the employees to do their work on the substituted holiday does not amount to a strike [Tata Iron and Steel Company Ltd. V. Their workmen case - AIR - 1972 - S.C. 1917], or where refusal to work by workmen according to the newly introduced rationalisation schemes contrary to Section 33 of the Industrial Disputes Act of 1947, the refusal to do the work on the part of workmen according to such schemes does not amount to a strike [North Brook Jute Company Ltd. V. Their workmen case - AIR 1960 - S. C. 879].

3.11.2 Important Provisions Relating to Strikes

(A) Provisions relating to prohibition of strike [Section 22]:

1. No person employed in a public utility service shall go on strike, in breach of contract –
   (a) Without giving a notice of strike to the employer, as herein-after provided, within six weeks before striking; or
   (b) Withing fourteen days of giving such notice, or
   (c) Before the expiry of the date of strike specified in such notice as aforesaid; or
   (d) During the pendency of any conciliation proceedings before a conciliation officer and seven days after the conclusion of such proceedings.
   [Section 22 (1)]

2. The notice of strike under the provisions mentioned above in Section 22 (1) shall not be necessary where there is already in existence a strike in public utility services. But, it is very essential for the employer to send an intimation of such a strike to such authority as may be specified by the appropriate Government, on

the day on which the strike is declared, either generally or for a particular area or for a particular class of public utility services [Section 22 (3)].

The notice of strike referred to in Section 22 (1) must be given by such number of persons to such person or persons and in such manner as may be prescribed [Section 22 (4)].

4. If on any day an employer receives from any person employed by him any such notices as are referred to in Section 22 (1), he must within five days, thereof report to the appropriate Government or to such authority as that appropriate Government may prescribe the number of such notices received on that date [Section 22 (6)].

(B) General prohibition of strike [Section 23]:

No workman who is employed in any industrial establishment will go on strike in breach of contract under the following circumstances.

1. During the pendency of conciliation proceedings before a Board and seven days after the conclusion of such proceedings.
2. During the pendency of proceedings before a Labour Court, an Industrial Tribunal or National Tribunal and two months after the conclusion of such proceedings.
3. During the pendency of arbitration proceedings before an arbitrator and two months after the conclusion of such proceedings, where a notification has been issued under Section 10-A(3-A), or
4. During any period in which a settlement or award is in operation, in respect of any of the matters covered by the settlement or award.

(C) Illegal strikes [Section 24]:

1. A strike shall be illegal if it is commenced or declared in contravention of Section 22 or Section 23 or if it is continued in contravention of an order made under section 10 (3) or under Section 10-A (4-A) [Section 24 (1)].
2. Where a strike in persuance of an industrial dispute has already commenced and is in existence at the time of the reference of the dispute to a Board, an arbitrator, a Labour Court, Tribunal or National Tribunal, the continuance of such strike shall not be deemed to be illegal, provided that such strike was not at its commencement in contravention of the provisions of this Act or the continuance thereof was not prohibited under Section 10 (3) or under Section 10-A (4-A) [Section 24 (2)].
3. Any strike declared in consequence of an illegal lock-out shall not be deemed to be illegal [Section 24 (3)].

3.11.3 Lock-outs

Lock-out has been defined in Section 2 (1) of this Act. Lock-out means the temporary closing of a place of employment, or the suspension of work, or the refusal by an employer to continue to employ any number of workmen employed by him. Thus, Lock-out is done by the employer and is resorted to enforce the employees to accept the employer's terms of working. Lock-out is a weapon available to the employer to persuade his demand by a coercive process. It is just the antithesis of a strike. But it must be remembered that lock-out should not be misunderstood as closure. Closure and Lock-out are two different terms.

From the above mentioned definition of lock-out and the discussion done so far, we come to know the following important characteristics of lock-out.

(a) Lock-out is an act of management and it is generally intended to put some pressure on the workers in order to make them agree to the terms and conditions of work of their employer.

(b) Mere suspension of work on account of shortage of raw materials, coal, supply of energy, water etc. is not lock-out.

(c) Lock-out indicates the temporary closure of the place of business and not the closure of the business itself.

(d) Lock-out is generally caused by strike, fear of disorder, fear of destruction of the properties of the firm, company etc. Most of these causes are the result of industrial disputes.

(e) Lock-out indicates the temporary closing of a place of employment, or the suspension of work, or the refusal of an employer to continue to employ any number of persons employed by him.

(f) Lock-out and discharge are not the same thing. In a lock-out, the relationship between an employer and his employees continues. But, in the case of discharge, this relationship is cut off.

(g) Lock-out does not indicate closure. Closure implies discontinuation of the business.

Important Provisions Relating to Lock-outs:

The important provisions made in the Act relating to Lock-out are as follows:

(A) Provisions relating to Prohibition of Lock-out [Section 22]:

1. It is mentioned in Section 22 (2) that, "No employer carrying on any public utility service shall lock-out any of his workmen –

    (a) Without giving them notice of lock-out as hereinafter provided, within six weeks before locking-out; or

    (b) Within fourteen days of giving such notice; or

    (c) Before the expiry of the date of lock-out specified in any such notice as aforesaid; or

    (d) During the pendency of any conciliation proceedings before a conciliation officer and seven days after the conclusion of such proceedings."

2. The notice of lock-out under Section 22 shall not be necessary where there is already in existence of a lock-out in the public utility service. However, the

employer shall send the intimation of such lock-out on the day on which it is declared, to such authority as may be specified by the appropriate Government either generally or for a particular area or for a particular class of public utility services [Section 22 (3)].

3. The notice of lock-out referred to Section 22 (2) is required to be given in such manner as may be prescribed [Section 22 (5)].

4. If on any day an employer gives to any persons employed by him any such notices as are referred to in Section 22 (2), he shall within five days thereof report to the appropriate Government or to such other authority as that Government may prescribe, the number of such notices given on that day [Section 22 (6)].

(B) Provisions relating to general prohibition of lock-out [Section 23]:

According to the provisions of Section 23,

No employer shall declare a lock-out –

1. During the pendency of conciliation proceedings before a Board and seven days after the conclusion of such proceedings;

2. During the pendency of proceedings before a Labour Court, Tribunal or National Tribunal and two months after the conclusion of such proceedings;

3. During the pendency of arbitration proceedings before an arbitrator and two months after the conclusion of such proceedings, where a notification has been issued under Section 10-A(3-A); or

4. During any period in which a settlement or award is in operation, in respect of any of the matters covered by the settlement or award.

(C) Provisions relating to illegal lock-out [Section 24]:

1. A lock-out shall be illegal, if (a) it is commenced or declared in contravention of Section 22 or Section 23 which are mentioned above, or (b) it is continued in contravention of an order made under Section 10 (3) or Section 10-A (4-A) [Section 24 (1)].

2. Where a lock-out in pursuance of an industrial dispute has already commenced and is in existence at the time of reference of the dispute to a Board, an arbitrator, a Labour Court, Tribunal or National Tribunal, the continuance of such lock-out shall not be deemed to be illegal, provided that such lock-out was not at its commencement in contravention of the provisions of this Act, or the continuance thereof was not prohibited under Section 10 (3) or under Section 10-A (4-A) [Section 24 (2)].

3. Any lock-out declared in consequence of an illegal strike shall not be deemed to be illegal [Section 24 (3)].

3.11.4 Prohibition of Strikes and Lock-outs in Public Utility Services [Section 22]

Provisions have been made to prohibit Strikes and Lock-outs in Public Utility Services in Section 22 which runs as follows –

No person employed in a public utility service shall go on strike in breach of contract (a) without giving to the employer notice of strike, as hereinafter provided, within six weeks before striking, or (b) within fourteen days of giving such notice; or (c) before the expiry of the date of strike specified in any such notice as aforesaid, or (d) during the pendency of any conciliation proceedings before a Conciliation Officer and seven days after the conclusion of such proceedings [Section 22 (1)].

No employer carrying on any public utility service shall lock-out any of his workmen (a) without giving them notice of lock-out; as hereinafter provided, within six weeks before locking-out; or (b) within fourteen days of giving such notice, or (c) before the expiry of the date of lock-out specified in any such notice as aforesaid, or (d) during the pendency of any conciliation proceedings before a Conciliation Officer and seven days after the conclusion of such proceedings [Section 22 (2)].

The notice of a strike or lock-out under section 22 shall not be necessary where there is already in existence a strike or Lock-out, as the case may be, in the public utility service, but the employer shall send a intimation of such strike or lock-out on the day on which it is declared; to such authority as may be specified by the appropriate Government either generally or for a particular area or for a particular class of public utility services [Section 22 (3)].

The notice of strike referred to in section 22 (1) shall be given by such number of persons to such person or persons and in such manner as may be prescribed [Section 22 (4)].

The notice of lock-out referred to Section 22 (2) shall be given in such manner as may be prescribed [Section 22 (5)].

If on any day, an employer receives from any persons employed by him any such notices as are referred to in Section 22 (1) or gives to any person employed by him any such notices as are referred to in Section 22 (2), he shall within five days thereof report to the appropriate Government or to such authority as that Government may prescribe, the number of such notice received or given on that day [Section 22 (6)].

3.11.5 General Prohibition of Strikes and Lock-outs [Section 23]

Section 23 of this Act makes provisions for the general prohibition of Strikes and Lockouts. The Section says that no workman who is employed in any industrial establishment shall go on strike in breach of contract and no employer of any such workmen shall declare a Lock-out (a) during the pendency of conciliation proceedings before a Board and seven days after conclusion of such proceedings, or (b) during the pendency of proceedings before a Labour Court, Tribunal or National Tribunal and two months after the conclusion of such proceedings, or (bb) during the pendency of arbitration proceedings before an arbitrator and two months after the conclusion of such proceedings, where a notification has been issued under Section 10-A (3-A) or (c) during any period in which a settlement or award is in operation in respect of any of the matters covered by the settlement or award.

3.11.6 Illegal Strikes and Lock-outs [Section 24]

A strike or lock-out shall be illegal (i) if it is commenced or declared in contravention of Section 22 or 23 or (ii) if it is continued in contravention of an order made under sub-section (3) of Section 10 or sub-section 4 (A) of Section 10-A [Section 24 (1)].

Where a strike or lock-out in pursuance of an industrial dispute has already commenced and is in existence at the time of the reference of the dispute to a board, an arbitrator, a Labour Court, Tribunal or National Tribunal, the continuance of such strike or Lock-out shall not be deemed to be illegal [Section 24 (2)].

Provided that such strike or lock-out was not at its commencement in contravention of the provisions of this Act or the continuance thereof was not prohibited under Section 10 (3) or 10-A (4-A) [Proviso to section 24 (2)].

A lock-out declared in consequence of an illegal strike or a strike declared in consequence of an illegal lock-out shall not be deemed to be illegal [Section 24 (3)].

Thus, Lock-outs and strikes declared in public utility services in the following circumstances are held illegal;

If strikes and lock-outs declared or commenced without giving proper notice in a prescribed manner or during the pendency of conciliation proceedings before a conciliation officer and after seven days after the conclusion of such proceedings.

Strikes and lock-outs whether declared or commenced in a public utility service are illegal if commenced or declared during the pendency of (a) conciliation proceedings before a Board and seven days after the conclusion of such proceedings; (b) Proceedings before Labour Court, an Industrial Tribunal or National Tribunal and two months after the conclusion of such proceedings (c) During any period in which a settlement or award is in operation in respect of any matters covered by the settlement or award.

3.11.7 Prohibition of Financial Assistance or Aid to Illegal Strikes and Lock-outs [Section 25]

It is provided in Section 25 of this Act that no person shall knowingly expend or apply any money in direct furtherance or support of any illegal strike or lock-out.

3.11.8 Penalties for illegal Strikes and Lock-outs [Section 26, 27, 28]

(a) **Penalty for illegal strike:** Any workman who commences, continues or acts otherwise in furtherance of a strike which is not legal under this Act, shall be punishable with imprisonment for a term which can be extended upto one month or with a fine which also can be extended upto ₹ Fifty or both [Section 26 (1)].

- (b) **Penalty for illegal lock-out:** Any employer who commences, continues or acts otherwise in pursuance of illegal lock-out under this Act, shall be punishable with imprisonment for a term which may be extended upon one month or with a fine which may be extended upto one thousand rupees or with both [Section 26 (2)].
- (c) **Penalty for instigating a strike or lock-out:** Any person who instigates or incites others to take part in, otherwise acts in furtherance of a strike or lock-out which is illegal under this Act, shall be punishable with imprisonment for a term which may be extended upto six months or with a fine which may be extended upto one thousand rupees or with both [Section 27].
- (d) **Penalty for providing financial assistance to illegal strikes and lock-out:** Any person who knowingly expends or applies any money in direct furtherance or support of any strike or lock-out which is illegal under this Act shall be punishable with imprisonment for a term which may extend to six months or with a fine which may extend to one thousand rupees or with both [Section 28].

3.11.9 Distinction Between Strike and Lock-out

	Strike		**Lock-out**
1.	'Strike' means a cessation of work by a body of persons employed in any industry acting in combination, or a concerted refusal, or a refusal under a common understanding of any number of persons who are or have been so employed to continue to work or to accept employment [Section 2 (q)].	1.	'Lock-out' means the temporary closing of a place of employment, or the suspension of work, or the refusal by an employer to continue to employ any number of persons employed by him [Section 2 (1)].
2.	A strike is the weapon which is used by employees or workmen acting together to force their employer to agree to the demands made by them.	2.	Lock-out is an act of management. It is the weapon in the hands of an employer which is used to put some pressure on the workers to make them agree to the terms and conditions of work of their employer. Lock-out can be described as the antithesis of a strike.
3.	A strike implies a stoppage or cessation of work by the employees acting together. A strike can be 'stay-in strike' or 'Go-slow' strike.	3.	Lock-out indicates the temporary closure of the place of business by an employer; but not the closure of the business itself.
4.	In the case of a strike, an employer is not liable to pay wages for period of the strike.	4.	In the case of a lawful lock-out, no compensation is payable by an employer. But, if it is illegal, an employer is liable to pay compensation for the period of lockout to his employees.

Strike	Lock-out
5. A strike declared in consequence of an illegal lock-out, such strike is not deemed to be illegal [Section 24 (3)].	5. A lock-out declared in consequence of an illegal strike, such lock-out is not deemed to be illegal [Section 24 (3)].
6. Any workman who commences, continues or otherwise acts in furtherance of a strike which is illegal, is punishable with imprisonment for a term which may extend to one month, or with a fine which may extend to ₹ Fifty, or with both [Section 26 (1)].	6. Any employer who commences, continues or otherwise acts in furtherance of a lock-out which is illegal, is punishable with imprisonment for a term which may extend to one month or with a fine which may extend to ₹ One Thousand, or with both [Section 26 (2)].

3.12 Lay-off and Retrenchment

Provisions related to lay-off and Retrenchment have been included in Chapter V-A of this Act. But the definitions of the terms lay-off and Retrenchment are given in Section 2 of this Act.

3.12.1 Lay-off

Section 2 (k k k) of this Act defines lay-off and accordingly lay-off means the refusal, failure or inability of an employer to provide or to give employment to a workman whose name is borne on the muster rolls of his industrial establishment and who has not been retrenched. Such failure, refusal or inability to provide employment to a workman may be due to one of the following causes.

(a) The accumulation of stocks.
(b) Shortages of coal, power, fuel or raw materials.
(c) The breakdown of machinery.
(d) Natural calamity.
(e) Any other connected reason –

A workman is deemed to have been laid off for any day if he presents himself for work at the establishment at the appointed time for the purpose and during the normal working hours on that day and is not given employment by the employer within two hours of his so presenting himself, but if the workman, instead of being given an employment at the commencement of any shift for any day is asked to present himself for the purpose during the second half of the shift for the day and is given employment then, he shall be deemed to have been laid off only for one-half of that day. It is further provided in the section that if he is not given any such employment even after so remaining present he shall not be deemed to have been laid-off for the second half of the shift for the day and shall be entitled to full basic wages and dearness allowance for that part of the day.

3.12.2 Retrenchment

The term 'Retrenchment' is defined in Section 2 (00) of the Industrial Disputes Act as follows:

Retrenchment means the termination by the employer of the service of a workman for any reason whatsoever, otherwise than as punishment inflicted by way of disciplinary act.

To retrench means to end, cease or to conclude. However, retrenchment does not include (i) voluntary retirement of a workman, or (ii) retirement of a workman on reaching the age of superannuation if the contract of the employment between the employer and the workman concerned contains a stipulation in that behalf, or (iii) termination of service of a workman on the ground of continued ill health or (iv) termination of service of the workmen as a result of the non-renewal of the contract of employment between the employer and the workmen concerned on its expiry or of such contract being terminated under a stipulation in that behalf contained therein.

Thus, it seems that it is only when the services of a workman are dispensed with on the grounds of surplus labour, then the termination of services of such workman may be called retrenchment.

3.12.3 Application of Provisions of this Act to Lay-off and Retrenchment

In chapter V-A, provisions related to lay-off and retrenchment have been made. Let us consider these provisions.

Application of Sections 25 C to 25 E:

The provisions included in Sections 25 C to 26 E are applicable only to industrial establishments in which fifty or more workmen on an average per working day have been employed in the preceding calendar month. Section 25 A to this Act states that Section 25-C to 25-E inclusive shall not apply to an industrial establishment to which Chapter V B applies or (a) to industrial establishments is less than fifty workmen on an average per working day have been employed in the preceding calendar month or (b) to industrial establishments which are of a seasonal character or in which work is performed only intermittently.

If a question arises whether an industrial establishment is of a seasonal character or whether work is performed therein only intermittently, the decision of the appropriate Government thereon shall be final [Section 25 A (2)].

In Sections 25 A; 25-C, 25-D and 25-E, the term industrial establishment means (i) a factory as defined in Section 2 (m) of the Factories Act 1948 or (ii) a mine as defined in Section 2 (j) of the Mines Act 1952 or (iii) a Plantations as defined in Section 2 (f) of the Plantations Labour Act, 1951.

3.12.4 Continuous Service [Section 25-B]

For the purposes of this chapter: a workman shall be deemed or said to be in continuous service for a period, if he is for that period in uninterrupted service, including service which may be interrupted on account of sickness or authorised leave or an accident or a strike which is not illegal or a lock-out or a cessation of work which is not due to any fault on the part of the workman [Section 25-B (1)].

Where a workman is not in continuous service within the meaning of Section 25-B (1) for a period of one year or six months, he shall be deemed to be in continuous service under an employer –

(a) For a period of one year, if the workman, during a period of twelve calendar months preceding the date with reference to which calculation is to be made, actually worked under the employer for not less than –

   (i) 190 days in the case of a workman employed below ground in mine; and

   (ii) 240 days in any other case.

(b) For a period of six months; if the workman, during a period of six calendar months preceding the date with reference to which calculation is to be made, has actually worked under the employer for not less than

   (i) 95 days, in the case of a workman employed below ground in a mine; and

   (ii) 120 days in any other case. [Section 25 B (2)].

For the purpose of above mentioned clause 2 of Section 25-B, the number of days in which a workman has actually worked under an employer shall include the days on which (i) he has been laid off under an agreement or as permitted by standing orders made under the Industrial Employment (Standing Orders) Act, 1946 or under this Act under any other law applicable to the industrial establishment; (ii) he has been on leave with full wages in the previous year (iii) he has been absent due to temporary disablement caused by accident arising out of and in the course of his employment and (iv) in the case of a female, she has been on maternity leave, so, however that the total period of such maternity leave does not exceed twelve weeks [Explanation to Section 25-B].

3.12.5 Right of Workman Laid-off for Compensation [Section 25-C]

The right is given to a workman to receive lay-off compensation. It is given to a workman to relieve the hardship on the grounds of human public policy. The principle of social justice is followed in awarding lay-off compensation. The provisions regarding the payment of compensation to a workman who is laid off are contained in Section 25-C which is reproduced below.

Whenever a workman, other than a badli or a casual workman, whose name is borne on the muster rolls of an industrial establishment and who has completed not less than one year of continuous service under an employer is laid-off, whether continuously or intermittently, he shall be paid by the employer for all days during which he is so laid-off, except for such weekly holidays as may intervene, compensation which shall be equal to fifty per cent of the total of the basic wages and dearness allowance that would have been payable to him had he not been so laid-off [Sections 25-C (i)]; provided that if during any period of twelve months, a workman is so laid-off for more than forty-five (45) days no such compensation shall be payable in respect of any period of the lay-off after the expiry of the first forty-five days, if there is an agreement to that effect between workman and the employer. It is further provided that it shall be lawful for the employer in any case falling within the foregoing proviso to retrench the workman according to the provisions contained in Section 25 F at the time after the expiry of the first forty-five days of the lay-off and when he does so, any compensation paid to the workman for having been laid-off during the preceding twelve months may be set-off against the compensation payable for retrenchment.

Here 'badli workman' means a workman who is employed in an industrial establishment in the place of another workman whose name is borne on the muster-rolls of the establishment but shall cease to be regarded as such for the purposes of this section, if he has completed one year of continuous service in the establishment [Explanation to Section 25-C].

The important provisions of Section 25-C can be summarised as follows:

(a) For entitlement to the compensation, the workman should not be a badli or casual workman and his name must appear on the muster-rolls of the industrial establishment.

(b) The workman must have completed not less than one full year of continuous service.

(c) When the above mentioned conditions are fulfilled, the workman, whether laid-off continuously or intermittently, shall be paid compensation by his employer for all days during which he is laid-off, of course except for such weekly holidays as may intervene.

(d) The rate at which the compensation is to be paid shall be equal to fifty per cent of the total basic wages as well as dearness allowance that would have been payable to the workman had he not been laid-off.

(e) Compensation shall not be payable to a workman during any period of twelve months after the expiry of the first forty-five days if there is an agreement to that effect between the employer and the workmen.

(f) Where a workman is laid-off for a period of forty-five days during the period of twelve months, the employer can retrench the workman according to the provisions contained in Section 25-F at any time after the expiry of the first forty-five days of lay-off.

(g) When the employer retrenches the workman, any compensation paid to the workman for having been laid-off during the preceding twelve months may be set-off against the compensation payable for retrenchment of the workman.

3.12.6 Duty of an Employer to Maintain Muster-rolls of Workmen [Section 25-D]

Section 25-D of this Act compels the employer to maintain muster-rolls of workmen notwithstanding that they have been laid-off. It shall also be the duty of the employer to provide muster-rolls for making of entries by workmen who may remain present themselves for work at the industrial establishment at the appointed time during normal working hours.

3.12.7 Workmen not Entitled to Compensation in Certain Cases [Section 25-E]

The Act provides that in certain cases workmen are not entitled to receive any compensation. Section 25-E of this Act states that no compensation shall be paid to a workman who has been laid off (i) if he refuses to accept any alternative employment in the same industrial establishment from which he has been laid-off; or in any other industrial establishment belonging to the same employer which is situated in the same town or village or within a radius of five miles from the establishment to which he belongs; if in the opinion of the employer, such alternative employment does not call for special skill or previous experience and can be done by the workman; provided that the wages which would normally have been paid to the workman are offered for the alternative employment also, (ii) if he does not present himself for work at the establishment at the appointed time during normal working hours at least once a day; (iii) if such laying-off is due to a striking or slowing down of production on the part of workmen in another part of the establishment.

3.12.8 Conditions Precedent to Retrenchment of Workmen [Section 25-F]

We have already studied the meaning of the term retrenchment. Now let us consider the conditions precedent to retrenchment of workmen under this Act.

No workman employed in an industry who has been in continuous service for not less than one year under an employer shall be retrenched by the employer until –

(i) The workman has been served one month's notice in writing indicating the reasons for retrenchment and the period of notice has expired or the workman has been paid in lieu of such notice, wages for the period of such notice.

(ii) The workman has been paid at the time of retrenchment, compensation which shall be equivalent to fifteen days average pay for every completed year of continuous service or any part thereof in excess of six months; and

(iii) Notice in the prescribed manner is served on the appropriate Government or such authority as may be specified by the appropriate Government by notification in the Official Gazette [Section 25 F].

3.12.9 Procedure for Retrenchment

Section 25-G of this Act makes clear the procedure for retrenchment. This Section 25-G applies the rule of 'Last come first go' to retrenchment. Section 25-G states that where any workman in an industrial establishment, who is a citizen of India, is to be retrenched and he belongs to a particular category of workmen in that establishment, in the absence of any agreement between the employer and the workman in this behalf, the employer shall ordinarily retrench the workman who was the last person to be employed in that category, unless for reasons to be recorded the employer retrenches any other workman.

3.12.10 Re-employment of Retrenched Workman [Section 25-H]

Provision has been made in Section 25-H of this Act to re-employ the retrenched workman which is as follows:

Where any workmen are retrenched and the employer proposes to take into his employment any persons, he shall, in such manner as may be prescribed, give an opportunity to the retrenched workmen who are citizens of India to offer themselves for re-employment and such retrenched workmen who offer themselves for re-employment shall have preference over other persons.

3.12.11 Compensation to Workmen in Case of Transfer of Undertakings [Section 25-FF]

Provisions have been made regarding the compensation to be paid to workmen in case of transfer of undertakings in Section 25-FF of this Act which is as follows:

Where the ownership of the management of an undertaking is transferred, whether by agreement or by operation, from the employer in relation to that undertaking to a new employer, every workman who has been in continuous service for not less than one year in that undertaking immediately before such transfer shall be entitled to notice and compensation in accordance with the provisions of Section 25-F as if the workman had been retrenched. It is also provided that nothing in Section 25-FF shall apply to a workman in any case where there has been a change of employers by reason of transfer, if (i) the service of workman has not been interrupted by such transfer; (ii) the terms and conditions of service applicable to the workman after such transfer are not in any way less favourable to the workman than those applicable to him immediately before the transfer; and (iii) the new employer is, under the terms of such transfer or otherwise, legally liable to pay to the workman, in the event of his retrenchment, compensation on the basis that his service has been continuous and has not been interrupted by the transfer.

3.12.12 Difference Between Lock-out and Lay-off

Lock-out is a temporary closing of the business whereas lay-off generally occurs in a continuing business. In the case of Lock-out the employer closes the business and locks out the whole body of workmen for reasons which are not concerned with the reasons of declaring layoff. In the case of lay-off because of the reasons given in Section 2 (k k k), the employer cannot provide employment to some or all of his workmen. Thus, the nature of these two concepts or terms is entirely different and therefore the consequences too are different. The following points make clear the distinction between these two terms.

	Lock-out		Lay-off
1.	Lock-out means the temporary closing of a place of employment or the suspension of work or the refusal by an employer to continue to employ any number of persons employed by him.	1.	Lay-off means the failure, refusal or inability of an employer on account of shortage of coal, power, fuel or raw materials or the accumulation of stock or the break down of machinery or natural calamity or of any other connected reasons to provide employment to a workman whose name is borne on the muster-rolls of this industrial establishment and who has not been retrenched.

Lock-out	Lay-off
2. Lock-out is resorted to by an employer to pressurise the workmen to accept his demand.	2. Lay-off is really not connected with economic reasons because of which it becomes difficult for an employer to provide employment and such reasons are beyond the control of an employer.
3. Lock-out is due to an industrial dispute. It continues during the period of dispute.	3. Lay-off is not concerned or connected with an industrial dispute.
4. When lock-out is to be declared, the employer is not bound to pay any compensation to the workmen.	4. When the workmen are laid off, employer has to pay compensation to those workmen who are laid-off.
5. When lock-out is to be declared, the employer has to fulfil certain conditions as prescribed in Section 22 and 23 of this Act.	5. No such conditions are required to be fulfilled before the declaration of a lay-off.
6. When lock-out is declared, workman is not required to remain present at the factory doors or at the doors of the establishment, at the commencement of working hours.	6. When workmen are laid-off, the laid-off workmen have to remain present for work at the time of the commencement of working hours.
7. In the case of lock-out, lock-out in excess of 45 days in a year does not give an employer any right or option to retrench the workmen.	7. The employer gets an option to retrench the workmen if lay-off continues for more than forty five days in a year.
8. When lock-out is declared, the workmen lose their full amount of wages.	8. When workmen are laid-off, they lose half the amount of their wages.
9. When lock-out is declared, no alternative employment is provided to the concerned workmen.	9. When workmen are laid-off, the laid-off workmen may be provided or offered an alternative employment.

3.12.13 Difference Between Retrenchment and Lock-out

Retrenchment	Lock-out
1. The term 'retrenchment' as used in this Act means the termination by the employer of the service of a workman for any reason whatsoever, otherwise than as punishment inflicted by way of disciplinary action. It does not include – (a) Voluntary retirement of a workman. (b) Retirement of a workman on reaching superannuation age. (c) Termination of service of workman as a result of non-renewal of the contract of employment.	1. Lock-out means the temporary closing of an employment place or suspension of work or the refusal by an employer to continue to employ any number of persons employed by the employer.

Retrenchment	Lock-out
(d) Termination of services on the ground of continued ill health of a workman.	
2. Retrenchment is done to remove surplus labour.	2. Lock-out is coercive and is declared for compelling the workmen to accept the demands of the employer.
3. Workmen may be retrenched independent of an industrial dispute.	3. Lock-out is declared because of an industrial dispute.
4. Retrenchment is permanent.	4. Lock-out is temporary.
5. Retrenchment puts an end to the relationship between an employer and his workmen.	5. In the case of lock-out, the relationship between the employer and his workmen continues.

3.12.14 Distinction between Retrenchment and Lay-off

Retrenchment	Lay-off
1. Meaning of retrenchment is the termination of service of a workman by an employer for any reason, whatsoever, otherwise than as punishment inflicted by way of disciplinary action. Retrenchment does not include voluntary retirement, because of reaching the super annuation, age, termination of services either because of continued ill health of a workman or because of non-renewal of employment contract.	1. Lay-off means the failure, refusal or inability of an employer to provide employment to the workmen employed by him on account of the following reasons: (a) Storage of coal, power, fuel, rawmaterials. (b) Accumulation of stock. (c) Breakdown of machinery. (d) Natural calamity, or (e) Any other connected reason. The names of workmen who are laid off must appear on the muster-rolls and they must not be retrenched.
2. Workmen are retrenched to remove surplus labour.	2. Workmen are laid off because of the reasons mentioned above which are beyond the control of the employer.
3. Retrenchment is permanent.	3. Lay-off is temporary.
4. In retrenchment, the relationship between the employer and his workmen comes to an end.	4. In lay-off, the relationship between the employer and his workmen is suspended temporarily.

3.13 Closure of an Industrial Undertaking [Section 25 FFA]

Provisions have been made in Section 25 FFA of this Act regarding the notice to be given for closing down any undertaking and accordingly an employer who intends to close down an undertaking shall serve, at least sixty days before the date on which the intended closure is to become effective, a notice, in the prescribed manner on the appropriate Government stating clearly the reason for the intended closure of the undertaking:

Provided that nothing in this section shall apply to:

(a) An undertaking in which
 (i) Less than fifty workmen are employed, or
 (ii) Less than fifty workmen were employed on an average per working day in the preceding twelve months,
(b) An undertaking set up for the construction of buildings, bridges, roads, canals, dams or for other construction work or project. [Section 25-FFA (i)].

Notwithstanding anything contained in sub-section (1), the appropriate Government may, if it is satisfied that owing to such exceptional circumstances as accident to the undertaking or death of the employer or the like it is necessary so to do, by order, direct that provisions of subsection (1) shall not apply in relation to such undertaking for such period as may be specified in the order [Section 25 FFA (2)].

3.13.1 Compensation to be Paid to Workmen in Case of Closing Down of an Undertaking [Section 25-FFF]

Closure of an undertaking means closing of industrial activity and as a consequence, workmen employed in such undertaking are rendered jobless. When an undertaking is closed, compensation is required to be paid to the workmen working in such undertaking. Provisions have been made in Section 25-FFF of this Act regarding the compensation to be paid to workmen in case of closing down of undertaking. These provisions are as follows:

Where an undertaking is closed down for any reason whatever, every workman who has been in continuous service for not less than one year in that undertaking immediately before such closure shall subject to the provisions of sub-section (2) be entitled to notice and compensation in accordance with the provisions of Section 25-F as if the workman has been retrenched [Section 25 FFF (i)].

It is also provided that where the undertaking is closed down on account of unavoidable circumstances beyond the control of the employer, the compensation to be paid to the workman under clause (b) of Section 25-F shall not exceed his average pay for three months [Proviso to Section 25 FFF (i)].

An undertaking which is closed down by reason merely of:
(i) Financial difficulties including financial loss; or
(ii) Accumulation of undisposed stocks, or
(iii) The expiry of the period of the lease or licence granted to it; or

(iv) In case where the undertaking is engaged in mining operations, exhaustion of the minerals in the area in which such operations are carried on, shall not be deemed to have been closed down on account of unavoidable circumstances beyond the control of the employer within the meaning of the proviso to this sub-section.

This section further states that notwithstanding anything contained in sub-section (1) where an undertaking engaged in mining operations is closed down by reason merely of exhaustion of the minerals in the area in which such operations are carried on, no workman referred to in that sub-section shall be entitled to any notice or compensation in accordance with the provisions of Section 25-F if –

(a) The employer provides the workman with alternative employment with effect from the date of closure at the same remunerations as he was entitled to receive, and on the same terms and conditions of service as were applicable to him, immediately before the closure,

(b) The service of workman has not been interrupted by such alternative employment; and

(c) The employer is, under the terms of such alternative employment or otherwise, legally liable to pay to the workman, in the event of his retrenchment, compensation on the basis that his service has been continuous and has not been interrupted by such alternative employment [Section 25 FFF (1-A)].

For the purposes of sub-sections (1) and (1A), the expressions "minerals" and " mining operations " shall have the meanings respectively assigned to them in clause (a) and (b) of section 3 of the Mines and Minerals (Regulation and Development) Act, 1957 [Section 25 FFF (1-B)].

Where any undertaking set up for the construction of building, bridges, canals, dams or other construction work is closed down on account of the completion of the work within two years from the date on which the undertaking had been set up, no workman employed therein shall be entitled to any compensation under clause (b) of Section 25-F but if the construction work is not so completed within two years, he shall be entitled to notice and compensation under that section for every completed year of continuous service or any part thereof in excess of six-months [Section 25 FFF (2)].

3.14 Special Provisions Relating to Lay-off, Retrenchment and Closure in Certain Establishments

The Industrial Disputes Act, 1947 was amended in 1976 and Chapter V-B has been introduced. This chapter, which contains Sections 25 k to 25 s, deals with special provisions of lay-off, retrenchment and closure in certain establishments employing one hundred or more than one hundred workmen. Section 25 k (1) states that the provisions of this chapter shall apply to an industrial establishment, not being an establishment of a seasonal character or in which work is performed only intermittently, in which not less than one hundred workmen were employed on an average per working day for the preceding twelve months. This section further states that if a question arises whether an industrial establishment is of a seasonal character or whether work is performed therein only intermittently, the decision of the appropriate Government thereon shall be final [Section 25 k (2)].

3.14.1 Industrial Establishment [Section 25-L]

For the purpose of chapter V - B, the definition of the term ' industrial establishment ' is given in Section 25-L (a) is as follows:

"Industrial Establishment" means –
- (i) A factory as defined in clause (m) of Section 2 of the Factories Act, 1948.
- (ii) A mine as defined in clause (i) of sub-section (1) of Section 2 of the Mines Act, 1952; or
- (iii) A plantation as defined in clause (f) of Section 2 of the Plantation Labour Act, 1951.

Section 25 L (b) gives the definition of an appropriate Government which is as follows:

- (i) Notwithstanding anything contained in sub-clause (ii) of clause (a) of Section 2,
- (i) In relation to any company in which less than fifty-one per cent of the paid-up share capital is held by the Central Government, or
- (ii) In relation to any corporation [not being a corporation referred to in sub-clause (i) of clause (a) of Section (2) established by or under any law made by Parliament, the Central Government shall be the appropriate Government.

3.14.2 Prohibition of Lay-off [Section 25-M]

Section 25-M of this Act provides for the prohibition of lay-off in certain cases. According to Section 25-M.

No workman other than a badli workman or a casual workman whose name is borne on the muster-rolls of an industrial establishment to which this Chapter applies shall be laid-off by his employer except with the prior permission of the appropriate Government or such authority as may be specified by that Government by notification in the Official Gazette (thereafter in this section referred to as the specified authority), obtained on an application made in this behalf, unless such lay-off is due to shortage of power or to natural calamity, and in the case of mine such lay-off is due also to fire, flood, excess of inflammable gas or explosion [Section 25 M (1)].

An application for permission under sub-section (I) shall be made by the employer in the prescribed manner stating clearly the reasons for the intended lay-off and a copy of such application shall also be served simultaneously on the workmen concerned in the prescribed manner [Section 25 M (2)].

Where the workmen (other than badli workmen or casual workmen) of an industrial establishment, being a mine, have been laid-off under sub-section (1) for reasons of fire, flood or excess of inflammable gas or explosion, the employer in relation to such establishment, shall within a period of thirty days from the date of commencement such lay-off, apply in the prescribed manner, to the appropriate Government or the specified authority for permission to continue the lay-off [Section 25 M (3)].

Where an application for permission under sub-section (1) or sub-section (3) has been made, the appropriate Government or the specified authority, after making such enquiry as it thinks fit and after giving a reasonable opportunity of being heard to the employer, the workmen concerned and the persons interested in such lay-off, may having regard to the genuineness and adequacy of the reasons for such lay-off, the interests of the workmen and all other relevant factors, by order and for reasons to be recorded in writing, grant or refuse to grant such permission and a copy of such order shall be communicated to the employer and the workmen. [Section 25 M (4)].

Where an application for permission under sub-section (I) or sub-section (3) has been made and the appropriate Government or the specified authority does not communicate the order granting or refusing to grant permission to the employer within a period of sixty days from the date on which such application is made, the permission applied for shall be deemed to have been granted on the expiration of the said period of sixty days [Section 25 M (5)].

An order of the appropriate Government or the specified authority granting or refusing to grant permission shall, subject to the provisions of subsection (7) be final and binding on all the parties concerned and shall remain in force for one year from the date of such order [Section 25 M (6)].

The appropriate Government or the specified authority may, either on its own motion or on the application made by the employer or any workmen, review its order granting or refusing to grant permission under sub-section (4) or refer the matter or, as the case may be, cause it to be referred to a Tribunal for adjudication [Section 25 M (7)].

It is also provided that where a reference has been made to a Tribunal under this subsection, it shall pass an award within a period of thirty days from the date of such reference [Proviso to Section 25 M].

Where no application for permission under sub-section (I) is made, or where no application for permission under sub-section (3) is made within the period specified therein or where the permission for any lay-off has been refused, such lay-off shall be deemed to be illegal from the date on which the workmen had been laid-off and the workmen shall be entitled to all the benefits under any law for the time being in force as if they had not been laid-off [Section 25-M (8)].

Notwithstanding anything contained in the foregoing provisions of this section, the appropriate Government may, if it is satisfied that owing to such exceptional circumstances as accident in the establishment or death of the employer or the like, it is necessary so to do, by order, direct that the provisions of sub-section (1), or as the case may be, sub-section (3) shall not apply in relation to such establishment for such period as may be specified in the order [Section 25 M (9)].

3.14.3 Conditions Precedent to Retrenchment of Workmen [Section 25-N]

Section 25-N has been substituted by the Industrial Disputes (Amendment), Act, 1984 and according to that section –

1. No workman employed in any industrial establishment to which this Chapter applies, who has been in continuous service for not less than one year under an employer shall be retrenched by that employer until;
   (a) The workman has been given three months notice in writing indicating the reasons for retrenchment and the period of notice has expired, or the workman has been paid in lieu of such notice, wages for the notice, and
   (b) The prior permission of the appropriate Government or such authority as may be specified by that Government by the notification in the Official Gazette (hereafter in this section referred to as the specified authority) has been obtained on an application made in this behalf [Section 25-N (1)].
2. An application for permission under sub-section (1) shall be made by the employer in the prescribed manner stating clearly the reasons for the intended retrenchment and a copy of such application shall also be served simultaneously on the workmen concerned in the prescribed manner [Section 25-N (2)].
3. Where an application for permission under sub-section (1) has been made, the appropriate Government or the specified authority, after making such enquiry as it thinks fit and after giving a reasonable opportunity of being heard to the employer, the workmen concerned and the persons interested in such retrenchment, may, having regard to the genuineness and adequacy of the reasons stated by the employer, the interests of the workmen and all other relevant factors, by order and for reasons to be recorded in writing, grant or refuse to grant such permission and a copy of such order shall be communicated to the employer and the workmen [Section 25-N (3)].
4. Where an application for permission has been made under sub-section (1) and the appropriate Government or the specified authority does not communicate the order granting or refusing to grant permission to the employer within a period of sixty days from the date on which such application is made, the permission applied for shall be deemed to have been granted on the expiration of the said period of sixty days [Section 25-N (4)].
5. An order of the appropriate Government or the specified authority granting or refusing to grant permission shall, subject to the provisions or subsection (6), be final and binding on all the parties concerned and shall remain in force for one year from the date of such order [Section 25-N (5)].
6. The appropriate Government or the specified authority may, either on its own motion or on the application made by the employer or any workmen, review its order granting or refusing to grant permission under sub-section (3) or refer the matter or as the case may be, cause it to be referred, to a Tribunal for adjudication [Section 25-N (6)]. It is also provided that where a reference has been made to a Tribunal under this sub-section, it shall pass an award within a period of thirty days from the date of such reference [Proviso to Section 25-N (6).

7. Where no application for permission under sub-section (1) is made, or where the permission for any retrenchment has been refused, such retrenchment shall be deemed to be illegal from the date on which the notice of retrenchment was given to the workman and the workman shall be entitled to all the benefits under any law for the time being in force as if no notice had been given to him [Section 25- N (7).
8. Notwithstanding anything contained in the foregoing provisions of this section, the appropriate Government may, if it is satisfied that owing to such exceptional circumstances as accident in the establishment or death of the employer or the like, it is necessary so to do, by order, direct that the provisions of sub-section (1) shall not apply in relation to such establishment for such period as may be specified in the order [Section 25-N (8)].
9. When permission for retrenchment has been granted under sub-section (3) or where permission for retrenchment is deemed to be granted under sub-section (4), every workman who is employed in that establishment immediately before the date of application for permission under this section shall be entitled to receive, at the time of retirement, compensation which shall be equivalent to fifteen days' average pay for every completed year of continuous service or any part thereof in excess of six months [Section 25-N (9)].

3.14.4 Procedure of Closing Down an Undertaking [Section 25-O]

Provisions relating to the procedure of closing down an undertaking, powers of an appropriate Government, compensation to be paid to the workmen etc. have been made in Section 25-O of this Act, Section 25-O is as follows:

1. An employer who intends to close down an undertaking of an industrial establishment to which this Chapter applies shall, in the prescribed manner, apply, for prior permission at least ninety days before the date on which the intended closure is to become effective, to the appropriate Government, stating clearly the reasons for the intended closure of the undertaking and copy of such application shall also be served simultaneously on the representatives of the workman in the prescribed manner [Section 25-O (1)]. It is also provided that nothing in this sub-section shall apply to an undertaking set up for the construction of buildings, bridges, roads, canals, dams or for other construction work [Proviso to section 25-O (1)].
2. Where an application for permission has been made under sub-section (1), the appropriate Government, after making such inquiry as it thinks fit and after giving a reasonable opportunity of being heard to the employer, the workmen and the persons interested in such closure may, having regard to the genuineness and adequacy of the reasons stated by the employer, the interests of the general public and all other relevant factors, by order and for the reasons to be recorded in writing, grant or refuse to grant such permission and a copy of such order shall be communicated to the employer and the workmen [Section 25-O (2).

3. Where an application has been made under sub-section (1) and the appropriate Government does not communicate the order granting or refusing to grant permission to the employer within a period of sixty days from the date on which such application is made, the permission applied for shall be deemed to have been granted on the expiration of the said period of sixty days [Section 25-O (3)].
4. An order of the appropriate Government granting or refusing to grant permission shall, subject to the provisions of sub-section (5), be final and binding on all the parties and shall remain in force for one year from the date of such order [Section 25-O (4)].
5. The appropriate Government may either on its own motion or on the application made by the employer or any workman, review its order granting or refusing to grant permission under sub-section (2) or refer the matter to a Tribunal for adjudication [Section 25-O (5)]. It is provided that where a reference has been made to a Tribunal under this sub-section, it shall pass an award within a period of thirty days from the date of such reference [Provision to Section 25-O (5)].
6. Where no application for permission under sub-section (1) is made within the period specified therein, or where the permission for closure has been refused, the closure of the undertaking shall be deemed to be illegal from the date of closure and the workmen shall be entitled to all the benefits under any law for the time being in force of if the undertaking had not been closed down [Section 25-O (6)].
7. Notwithstanding anything contained in the foregoing provisions of this section, the appropriate Government may, if it is satisfied that owing to such exceptional circumstances as accident in the undertaking or death of employer or the like it is necessary so to do, by order, direct that the provisions of sub-section (I) shall not apply in relation to such undertaking for such period as may be specified in the order [Section 25-O (7)].
8. Where an undertaking is permitted to be closed down under sub-section (2) or where permission for closure is deemed to be granted under sub-section, (3), every workman who is employed in that undertaking immediately before the date of application for permission under this section, shall be entitled to receive compensation which shall be equivalent to fifteen days' average pay for every completed year of continuous service or any part thereof in excess of six months [Section 25-O (8)].

3.14.5 Special Provision as to Restarting of Undertakings Closed Down Before Commencement of the Industrial Disputes (Amendment) Act, 1976 [Section 25-P]

If the appropriate Government is of opinion in respect of any undertaking of an industrial establishment to which this Chapter applies and which was closed down before commencement of the Industrial Disputes (Amendment) Act, 1976 –

(a) That such undertaking was closed down otherwise than on account of unavoidable circumstances beyond the control of the employer;

(b) That there are possibilities of restarting the undertaking;

(c) That it is necessary for the rehabilitation of the workmen employed in such undertaking before its closure or for the maintenance of supplies and services essential to the life of the community to restart the undertaking or both, and

(d) That the restarting of the undertaking will not result in hardship to the employer in relation to the undertaking, it may, after giving an opportunity to such employer and workmen direct, by order published in the Official Gazette, that the undertaking shall be restarted within such time (not being less than one month from the date of the order) as may be specified in the order.

3.14.6 Difference Between Closure and Retrenchment

Retrenchment means the termination of services of a workman by an employer for any reason whatsoever, otherwise than as punishment inflicted by way of disciplinary action. It does not include (1) Voluntary retirement of the workmen (2) retirement of the workmen on, reaching the superannuation age (3) termination of the services of the workmen as a result of the non-renewal of the contract of employment (4) termination of the services of the workmen on the ground of continued ill health.

The term closure implies closing of industrial activity as a consequence of which workmen are rendered jobless. The closure cannot be always permanent and irrevocable. An employer may revive the industrial activity which was closed because of certain reasons. But closure can be a permanent suspension of industrial activity which takes place on account of trade or business reasons and it discontinues the relationship between an employer and his workmen. Closure affects almost all workmen employed in the undertaking. In retrenchment, some workmen are retrenched and not all; the industrial activity or the business continues.

3.14.7 Difference Between Lay-off and Closure

The difference between lay-off and closure is discernible. Closure is nothing but *the closing of the business or undertaking permanently or temporarily for an indefinite period by an employer.* While lay-off means *the failure, inability or refusal on the part of an employer to provide employment to a workman or workmen whose names are borne on the muster roll of the industrial establishment or undertaking or business.* Such refusal or inability on the part of an employer to provide an employment may be due to causes such as shortage of fuel, coal, raw-materials, natural calamity etc. which we have already considered. The other points making clear the difference between lay-off and closure are as under.

Lay-off	Closure
1. Lay-off is a temporary suspension of an industrial activity of business.	1. Closure is permanently discontinuation of an industrial activity.
2. In lay-off, the workmen do not cease to be in the service of their employer.	2. In closure, the workmen are discharged and do not remain in service.

Lay-off	Closure
3. In lay-off the relationship between the workmen and their employer continues.	3. Closure does not continue the relationship between the workmen and their employer.
4. In lay-off, alternative employment can be offered to the workmen employed whose names appear on the muster-rolls and who are not retrenched.	4. In closure, no question arises to provide alternative employment to the workmen employed in the undertaking.
5. In lay-off, no notice is required to be given to the workmen employed.	5. When an undertaking is closed down, at least sixty days notice is required to be given to the appropriate Government.

3.14.8 Distinction Between Lock-out and Closure

The distinction between lock-out and closure is also obvious. Lock-out is nothing but a temporary closing of a place of an employment or the suspension of work or the refusal by an employer to continue to employ any number of persons employed by an employer. While closure implies the closing of an industrial activity as the consequence of which workmen become unemployed. Other points of distinction are given below.

Lock-out	Closure
1. Lock-out indicates the temporary closure of the business place or place of employment. It is not the closure of an undertaking or business.	1. Closure indicates the final termination of the business or undertaking. In other words, closure is a permanent suspension of business or undertaking.
2. Lock-out is an action of employer to enforce his demands on the workmen. In a way lock-out is a weapon of coercion in the hands of an employer.	2. The business or undertaking is closed down for trade reasons or other reasons. Closure is generally done for economic reasons.
3. In lock-out, the relationship between the workmen and their employer continues.	3. Closure discontinues the relationship between the workmen and their employer.
4. A lock-out is caused by the existence or apprehension or fear of an industrial dispute.	4. Closure is not the consequence of any industrial dispute.
5. If the lock-out is legal, the employer is not required to pay any compensation to the workmen.	5. If an undertaking is closed, the employer of the workmen employed in such undertaking is required to pay compensation according to the provisions of this act.

3.15 Offences and Penalties

Provisions have been made in various sections of the Act relating to the penalties for various offences. These provisions are as under –

3.15.1 Penalty for Lay-off and Retrenchment without Previous Permission [Section 25-Q]

Any employer who contravenes the provisions of Section 25-M or of Section 25-N of this Act is punishable with imprisonment for a period which may be extended upto six months or with a fine which also can be extended to rupees one thousand or with both.

3.15.2 Penalty for Closure [Section 25-R]

Any employer who closes down an undertaking without complying with the provisions of sub-section (1) of Section 25-O shall be punishable with imprisonment for a term which may extend to six months or with fine which may extend to five thousand rupees or with both [Section 25-(1)].

Any employer, who contravenes an order refusing to grant permission to close down an undertaking under sub-section (2) or Section 25-O or a direction given under Section 25-P shall be punishable with imprisonment for a term which may extend to one year, or with fine which may extend to five thousand rupees, or with both, and where the contravention is a continuing one, with a further fine which may extend to two thousand rupees for every day during which the contravention continues after the conviction [Section 25-R (2)].

3.15.3 Penalty for Committing Unfair Labour Practices [Section 25-U]

No employer or workman or a trade union, whether registered under the Trade Union Act, 1926 or not shall commit any unfair labour practice [Section 25-T]. Unfair labour practice means any of the practices specified in the fifth Schedule [Section 2 (ra)]. Any person who commits any unfair labour practice is punishable with imprisonment for a term which may extend to six months or with fine which may extend to rupees one thousand or with both [Section 25-U].

3.15.4 Penalty for Illegal Strikes and Lock-outs [Section 26]

Any workman who commences, continues or otherwise acts in furtherance of a strike which is not legal under this Act is punishable with imprisonment for a period which may be extended to one month or with a fine which may be extended upto fifty rupees or with both [Section 26 (1)].

Any employer who commences, continues or otherwise acts in furtherance of a lock-out which is not legal under this Act, is punishable with imprisonment for a term which may extend to one month or with a fine which may be imposed upto rupees one thousand or with both [Section 26 (2)].

The remedy which is indicated in this Section 26 is the statutory remedy. No other relief outside this Act can be available on general principles of jurisprudence. The relief, therefore, of compensation by proceedings in arbitration is contrary to law.

3.15.5 Penalty for Instigation [Section 27]

The terms 'Instigation' or 'Incitation' have some deeper meaning than a mere asking a person to do any particular act. These words or terms seem to convey the meaning "to goad or urge forward or to encourage the doing of an act. Any person who instigates or incites others to take part in, or otherwise acts in furtherance of a strike or lock-out which is not legal under this Act, is punishable with imprisonment for a term which may extend to six months or with a fine which may also be imposed up to Rupee one thousand or with both.

3.15.6 Penalty for Giving Financial Aid to Illegal Strikes and Lock-outs [Section 28]

Any person who knowingly applies or expends any money in direct furtherance or supports any illegal strikes or lock-out is punishable with imprisonment for a term which may be extended upto six months or with fine which may be extended upto one thousand rupees or with both.

3.15.7 Penalty for Breach of Settlement or Award [Section 29]

Any person who commits a breach of any term of any settlement or award, which is binding on such person under this Act, is punishable with imprisonment for a period which may extend to six months or with a fine or with both; and where the breach is a continuing one, with a further fine which may extend to two hundred rupees for every day during which the breach continues after the conviction for the first breach and the Court trying the offence, if it imposes a fine on the offender, may direct that the whole or any part of the fine realised from him shall be paid, by way of compensation, to any person who, in the opinion of the Court, has been injured by such breach.

This Section 29 of this Act covers strikes in violation of settlement.

3.15.8 Penalty for Disclosing Confidential Information [Section 30]

Any person who purposely or wilfully discloses any such information as is referred to in Section 21 of this Act in contravention of the provisions of that Section 21 is, on complaint made by or on behalf of the trade union or individual whose business is affected, is punishable with imprisonment for a term which may extend to six months, or with a fine which may extend to one thousand rupees or with both [Section 30].

3.15.9 Penalty for Closure without Notice [Section 30-A]

Any employer who closes down any undertaking without complying with the provisions of Section 25-FFA of this Act is punishable with imprisonment for a period which may be extended to six months, or with a fine which may extend to rupees five thousand or with both [Section 30-A].

3.15.10 Penalty for other Offences [Section 31]

Any employer who contravenes the provisions of Section 33 of this Act is punishable with the imprisonment for a period which may extend to six months or with fine which may extend to one thousand rupees or with both [Section 31 (1)].

Any person who contravenes any provisions of this Act or any rule made thereunder is punishable, if no other penalty elsewhere is provided by or under this Act for such contravention, with fine which may extend to one hundred rupees [Section 31 (2)].

3.15.11 Offence by Companies, Associations of Persons etc.

According to Section 32 of this Act. "Where a person committing an offence under this Act is a company, or other body corporate, or an association of persons (whether incorporated or not), every director, manager, secretary, agent or other officer or person concerned with the management thereof shall, unless he proves that the offence was committed without his knowledge or consent, be deemed to be guilty of such offence."

3.15.12 Cognizance of Offences [Section 34]

1. No Court shall take cognizance of any offence punishable under this Act or of the abetment of any such offence, save on complaint made by or under the authority of the appropriate Government [Section 34 (1)].
2. No Court inferior to that of [a Metropolitan Magistrate or a Judicial Magistrate of the first class] shall try any offence punishable under this Act [Section 34 (2)].

3.16 Conditions of Service to remain Unchanged

3.16.1 Conditions of Service, etc., to Remain Unchanged under certain Circumstance during Pendency of Proceedings [Section 33]

1. During the pendency of any conciliation proceeding before a conciliation officer or a Board or of any proceeding before an arbitrator or a Labour Court or Tribunal or National Tribunal in respect of an industrial dispute, no employer shall:
   (a) In regard to any matter connected with the dispute, alter, to the prejudice of the workmen concerned in such dispute, the conditions of service applicable to them immediately before the commencement of such proceeding; or
   (b) For any misconduct connected with the dispute, discharge or punish, whether by dismissal or otherwise, any workmen concerned in such dispute; save with the express permission in writing of the authority before which the proceeding is pending [Section 33 (1)].
2. During the pendency of any such proceeding in respect of an industrial dispute, the employer may, in accordance with standing orders applicable to a workman concerned in such dispute or, where there are no such standing orders, in accordance with the terms of the contract, whether express or implied, between him and the workman –

(a) Alter, in regard to any matter not connected with the dispute, the conditions of service applicable to that workman immediately before the commencement of such proceeding; or

(b) For any misconduct not connected with the dispute, discharge or punish, whether by dismissal or otherwise, that workman [Section 33 (2)].

Provided that no such workman shall be discharged or dismissed, unless he has been paid wages for one month and an application has been made by the employer to the authority before which the proceeding is pending for approval of the action taken by the employer [Proviso to Section 33 (2)].

3. Notwithstanding anything contained in sub-section (2), no employer shall, during the pendency of any such proceeding in respect of an industrial dispute, take any action against any protected workman concerned in such dispute –

(a) By altering, to the prejudice of such protected workman, the conditions of service applicable to him immediately before the commencement of such proceedings; or

(b) By discharging or punishing, whether by dismissal or otherwise, such protected workman, save with the express permission in writing of the authority before which the proceeding is pending [Section 33 (3)].

Meaning of "Protected Workman"

For the purposes of this sub-section a "protected workman", in relation to an establishment, means a workman who, being a member of the executive or other office bearer of a registered trade union connected with the establishment, is recognised as such in accordance with rules made in this behalf [Explanation to Section 33 (3)].

In every establishment, the number of workmen to be recognised as protected workmen for the purposes of sub-section (3) shall be one per cent of the total number of workmen employed therein subject to a minimum number of five protected workmen and a maximum number of one hundred protected workmen and for the aforesaid purpose, the appropriate Government may make rules providing for the distribution of such protected workmen among various trade unions, if any, connected with the establishment and the manner in which the workmen may be chosen and recognised as protected workmen [Section 33 (4)].

Where an employer makes an application to a conciliation officer, Board, an arbitrator, a Labour Court, Tribunal or National Tribunal under the proviso to sub-section (2) for approval of the action taken by him, the authority concerned shall, without delay, hear such application and pass, within a period of three months from the date of receipt of such application, such order in relation thereto as it deems fit.

It is also provided that where any such authority considers it necessary or expedient so to do, it may, for reasons to be recorded in writing, extend such period by such further period as it may think fit [Proviso to Section 33 (5)].

It is provided further that no proceedings before any such authority shall lapse merely on the ground that any period specified in this sub-section had expired without such proceedings being completed [Proviso to Section 33 (5)].

3.16.2 Special Provision for Adjudication as to Whether Conditions of Service, etc., Changed during Pendency of Proceedings

Where an employer contravenes the provisions of Section 33 during the pendency of proceedings before a conciliation officer, Board, an arbitrator, a Labour Court, Tribunal or National Tribunal, any employee aggrieved by such contravention, may make a complaint in writing, in the prescribed manner –

(a) To such conciliation officer of Board, and the conciliation officer or Board shall take such complaint into account in mediating in, and promoting the settlement of, such industrial dispute; and

(b) To such arbitrator, Labour Court, Tribunal or National Tribunal and on receipt of such complaint, the arbitrator, Labour Court, Tribunal or National Tribunal, as the case may be, shall adjudicate upon the complaint as if it were a dispute referred to or pending before it, in accordance with the provisions of this Act and shall submit his or its award to the appropriate Government and the provisions of this Act shall apply accordingly [Section 33-A].

3.17 Recovery of Money Due from an Employer

1. Where any money is due to a workman from an employer under a settlement or an award or under the provisions of Chapter V-A or Chapter V-B, the workman himself or any other person authorised by him in writing in this behalf, or, in the case of the death of the workman, his assignee or heirs may, without prejudice to any other mode of recovery, make an application to the appropriate Government for the recovery of the money due to him, and if the appropriate Government is satisfied that any money is so due, it shall issue a certificate for that amount to the Collector who shall proceed to recover the same in the same manner as an arrear of land revenue [Section 33 (1)].

It is provided that every such application shall be made within one year from the date on which the money became due to the workman from the employer [Proviso 1 to Section 33-C (1)].

It is provided further that any such application may be entertained after the expiry of the said period of one year, if the appropriate Government is satisfied that the applicant had sufficient cause for not making the application within the said period [Proviso 2 to Section 33-C (1)].

2. Where any workman is entitled to receive from the employer any money or any benefit which is capable of being computed in terms of money and if any question arises as to the amount of money due or as to the amount at which such benefit should be computed, then the question may, subject to any rules that may be made under this Act, be decided by such Labour Court as may be specified in this behalf by the appropriate Government within a period not exceeding three months [Section 33-C (2)].

It is also provided that where the presiding officer of a Labour Court considers it necessary or expedient so to do, he may, for reasons to be recorded in writing, extend such period by such further period as he may think fit [Proviso to Section 33-C (2)].

3. For the purposes of computing the money value of a benefit, the Labour Court may, if it is so thinks fit, appoint a Commissioner who shall, after taking such evidence as may be necessary, submit a report to the Labour Court and the Labour Court shall determine the amount after considering the report of the Commission and other circumstances of the case [Section 33-C (3)].

4. The decision of the Labour Court shall be forwarded by it to the appropriate Government and any amount found due by the Labour Court may be recovered in the manner provided for in sub-section (1) of Section 33-C [Section 33-C (4)].

5. Where workmen employed under the same employer are entitled to receive from him any money or any benefit capable of being computed in terms of money, then, subject to such as may be made in this behalf, a single application for the recovery of the amount due may be made on behalf of or in respect of any member of such workmen [Section 33-C (5)]

In this section "Labour Court" includes any Court constituted under any law relating to investigation and settlement of industrial disputes in force in any State [Explanation to Section 33-C].

3.18 Representation of Parties

Provisions relating to the representation of parties to a dispute have been made in Section 36 of this Act which are as follows:

1. A workman who is a party to a dispute shall be entitled to be represented in any proceeding under this Act by –
   (a) Any member of the executive or other office bearer of a registered trade union of which he is a member;
   (b) Any member of the executive or other office bearer of a federation of trade unions to which the trade union referred to in clause (a) is affiliated;
   (c) Where the worker is not a member of any trade union, by any member of the executive or other office bearer of any trade union connected with, or by any other workman employed in the industry in which the worker is employed and authorised in such manner as may be prescribed [Section 36 (1)].

2. An employer who is a party to a dispute shall be entitled to be represented in any proceeding under this Act by,
   (a) An officer of an association of employers of which he is a member;
   (b) An officer of a federation of association of employers to which the association referred to in clause (a) is affiliated;
   (c) Where the employer is not a member of any association of employers, by an officer of any association of employers connected with, or by any other employer engaged in, the industry in which the employer is engaged and authorised in such a manner as may be prescribed [Section 36 (2)].

3. No party to a dispute shall be entitled to be represented by a legal practitioner in any conciliation proceedings under this Act or in any proceedings before a Court [Section 36 (3)].

4. In any proceeding before a Labour Court, Tribunal or National Tribunal, a party to a dispute may be represented by a legal practitioner with the consent of the other parties to the proceeding and with the leave of the Labour Court, Tribunal or National Tribunal, as the case may be [Section 36 (4)].

3.19 Protection Given to a Person or Persons under this Act

3.19.1 Protection of Action taken under the Act

No suit, prosecution or other legal proceeding shall lie against any person for anything which is in good faith done or intended to be done pursuance of this Act or any rules made thereunder [Section 37].

3.19.2 Protection of Persons

1. No person refusing to take part or to continue to take part in any strike or lock-out which is illegal under this Act, shall by reason of such refusal or by reason of any action taken by him under this section, be subject to expulsion from any trade union or society, or to any fine or penalty; or to deprivation of any right or benefit to which he or his legal representatives would otherwise be entitled, or be liable to be placed in any respect, either directly or indirectly, under any disability or at any disadvantage as compared with other members of the union or society, anything to the contrary in rules of a trade union or society notwithstanding [Section 35 (1)].

2. Nothing in the rules of a trade union or society requiring the settlement of disputes in any manner shall apply to any proceeding for enforcing any right or exemption secured by this section, and in any such proceeding the Civil Court may, in lieu of ordering a person who has been expelled from membership of a trade union or society to be restored to membership, order that he be paid out of the funds of the trade union or society such sum by way of compensation or damages as that Court thinks just [Section 35 (2)].

3.20 Powers given to an Appropriate Government

3.20.1 Power of the Appropriate Government to Transfer Certain Proceedings [Section 33-B]

1. The appropriate Government may, by order in writing and for reasons to be stated therein, withdraw any proceeding under this Act pending before a Labour Court, Tribunal or National Tribunal and transfer the same to another Labour Court, Tribunal or National Tribunal, as the case may be, for the disposal of the proceeding and the Labour Court, Tribunal or National Tribunal to which the proceedings is so transferred may, subject to special directions in the order of transfer, proceed either de novo or from the stage at which it was so transferred [Section 33-B (1)].

Provided that where a proceeding under Section 33 or Section 33-A is pending before a Tribunal or National Tribunal, the proceeding may also be transferred to a Labour Court [Proviso to Section 33-B (1)].

2. Without prejudice to the provisions of sub-section (1), any Tribunal or National Tribunal, if so authorised by the appropriate Government, may transfer any proceeding under Section 33 or Section 33-A pending before it to any one of the Labour Courts specified for the disposal of such proceedings by the appropriate Government by notification in the Official Gazette and the Labour Court to which the proceedings is so transferred shall dispose of the same [Section 33-B (2)].

3.20.2 Power of the Appropriate Government to Remove Difficulties [Section 36-A]

1. If, in the opinion of the appropriate Government, any difficulty or doubt arises as to the interpretation of any provision of an award or settlement, it may refer the question to such Labour Court, Tribunal or National Tribunal as it may think fit [Section 36-A (1)].
2. The Labour Court, Tribunal or National Tribunal to which such question is referred shall, after giving the parties an opportunity of being heard, decide such question and its decision shall be final and binding on all such parties [Section 36-A (2)].

3.20.3 Power of the Appropriate Government to Exempt

Where the appropriate Government is satisfied in relation to any industrial establishment or undertaking or any class of industrial establishments or undertakings carried on by a department of that Government that adequate provisions exist for the investigation and settlement of industrial disputes in respect of workmen employed in such establishment or undertaking or class of establishments or undertakings, it may, by notification in the Official Gazette, exempt, conditionally or unconditionally such establishment or undertaking or class of establishments or undertakings from all or any of the provisions of this Act [Section 36-B].

3.20.4 Power to Make Rules [Section 38]

1. The appropriate Government may, subject to the condition of previous publication, make rules for the purpose of giving effect to the provisions of this Act [Section 38 (1)]
2. In particular and without prejudice to the generality of the foregoing power, such rules may provide for all or any of the following matters, namely –
    (a) The powers and procedure of conciliation officers, Boards Courts, Labour Courts, Tribunals and National Tribunals including rules as to the summoning of witnesses, the production of documents relevant to the subject-matter of an inquiry or investigation, the number of members necessary to form a quorum and the manner of submission of reports and awards;
    (aa) The form of arbitration agreement, the manner in which it may be signed by the parties, the manner in which a notification may be issued under sub-section (3-A) of Section 10-A, the powers of the arbitrator named in the arbitration agreement and the procedure to be followed by him;

(aaa) The appointment of assessors in proceedings under this Act;
(b) The constitution and functions of and the filling of vacancies in Works Committees, and the procedure to be followed by such Committees in the discharge of their duties;
(c) The allowances admissible to members of Courts and Boards and presiding officers of Labour Courts, Tribunals and National Tribunal and to assessors and witnesses;
(d) The ministerial establishment which may be allotted a Court, Board Labour Court, Tribunal or National Tribunal and the salaries and allowances payable to members of such establishment;
(e) The manner in which and the persons by and to whom notice of strike or lockout may be given and the manner in which such notice shall be communicated;
(f) The conditions subject to which parties may be represented by legal practitioners in proceedings under this Act before a Court, Labour Court, Tribunal or National Tribunal;
(g) Any other matter which is to be or may be prescribed [Section 38 (2)].
3. Rules made under this section may provide that a contravention thereof shall be punishable with fine not exceeding fifty rupees [Section 38 (3)].
4. All rules made under this section shall, as soon as possible after they are made, be laid before the State Legislature or, where the appropriate Government is the Central Government, before both Houses of Parliament [Section 38 (4)].
5. Every rule made by the Central Government under this section shall be laid, as soon as may be after it is made, before each House of Parliament while it is in session for a total period of thirty days which may be comprised in one session or in two or more successive sessions, and if before the expiry of the session immediately following the sessions or the successive sessions aforesaid both Houses agree in making any modification in the rule, or both Houses agree that the rule should not be made, the rule shall thereafter have effect only in such modified form or be of no effect, as the case may be; so, however, that any such modification or annulment shall be without prejudice to the validity of anything previously done under that rule [Section 38 (5)].

3.20.5 Provisions Relating to Delegation of Powers

The appropriate Government may, by notification in the Official Gazette, direct that any power exercisable by it under this Act or rules made thereunder shall, in relation to such matters and subject to such conditions, if any, as may be specified in the direction, be exercisable also –

(a) Where the appropriate Government is the Central Government, by such officer or authority subordinate to the Central Government or by the State Government, or by such officer or authority subordinate to the State Government, as may be specified in the notification; and

(b) Where the appropriate Government is a State Government, by such officer or authority subordinate to the State Government as may be specified in the notification [Section on 39].

3.20.6 Powers of the Appropriate Government to Amend Schedules [Section 40]

1. The appropriate Government may, if it is of opinion that it is expedient or necessary in the public interest so to do, by notification in the Official Gazette, add to the First Schedule any industry, and on any such notification being issued, the First Schedule shall be deemed to be amended accordingly [Section 40 (1)].

2. The Central Government may, by notification in the Official Gazette, add to or alter or amend the Second Schedule or the Third Schedule and on any such notification being issued, the Second Schedule or the Third Schedule, as the case may be, shall be deemed to be amended accordingly [Section 40 (2)].

3. Every such notification shall, as soon as possible after it is issued, be laid before the Legislature of the State, if the notification has been issued by a State Government, or before Parliament, if the notification has been issued by the Central Government [Section 40 (3)].

Questions for Discussion

1. What is the object underlying the Industrial Disputes Act, 1947?
2. Explain the objects and the scope of Industrial Disputes Act, 1947.
3. Define the following terms as used in the Industrial Disputes Act, 1947.
    (a) Average Pay
    (b) Banking Company
    (c) Closure
    (d) Conciliation Officer
    (e) Conciliation Proceeding
    (f) Controlled Industry
    (g) Employer
    (h) Executive
    (i) Independent person
    (j) Labour Court
    (k) National Tribunal
    (l) Trade Union
    (m) Wages
    (n) Tribunal.
4. Define and Explain fully the following terms as used in the Industrial Disputes Act, 1947.
    (a) Appropriate Government
    (b) Industrial Dispute
    (c) Industrial Dispute
    (d) Industrial Establishment
    (e) Lay-off
    (f) Lock-out
    (g) Public Utility Service
    (h) Retrenchment
    (i) Settlement
    (j) Strike
    (k) Unfair labour practices
    (l) Workman.

5. What is an industrial dispute? Explain its essentials. Who can give rise to an industrial dispute? When does an individual dispute become an industrial dispute?
6. Explain fully the machinery that is in existence under the Industrial Disputes Act, 1947 for the settlement of industrial disputes.
7. Which authorities have been appointed under this Act to investigate and settle Industrial disputes?
8. Explain the various methods for the settlement of industrial disputes under the Industrial Disputes Act, 1947.
9. Define 'Appropriate Government' under the Industrial Disputes Act, 1947 and explain its relevance.
10. What is works committee? Explain its constitution and duties or functions.
11. How are conciliation officers appointed? Explain their functions.
12. What is a conciliation? Explain the principles underlying conciliation.
13. How is the Board of Conciliation appointed? Explain the duties of the Board. How the reference of an industrial disputes is made to the Board?
14. How are the Courts of Inquiry appointed under this Act and what is their constitution? Explain the powers and the duties of the Courts of Inquiry.
15. Write a note on the constitution of Labour Courts, Industrial Tribunals and National Tribunals.
16. Explain the duties, powers of Conciliation Officers, Works Committees, Boards of Conciliation, Labour Courts, Industrial Tribunals and National Tribunals in the Settlement of industrial dispute under the Industrial Disputes Act.
17. State the explain the provisions of the Industrial Disputes Act 1947, relating to notice for changing the conditions of service. What are the matters in respect of which notice of change is prescribed in this Act?
18. "Section 10 of the Industrial Disputes Act, 1947 confers a power rather than imposes duty on the appropriate Government in the matter of reference of duties". Elaborate.
19. What is 'Industrial Dispute'? Explain the procedure for voluntary reference of disputes to arbitration.
20. Define the terms 'award' and 'settlement' and distinguish between them.
21. Define 'award' and 'settlement'. Who are the persons on whom settlements and awards are binding?
22. Discuss provisions of the Industrial Disputes Act of 1947 relating to voluntary reference of disputes to arbitration.

23. State the provisions of the Industrial Disputes Act of 1947 relating to the commencement of award; persons on whom settlements and award are binding; and the period of operation of settlements and awards.
24. Write a note on 'Grievance Settlement Authority'.
25. Define and explain the terms 'strike and lock-out' as used in the Industrial Disputes Act, 1947. When does a strike or lock-out become illegal?
26. Explain the provisions of this Act relating to strikes and lock-up in public utility services.
27. Distinguish between strikes and lock-outs and explain the penalties for illegal strikes and lock-outs.
28. Can a lock-out be declared in consequence of an illegal strike? If in consequence of an illegal strike, a lock-out is declared, will such lock-out be illegal?
29. State and explain the provisions of the Industrial Disputes Act, 1947 relating to lay-off and retrenchment.
30. Define the term 'continuous service' and its importance.
31. Explain the right of workmen who have been laid-off to receive compensation.
32. Explain the term 'closure' and provision of this Act relating to compensation to be paid to workmen in the case of closing down of undertaking.
33. What are the special provisions of this Act relating to lay-off, retrenchment and closure in certain establishments?
34. Explain the provisions of this Act, relating to the prohibition of lay-off.
35. What are the conditions precedent to retrenchment of workmen under the Industrial Disputes Act, 1947?
36. Explain fully the procedure of closing down an undertaking.
37. Explain the penalties provided for in this Act for the following offences:
    (a) Lay-off and retrenchment without previous permission;
    (b) Closure, without notice;
    (c) Committing unfair labour practices;
    (d) Illegal strikes and lock-outs;
    (e) Instigation;
    (f) Penalty for providing financial aid to illegal strikes and lock-outs.
    (g) Breach of settlement;
    (h) Disclosing confidential information.

38. Distinguish between:
    (a) Lock-out and lay-off
    (b) Closure and retrenchment
    (c) Retrenchment and lock-out
    (d) Retrenchment and lay-off
    (e) Lay-off and closure
    (f) Lock-out and closure.
39. Write notes on the following:
    (a) Machinery for settlement of industrial disputes
    (b) National Tribunals
    (c) Assessors
    (d) Filling of vacancy and finality of orders
    (e) Conditions, precedent to retrenchment of workmen
    (f) Re-employment of retrenched workmen
    (g) Compensation to workmen in the case of transfer of undertaking
    (h) Industrial establishment
    (i) Prohibition of lay-off
    (j) Closure of an industrial undertaking
    (k) Procedure of closing down an undertaking
    (l) Offences and Penalties under the Industrial Disputes Act 1947.

Task for Practicals

1. Explain with reasons whether the following acts amount to retrenchment.
   (a) Non-absorption of workmen gone on strike.
   (b) Termination of services of workmen on the ground of continued ill-health.
   (c) Voluntary retirement.
   (d) Termination of services on the ground of surplus labour.
   [**Answers:** (a) No, (b) No, (c) No, (d) Yes.]

2. Mr. 'X' is employed in the technical post in Railway and drawing Rs. 1600/- per month. He claims that he is a workman under the Industrial Disputes Act, 1947. Can his claim be justified?

   [**Answer:** According to Section 2 (5) of this Act, he is a workman and his claim is justified].

3. 'X' Insurance Company is carrying on its business in Pune only. An industrial dispute has arisen between the company and its workmen. The Maharashtra Government has referred the dispute to the Industrial Tribunal. Is this reference valid?

   [**Answer:** The reference made by the Maharashtra Government is not valid at all because according to Section 2 (a), the appropriate Government in the case of Insurance Company is the Central Government and not the State Government].

4. An industrial dispute took place between employer and his workmen. Their number was 85 regarding the retrenchment. The appropriate Government referred the matter to the Labour Court, was the reference valid?

    [**Answer:** The reference was valid for (a) An appropriate Government referred the matter. (b) Concern employed less than 100 workmen. (c) Retrenchment is the matter included in the Third Schedule. (d) The Labour Court has the power to adjudicate the matters included in the Third Schedule.

5. Mr. 'A' who was employed for 10 months before he was laid-off. During the period of 10 months, he worked for 212 days. Is Mr. 'A' entitled to receive compensation under the Industrial Disputes Act, 1947?

    [**Answers:** No. Mr. 'A' is not entitled to receive any compensation under this Act as he was not in a continuous service for one year].

Chapter **4**...

The Maternity Benefit Act, 1961 (Social Security Legislation)

Contents ...

4.1 The Basic Object, Extent and Coverage of the Act [Sections 1 and 2]
4.2 Important Features of the Maternity Benefit Act, 1961
4.3 Definitions [Section 3]
4.4 Prohibition of Employment by Women during Certain Period [Section 4]
4.5 Provisions Relating to the Maternity Benefit and Other Benefits [Sections 5 to 13]
4.6 Appointment, Powers and Duties of the Inspectors [Sections 14 to 17]
4.7 Forfeiture of Maternity Benefit [Section 18]
4.8 Miscellaneous Provisions of the Act [Sections 19, 21 and 30]
4.9 The Maharashtra Maternity Benefits Rules of 1965
• Questions for Discussion

The concept of 'social security' implies that there should be protection provided by society to its members against providential mishaps over which an individual has no control. The idea of social security is that the State must make itself responsible for ensuring some minimum standard of material welfare to all its citizens on a basis wide enough to cover the main contingencies of life.

It can easily be observed that in the life of a human being, there are two important stages of dependency i.e. childhood and old age. The social security system aims to help the people in such times of dependency. The main risks of insecurity include mainly sickness, invalidity, maternity, accident, unemployment, death of bread-winners and other such emergencies.

The Directive Principles of State Policy as embodied in the Constitution of India lay special stress on the goal of a Welfare State; which are essential in order to secure a social order for the purpose of promoting welfare of the people. No doubt, there is need for social security in India.

In view of the wide-spread poverty of the masses, the wide prevalence of various diseases, the high incidence of maternal and infantile mortality, the low expectation of life, unemployment, indebtedness etc. there is a need of a comprehensive social security programme.

Various Acts have thus been passed to provide for social security for workers such as the Workmen's Compensation Act of 1923, the Employees' State Insurance Act of 1948. The Maternity Benefit Act of 1961 is one such act.

The object of this act is to protect the dignity of motherhood by providing for the full and healthy maintenance of women and her child when she is not working. As a matter of fact, maternity benefit is an indemnity for the loss of wages incurred by a woman who has to remain absent from work for a certain period before her child-birth and even thereafter in the interest of the health of her child and herself.

The I.L.O. Convention of 1919 prescribed a leave period of twelve weeks. However, the Government of India did not ratify the Convention because of certain difficulties such as the migratory habit of women workers, their customs of going home before confinement, shortage of necessary medical services etc.

The State Government passed the legislation on this subject from time to time. The Acts passed by different State Governments prior to and even after Independence vary considerably with regard to qualifying conditions for obtaining maternity benefit and other related benefits.

With the passage of the Employees' State Insurance Act of 1948, the maternity benefit and the other related benefits became the responsibility of the Employees' State Insurance Corporation and the State Acts applied to residuary employments till the enactment of the Maternity Benefit Act of 1961. This Act was passed to regulate the employment of women in certain establishments for certain periods before and after child-birth and also to provide for maternity and certain other benefits. The Act was amended from time to time.

The latest amendment was made in 2008 by notification in order to increase the Medical Bonus by the Central Government. The medical bonus to be paid to every woman entitled to maternity benefit under this Act is now ₹ 2,500 subject to the conditions mentioned in Section 8 of the Act and also empowering the Central Government to increase it from time to time before every three years, by way of notification in the Official Gazette, subject to a maximum of ₹ 20,000/-.

4.1 The Basic Object, Extent and Coverage of the Act [Sections 1 and 2

The Maternity Benefit Act of 1961 has been passed to regulate the employment of women in certain establishments for a certain period before and after child-birth and also to provide for maternity benefit and certain other benefits. Thus, the Act is intended to achieve the object of providing social justice and social security to women workers or employees.

The Act extends to the whole of India [Section 1 (2)]. According to Section 2 (1), this Act applies, in the first instance,
   (a) to every establishment being a factory, mine or plantation including any such establishment belonging to Government and to every establishment wherein persons are employed for the exhibition of equestrian, acrobatic and other performances;
   (b) to every shop or establishment within the meaning of any law for the time being in force in relation to shops and establishments in a State, in which ten or more persons are employed, or were employed, on any day of the preceding twelve months.

In the Proviso to Section 2 (1), it has been made clear that the State Government may extend all or any of the provisions of the Act to any other establishment or class of establishments, industrial, commercial, agricultural or otherwise. However, the State Government can do so only with the approval of the Central Government after giving not less than two months notice by notification in the Official Gazette of its intention to do so. But it is also mentioned in Section 2 (2) that, "Save as otherwise provided in Sections 5A and 5B nothing contained in this Act, shall apply to any factory or other establishment to which the provisions of the Employees' State Insurance Act, 1948 (34 of 1948), apply for the time being.

This Act expressly provides for maternity leave and payment of certain maternity benefits to be paid to the women workers during the period when they are out of employment because of their pregnancy. Besides this, the Act prohibits the working of pregnant women for a specified period before and after delivery. Moreover, the services of a woman worker cannot be terminated during the period of absence on account of pregnancy except for gross misconduct.

4.2 Important Features of the Maternity Benefit Act, 1961

From the provisions of the Maternity Benefit Act, 1961, we come to know the certain important features of the Act which are as follows :

(a) There are certain Acts which provide for social security for workers and the Maternity Benefit Act, 1961 is one such Act. The Workmen's Compensation Act of 1923, The Employees' State Insurance Act of 1948, The Payment of Gratuity Act etc. are the other Acts which provide for social security for workers.

(b) This Act regulates the employment of women in certain establishments for a certain period before and after child-birth and it also provides for maternity benefit and certain other benefits. Maternity benefit is an indemnity for the loss of wages incurred by a woman who voluntarily before child-birth and compulsorily thereafter abstains from work in the interest of the health of her child and herself. In short, the Act intends to achieve the object of providing social justice and social security to women workers or employees.

(c) The Act expressly provides for maturity leave and payment of certain maturity benefits to be paid to the women workers during the period when they are out of employment because of their pregnancy.

(d) There is a provision relating to the payment of medical bonus in the Act. Every woman is entitled to receive a medical bonus of ₹ Two Thousand and Fifty besides maternity benefit from her employer if no pre-natal confinement and postnatal care is provided by the employer free of charge.

(e) The maximum period for which any woman is entitled to maternity benefit is given in the Act. Such period is **Twelve** weeks, that is to say, **six** weeks upto and including the day of her delivery and **six** weeks immediately following that day.

(f) How many days a woman has to work in order to be entitled for maternity benefit is also made clear in the provision of the Act. A woman is entitled to maternity benefit is she actually works in an establishment of the employer from whom she claims maternity benefit for a period of not less than **Eighty** days in the **Twelve** months immediately preceding the date of her expected delivery.

(g) There is the provision to receive the amount of maternity benefit to the nominated person in case of a death of a woman. If a woman entitled to the maternity benefit dies before receiving such benefit, the employer is bound to pay such benefit to the person nominated by that woman. If there is no such nominee, it is paid to her legal representative.

(h) There are provisions relating to leave for miscarriage, illness arising out of pregnancy, delivery, premature birth of child, medical termination of pregnancy, tubectomy operation etc. in Sections 9 and 10 of the Act.

(i) Two nursing breaks in the course of the daily work are allowed of the prescribed duration for nursing the child until the child attains the age of **fifteen** months. When a woman returns to duty after the delivery and such nursing breaks allowed are in addition to the interval for rest allowed to her.

(j) The time for payment of maturity benefit is given in the act. The amount of maternity benefit for the period preceding the date of her expected delivery is required to be paid in advance to the woman on production of proof that the woman is pregnant. While the amount due for the subsequent period is required to be paid to the woman within **Forty-Eight** hours of production of proof that the woman has delivered a child. The medical bonus is also paid along with the second instalment of the maternity benefit.

(k) If a pregnant woman does not give the notice to her employer for receiving the maternity and other benefits according to the provisions of the Act, it does not disentitle the woman to maternity and other benefits under the Act. If maternity and other benefits are not paid according to provisions of the Act, an Inspector may, either on his own motion or on application made to him by the concerned woman, order the payment of the amount of maternity and other benefits within such period as may be specified in the order.

(*l*) Provisions have been made in the Act to appoint the Inspectors for the purposes of this Act by giving them necessary powers.

(m) There is the provision to forfeit the maternity benefits. If a woman works in any other establishment after she has been permitted by her employer to remain absent herself according to the provisions of the Act for any period during such authorised absence, her claim to the maternity benefits is forfeited for such period.

(n) The punishments are stated in the Act [Sections 21 and 22] for the contravention of the provisions of the Act.

4.3 Definitions [Section 3]

Definitions of certain words, terms etc. are given in Section 3 of the Act which are given below.

1. **Appropriate Government [Section 3 (a)]:**

   "Appropriate Government" means, in relation to an establishment being a mine or an establishment wherein persons are employed for the exhibition of equestrian, acrobatic and other performances the Central Government and in relation to any other establishment the State Government.

2. **Child [Section 3 (b)]:**

   "Child" includes a still-born child;

3. **Delivery [Section 3 (c)]:**

   "Delivery" means the birth of a child;

4. **Employer [Section 3 (d)]:**

   "Employer" means –

   (i) in relation to an establishment which is under the control of the Government, a person or authority appointed by the Government for the supervision and control of employees or where no person or authority is so appointed, the head of the department;

   (ii) in relation to an establishment under any local authority, the person appointed by such authority for the supervision and control of employees or where no person is so appointed, the chief executive officer of the local authority;

   (iii) in any other case, the person who, or the authority which has the ultimate control over the affairs of the establishment and where the said affairs are entrusted to any other person whether called a manager, managing director, managing agent, or by any other name, such person.

5. **Establishment [Section 3 (e)]:**

   "Establishment" means –

   (i) a factory;

   (ii) a mine;

   (iii) a plantation;

   (iv) an establishment wherein persons are employed for the exhibition of equestrian, acrobatic and other performances;

   (iva) a shop or establishment;

   (v) an establishment to which the provisions of this Act have been declared under sub-section (1) of section 2 to be applicable.

6. Factory [Section 3 (f)] :

"Factory" means a factory as defined in clause (m) of Section 2 of the Factories Act, 1948 (63 of 1948);

7. Inspector [Section 3 (g)] :

"Inspector" means an Inspector appointed under Section 14 under this Act.

8. Maternity Benefit [Section 3 (h)] :

"Maternity benefit" means the payment referred to in sub-section (1) of Section 5;

9. Medical Termination of Pregnancy [Section 3 (ha)] :

"Medical termination of pregnancy" means the termination of pregnancy permissible under the provisions of the Medical Termination of Pregnancy Act, 1971 (34 of 1971).

10. Mines [Section 3 (i)] :

"Mine" means a mine as defined in clause (j) of Section 2 of the Mines Act, 1952 (35 of 1952);

11. Miscarriage [Section 3 (j)] :

"Miscarriage" means expulsion of the contents of a pregnant uterus at any period prior to or during the twenty-sixth week of pregnancy but does not include any miscarriage, the causing of which is punishable under the Indian Penal Code (45 of 1860);

12. Plantation [Section 3 (k)] :

"Plantation" means a plantation as defined in clause (f) of Section 2 of the Plantations Labour Act, 1951(69 of 1951).

13. Prescribed [Section 3 (*l*)] :

"Prescribed" means prescribed by rules made under this Act;

14. State Government [Section 3 (m)] :

"State Government", in relation to a Union Territory, means the Administrator thereof.

15. Wages [Section 3 (n)] :

"Wages" means all remuneration paid or payable in cash to a woman, if the terms of the contract of employment, express or implied, were fulfilled and includes :

(1) such cash allowances (including dearness allowance and house rent allowance) as a woman is for the time being entitled to;

(2) incentive bonus; and

(3) the money value of the concessional supply of foodgrains and other articles, but does not include –

   (i) Any bonus other than incentive bonus;

   (ii) overtime earnings and any deduction or payment made on account of fines;

   (iii) any contribution paid or payable by the employer to any pension fund or being fund or for the benefit of the woman under any law for the time being in force; and

   (iv) any gratuity payable on the termination of service.

It may be noted that for the purpose of computation of maternity benefit, the week includes Sunday as well as rest days which are wageless holidays.

16. Woman [Section 3 (O)] :

"Woman" means a woman employed, whether directly or through any agency, for wages in any establishment.

4.4 Prohibition of Employment by Women During Certain Period [Section 4]

The provisions have been made in Section 4 of the Act to prohibit the employment of women or work by women during certain period. These provisions are as under :

I. No employer shall knowingly employ a woman in any establishment during the six weeks immediately following the day of her delivery, miscarriage or medical termination of pregnancy [Section 4 (1)].

II. No woman shall work in any establishment during the six weeks immediately following the day of her delivery or her miscarriage [Section 4 (2)].

III. Without prejudice to the provisions of Section 6, no pregnant woman shall, on a request being made by her in this behalf, be required by her employer to do during the period specified in sub-section (4) any work which is of an arduous nature or which involves long hours of standing, or which in any way is likely to interfere with her pregnancy or the normal development of the foetus, or is likely to cause her miscarriage or otherwise to adversely affect her health [Section 4 (3)].

IV. The period referred to in sub-section (3) shall be –
   (a) the period of one month immediately preceding the period of six weeks, before the date of her expected delivery;
   (b) any period during the said period of six weeks for which the pregnant woman does not avail of leave of absence under Section 6 [Section 4 (4)].

It is obvious that the above mentioned provisions have been made in the interest of the health of pregnant women and their children.

4.5 Provisions Relating to the Maternity Benefit and Other Benefits [Sections 5 to 13]

Sections from 5th to 13th throws light on different benefits under the Act. The provisions of all these nine sections are given below.

4.5.1 Right to Payment of Maternity Benefits [Section 5]

The provisions of Section 5 (1) make clear the right to the payment of maternity benefits while provisions of Section 5 (2) and 5 (3) include certain conditions for the payment of maternity benefit.

According to Section 5 (1), "Subject to the provisions of this Act, every woman shall be entitled to, and her employer shall be liable for, the payment of maternity benefit at the rate of the average daily wage for the period of her actual absence, that is to say, the period immediately preceding the day of her delivery, the actual day of her delivery and any period immediately following that day".

The meaning of the 'Average Daily Wage' is given in the explanation to Section 5 (1) which is as follows :

"For the purpose of this sub-section, the average daily wage means the average of the woman's wages payable to her for the days on which she has worked during the period of three calendar months immediately preceding the date from which she absents herself on account of maternity. (The minimum rate of wage fixed or revised under the Minimum Wages Act, 1948 (11 of 1948) or ten rupees, whichever is the highest) [Explanation to Section 5 (1)].

The following conditions are required to be fulfilled before maternity benefit becomes payable to a woman worker in an establishment to which this Act is applicable.

(a) The qualifying condition to get benefit is that the claimant must have actually worked in the establishment concerned for a period of not less than eighty days in the twelve months immediately preceding the date of her expected delivery. Section 5 (2) clearly states that, "No woman shall be entitled to maternity benefit unless she has actually worked in an establishment of the employer from whom she claims maternity benefit, for a period of not less than eighty days in the twelve months immediately preceding the date of her expected delivery".

However, it is provided that, "The qualifying period of eighty days aforesaid shall not apply to a woman who has immigrated into the State of Assam and was pregnant at the time of the immigration" [Proviso to Section 5 (2)].

"For the purpose of calculating under this sub-section the days on which a woman has actually worked in the establishment, the days for which she has been laid off or was on holidays declared under any law for the time being in force to be holidays with wages during the period of twelve months immediately preceding the date of her expected delivery shall be taken into account" [Explanation to Section 5 (2)].

(b) Condition relating to maternity benefit in respect of maximum period is laid down in Section 5 (3). This section states that, "the maximum period for which any woman shall be entitled to maternity benefit shall be twelve weeks of which not more than six weeks shall precede the date of her expected delivery". However, it is also made clear that, "Where a woman dies during this period, the maternity benefit shall be payable only for the day upto and including the day of her death" [Proviso 1 to Section 5 (3)]. It is provided further that where a woman, having been delivered of a child, dies during her delivery or during the period immediately following the date of her delivery for which she is entitled for the maternity benefit, leaving behind in either case the child, the employer shall be liable for the maternity benefit for that entire period but if the child also dies during the said period, then for the days up to and including the date of the death of the Child" [Proviso 2 to Section 5 (3)].

4.5.2 Continuance of Payment of Maternity Benefit in Certain Cases [Section 5-A]

This Section 5-A has been inserted by amending the Act in 1972. This Section makes it clear that, "Every woman entitled to the payment of maternity benefit under this Act shall, notwithstanding the application of the Emloyees' State Insurance Act, 1948 (34 of 1948), to the factory or other establishment in which she is employed, continue to be so entitled until she becomes qualified to claim maternity benefit under Section 50 of the Act".

Section 50 of the E.S.I. Act of 1948 throws light on the maternity benefit and Section 50 states that, "The qualification of an insured woman to claim maternity benefit, the conditions subject to which such benefit may be given, the rates and period thereof shall be such as may be prescribed by the Central Government".

4.5.3 Payment of Maternity Benefit in Certain Cases [Section 5-B]

"Every woman –
(a) who is employed in a factory or other establishment to which the provisions of the Employees' State Insurance Act, 1948 (34 of 1948), apply;
(b) whose wages (excluding remuneration for over-time work) for a month exceed the amount specified in sub-clause (b) of clause (9) of Section 2 of that Act; and
(c) who fulfils the conditions specified in sub-section (2) of Section 5, shall be entitled to the payment of maternity benefit under this Act".

Thus, provisions of Section 5-B make clear as to whom the maternity benefit is payable in certain cases which are mentioned in this section. Provision of sub-clause (b) of clause (9) of Section 2 of the E.S.I. Act of 1948 is as follows.

"Any person so employed (in a factory or establishment to which the E.S.I. Act is applicable) whose wages (excluding remuneration for overtime work) exceed such wages as may be prescribed by the Central Government". Before 1st February, 1991, amount of wages was ₹ 1,600. But by amending the E.S.I Act, instead of ₹ 1,600, the words "such wages as may be prescribed by the Central Government have been inserted.•

When we consider the maternity benefits available under this Act, we must take into consideration the provisions of Section 18 which are related to forfeiture of maternity benefit. According to Section 18, "If a woman works in any establishment after she has been permitted by her employer to absent herself under the provisions of Section 6 for any period during such authorised absence, she shall forfeit her claim to the maternity benefit for such period.

4.5.4 Notice of Claim for Maternity Benefit and Payment Thereof [Section 6]

Provisions relating to notice of claim for maternity benefit, payment thereof, mode of payment etc. have been done in Section 6 of the Act.

According to Section 6 (1), "Any woman employed in an establishment and entitled to maternity benefit under the provisions of this Act may give notice in writing in such form as may be prescribed, to her employer, stating that her maternity benefit and any other amount to which she may be entitled under this Act may be paid to her or such person as she may nominate in the notice and that she will not work in any establishment during the period for which she receives maternity benefit".

In Rule 3 of the Maharashtra Maternity Benefit Rules of 1965, it is mentioned that the notice to be given by a woman entitled to maternity benefit under the provisions of the Act shall be in Form I. This Form I is given below for information.

> **FORM I**
>
> **[Rule 3]**
>
> *Notice under Section 6 of the Maternity Benefit Act of 1961*
>
> To,
>
> ....
>
> (Name of employer)
>
> I, ... (name of woman) *wife/*daughter of .... employed as .... at .... hereby give you notice that I *expect to be confined within six weeks from the date of this notice and shall be absent from work from .... /*have given birth to a child on ....
>
> The maternity benefit and any other amount to which I am entitled under the provisions of the Maternity Benefit Act, 1961, may be paid to .... *Me/*Shri/Shrimathi/Kumari
>
> I shall not work in any establishment during the period for which I receive maternity benefit.
>
> Date ....
>
> Signature of an attestor in case the woman is   Signature or thumb impression
> not able to sign and affixes thumb impression   of woman
>
> *To be struck off when not applicable.

"In the case of a woman who is pregnant, such notice shall state the date from which she will be absent from work, not being a date earlier than six weeks from the date of her expected delivery" [Section 6 (2)].

"Any woman who has not given the notice when she was pregnant may give such notice as soon as possible after the delivery" [Section 6 (3)].

"On receipt of the notice, the employer shall permit such woman to absent herself from the establishment during the period for which she receives the maternity benefit" [Section 6 (4)].

"The failure to give notice under this section shall not disentitle a woman to maternity benefit or any other amount under this Act if she is otherwise entitled to such benefit or amount and in any such case an Inspector may either of his own motion or on an application made to him by the woman, order the payment of such benefit or amount within such period as may be specified in the order" [Section 6 (6)].

4.5.5 Mode of Payment of Maternity Benefit

"The amount of maternity benefit for the period preceding the date of her expected delivery shall be paid in advance by the employer to the woman on production of such proof as may be prescribed that the woman is pregnant, and the amount due for the subsequent period shall be paid by the employer to the woman within the forty-eight hours of production of such proof as may be prescribed that the woman has been delivered of a child" [Section 6 (5)].

4.5.6 Payment of Maternity Benefit in case of Death of a Woman [Section 7]

According to the provisions of Section 7, "If a woman entitled to maternity benefit or any other amount under this Act, dies before receiving such maternity benefit or amount, or where the employer is liable for maternity benefit under the second proviso to sub-section (3) of Section 5, the employer shall pay such benefit or amount to the person nominated by the woman in the notice given under Section 6 and in case there is such nominee, to her legal representative".

4.5.7 Payment of Medical Bonus

(1) "Even woman entitled to benefit under this Act shall also be entitled to receive from her employer a medical bonus of Two Thousand Five Hundred Rupees (₹ 2,500), if no pre-natal confinement and post-natal care is provided for by the employer free of charge" [Section 8 (1)].

(2) "The Central Government may from time to time, by notification in the *Official Gazette,* increase the amount of medical bonus subject to the maximum of twenty thousand rupees" [Section 8 (2)].

Prior to the amendment of 2007, the amount of medical bonus was ₹ 250/- only. But after the amendment, the amount had has been increased and made ₹ One Thousand subject to the conditions mentioned in Section 8 (1). This amount was Two Thousand Five Hundred Rupees (₹ 2,500) in 2008. This amount can be increased to the maximum of Twenty thousand rupees (20,000) [Section 8(2)].

4.5.8 Provisions of the Act relating to Leave and Nursing Breaks

In the Act, provisions have been made for the following types of leave in addition to authorised absence under Section 6.

(A) Leave for Miscarriage, Termination of Pregnancy :

"In case of miscarriage or medical termination of pregnancy, a woman shall, on production of such proof as may be prescribed, be entitled to leave with wages at the rate of maternity benefit for a period of six weeks immediately following the day of her miscarriage or as the case may be, her medical termination of pregnancy" [Section 9].

(B) Leave with Wages for Tubectomy Operation :

"In case of tubectomy operation, a woman shall, on production of such proof as may be prescribed, be entitled to leave with wages at the rate of maternity benefit for a period of two weeks immediately following the day of her tubectomy operation" [Section 9 [A]].

(C) Leave for illness arising out of pregnancy, delivery, premature birth of child, miscarriage, medical termination of pregnancy or tubectomy operation :

"A woman suffering from illness arising out of pregnancy, delivery, premature birth of child, miscarriage, medical termination of pregnancy or tubectomy operation shall, on production of such proof as may be prescribed, be entitled in addition to the period of absence allowed to her under Section 6, or, as the case may be, under Section 9, to leave with wages at the rate of maternity benefit for a maximum period of one month" [Section 10].

Provisions relating to "**Nursing Breaks**" have been made in Section 11 of the Act which are as follows:

"Every woman delivered of a child who returns to duty after such delivery shall, in addition to the interval for rest allowed to her, be allowed in the course of her daily work two breaks of prescribed duration for nursing the child until the child attains the age of fifteen months".

From these provisions of Section 11, we come to know the following two important points in respect of "Nursing Breaks".

(i) After having delivered a child, where a woman returns to duty after such delivery, she is allowed in the course of her daily work two breaks of prescribed duration for nursing the child until that child attains the age of fifteen months.

(ii) These nursing breaks are given in addition to the interval for rest allowed to the woman.

According to Rule 6 of The Maharashtra Maternity Benefit Rules of 1965, "Each of the two breaks allowed to a woman under Section 11 shall be of Fifteen minutes duration".

4.5.9 Dismissal during Absence of Pregnancy

"When a woman absents herself from work in accordance with the provisions of this Act, it shall be unlawful for her employer to discharge or dismiss her during or on account of such absence or to give notice of discharge or dismissal on such a day that the notice will expire during such absence, or to vary to her disadvantage any of the conditions of her service" [Section 12 (1)].

"The discharge or dismissal of a woman at any time during her pregnancy, if the woman but for such discharge or dismissal would have been entitled to maternity benefit or medical bonus referred to in Section 8, shall not have the effect of depriving her of the maternity benefit or medical bonus" [Section 12 (2) (a)].

However, it is also provided that "where the dismissal is for any prescribed gross misconduct, the employer may, by order in writing communicate to the woman, deprive her of the maternity benefit or medical bonus or both" [Proviso to Section 12 (2) (a)].

In Rule 7 of the Maharashtra Maternity Benefit Rule of 1965, the Acts which constitute gross misconduct are given. The Rule 7 is as follows:

"Acts constituting gross misconduct

The following acts shall, for the purpose of proviso to clause (a) of sub-section (2) of Section 12, constitute gross misconduct, namely:

(a) willfully destroying goods or property of the employer;
(b) assaulting superiors or colleagues at the place of duty;
(c) criminal offence involving moral turpitude resulting in conviction by a Court of law;
(d) theft, fraud or dishonesty in relation to the employer's business or in relation to the employer's property at the premises where the woman is employed;
(e) willful failure to observe the safety measures or the rules on that subject;
(f) willfully interfering with safety devices or fire fighting equipment".

The provisions of Section 12 (2) (b) also make clear that, "any woman deprived of maternity benefit or medical bonus, or both, or discharged or dismissed during or on account of her absence from work in accordance with the provisions of this Act, may, within sixty days from the date on which order of such deprivation or discharge or dismissal is communicated to her, appeal to such authority as may be prescribed, and the decision of that authority on such appeal, whether the woman should or should not be deprived of maternity benefit or medical bonus, or both, or discharged or dismissed shall be final".

According to Section 12 (2) (c), "Nothing contained in this sub-section shall affect the provisions contained in sub-section (1)". This means provisions of Section 12 (2) do not affect the provisions contained in Section 12 (1).

4.5.10 No Deduction of Wages in Certain Cases [Section 13]

"No deduction from the normal and usual daily wages of a woman entitled to maternity benefit under the provisions of this Act shall be made by reason only of:

(a) the nature of work assigned to her by virtue of the provisions contained in sub-section (3) of Section 4. This means the nature of work assigned to her by virtue of the provisions contained in Section 4 (3) is not of arduous nature, or that the pregnant woman has been given a difficult nature of work. The meaning of word 'arduous' is difficult or strenuous.
(b) No deduction from the normal and usual daily wages of a woman entitled to maternity benefit under the provisions of this Act is allowed for breaks for nursing the child which is allowed to her under the provisions of Section 11".

4.6 Appointment, Powers and Duties of the Inspectors [Sections 14 to 17]

4.6.1 Appointment of Inspectors [Section 14]

"The appropriate Government may, by notification in the *Official Gazette*, appoint such officers as it thinks fit to be Inspectors for the purpose of this Act and may define the local limits of the jurisdiction within which they shall exercise their functions under this Act".

It is further made clear in Section 16 of this Act that, "Every Inspector appointed under this Act shall be deemed to be a public servant within the meaning of Section 21 of the Indian Penal Code (45 of 1860)".

4.6.2 Powers and Duties of the Inspectors [Section 15]

The powers given to the Inspectors under this Act are mentioned in Section 15. The provisions of Section 15 are as under:

"An Inspector may, subject to such restrictions or conditions as may be prescribed, exercise all or any of the following powers, namely:

(a) enter at all reasonable times with such assistants, if any, being persons in the service of the Government or any local or other public authority, as he thinks fit, any premises or place where women are employed or work is given to them in an establishment, for the purposes of examining any registers, records and notices required to be kept or exhibited by or under this Act and required their production for inspection;

(b) examine any person whom he finds in any premises or place and who, he has reasonable cause to believe, is employed in the establishment:

Provided that no person shall be compelled under this section to answer any question or give any evidence tending to incriminate himself;

(c) require the employer to give information regarding the names and addresses of women employed, payments made to them, and applications or notices received from them under this Act; and

(d) take copies of any registers and records or notices or any portions thereof".

4.6.3 Power of Inspector to Direct Payments to be made Section 17]

Section 17 empowers an Inspector appointed under this Act to direct payments to be made. The Section 17 has been amended by the Amendment Act of 1988 and its provisions has been made applicable with effect from 10-01-1989. The provisions of Section 17 are given below :

(1) Any woman claiming that –
   (a) maternity benefit or any other amount to which she is entitled under this Act and any person claiming that payment due under Section 7 has been improperly withheld;
   (b) her employer has discharged or dismissed her during or on account of her absence from work in accordance with the provisions of this Act, may make a complaint to the Inspector [Section 17 (1)].

(2) The inspector may, of his own motion or on receipt of a complaint referred to in sub-section (1), make an inquiry or cause an inquiry to be made and if satisfied that:
   (a) payment has been wrongfully withheld, may direct the payment to be made in accordance with his orders;
   (b) she has been discharged or dismissed during or on account of her absence from work in accordance with the provisions of this Act, may pass such orders as are just and proper according to the circumstances of the case [Section 17 (2)].

(3) Any person aggrieved by the decision of the Inspector under sub-section (2) may, within thirty days from the date on which such decision is communicated to such person, appeal to the prescribed authority [Section 17 (3)].

(4) The decision of the prescribed authority where an appeal has been preferred to it under sub-section (3) or of the Inspector where no such appeal has been preferred shall be final [Section 17 (4)].

(5) Any amount payable under this section shall be recoverable by the Collector on a certificate issued for that amount by the Inspector as an arrear of land revenue [Section 17 (5)].

4.7 Forfeiture of Maternity Benefit [Section 18]

If a woman works in any establishment after she has been permitted by her employer to absent herself under the provisions of Section 6 for any period during such authorised absence, she shall forfeit her claim to the maternity benefit for such period.

4.8 Miscellaneous Provisions of the Act [Sections 19, 21 to 30]

There are in all 30 Sections. Of these sections, we have considered the provisions of 18 sections. Provisions of Sections 21, 22, 23 are related to penalties and offences while remaining sections deal with abstracts, registers, power to exempt establishment etc. Now let us first consider the provisions relating to penalties and offences.

4.8.1 Penalties and Offences

(A) Penalty for Contravention of Act by Employer [Section 21]:

(1) "If any employer fails to pay any amount of maternity benefit to a woman entitled under this Act or discharges or dismisses such woman during or on account of her absence from work in accordance with the provisions of this Act, he shall be punishable with imprisonment which shall not be less than three months but which may extend to one year and with fine which shall not be less than two thousand rupees but which may extend to five thousand rupees" [Section 21 (1)]. However, it is provided that "The Court may, for sufficient reasons to be recorded in writing, impose a sentence of imprisonment for a lesser term or fine only in lieu of imprisonment" [Proviso to Section 21 (1)]. Further it is made clear in Section 21 (2) that, "If any employer contravenes the provisions of this Act or the rules made thereunder, he shall, if no other penalty is elsewhere provided by or under this Act for such contravention, be punishable with imprisonment which may extend to one year, or with fine which may extend to five thousand rupees, or with both".

But "where the contravention is of any provision regarding maternity benefit or regarding payment of any other amount and such maternity benefit or amount has not already been recovered, the Court shall, in addition, recover such maternity benefit or amount as if it were a fine and pay the same to the person entitled thereto" [Proviso to Section 21 (2)].

(B) Penalty for Obstructing Inspector [Section 22]:

It is stated in Section 22 that, "Whoever fails to produce on demand by the Inspector any register or document in his custody kept in pursuance of this Act or the rules made thereunder or conceals or prevents any person from appearing before or being examined by an Inspector shall be punishable with imprisonment which may extend to one year, or with fine which may extend to five thousand rupees, or both".

(C) Cognizance of Offences [Section 23] :

(1) "Any aggrieved woman, an office-bearer of a trade union registered under the Trade Unions Act, !926 (16 of 1926) of which such woman is a member or a voluntary organisation registered under the Societies Registration Act, 1860 (21 of 1860) or an Inspector may file a complaint regarding the commission of an offence under this Act in any Court of competent jurisdiction and no such complaint shall be filed after the expiry of one year from the date on which the offence is alleged to have been committed" [Section 23 (1)].

(2) "No Court inferior to that of a Metropolitan Magistrate or a Magistrate of the first class shall try any offence under this Act" [Section 23 (2)].

(D) Protection of Action taken in Good Faith [Section 24] :

"No suit, prosecution or other legal proceedings shall lie against any person for anything which is in good faith done or intended to be done in pursuance of this Act or of any rule or order made thereunder".

4.8.2 Abstract of Act and Rules thereunder to be Exhibited [Section 19]

An abstract of the provisions of this Act and the rules made thereunder in the language or languages of the locality shall be exhibited in a conspicuous place by the employer in every part of the establishment in which women are employed.

4.8.3 Maintenance of Records, Registers etc. [Section 20]

Every employer shall prepare and maintain such registers, records and muster-rolls and in such manner as may be prescribed.

4.8.4 Effect of Laws and Agreements Inconsistent with this Act [Section 27]

(1) The provisions of this Act shall have effect notwithstanding anything inconsistent therewith contained in any other law or in the terms of any award, agreement or contract of service, whether made before or after the coming into force of this Act [Section 27 (1)].

But it is provided that "where under any such award, agreement, contract of service or otherwise, a woman is entitled to benefits in respect of any matter which are more favourable to her than those to which she would be entitled under this Act, the woman shall continue to be entitled to the more favourable benefits in respect of that matter, notwithstanding that she is entitled to receive benefits in respect of other matters under this Act" [Proviso to Section 27 (1)].

(2) "Nothing contained in this Act shall be construed to preclude a woman from entering into an agreement with her employer for granting her rights or privileges in respect of any matter which are more favourable to her than those to which she would be entitled under this Act" [Section 27 (2)].

4.8.5 Powers of Government

[A] Power of Central Government to give Directions [Section 25] :

The Central Government may give such directions as it may deem necessary to a State Government regarding the carrying into execution of the provisions of this Act and the State Government shall comply with such direction.

[B] Power to Exempt Establishments [Section 26] :

If the appropriate Government is satisfied that having regard to an establishment or a class of establishments providing for the grant of benefits which are not less favourable than those provided in this Act, it is necessary so to do, it may, by notification in the Official Gazette, exempt, subject to such conditions and restrictions, if any, as may be specified in the notification, the establishment or class of establishments from the operation of all or any of the provisions of this Act or of any rule made thereunder.

[C] Power to Make Rules [Section 28] :

(1) The appropriate Government may, subject to the condition of previous publication and by notification in the *Official Gazette*, make rules for carrying out the purposes of this Act [Section 28 (1)].

(2) In particular, and without prejudice to the generality of the foregoing power, such rules may provide for –

   (a) the preparation and maintenance of registers, records and muster rolls;

   (b) the exercise of powers (including the inspection of establishments) and the performance of duties by Inspectors for the purposes of this Act;

   (c) the method of payment of maternity benefit and other benefits under this Act as far as provision has not been made therefore in this Act;

   (d) the form of notices under Section 6;

   (e) the nature of proof required under the provisions of this Act;

   (f) the duration of nursing breaks referred to in Section 11;

   (g) acts which may constitute gross misconduct for purposes of Section 12;

   (h) the authority to which an appeal under clause (b) of sub-section (2) of Section 12 shall lie; the form and manner in which such appeal may be made and the procedure to be followed in disposal thereof,

   (i) the authority to which an appeal shall lie against the decision of the Inspector under Section 17; the form and manner in which such appeal may be made and the procedure to be followed in disposal thereof,

   (j) the form and manner in which complaints may be made to Inspectors under sub-section (1) of Section 17 and the procedure to be followed by them when making inquiries or causing inquiries to be made under sub-section (2) of that section;

   (k) any other matter which is to be, or may be, prescribed [Section 28 (2)].

(3) Every rule made by the Central Government under this section shall be laid as soon as may be after it is made, before each House of Parliament while it is in session for a total period of thirty days which may be comprised in one session or in two or more successive sessions, and if, before the expiry of the session immediately following the session or the successive sessions aforesaid, both Houses agree in making any modification in the rule or both Houses agree that the rule should not be made, the rule shall thereafter have effect only in such modified form to be of no effect, as the case may be; so, however that any such modification or annulment shall be without prejudice to the validity of anything previously done under that rule [Section 28 (3)].

4.8.6 Amendment of Act 69 of 1951 [Section 29]

In Section 32 of the Plantations Labour Act, 1951:

(a) in sub-section (1), the letter and brackets "(a)" before the words "in the case of sickness", the word "and" after the words "sickness allowance" and clause (b) shall be omitted;

(b) in sub-section (2), the words, "or maternity" shall be omitted.

4.8.7 Repeal [Section 30]

On the application of this Act :

(i) to mines, the Mines Maternity Benefit Act, 1941 (19 of 1941); and

(ii) to factories situated in the Union Territory of Delhi, the Bombay Maternity Benefit Act, 1929 (Bom. Act VII of 1929); as in force in that territory, shall stand repealed.

Thus, when the Maternity Benefit Act of 1961 has been made applicable to mines, the Mines Maternity Benefit Act of 1941 was repealed. Likewise, when this Act has been made applicable to factories situated in the Union Territory of Delhi, the Bombay Maternity Benefit Act of 1929 which was in force in that territory also stood repealed.

4.9 The Maharashtra Maternity Benefit Rules of 1965

In exercise of the powers conferred by Section 28 of the Maternity Benefit Act, 1961 (53 of 1961), the Government of Maharashtra has made the following Rules.

These Rules have been amended from time to time. The Rules and various forms thereunder are given below:

Rule 1. Short Title and Commencement:

(1) These rules may be called Maharashtra Maternity Benefit Rules, 1965.

(2) They shall come into force on such date as the State Government may appoint in this behalf.

Rule 2. Definitions:

In these rules, unless the context otherwise requires,

(a) "Act" means the Maternity Benefit Act, 1961;

(b) "Competent Authority" means an officer appointed by the appropriate Government;

(c) "Form" means a form appended to these rules;

(d) "Registered medical practitioner" means a person registered under any law for the time being in force relating to registration of medical practitioners;

(e) "Registered midwife" means a midwife registered under any law for the time being in force relating to registration of midwives;

(f) "Section" means a section of the Act.

Rule 3. Form of Notice under Section 6:

The notice to be given by a woman entitled to maternity benefit under the provisions of the Act shall be in Form I. Form I has already been given.

Rule 4. Method of Payment of Maternity Benefit and other Benefits:

(1) The medical bonus payable to a woman under Section 8 shall be paid along with the amount of maternity benefit payable in respect of the period of six weeks immediately following the date of her delivery.

(2) The wages payable to a woman in respect of leave for miscarriage under Section 9 or leave for illness arising out of pregnancy, delivery, premature birth of a child or miscarriage under Section 10 shall be paid within forty-eight hours of production of proof of such miscarriage or illness.

Rule 5. Proof of Pregnancy Death, etc.:

(1) The production of a certificate in Form 2 from a registered medical practitioner certifying the pregnancy, delivery, miscarriage or illness arising out of pregnancy, delivery, premature birth of child or miscarriage of a woman shall, for the purpose of the Act and these rules, be proof of such pregnancy, delivery, miscarriage or, as the case may be, illness.

Provided that, the production of –

(a) a certificate from a registered midwife in Form 3 in evidence of the confinement or miscarriage of a woman, or

(b) a certificate from a police *patil* or a certified extract from a register of births maintained under the provisions of any law for the time being in force relating to registration of births, in evidence of the confinement of a woman, shall also be proof of the confinement, or as the case may be, miscarriage of a woman.

(2) The production of a certificate in Form 4 from a registered medical practitioner or of a certified extract from any register of deaths maintained under the provisions of any law for the time being in force, relating to registration of deaths certifying the death of a woman or of a child shall, for the purposes of the Act and these rules, be proof of such death.

Form 2, Form 3 and Form 4 are given below.

FORM 2

[Rule 5 (1)]

This is to certify that I examined ....*wife/*daughter of .... a woman employed in .... on ....and *found that she is pregnant and is expected to deliver a child within .... (mention months and days) from the above-mentioned date/*found that she is delivered of a child on .... /* found that she had miscarriage on ..../ *found that she is suffering from .... an illness arising out of her *pregnancy/*delivery/*premature birth of a child/*miscarriage.

Date ....
           Signature, qualifications and designation,
           if any, of registered medical practitioner.

Note : The expressions "child" and "miscarriage" are defined in the Act as follows :

(1) "child" includes a still-born child,

(2) "Miscarriage" means expulsion of the contents of a pregnant uterus at any period prior to or during the twenty-sixth week of pregnancy but shall not include any miscarriage, causing of which is punishable under the Indian Penal Code (45 of 1880).

*To be struck off when not applicable

FORM 3

[See proviso to rule 5(1)]

This is to certify that I examined .... *wife/*daughter of .... a woman employed in .... and found that *she has been delivered of a child on .... *she had miscarriage on ....

Date : ....   Signature of a registered midwife

Note : The expressions "child" and "miscarriage" are defined in the Act as follows :

(1) "child" includes a still-born child;

(2) "Miscarriage" means expulsion of the contents of a pregnant uterus at any period prior to or during the twenty-sixth week of pregnancy but shall not include any miscarriage, causing of which is punishable under the Indian Penal Code (45 of 1860).

*To be struck off if not applicable

FORM 4

[See rule 5(2)]

This is to certify that Smt. .... *wife/*daughter of .... employed in ....expired on........................... before/* during/* after confinement. The child *died on .... /*survives her.

Date : ....

Signature, qualifications and designation, if any, of registered medical practitioner.

*To be struck off if not applicable.

Rule 6. Duration of Breaks allowed under Section 11:

Each of the two breaks allowed to a woman under Section 11 shall be of fifteen minutes duration.

But it is provided that, having regard to the time reasonably required to a woman, for reaching the creche or the place where her child is kept by her while on duty and for coming back to the place of duty, the duration of each such break shall be extended by not less than five and not more than fifteen minutes and where there is a dispute as regards the time reasonably required by a woman for the aforesaid purpose, each such break shall be extended by such time as may be determined by the Competent Authority.

Rule 7

The provisions of Rule 7 have already been considered while studying the provisions of Section 12 (2) (a).

Rule 8. Appeal under Section 12:

(1) Every appeal under clause (b) of sub-section (2) of Section 12 shall be made to the Competent Authority as early as may be in Form 5. It shall be handed over to the Competent Authority personally, or sent to it by registered post.

(2) After the appeal is received, the Competent Authority shall furnish a copy thereof to the employer and serve a notice on him calling upon him to send his reply to the appeal and produce such documents relating to the appeal as may be specified in the notice, on or before the date specified in the notice. The notice shall also state that if the employer fails to send his reply or produce the documents on or before the date specified in the notice, the appeal shall be decided *ex parte*.

(3) After considering the facts presented to it by the appellant and the employer and after ascertaining them from the documents, if any, produced by the employer, the Competent Authority shall give its decision on the appeal. Where the employer fails to send his reply and produce documents as required by the notice served on him under, sub-rule (2), the Competent Authority shall give its decision *ex parte*.

FORM 5
[Rule 8 (1), Section 12 (2) (b)]

To

THE COMPETENT AUTHORITY,

Sir,

I, ... the undersigned, woman employee of .... (name of the factory and address) having been wrongly deprived by the employer of *maternity benefit/*medical bonus/*maternity benefit and medical bonus to which I am entitled under the Maternity Benefit Act, 1961 prefer this appeal under clause (b) of sub-section (2) of Section 12 of that Act and request that the said employer be ordered to pay me the *maternity benefit/*medical bonus/*maternity benefit and medical bonus to which I am entitled. A copy of the order of the employer in this behalf is enclosed. The order was communicated to me on ....

Date : ....

Signature of an attester in case the woman Signature or thumb impression
is not able to sign, and affixes thumb impression. of the woman.

*Strike off if not applicable.

Rule 9. Complaint under Section 17 :

(1) Every complaint under Section 17 shall be made as nearly as may be in Form 6, where the complainant is a woman entitled to the benefits in respect of which the complaint is made and in Form 7, where the complainant is any person claiming such benefits under Section 7.

(2) After a complaint is received under Section 17, an Inspector shall, before issuing orders under sub-section (2) of that section, examine all records maintained by the employer which he considers to be relevant for making inquiry into the complaint and examine any person employed by the employer and take down necessary statements from such person.

FORM 6
[Rule 9 (1)]

To

THE INSPECTOR,

Sir,

I, ... employed in .... having fulfilled the conditions laid down in the Maternity Benefit Act, 1961, and the rules thereunder am entitled to .... ₹ .... as maternity benefit/ * and ₹ ....as medical bonus/ *and ₹ .... as wages in respect of the leave admissible to me under*section 9/ *section 10/ *Sections 9 and 10. The said amount has been improperly withheld by my employer. He may, therefore, be ordered to pay the said amount to me.

Date : ....

Signature of an attester in case the woman is unable to sign, and affixes thumb impression.

Signature or thumb impression of the woman.
Full address of the woman

*Strike off if not applicable.

FORM 7
[Rule 9 (1)]

1, ... *a person nominated under Section 6 of the Maternity Benefit Act, 1961 by/ *a legal representative of/ ....(name of woman) employed in .... have to complain that the said woman having fulfilled the conditions laid down in the Maternity Benefit Act, 1961 and the rules thereunder is entitled to ₹ .... *as maternity benefit/ * and ₹ .... as medical bonus/ * and ₹ .... as wages in respect of the leave admissible to her under Section 9/* Section 10/ * Sections 9 and 10.

The said amount has been improperly withheld by the employer of the said .... (name of the woman). He may, therefore, be ordered to pay the said amount to me.

Date : ....

Signature of an attester in case the nominee legal representative is unable to sign, and affixes thumb impression.

Signature or thumb impression of the nominee/legal representative.

*Strike off if not applicable.

Rule 10. Appeal under Section 17 :

(1) Every appeal under sub-section (3) of section 17 shall be made to the Competent Authority as early as may be in Form 8.

Provided that, where the appeal is against the decision of the Competent Authority itself, the appeal shall be made to the State Government or to such other authority as the State Government may appoint in that behalf in the form of a memorandum setting forth concisely the grounds of objections to the decision.

(2) Where the appeal is received by the Competent Authority, the Competent Authority shall on receipt of the appeal, call upon the Inspector against whose decision the appeal is made to furnish before a specified date all records relevant to the appeal, recorded statements of the appellant and the Inspector, if necessary, take into account the documents and evidence produced before it and the facts as presented to it or as ascertained by it and then give its decision.

FORM 8
[Rule 10 (1), Section 17 (3)]

To

THE COMPETENT AUTHORITY,

Sir,

I, ..., being aggrieved by the decision of Shri. .... an Inspector, given under sub-section (2) of Section 17 of the Maternity Benefit Act, 1961, prefer this appeal to you under sub-section (3) of the said Section 17. A copy of the decision of the Inspector is attached hereto. The decision was communicated to me on ....

I request that in view of the facts and grounds of appeal mentioned in the memorandum attached hereto, the said decision may be set aside.

Date : ....

Signature of aggrieved person and his full address.

Rule 11. Form of abstracts to be exhibited under Section 19:

The abstracts of the provisions of the Act and the rules made thereunder to be exhibited under Section 19 shall be in Form 9.

FORM 9
[Rule 11, Section 19]
(ABSTRACT OF THE MATERNITY BENEFIT ACT, 1961 AND THE RULES MADE THEREUNDER

1. No employer shall knowingly employ a woman in any establishment during the six weeks immediately following the day of her delivery or miscarriage and no woman shall work in any establishment during the said period.
2. No pregnant woman shall, on a request being made by her in this behalf, be required by her employer to do, during the period of one month immediately preceding the period of six weeks, before the date of her expected delivery and at any time during this period of six weeks or which involves long-hours of standing or which in any way is likely to interfere with her pregnancy or the normal development of the foetus, or is likely to cause her miscarriage or otherwise to adversely affect her health.
3. (1) Subject to the provisions of the Act, every woman who has actually worked in an establishment of the employer from whom she claims maternity benefit for a period of not less than one hundred and sixty days, in the twelve months immediately preceding the date of her expected delivery (including the days during which she was laid off during the period of such twelve months), shall be entitled to, and her employer shall be liable for the payment of maternity benefit at the rate of her average daily wage, or one rupee a day, whichever is higher, for the period of her actual absence not exceeding six weeks immediately preceding and including the day of her delivery and for the six weeks immediately following that day.

Provided that –
(i) where a woman dies during the period for which maternity benefit is payable to her, the benefit shall be payable only for the days up to and including the day of her death.
(ii) where the woman having been delivered of a child, dies, during her delivery or during the period of six weeks immediately following the date of her delivery, leaving behind in either case the child, the employer shall be liable for the payment of maternity benefit for the entire period of six weeks immediately following the day of her delivery but if the child also dies during the said period, then for the days up to and including the day of the death of the child.

4. The amount of benefit for the period preceding the date of her expected delivery shall be paid in advance by the employer to the woman on production of a certificate from a registered medical practitioner in Form 2 appended to the Maharashtra Maternity Benefit Rules, 1961 (hereinafter referred to as "the Maternity Benefit Rules") in evidence of the fact that she is pregnant and expected to be deliver of a child within six weeks of the date on which the certificate is produced by her, and the amount due for the subsequent period shall be paid by the employer to the woman within forty-eight hours of production of a certificate in the aforesaid Form from a registered medical practitioner or of a certificate from a registered midwife in Form 3 appended to the Maternity Benefit Rules or of a certified extract from any register of birth maintained under the provisions of any law for the time being in force relating to registration of births, in evidence of the fact that she has been delivered of a child.

5. (i) Any woman employed in an establishment and entitled to maternity benefit under the provisions of the Act may give notice in writing in Form 1 appended to the Maternity Benefit Rules to her employer, stating that her maternity benefit and any other amount to which she may be entitled under the Act may be paid to her or to such person as she may nominate in the notice and that she will not work in any establishment during the period for which she receives maternity benefit.
(ii) In the case of a woman who is pregnant, such notice shall state the date from which she will be absent from work, not being a date earlier than six weeks from the date of her expected delivery.
(iii) Any woman who has not given the notice when she was pregnant may give such notice as soon as possible after the delivery.
(iv) On receipt of the notice, the employer shall permit such woman to absent herself from the establishment until the expiry of six weeks after the day of her delivery.

6. (i) Every woman entitled to maternity benefit under the Act shall also be entitled to receive from her employer a medical bonus of twenty five rupees, if no pre-natal confinement and post-natal care is provided for by the employer free of charge. The medical bonus shall be paid along with the second installment of the maternity benefit

(ii) In case of miscarriage, a woman shall, on production of a certificate from a registered medical practitioner in Form 2 appended to the Maternity Benefit Rules or of a certificate from a registered midwife in Form 3 appended to those rules be entitled to leave with wages at the rate of maternity benefit, for a period of six weeks immediately following the day of her miscarriage. The said wages shall be paid within forty-eight hours of production of the certificate in Form 2 or Form 3, as the case may be.

(iii) A woman suffering from illness arising out of pregnancy, delivery, premature birth of child or miscarriage shall, on production of a certificate from a registered medical practitioner in Form 2 appended to the Maternity Benefit Rules be entitled, in addition to the period of absence allowed to her on account of maternity or miscarriage, as the case may be, to leave with wages at the rate of maternity benefit for a maximum period of one month. The wages for the leave period shall be paid within forty-eight hours of production of proof of such illness.

7. Every woman delivered of a child who returns to duty after such delivery shall, in addition to the interval for rest allowed to her, be allowed in the course of her daily work two breaks of fifteen minutes duration each for nursing the child until the child attains the age of fifteen months.

Provided that, having regard to the time reasonably required to a woman for reaching the creche or the place where her child is kept by her while on duty and for coming back to the place of duty, the duration of each such break shall be extended by not less than five and not more than fifteen minutes, and where there is a dispute as regards the time reasonably required by a woman for the aforesaid purpose, each such break shall be extended by such time as may be determined by the Competent Authority.

8. (1) When a woman absents herself from work in accordance with the provisions of the Act, it shall be unlawful for her employer to discharge or dismiss her during or on account of such absence or to give notice of discharge or dismissal on such a day that the notice will expire during such absence, or to vary to her disadvantage any of the conditions of her service.

(2) (a) The discharge or dismissal of a woman at any time during her pregnancy, if the woman but for such discharge or dismissal would have been entitled to maternity benefit or medical bonus shall not have the effect of depriving her of the maternity benefit or medical bonus or both.

Provided that, where the dismissal is for any of the following acts, the employer may by order in writing communicated to the woman, deprive her of the maternity benefit or medical bonus or both –

(i) willfully destroying the goods or property of the employer;
(ii) assaulting superiors or colleagues at the place of duty;
(iii) criminal offence involving moral turpitude resulting in conviction by a court of law;

(iv) theft, fraud or dishonesty in relation to the employer's business or in relation to the employer's property at the premises where the woman is employed;
(v) willful failure to observe the safety measures of the rules on that subject;
(vi) willfully interfering with safety devices or fire fighting equipment.
(b) Any woman deprived of maternity benefit or medical bonus or both may, within sixty days from the date on which the order of such deprivation is communicated to her, appeal in Form 5 appended to the Maternity Benefit Rules to the Competent Authority and the decision of that authority on such appeal, whether the woman should or should not be deprived of maternity benefit or medical bonus or both, shall be final.
9. If a woman working in any establishment after she has been permitted by her employer to absent herself under the provisions of the Act for any period during such authorised absence, she shall forfeit her claim to the maternity benefit for such period.
10. (i) Any woman or her nominee or legal representative claiming that maternity benefit or any other amount to which she is entitled under the Act has been improperly withheld may make a complaint to the Inspector in writing in Forms 6 or, as the case may be, Form 7 appended to the Maternity Benefit Rules.
(ii) The Inspector may, of his own motion or on receipt of a complaint in Form 6 or 7 make an inquiry or cause an inquiry to be made and if satisfied the payment has been wrongfully withheld, may direct the payment to be made in accordance with his orders.
(iii) Any person aggrieved by the decision of the Inspector may, within thirty days from the date on which such decision is communicated to such person, appeal to the Competent Authority.
(iv) The decision of the Competent Authority where an appeal has been referred to it or of the Inspector where no such appeal has been preferred shall be final.
11. (i) The employer shall supply to every woman employed by him at her request copies of all Forms appended to the Maternity Benefit Rules other than Forms 9, 10 and 11.
(ii) Where a notice, appeal or complaint has been received in a form other than the form prescribed under the Act, the person receiving such notice, appeal or complaint shall, within fifteen days of the receipt of such notice, appeal or complaint, require the woman to submit the notice, appeal or complaint, as the case may be, in the prescribed Form.
12. (i) The employer of every factory in which women are employed shall prepare and maintain an up-to-date maternity benefit register in Form 10 appended to the Maternity Benefit Rules and shall enter therein particulars of all women workers in the factory.
(ii) All entries in the register shall be made in ink and it shall always be available for inspection by the Inspector during working hours.
(iii) The employer of every factory shall on or before the 15th day of January in each year submit to the Competent Authority a return in Form 11 appended to the Maternity Benefit Rules.

Rule 12. Maternity Benefit Register:

(1) Every employer of a factory wherein women are employed shall prepare and maintain up-to-date a maternity benefit register in Form 10.

(2) All entries in the register shall be made in ink and the register shall be kept open for inspection by the Inspector during working hours.

(3) It shall be lawful for the employer to enter such particulars in the register as he may consider to be necessary for the purposes of the Act.

FORM 10
[Rule 12 (1)]
Maternity Benefit Register

1. Name of the woman: ....
2. Date of appointment: ....
3. Department in which employed: ....
4. Nature of work: ....
5. Dates (with month and year) on which she is laid off and not employed: ....
6. Total days employed in the: ....
7. Date on which woman gives payment period:
   Notice under Section 6 of the Maternity Benefit Act, 1961. ....
8. Date of birth of child: ....
9. Date of production of proof of pregnancy under Section 6 of the Maternity Benefit Act, 1961: ....
10. Date of production of proof of delivery/miscarriage/death: ....
11. Where the maternity benefit is paid in advance before delivery, the date on which it is paid and the amount thereof: ....
12. Date on which subsequent payment of maternity benefit is made and the amount thereof: ....
13. Where the medical bonus is paid, the date on which it is paid and amount thereof: ....
14. Date on which wages on account of leave are paid and amount thereof: ....
15. Name of the person nominated by the woman: ....
16. If the woman dies, the date of her death, the name of the person to whom maternity benefit and/or other amount was paid, the amount thereof, and the date of payment: ....
17. If the woman dies and the child survives, the name of the person to whom the amount of maternity benefit was paid on behalf of the child and the period for which it was paid: ....
18. Remarks column for the use of Inspector: ....

Rule 13. Supply of Forms:

Every employer shall, on an application made by a woman, supply her with copies of any of the Forms other than Forms 9, 10 and 11.

Rule 14. Failure to submit notice etc. in prescribed forms:

Where any notice, appeal, or complaint is not given or made as nearly as may be in the form in which it is required to be given or made under these rules, the person receiving such notice, appeal or as the case may be, complaint shall, within fifteen days of the receipt of such notice, appeal or complaint, require the persons giving such notice, appeal or complaint to give it in the form in which it is required to be given under these rules and the said person shall thereupon give the notice in the prescribed form within one month.

Rule 15. Return:

Every employer shall furnish to the Competent Authority by the 15th day of January each year a return in Form 11 which is given below.

FORM 11

Return to be submitted to the Competent Authority on or before the 15th January each year.

1. Name of the Factory   ....
2. Name of Occupier   ....
3. Name of the Manager   ....
4. Year ending 31st December, 20   ....
5. Average number of women employed daily
6. Number of women who claimed maternity benefit under Section 6 of the Maternity Benefit Act, 1961   ....
7. Number of women who were paid maternity benefit for actual birth   ....
8. Number of other persons who were paid maternity benefit under Section 7 of the Maternity Benefit Act, 1961   ....
9. Total amount of maternity benefit paid   ....
10. Amount of medical bonus paid   ....

Signature of employer.

Rule 16. Records :

All records kept as required by the provisions of the Act and these rules shall be preserved for a period of three years commencing from the date of the last entry made therein.

Questions For Discussion

1. Explain the objects, extent and coverage of the Act.
2. Define the following terms as used in the Act.
   (a) Employer
   (b) Establishment
   (c) Miscarriage
   (d) Wages
   (e) Woman
3. Explain the features of the Maternity Benefit Act.
4. Describe the conditions for the payment of maternity benefit under this Act. When is maternity benefit forfeited?
5. Explain the requirements for maternity benefits.
6. What is maternity benefit? During which periods of time are maternity benefits payable?
7. Can an employer dismiss or discharge a woman during or on account of absence from work during pregnancy?
8. Explain the provisions of the Act relating to maternity benefit and other benefits available under the Act. How are these benefits paid?
9. Explain fully the provisions of Section 5-A and 5-B.
10. What are the leaves to which a woman is entitled in case of miscarriage or illness arising out of pregnancy?
11. Can any deductions be made from the normal and usual daily wages of a woman entitled to maternity benefit under the Act?
12. Explain the powers and duties of Inspectors appointed under this Act.
13. Explain the provisions of the Act relating to penalty for contravention of the provisions of the Act by an employer.
14. Write notes on the following:
    (a) Payment of medical bonus under this Act
    (b) Dismissal during absence of Pregnancy
    (c) Provisions relating to 'Nursing Breaks'
    (d) Forfeiture of maternity benefit
    (e) Penalties and Offences under the Maternity Benefit Act of 1961
    (g) Mode of Payment of Maternity Benefit.

Chapter 5...

The Payment of Gratuity Act, 1972

Contents ...
- 5.1 Nature of Gratuity Payment
- 5.2 Objects of the Payment of Gratuity Act of 1972
- 5.3 Important Features of the Payment of Gratuity Act, 1972
- 5.4 Scope and Extent of the Act
- 5.5 Definitions
- 5.6 Payment of Gratuity
- 5.7 Calculation of Gratuity
- 5.8 Provisions Relating to Better Terms of Gratuity
- 5.9 Forfeiture of Gratuity
- 5.10 Power of an Appropriate Government to Exempt
- 5.11 Compulsory Insurance [Section 4-A]
- 5.12 Nomination
- 5.13 Determination of the Amount of Gratuity
- 5.14 Recovery of Gratuity
- 5.15 Protection of Gratuity
- 5.16 Appointment and Powers of Inspectors
- 5.17 Penalties
- 5.18 Exemption of the Employer from Liability in Certain Cases
- 5.19 Cognisance of Offences [Section 11]
- 5.20 Protection of Action taken in Good Faith
- 5.21 Act to Override Other Enactments
- 5.22 Power to make Rules
- 5.23 Display of Abstract of the Act and Rules
- • Questions for Discussion

Labour welfare and Social security are the major aspects of national programmes towards bettering the lot of workers and creating a life and work environment of decent comfort for this class of population. Social security of workers refers to protection provided to the workers against providential mishaps over which they have no control.

The idea of social security implies that the State shall make itself responsible for ensuring some minimum standard of material welfare to its citizens to cover various main contingencies of life. Childhood and old age are the two stages of dependency in the life of a man. The social security system aims to help individuals in such time of dependency. Besides this, there are many risks of insecurity to which human life is liable.

the main risks of insecurity are incidents of life occurring right from childhood up to old age and death and they mainly include sickness, invalidity, accidents, industrial disease, unemployment, old age, death of the bread-winner and other such emergencies.

Considering these aspects, various social security measures are required to be introduced and implemented. In India, there is a network of legislation which provides for social security for the workers.

The Workmen's Compensation Act of 1923; The Employee's State Insurance Act of 1948; The Maternity Benefit Act of 1961; The Employee's Provident Funds and Miscellaneous Provisions Act of 1952; The Payment of Gratuity Act of 1972 and other such Acts have been passed to provide social security to workers in India. In this chapter, various important provisions of the Payment of Gratuity Act of 1972 are considered.

Prior to enactment of the Payment of Gratuity Act of 1972, there was no Central Act in existence to regulate the payment of gratuity to industrial workers except the Working Journalists (Conditions of Service) and Miscellaneous Provisions Act of 1955. However, the Government of Kerala enacted legislation in 1970-71 for the payment of gratuity to workers employed in factories, plantations, shops and establishments. The Governor of West Bengal promulgated an ordinance on 3rd June, 1971 prescribing a scheme of gratuity. The ordinance was subsequently replaced by the West Bengal Payment of Compulsory Gratuity Act of 1971. After the enactment of the above mentioned two Acts, some other State Governments also voiced their intention of enacting similar measures in their respective states. Therefore, a central law on the subject became necessary to ensure a uniform pattern of payment of gratuity to the employees throughout the country. As a result, the Payment of Gratuity Act of 1972 was passed by the Parliament in August, 1972. It came into force on 16th September, 1972. It was amended in 1984, 1987, 1994, 1998 and the latest amendment to the Act was made in 2010.

5.1 Nature of Gratuity Payment

Provident Fund and pension are retirement benefits. Gratuity is also one kind of retirement benefit. It is, in fact, a payment to be made to the employees to help them after their retirement whether such retirement is the result of the rules of superannuation or of some physical disability. Any employee should be entitled to claim a certain amount of payment as a retirement benefit for his faithful service over a certain period of his employment is the general principle underlying any gratuity scheme. This implies that a gratuity is received by an employee as a reward for meritorious and long service.

5.2 Objects of the Payment of Gratuity Act of 1972

The basic objects of the Payment of Gratuity Act of 1972 are –
(1) To ensure a uniform pattern of payment of gratuity to the employees throughout the country.
(2) To avoid different treatment to the employees of establishments which have branches in more than one state when the employees are liable to transfers from one state to another under the conditions of their service.
(3) To provide, according to the provisions of the Act, to pay the amount of gratuity to an employee on his superannuation, or on his retirement, or on his resignation, or on his death, or total disablement due to accident or disease as the case may be.

5.3 Important Features of the Payment of Gratuity Act, 1972

From the various provisions of the Payment of Gratuity Act of 1972, we come to know certain important features of the Act which are as follows:

(a) Meaning and Nature of Gratuity:

Gratuity is a lump sum payment to an employee when he retires or leaves his service. It is basically a retirement benefit to an employee so that he can live life comfortably after his retirement. However, gratuity is payable even to an employee who resigns after completing at least **Five** years of service under the Payment of Gratuity Act of 1972.

(b) Application of the Act:

The Act applies to every factory, mine, plantation, shop and establishment when ten or more persons are employed. It is also applicable to motor transport undertakings, club, chambers of commerce and associates, local bodies, solicitors' offices employing 10 or more persons.

(c) Employees Eligible for Gratuity:

The Act applies to all employees, workers employed in all those organisations to which this Act is applicable.

Gratuity is payable to an employee on (i) resignation, (ii) termination of service on account of death or disablement due to accident or disease, (iii) retirement. Gratuity is normally payable only after an employee completes five years of continuous service. However, in case of death or disablement of an employee, the condition of minimum service of Five years is not applicable. The Act is applicable to all employees irrespective of the amount of his salary. Earlier ceiling on the amount of salary was there. But that ceiling on salary of ₹ 2,500 was removed w.e.f. 24th May, 1994 by an amendment to the Act.

(d) Requirement of the Act in respect of 'Continuous Service':

For the purpose of the payment, an employee must be in continuous service is one of the essential conditions. But when an employee remains absent on account of leave, accident, sickness, lay-off, lock-out or strike, the employee is treated on 'continuous service'.

(e) Amount of Gratuity Payable:

Gratuity is payable @ **Fifteen** days' wages for every year of completed service. If the employee has completed more than **six** months in the last year of his service, it will be treated as full year for the purpose of gratuity.

In the case of seasonal employment, gratuity is payable @ **Seven** days' wages for each season. Wages for the purpose of gratuity consist of basic salary plus D.A. as per last drawn salary. Allowances like bonus, H.R.A., overtime, commission, etc. are not considered for the purpose of calculating gratuity. It should be noted that employees who are paid on monthly wages basis, wages per day should be calculated by dividing monthly salary by **Twenty six** days in order to arrive at daily wages.

At present, the maximum gratuity payable under the Act is ₹ **Ten** lakhs. However, employers can offer better terms to their employees than those specified under the Act.

(f) Compulsory Insurance of Gratuity Liability:

Provisions have been made in the Act for compulsory insurance of employer's liability to pay gratuity to their employees or in the alternate for setting up of a gratuity funds in relation to establishments employing 500 or more employees in Section 4-A. This Section 4-A has been inserted by the Payment of Gratuity Amendment Act of 1987 made effective from 1st October 1987.

(g) Nomination:

We find the provisions relating to nomination in Section 6 of the Payment of Gratuity Act of 1972. Rules relating to nominations have also been made in Payment of Gratuity (Central) Rules, 1972.

(h) Payment of the Amount of Gratuity:

Section 4 (1) provides for the time of payment of gratuity. It states that, "Gratuity shall be payable to an employee on the termination of his employment after he has rendered continuous service for not less than five years –

(a) on his superannuation, or
(b) on his retirement or resignation, or
(c) on his death or disablement due to accident or disease

It is provided that the completion of continuous service of five years shall not be necessary where the termination of the employment of any employee is due to death or disablement. [Proviso 1 to Section 4 (1)].

It is further provided that in the case of death of the employee, gratuity payable to him shall be paid to his nominee or, if no nomination has been made, to his heirs, and where any such nominees or heirs is a minor, the share of such minor, shall be deposited with the controlling authority who shall invest the same for the benefit of such minor in such bank or other financial institution, as may be prescribed, until such minor attains majority. [Proviso 2 to Section 4 (1)].

For the purposes of this section, disablement means something that incapacitates an employee for the work which he was capable of performing before the accident or disease. [Explanation to Section 4 (1)]. The employer is under obligation to pay the gratuity within **Thirty** days from the date it becomes payable.

(i) Gratuity cannot be Attached:

Gratuity payable to an employee cannot be attached in execution of any decree or order of any civil, revenue or criminal court according to the provisions of Section 13 of the Payment of Gratuity Act of 1972.

(j) Forfeiture and Deduction of Gratuity:

Provisions relating to forfeiture and deduction of gratuity have been made in Section 4 (6). This section states the case in which gratuity payable to an employee can be forfeited; notwithstanding anything contained in Section 4 (1).

According to Section 4 (6) (a), "the gratuity of an employee, whose services have been terminated for any act, wilful omission or negligence causing any damage or loss to, or destruction of, property belonging to the employer, shall be forfeited to the extent of the damage or loss so caused".

While Section 4 (6) (b) states that, "the gratuity payable to an employee may be wholly or partially forfeited" –
  (i) if the services of such an employee have been terminated for his riotous or disorderly conduct or any other act of violence on his part, or
  (ii) if the services of such employee have been terminated for any act which constitutes an offence involving moral turpitude, provided that such an offence is committed by him in the course of his employment.

Gratuity is paid to the employees besides other objectives for their good behaviour or conduct in their period of employment which must be more than five years. But, when an employee is dismissed for misconduct, he cannot be deprived altogether of the benefit of gratuity to be received for his services. He must be paid his dues of gratuity after deducting the loss, if any, caused because of his misconduct to his employer. However, in the case of theft, which is an offence involving moral turpitude, the gratuity payable to an employee under the provisions of this Act stands forfeited in view of Section 4 (6) (b) (ii).

(k) Recovery of Gratuity:

As gratuity is a compulsory payment according to the provisions of this Act, it must be paid to an employee on fulfilling the conditions laid down in the Act by his employer. If the amount of gratuity payable under this Act is not paid by the employer within the time limit prescribed for the payment, he must make an application to the controlling authority. On receiving the application by the aggrieved person, the controlling authority issues the certificate for that amount to the collector who recovers the same together with compound interest. The provisions relating to the recovery of the amount of gratuity are made in Section 8 which are as follows:

"If the amount of gratuity payable under this Act is not paid by the employer, within the prescribed time, to the person entitled thereto, the controlling authority shall, on an application made to it in this behalf by the aggrieved person, issue a certificate for that amount to the Collector, who shall recover the same, together with compound interest thereon at such rate as the Central Government may, by notification, specify from the date of expiry of the prescribed time, as arrears of land revenue and pay the same to the person entitled thereto". [Section 8].

It is also provided that the controlling authority shall, before issuing a certificate under this section, give the employer a reasonable opportunity of showing cause against the issue of such certificate [Proviso 1 to Section 8].

It is also provided that the amount payable under this Section 8 shall, in no case, exceed the amount of gratuity payable under this Act.

(*l*) Appoint of Inspectors:

Provisions have been made in the Act to appoint Inspectors. Necessary powers are given to the Inspectors to perform the duties entrusted to them under the Act.

(m) Provisions for imposing penalties:

Provisions have been made in Section 9 of this Act for imposing penalties for false statement, for false representation and also for contravention of the provisions of the Act.

5.4 Scope and Extent of the Act

The Act expressly provides for a scheme of compulsory payment of gratuity by the management of factories, mines, oilfields, plantations, ports, railway companies, shops and other establishments to which the Act applies in the event of superannuation, retirement, resignation and death or disablement due to accident or disease.

As regards the quantum of gratuity, the Act provides that for every completed year of service or part thereof in excess of six months, the employer is liable to pay to his employee at the rate of fifteen days' wages for every completed year of service or part thereof in excess of six months subject to a maximum of ₹ Three lakhs and fifty thousand.

Though a workman has the right to claim gratuity, this right to claim gratuity of a workman can be forfeited by his employer under certain circumstances [Section 4 (6)]. The gratuity of an employee can be forfeited to the extent of the damages or loss caused to the property of the employer by the wilful negligence or omission by his employee whose services have been terminated for any such act. The gratuity of an employee can be wholly forfeited provided that the services of such employee have been terminated for his disorderly conduct or riotous conduct or for any other violent act on his part or for any offence involving moral turpitude committed by him during the course of his employment. However, provisions have been made in the Act relating to grant of exemption by notification of appropriate Government and also for the settlement of any dispute relating to the amount of gratuity payable to an employee under the Act. Provisions also have been made in the Act relating to the admissibility of any claim for payment of gratuity, recovery of gratuity from defaulting employer's penalties for offences, protection of action in good faith etc.

Section 1 (2), makes it clear that the Act extends to the whole of India. However, it is expressly provided that in so far as it relates to plantations or ports, it shall not extend to the State of Jammu and Kashmir.

Scope of coverage of this Act is made clear in Sections 1 (3) and 3 (A).

Section 1 (3) states that the Act shall apply to –

(a) every factory, mine, oilfield, plantation, port and railway company;

(b) every shop or establishment within the meaning of any law for the time being in force in relation to shops and establishments in a State, in which ten or more persons are employed, or were employed, on any day of the preceding twelve months;

(c) such other establishments or class of establishments, in which ten or more employees are employed, or were employed, on any day of the preceding twelve months, as the Central Government may, by notification, specify in this behalf.

While Section 3 (A) states that, "A shop or establishment to which this Act has become applicable shall continue to be governed by this Act notwithstanding that the number of persons employed therein at any time after it has become so applicable falls below ten". The main intention to make this provision is obviously to check the tendency among the employers to reduce artificially the number of employees so as to get out of coverage under this Payment of Gratuity Act. It should also be noted that the municipalities are also covered by Section 1 (3) in view of giving more extensive application as this Act is a social legislation.

The Act has been applied to the following establishments in which ten or more persons are employed or were employed on any day of the preceding twelve months w.e.f. the dates and the notifications against each.

(1)	Motor Transport	w.e.f. 8-4-1974	G.S.R. 415, dt. 8-4-1974
(2)	Clubs	w.e.f. 8-10-1979	G.S.R. 1255, dt. 17-9-1979
(3)	Chambers of Commerce and Industry and Associated / Federation of Chambers of Commerce and Industry	w.e.f. 15-11-1980	S.O. 3203, dt. 30-10-1980
(4)	Inland Water Transport Establishments	w.e.f. 10-1-1981	S.O. 133, dt. 24-12-1980
(5)	Local Bodies	w.e.f. 23-1-1982	S.O. 239, dt. 8-1-1982
(6)	Solicitor's offices	w.e.f. 9-1-1982	S.O. 111, dt. 28-12-1982

However, the Act does not apply to apprentices and persons holding civil posts under the Central Government or a State Government and are governed by any other Act or by the rules providing for the payment of gratuity.

Section 5 (1) empowers the Government to exempt, subject to the conditions as may be specified in the notification, any establishment, factory, mine etc. to which this Act is applicable from the operation of the provisions of this Act, if in the opinion of the appropriate Government, the employees in such establishment, factory, mine etc. are in receipt of gratuity or pension benefits not less favourable than the benefits conferred under this Act.

5.5 Definitions

The definitions of various terms, words, concepts pertaining to the provisions of this Act are given in Section 2. These definitions are as follows:

Appropriate Government [Section 2 (a)]:

"Appropriate Government", means –
(i) in relation to an establishment -
  (a) belonging to, or under the control of the Central Government,
  (b) having branches in more than one State,
  (c) of a factory belonging to, or under the control of the Central Government,
  (d) of a major port, mine, oilfield or railway company, the Central Government,
(ii) in any other case, the State Government.

Thus, in relation to establishments mentioned above in (a) to (d) clauses, the Central Government is an appropriate Government. While in any other case, the State Government is an appropriate Government.

Continuous Service [Section 2 (c) and Section 2-A]:

The payment of gratuity is a retirement benefit. For the purpose of getting this benefit, the service of an employee should be a continuous one. However, interrupted service by the reason of leave, sickness, lay-off, strike etc. not due to any fault of an employee concerned should not be treated as a break in his continuous service. Considering this point, the concept of continuous service is defined. According to Section 2 (c), continuous service means continuous service as defined in Section 2-A. Section 2-A is as follows:

"For the purposes of this Act –
(1) an employee shall be said to be in continuous service for a period if he has, for that period, been in uninterrupted service, including service which may be interrupted on account of sickness, accident, leave, absence from duty without leave (not being an absence in respect of which an order treating the absence as a break in service has been passed in accordance with the standing orders, rules or regulations governing the employees of the establishment), lay-off, strike or a lock-out or cessation of work not due to any fault of the employee, whether such uninterrupted or interrupted service was rendered before or after the commencement of this Act [Section 2-A (1)];
(2) where an employee (not being an employee employed in a seasonal establishment) is not in continuous service within the meaning of clause (1), for any period of one year or six months, he shall be deemed to be in continuous service under the employer –
    (a) for the said period of one year, if the employee during the period of twelve calendar months preceding the date with reference to which calculation is to be made, has actually worked under the employer for not less than –
        (i) one hundred and ninety days, in the case of an employee employed below the ground in a mine or in an establishment which works for less than six days in a week; and
        (ii) two hundred and forty days, in any other case;
    (b) for the said period of six months, if the employee during the period of six calendar months preceding the date with reference to which the calculation is to be made, has actually worked under the employer for not less than –
        (i) ninety-five days, in the case of an employee employed below the ground in a mine or in an establishment which works for less than six days in a week; and
        (ii) one hundred and twenty days, in any other case [Section 2-A (2)];

For the purposes of clause (2), the number of days on which an employee has actually worked under an employer shall include the days on which –
   (i) he has been laid-off under an agreement or as permitted by standing orders made under the Industrial Employment (Standing Orders) Act, 1946 (20 of 1946), or under the Industrial Disputes Act, 1947 (14 of 1947), or under any other law applicable to the establishment;
   (ii) he has been on leave with full wages, earned in the previous year;
   (iii) he has been absent due to temporary disablement caused by an accident arising out of and in the course of his employment; and

(iv) in the case of a female, she has been on maternity leave; so, however, that the total period of such maternity leave does not exceed twelve weeks [Explanation to Section 2-A (2)].

(3) where an employee, employed in a seasonal establishment, is not in continuous service within the meaning of clause (1), for any period of one year or six months, he shall be deemed to be in continuous service under the employer for such period if he has actually worked for not less than seventy-five percent of the number of days on which the establishment was in operation during such period [Section 2-A (3)].

Completed Year of Service [Section 2 (b)]:

According to Section 2 (b), completed year of service means continuous service for one year.

Controlling Authority [Section 2 (d)]:

Controlling authority means an authority appointed by the appropriate Government under Section 3. Section 3 is reproduced as follows.

"The appropriate Government, may, by notification, appoint any officer to be a controlling authority, who shall be responsible for the administration of this Act and different controlling authorities may be appointed for different areas".

The provision of Section 3 implies that the controlling officer is responsible for the administration of this Act.

Employee [Section 2 (e)]:

(e) "Employee" means any person (other than an apprentice) employed on wages in any establishment, factory, mine, oilfield, plantation, port, railway company or shop, to do any skilled, semi-skilled, or unskilled, manual, supervisory, technical or clerical work, whether the terms of such employment are expressed or implied, and whether or not such person is employed in a managerial or administrative capacity, but does not include any such person who holds a post under the Central Government or a State Government and is governed by any other Act or by any rules providing for payment of gratuity [Section 2 (e)].

The definition of an employee is quite comprehensive. An employee does not include an apprentice nor a person holding a post under the Central or State Government and is governed by any other Act or by any other rules providing payment of gratuity. Explanation to this Section 2 (e) making clear the wage limit of an employee has been omitted by the Payment of Gratuity Amendment Act of 1994 with effect from 24-5-1994.

Employer [Section 2 (f)]:

According to Section 2 (f)

"Employer" means, in relation to any establishment, factory, mine, oilfield, plantation, port, railway company or shop –

(i) belonging to, or under the control of the Central Government or a State Government, a person or authority appointed by the appropriate Government for

the supervision and control of employees, or where no person or authority has been so appointed, the head of the Ministry or the Department concerned,
 (ii) belonging to, or under the control of, any local authority, the person appointed by such authority for the supervision and control of employees or where no person has been so appointed, the chief executive officer of the local authority,
 (iii) in any other case, the person, who, or the authority which, has the ultimate control over the affairs of the establishment, factory, mine, oilfield, plantation, port, railway company or shop, and where the said affairs are entrusted to any other person, whether called a manager, managing director or by any other name.

Factory [Section 2 (g)]:

For the purposes of this Act, 'Factory' has the same meaning as assigned to it in clause (m) of Section 2 of the Factories Act of 1948.

According to Section 2 (m), 'Factory' means any premises including the precincts thereof –
 (i) whereon 10 or more workers are working or were working on any day of the preceding 12 months, and in any part of which a manufacturing process is being carried on with the aid of power, or is ordinarily so carried on, or
 (ii) wheren 20 or more workers are working or were working on any day of the preceding 12 months, and in any part of which a manufacturing process is being carried out without the aid of power, or is ordinarily so carried out.

The term 'factory' does not include a mine subject to the operation of the Indian Mines Act, 1952 or a mobile unit belonging to the armed forces of the Union, a railway running shed or a hotel, restaurant or eating place.

Family [Section 2 (h)]:

According to Section 2 (h), "family", in relation to an employee, shall be deemed to consist of –
 (i) in the case of a male employee, himself, his wife, his children, whether married or unmarried, his dependent parents [and the dependent parents of his wife and the widow] and children of his pre-deceased son, if any;
 (ii) in the case of a female employee, herself, her husband, her children, whether married or unmarried, her dependent parents and the dependent parents of her husband and the widow and children of her pre-deceased son, if any.

However, where the personal law of an employee permits the adoption by him of a child, any child lawfully adopted by him shall be deemed to be included in his family, and where a child of an employee has been adopted by another person and such adoption is, under the personal law of the person making such adoption lawful, such child shall be deemed to be excluded from the family of the employee [Explanation to Section 2 (f)].

Major Port [Section 2 (i)]:

"Major port" has the meaning assigned to it in clause (8) of Section 3 of the Indian Ports Act, 1908 (15 of 1908);

Mine [Section 2 (j)]:

"Mine" has the meaning assigned to it in clause (j) of sub-section (1) of Section 2 of the Mines Act, 1952 (35 of 1952);

Notification [Section 2 (k)]:

"Notification" means a notification published in the Official Gazette;

Oilfield [Section 2 (l)]:

"Oilfield" has the meaning assigned to it in clause (e) of Section 3 of the Oilfields (Regulation and Development) Act, 1948 (53 of 1948);

Plantation [Section 2 (m)]:

"Plantation" has the meaning assigned to it in clause (f) of Section 2 of the Plantations Labour Act, 1951 (69 of 1951);

Port [Section 2 (n)]:

"Port" has the meaning assigned to it in clause (4) of Section 3 of the Indian Ports Act, 1908 (15 of 1908);

Prescribed [Section 2 (o)]:

"Prescribed" means prescribed by rules made under this Act;

Railway Company [Section 2 (p)]:

"Railway company" has the meaning assigned to it in clause (5) of Section 3 of the Indian Railways Act, 1809 (9 of 1890);

Retirement [Section 2 (q)]:

"Retirement" means termination of the service of an employee otherwise than on superannuation;

Superannuation [Section 2 (r)]:

"Superannuation", in relation to an employee, means the attainment by the employee of such age as is fixed in the contract or conditions of service as the age on the attainment of which the employee shall vacate the employment.

Wages [Section 2 (s)]:

"Wages" means all emoluments which are earned by an employee while on duty or on leave in accordance with the terms and conditions of his employment and which are paid or are payable to him in cash and include dearness allowance but does not include any bonus, commission, house rent allowance, overtime wages and any other allowance.

5.6 Payment of Gratuity

Section 4 of the Act throws light on the circumstances under which gratuity becomes payable to an employee. The payment of gratuity by an employer to his employees as defined under this Act is mandatory. However, provisions have been made in this Act to forfeit the gratuity. Section 4 also deals with the cases when gratuity can be forfeited.

5.6.1 When is Gratuity Payable?

Section 4 (1) states that, "Gratuity shall be payable to an employee on the termination of his employment after he has rendered continuous service for not less than five years –

(a) on his superannuation, or
(b) on his retirement or resignation, or
(c) on his death or disablement due to accident or disease.

It is provided that the completion of continuous service of five years shall not be necessary where the termination of the employment of any employee is due to death or disablement [Proviso 1 to Section 4 (1)].

It is further provided that in the case of death of the employee, gratuity payable to him shall be paid to his nominee or, if no nomination has been made, to his heirs, and where any such nominees or heirs is a minor, the share of such minor, shall be deposited with the controlling authority who shall invest the same for the benefit of such minor in such bank or other financial institution, as may be prescribed, until such minor attains majority [Proviso 2 to Section 4 (1)].

For the purposes of this section, disablement means such disablement as incapacitates an employee for the work which he was capable of performing before the accident or disease resulting in such disablement [Explanation to Section 4 (1)].

Some important points relating to the payment of gratuity are as follows:

(1) Gratuity is payable to an employee, (a) on the termination of his employment after he has rendered continuous service for not less than five years. The meaning of continuous service is given in Section 2-A; (b) or on his superannuation, where an employee continues his service even after the date of superannuation, he is entitled to receive gratuity for the full period of his service and not merely up to the age of superannuation; or (c) on his resignation; or (d) on his retirement; or (e) on his death; or (f) on becoming disable due to accident or disease. Here disablement implies such disablement which incapacitates an employee to do the work which he was capable of doing before the accident or disease..

(2) The completion of continuous service of five years is not necessary when the termination of the employment of any employee is due to either death or disablement.

(3) In the case of the death of an employee, gratuity payable to him must be paid to his nominee. However, if no such nomination is made, it is to be paid to his heirs. If any of such nominees or heirs is a minor, the share of such minor is to be deposited with the controlling authority. The appropriate Government appoints, by notification, an officer as a controlling authority who is responsible for the administration of this Act. Different controlling authorities are appointed for the different areas. It is the responsibility of the concerned controlling authority to invest the amount of gratuity for the benefit of a minor in such bank or in any other financial institutions, as may be prescribed, until such minor attains majority.

(4) Section 4 (4) provides for the computation of the gratuity payable to an employee employed on reduced wages after his disablement. It states that, "for the purpose of computing the gratuity payable to an employee who is employed, after his disablement, on reduced wages, his wages for the period preceding his disablement shall be taken to be the wages received by him during that period, and his wages for the period subsequent to his disablement shall be taken to be the wages as so reduced".

5.6.2 Rate of Gratuity

Section 4 (2) deals with the rate of gratuity. While making the provisions relating to fixing the rate of gratuity to be paid to employees, attention has also been paid to the piece-rated employees and employees working in seasonal establishments.

Section 4 (2) lays down that, "for every completed year of service or part thereof in excess of six months, the employer shall pay gratuity to an employee at the rate of fifteen days' wages based on the rate of wages last drawn by the employee concerned".

It is provided that in the case of a piece-rated employee, daily wages shall be computed on the average of the total wages received by him for a period of three months immediately preceding the termination of his employment, and, for this purpose, the wages paid for any overtime work shall not be taken into account [Proviso 1 to Section 4 (2)].

It is further provided that in the case of an employee who is employed in a seasonal establishment and who is not so employed throughout the year, the employer shall pay the gratuity at the rate of seven days' wages for each season [Proviso 2 to Section 4 (2)].

In the case of a monthly rated employee, the fifteen day's wages shall be calculated by dividing the monthly rate of wages last drawn by him by twenty-six and multiplying the quotient by fifteen [Explanation to Section 4 (2)].

A month is a period of 30 days including days of rest and holidays. If wages are to be calculated on monthly rate, 15 days' wages would be what an employee would earn within the period of 15 days and not in 15 working days [Swamy V. Controlling Authority, Hyderabad, 1978. Lab. I.C. 1285].

5.6.3 Maximum Amount of Gratuity

The amount of gratuity payable to an employee shall not exceed "₹ **Three Lakhs and Fifty Thousand**" [Section 4 (3)]. The Amendment Act of 1987 replaced the then existing ceiling of 20 months' wages for payment of gratuity by a monetary ceiling of ₹ 50,000. Then the Amendment Act of 1994 (w.e.f. 24-5-1994) increased the amount of maximum gratuity to ₹ One lakh and thereafter, the Payment of Gratuity (Amendment) Act of 1998 increased this limit to ₹ Three lakhs and fifty thousand. Further, by amending the Act in 2010, this limit has been increased to ₹ **Ten Lakhs**.

5.7 Calculation of Gratuity

We have considered various aspects such as when the gratuity is payable, rate of gratuity, maximum amount of gratuity etc. Now, let us study how the amount of gratuity payable to an employee is calculated by taking a few illustrations.

Illustration 1:
Mr. A is the employee whose last drawn salary which included basic salary and DA is ₹ 5,200/- per month. He has completed **Thirty Five** years of service. Calculate the amount of gratuity payable to him.

Solution:
The last drawn salary which includes basic salary and D.A. is ₹ 5,200 per month. Hence, his salary per day is ₹ 200 [₹ 5,200 divided by 26].

Therefore, he is entitled to get the gratuity of ₹ 3,000 [15 days multiplied by ₹ 200] for every year of completed service. He has served for 35 years continuously. So, he is entitled to get a gratuity of ₹ 1,05,000 [₹ 3,000 multiplied by 35 years].

Thus, the gratuity payable to Mr. A is ₹ 1,05,000.

Illustration 2:
Mr. Malik has served 30 years continuously and retired. His basic salary is ₹ 2,000, D.A. ₹ 1,120. Commission ₹ 1,000, House Rent ₹ 700 per month on his retirement. Calculate the amount of gratuity payable to Mr. Malik.

Solution:
For the purpose of calculating gratuity payable to Mr. Malik, we have to consider only his basic salary and D.A. Other allowances like H.R.A.; Commission etc. are not to be considered for calculating the amount of gratuity.

Hence, his last drawn salary comes to ₹ 3,120 [Basic Salary ₹ 2,000 plus D.A. ₹ 1,120]. It means his salary per day is ₹ 120 [₹ 3,120 divided by 26] and he is entitled to get the gratuity of ₹ 1,800 [15 days multiplied by ₹ 120] for every year of completed service.

As his total eligible service for the purpose of getting gratuity is 30 years, he is entitled to receive the gratuity of ₹ 54,000 [₹ 1,800 multiplied by 30 years].

Thus, the gratuity payable to Mr. Malik is ₹ 54,000/-.

Illustration 3:
Mr. Parag Ghamandi's monthly wages at the time of retirement were ₹ 4,004. He retired after 20 years and 4 months continuous service. Calculate the amount of gratuity payable to him.

Solution:

Facts:
1. Mr. Parag Ghamandi's last drawn monthly salary - ₹ 4,004.
2. His continuous service on retirement - 20 years and 4 months. But for calculating gratuity his continuous service - 20 years. It is so because if an employee completes more than **six** months in the last year of his service, then it is treated as a full year for the purpose of gratuity.
3. His salary per day - ₹ 154 [₹ 4,004 ÷ 26 days]
4. He is entitled to get gratuity for every year of completed service –
   ₹ 2,310 [₹ 154 daily salary × 15 days].
5. Total gratuity payable to him - ₹ 46,200 [₹ 2,310 multiplied by 20 years of continuous service].

Thus, the gratuity payable to Mr. Parag Ghamandi is ₹ 46,200/-.

5.8 Provisions relating to Better Terms of Gratuity

Sometimes an employee may get more amount and better terms of gratuity under an award or contract or agreement with his employer. Hence, it is stated in Section 4 (5) that, "Nothing in this section shall affect the right of an employee to receive better terms of gratuity under any award or agreement or contract with the employer". This simply implies that the provisions of Section 4 do not affect any right of an employee if he is to get more beneficial terms of gratuity from his employer under contract or agreement made with him. Thus, the scheme envisaged by the enactment not only secures the minimum of gratuity for the employees but the Act also provides for better terms of gratuity wherever possible.

5.9 Forfeiture of Gratuity

Provisions relating to forfeiture of gratuity have been made in Section 4 (6). This section states the case in which gratuity payable to an employee can be forfeited; notwithstanding anything contained in Section 4 (1).

According to Section 4 (6) (a), "the gratuity of an employee, whose services have been terminated for any act, wilful omission or negligence causing any damage or loss to, or destruction of property belonging to the employer, shall be forfeited to the extent of the damage or loss so caused".

While Section 4 (6) (b) states that, the gratuity payable to an employee may be wholly or partially forfeited –

(i) if the services of such an employee have been terminated for his riotous or disorderly conduct or any other act of violence on his part, or

(ii) if the services of such an employee have been terminated for any act which constitutes an offence involving moral turpitude, provided that such offence is committed by him in course of his employment.

Gratuity is paid to the employees besides other objectives for their good behaviour or conduct in their period of employment which must be more than five years. But, when an employee is dismissed for misconduct, he cannot be deprived altogether of benefit of gratuity to be received for his services. He must be paid his dues of gratuity after deducting the loss, if any, caused because of his misconduct to his employer. However, in the case of theft, which is an offence involving moral turpitude, the gratuity payable to an employee under the provisions of this Act stands forfeited in view of Section 4 (6) (b) (ii).

5.10 Power of an Appropriate Government to Exempt

There are three sub-sections of Section 5 which throw light on the power of an appropriate Government to exempt. Section 5 (1) empowers the appropriate Government to exempt by notification in the Official Gazette any establishment, factory, mine etc. to which this Act applies from the operation of the provisions of this Act under certain circumstances. Section 5 (2) has been incorporated in the Act by the Payment of Gratuity (Second) Amendment Act of 1984 which authorises the appropriate Government to exempt any employee or class of employees in similar circumstances. While Section 5 (3) authorises the appropriate Government to issue notification restrospectively. However, it is also made clear that such notification shall not be issued so as to prejudicially affect the interests of any person. Section 5 is reproduced as follows.

"The appropriate Government may, by notification, and subject to such conditions as may be specified in the notification, exempt any establishment, factory, mine, oilfield, plantation, port, railway company or shop to which this Act applies from the operation of the provisions of this Act if, in the opinion of the appropriate Government, the employees in such establishment, factory, mine, oilfield, plantation, port, railway company or shop are in receipt of gratuity or pensionary benefits not less favourable than the benefits conferred under this Act" [Section 5 (1)].

"The appropriate Government may, by notification and subject to such conditions as may be specified in the notification, exempt any employee or class of employees employed in any establishment, factory, mine, oilfield, plantation, port, railway company or shop to which this Act applies from the operation of the provisions of this Act, if, in the opinion of the appropriate Government, such employee or class of employees are in receipt of gratuity or pensionary benefits not less favourable than the benefits conferred under this Act" [Section 5 (2)].

"A notification issued under sub-section (1) or sub-section (2) may be issued retrospectively a date not earlier than the date of commencement of this Act, but no such notification shall be issued so as to prejudicially affect the interests of any person" [Section 5 (3)].

5.11 Compulsory Insurance [Section 4-A]

Provisions have been made in the Act for compulsory insurance of employer's liability to pay gratuity to his employees or in the alternate for setting up of a gratuity fund in relation to establishments employing 500 or more employees in Section 4-A. This Section 4-A has been inserted by the Payment of Gratuity Amendment Act of 1987 made effective from 1st October 1987. Section 4-A is as follows:

(1) With effect from such date as may be notified by the appropriate Government in this behalf, every employer, other than an employer or an establishment belonging to, or under the control of, the Central Government or a State Government, shall, subject to the provisions of sub-section (2), obtain an insurance in the manner prescribed, for his liability for payment towards the gratuity under this Act, from the Life Insurance Corporation of India established under the Life Insurance Corporation of India Act, 1956 (31 of 1956) or any other prescribed insurer [Section 4-A (1)].

It is provided that different dates may be appointed for different establishments or class of establishments or for different areas [Proviso to Section 4-A (1)].

(2) The appropriate Government may, subject to such conditions as may be prescribed, exempt every employer who had already established an approved gratuity fund in respect of his employees and who desires to continue such arrangement, and every employer employing five hundred or more persons who establishes an approved gratuity fund in the manner prescribed from the provisions of sub-section (1). [Section 4-A (2)].

(3) For the purpose of effectively implementing the provisions of this section, every employer shall within such time as may be prescribed get his establishment registered with the controlling authority in the prescribed manner and no employer shall be registered under the provisions of this section unless he has taken an insurance referred to in sub-section (1) or has established an approved gratuity fund referred to in sub-section (2) [Section 4-A (3)].

(4) The appropriate Government may, by notification, make rules to give effect to the provisions of this section and such rules may provide for the composition of the Board of Trustees of the approved gratuity fund and for the recovery by the controlling authority of the amount of the gratuity payable to an employee from the Life Insurance Corporation of India or any other insurer with whom an insurance has been taken under sub-section (1), or as the case may be, the Board of Trustees of the approved gratuity fund [Section 4-A (4)].

(5) Where an employer fails to make any payment by way of premium to the insurance referred to in sub-section (1) or by way of contribution to an approved gratuity fund referred to in sub-section (2), he shall be liable to pay the amount of gratuity due under this Act (including interest, if any, for delayed payments) forthwith to the controlling authority [Section 4-A (5)].

(6) Whoever contravenes the provisions of sub-section (5) shall be punishable with fine which may extend to ten thousand rupees and in the case of a continuing offence with a further fine which may extend to one thousand rupees for each day during which the offence continues [Section 4-A (6)].

Explanation: In this section "approved gratuity fund" shall have the same meaning as in clause (5) of Section 2 of the Income-tax Act, 1961 (43 of 1961) [Explanation to Section 4-A].

Thus, according to Section 4-A (1), it is the responsibility of every employer to obtain an insurance for his liability in respect of payment of gratuity under this Act from the Life Insurance Corporation or any other prescribed insurer as notified by the appropriate Government in this behalf. Provisions of Section 4-A (1) do not apply to an employer or an establishment belonging to, or under the control of the Central or State Government. However, according to the provisions of Section 4-A (2), the Appropriate Government may exempt (1) every employer who has already established an approved gratuity fund in respect of his employees and desiring to continue such agreement and (2) every employer employing 500 or more persons who establishes an approved gratuity fund in the manner prescribed from the provisions of Section 4-A (1).

Provisions of Section 4-A (3) make it clear that every employer has to get his establishment registered within such time as may be prescribed with the controlling authority in the prescribed manner. An employer shall not be registered under the provisions of Section 4-A unless he has taken an insurance referred to in Section 4-A (1) or established an approved gratuity fund referred to in Section 4-A (2).

The Appropriate Government is empowered to make rules by notification in the Official Gazette to give effect to the provisions of this Section [Section 4-A (4)]. Section 4-A (4) further provides that the rules thus made may provide for the composition of the Board of

Trustees of the approved controlling authority of the amount of the gratuity payable to an employee from the Life Insurance Corporation or any other insurer with whom an insurance has been taken under Section 4-A (1) or as the case may be, the Board of Trustees of the approved gratuity fund.

The provisions also have been made in Section 4-A (5) for the failure to pay insurance premium or contribution, if any. It states that where an employee fails to make any payment by way of premium to the insurance referred to in Section 4-A (1) or by way of contribution to an approved gratuity fund as referred to in Section 4-A (2), such employer is liable to pay the amount of gratuity due under this Act, including interest for delayed payments, forthwith to the controlling authority. Whoever contravenes these provisions of Section 4-A (5) is punishable with fine which may extend to ten thousand rupees and in the case of continuing offence with a further fine which may extend to one thousand rupees for each day during which the offence continues [Section 4-A (6)].

5.12 Nomination

Provisions relating to nomination exist in Section 6 of the Payment of Gratuity Act of 1972. Rules relating to nominations have also been made in Payment of Gratuity (Central) Rules, 1972. The provisions of Section 6 and rules pertaining to nominations are given as follows.

Section 6: Nomination:

(1) Each employee, who has completed one year of service, shall make, within such time, in such form and in such manner, as may be prescribed, nomination for the purpose of the second proviso to sub-section (1) of Section 4 [Section 6 (1)].

(2) An employee may, in his nomination, distribute the amount of gratuity payable to him under this Act amongst more than one nominee [Section 6 (2)].

(3) If an employee has a family at the time of making a nomination, the nomination shall be made in favour of one or more members of his family, and any nomination made by such employee in favour of a person who is not a member of his family, shall be void [Section 6 (3)].

(4) If at the time of making a nomination the employee has no family, the nomination may be made in favour of any person or persons but if the employee subsequently acquires a family, such nomination shall forthwith become invalid and the employee shall make, within such time as may be prescribed, a fresh nomination in favour of one or more members of his family [Section 6 (4)].

(5) A nomination may, subject to the provisions of sub-sections (3) and (4) be modified by an employee at any time, after giving to his employer a written notice in such form and in such manner as may be prescribed, of his intention to do so. [Section 6 (5)].

(6) If a nominee predeceases the employee, the interest of the nominee shall revert to the employee who shall make a fresh nomination, in the prescribed form, in respect of such interest [Section 6 (6)].

(7) Every nomination, fresh nomination or alteration of nomination, as the case may be, shall be sent by the employee to his employer, who shall keep the same in his safe custody [Section 6 (7)].

Rule 6 which pertains to nominations is given below:

Rule 6. Nominations:

(1) A nomination shall be in Form 'F' and submitted in duplicate by personal service by the employee, after taking proper receipt or by sending through registered post acknowledgement due to the employer –

    (i) in the case of an employee who is already in employment for a year or more on the date of commencement of these rules, ordinarily within ninety days from such date, and

    (ii) in the case of an employee who completes one year of service after the date of commencement of these rules, ordinarily, within thirty days of the completion of one year of service.

Provided that nomination in Form 'F' shall be accepted by the employer after the specified period, if filed with reasonable grounds for delay, and no nomination so accepted shall be invalid merely because it was filed after the specified period.

(2) Within thirty days of the receipt of a nomination in Form 'F' under sub-rule (1), the employer shall get the service particulars of the employee, as mentioned in the form of nomination, verified with reference to the records of the establishment and return to the employee, after obtaining a receipt thereof, the duplicate copy of the nomination in Form 'F' duly attested either by the employer or an officer authorised in this behalf by him, as a token of recording of the nomination by the employer and the other copy of the nomination shall be recorded.

(3) An employee who has no family at the time of making a nomination shall, within ninety days of acquiring a family, submit in the manner specified in sub-rule (1), a fresh nomination, as required under sub-section (4) of Section 6, in duplicate in Form 'G' to the employer, and thereafter the provisions of sub-rule (2) shall apply *mutatis mutandis* as if it was made under sub-rule (1).

(4) A notice of modification of a nomination, including cases where a nominee pre-deceases an employee, shall be submitted in duplicate in Form 'H' to the employer in the manner specified in sub-rule (1), and thereafter the provisions of sub-rule (2) shall apply *mutatis mutandis* as if it was made under sub-rule (1).

(5) A nomination or a fresh nomination or a notice of modification of nomination shall be signed by the employee or, if illiterate, shall bear his thumb-impression, in the presence of two witnesses, who shall also sign a declaration to that effect in the nomination, fresh nomination or notice of modification of nomination, as the case may be.

(6) A nomination, fresh nomination or notice of modification of nomination shall take effect from the date of receipt thereof by the employer.

Various forms in which information pertaining to nominations are given below:

FORM 'F'

[*See sub-rule* (1) of Rule 6]

Nomination

To,

(Give here name or description of the establishment with full address)

1. Shri/Shrimati/Kumari ....

(name in full here)

whose particulars are given in the statement below, hereby nominate the person(s) mentioned below to receive the gratuity payable after my death as also the gratuity standing to my credit in the event of my death before the amount payable, or having become payable has not been paid and direct that the said amount of gratuity shall be paid in the proportion indicated against the name(s) of the nominee(s).

2. I hereby certify that the person(s) mentioned is/are a member(s) of any family within the meaning of clause (*h*) of Section 2 of the Payment of Gratuity Act, 1972.

3. I hereby declare that I have no family within the meaning of clause (*h*) of Section 2 of the said Act.

4. (a) My father/mother/parents is/are not dependant on me.

   (b) My husband's father/mother/parents is/are not dependant on my husband.

5. I have excluded my husband from my family by a notice dated the .... to the controlling authority in terms of the proviso to clause (*h*) of Section 2 of the said Act.

6. Nomination made herein invalidates my previous nomination.

Nominee(s)

Name in full with full address of nominee(s)	Relationship with the employee	Age of nominee	Proportion by which the gratuity will be shared
(1)	(2)	(3)	(4)

1.
2.
3.
so on.

Statement

1. Name of the employee in full
2. Sex
3. Religion
4. Whether unmarried/married/widow/widower
5. Department/Branch/Section where employed
6. Post held with Ticket or, Serial No., if any
7. Date of appointment
8. Permanent address:

Village	Thana	Sub-division ......
Post office	District	State ......

Place ....
Date ....   Signature/Thumb-impression of the Employee

Declaration by Witnesses

Nomination signed/thumb-impressed before me

Name in full and full address of witnesses   Signature of witnesses
1.   1.
2.   2.

Place ....
Date ....

Certificate by the Employer

Certified that the particulars of the above nomination have been verified and recorded in this establishment.

Employer's Reference No., if any authorised   Signature of the Employer/Officer

                                                                         Designation

Date ....   Name and address of the establishment or rubber stamp thereof

Acknowledgement by the Employee

Received the duplicate copy of nomination in Form 'F' filed by me and duly certified by the employer.

Date ....   Signature of the Employee

Note: Strike out the words/paragraphs not applicable.

FORM 'G'

[*See* sub-rule (3) of Rule 6]

Fresh Nomination

To,

(Give here name or description of the establishment with full address)

1. Shri/Shrimati/Kumari ....

(Name in full here)

whose particulars are given in the statement below, have acquired a family within the meaning of clause (h) of Section 2 of the Payment of Gratuity Act, 1972 with the effect from the .... (date here) .... in the manner indicated below and therefore nominate between the person(s) mentioned below to receive the gratuity payable after my death as also the gratuity standing to my credit in the event of my death before the amount has become payable, or having become payable has not been paid and direct that the said amount of gratuity shall be paid in the proportion indicated against the name(s) of the nominee(s).

2. I hereby certify that the person(s) mentioned is/are a member(s) of any family within the meaning of clause (*h*) of Section 2 of the said Act.

3. (a) My father/mother/parents is/are not dependent on me.

    (b) My husband's father/mother/parents is/are not dependant on my husband.

4. I have excluded my husband from my family by a notice dated the .... to the Controlling Authority in terms of the proviso to clause (*h*) of Section 2 of the said Act.

Nominee(s)

Name in full with full address of nominee(s)	Relationship with the employee	Age of nominee	Proportion by which the gratuity will be shared
(1)	(2)	(3)	(4)
1.			
2.			
3.			
so on.			

Manner of acquiring a "Family"

(Here give details as to how a family was acquired, i.e. whether by marriage or parents being rendered dependant or through other process like adoption).

Statement

1. Name of the employee in full
2. Sex
3. Religion
4. Whether unmarried/married/widow/widower
5. Department/Branch/Section where employed
6. Post held with Ticket or, Serial No., if any
7. Date of appointment
8. Permanent address:

| Village .... | Thana .... | Sub-division ...... |
| Post office .... | District ..... | State ...... |

Place ....
Date ....
Signature/Thumb-impression of the Employee

Declaration by Witnesses

Fresh nomination signed/thumb-impressed before me.

Name in full and full address of witnesses
1. ....
2. ....

Signature of witnesses
1. ....
2. ....

Place ....
Date ....

Certificate by the Employer

Certified that the particulars of the above nomination have been verified and recorded in this establishment.

Employer's Reference No., if any authorised

Date ....

Signature of the Employer/Officer

Designation ....

Name and address of the establishment or rubber stamp thereof

Acknowledgement by the Employee

Received the duplicate copy of nomination in Form ...... filed by me on ...... duly certified by the employer.

Date ....
Signature of the Employee

Note: Strike out the words/paragraphs not applicable.

FORM 'H'
[*See* sub-rule (4) of Rule 6]
Modification of Nomination

To,

    (Give here name or description of the establishment with full address)

I,   Shri/Shrimati/Kumari ....

                                                               (Name in full here)

whose particulars are given in the statement below, hereby give notice that the nomination filed by me on .... and recorded under your reference No. ....

(date) .... No .... dated .... shall stand modified in the following manner –

....
....
....

                       (Here give details of the modification intended)

Statement

1. Name of the employee in full
2. Sex
3. Religion
4. Whether unmarried/married/widow/widower
5. Department/Branch/Section where employed
6. Post held with Ticket No., or Serial No., if any
7. Date of appointment
8. Address in full

Place ....   Signature/Thumb-impression of the Employee

Date ....

Declaration by Witnesses

Modification of nomination signed/thumb-impressed before me.

Name in full and full address of witnesses   Signature of Witnesses

1. ....   1. ....
2. ....   2. ....

Place ....

Date ....

Certificate by the Employer

Certified that the above modifications have been recorded.

Employer's reference No., if any   Signature of the employer/officer authorised
                                          Designation

Date ....   Name and address of the establishment or
                                          rubber stamp thereof

Acknowledgement by the Employee

Received the duplicate copy of the notice for modification in Form 'H' filed by me on .... duly certified by the employer.

Date ....   Signature of the Employee

Note: Strike out the words not applicable.

Important points relating to nomination are given below:

(a) Nomination is required to be done within 30 days.

(b) Information relating to nomination is required to be submitted in Form 'F' in duplicate.

(c) An employee has a right to distribute the amount of gratuity payable to him under this Act among more than one nominee.

(d) Nomination is required to be done in favour of one or more members of the family of an employee in order to protect the interests of his family. If any nomination is made in favour of a person who is not a member of his family, such nomination is considered as void.

(e) However, if the employee has no family at the time of making nomination, nomination can be made in favour of any person or persons. But, if the employee acquires the family subsequently, the nomination already made becomes invalid and the concerned employee has to make a fresh nomination in favour of one or more members of his family within 90 days.

For this purpose, Form 'G' in duplicate is required to be submitted with necessary details.

(f) An employee has a right to modify his nomination at any time. For that purpose, he has to give a notice in writing to his employer by giving necessary details in Form 'H'.

(g) If a nominee pre-deceases the employee, then in such case, the interest of the deceased nominee is reverted to the employee. Thereafter, the employee has to make a fresh nomination in respect of such interest.

(h) Every nomination is required to be sent by an employee to his employer. The employer has to keep it safe in his custody.

(i) Nomination takes effect from the date of the receipt of the nomination by the employer.

5.13 Determination of the Amount of Gratuity

Provisions relating to application for gratuity [Section 7 (1)], determination of the amount of gratuity [Section 7 (2)]; Payment of gratuity [Section 7 (3)], Payment of interest on the amount of gratuity [Section 7 (3-A)], dispute as to gratuity [Section 7 (4)], Powers of controlling authority [Section 7 (5)], appeal etc. have been made in the Payment of Gratuity Act of 1972. Section 7 is reproduced below for your information.

Section 7 – Determination of the amount of gratuity:

(1) A person who is eligible for payment of gratuity under this Act or any person authorised, in writing, to act on his behalf shall send a written application to the employer, within such time and in such form as may be prescribed for payment of such gratuity [Section 7 (1)].

(2) As soon as gratuity becomes payable, the employer shall, whether an application referred to in sub-section (1) has been made or not, determine the amount of gratuity and give notice in writing to the person to whom the gratuity is payable and also to the controlling authority specifying the amount of gratuity so determined [Section 7 (2)].

(3) The employer shall arrange to pay the amount of gratuity within thirty days from the date it becomes payable to the person to whom the gratuity is payable. [Section 7 (3)].

(3-A) If the amount of gratuity payable under sub-section (3) is not paid by the employer within the period specified in sub-section (3), the employer shall pay, from the date on which the gratuity becomes payable to the date on which it is paid, simple interest at such rate, not exceeding the rate notified by the Central Government from time to time for repayment of long-term deposits, as that Government may, by notification specify [Section 7 (3-A)].

It is provided that no such interest shall be payable if the delay in the payment is due to the fault of the employee and the employer has obtained permission in writing from the controlling authority for the delayed payment on this ground [Proviso to Section 7 (3-A)].

(4) (a) If there is any dispute as to the amount of gratuity payable to an employee under this Act or as to the admissibility of any claim of, or in relation to an employee for payment of gratuity, or as to the person entitled to receive the gratuity, the employer shall deposit with the controlling authority such amount as he admits to be payable by him as gratuity [Section 7 (4) (a)].

(b) Where there is a dispute with regard to any matter or matters specified in clause (a), the employer or employee or any other person raising the dispute may make an application to the controlling authority for deciding the dispute [Section 7 (4) (b)].

(c) The controlling authority shall, after due inquiry and after giving the parties to the dispute a reasonable opportunity of being heard, determine the matter or matters in dispute and if, as a result of such inquiry any amount is found to be payable to the employee, the controlling authority shall direct the employer to pay such amount or, as the case may be, such amount as reduced by the amount already deposited by the employer [Section 7 (4) (c)].

(d) The controlling authority shall pay the amount deposited, including the excess amount, if any, deposited by the employer, to the person entitled thereto. [Section 7 (4) (d)].

(e) As soon as may be after a deposit is made under clause (a), the controlling authority shall pay the amount of the deposit –
- (i) to the applicant where he is the employee; or
- (ii) where the applicant is not the employee, to the nominee or, as the case may be, the guardian of such nominee or heir of the employee if the controlling authority is satisfied that there is no dispute as to the right of the applicant to receive the amount of gratuity [Section 7 (4) (e)].

(5) For the purpose of conducting an inquiry under sub-section (4), the controlling authority shall have the same powers as are vested in a court, while trying a suit, under the Code of Civil Procedure, 1908 (5 of 1908), in respect of the following matters, namely –
- (a) enforcing the attendance of any person or examining him on oath;
- (b) requiring the discovery and production of documents;
- (c) receiving evidence on affidavits;
- (d) issuing commissions for the examination of witnesses [Section 7 (5)].

(6) An inquiry under this section shall be a judicial proceeding within the meaning of Sections 193 and 228, and for the purpose of Section 196, of the Indian Penal Code, 1860 (45 of 1860) [Section 7 (6)].

(7) Any person aggrieved by an order under sub-section (4), may, within sixty days from the date of the receipt of the order, prefer an appeal to the appropriate Government or such other authority as may be specified by the appropriate Government in this behalf [Section 7 (7)].

It is also provided that the appropriate Government or the appellate authority, as the case may be, may, if it is satisfied that the appellant was prevented by sufficient cause from preferring the appeal within the said period of sixty days, and extended the said period by a further period of sixty days [Proviso 1 to Section 7 (7)].

It is further provided that no appeal by an employer shall be admitted unless at the time of preferring the appeal, the appellant either produces a certificate of the controlling authority to the effect that the appellant has deposited with him an amount equal to the amount of gratuity required to be deposited under sub-section (4), or deposits with the appellate authority such amount [Proviso 2 to Section 7 (7)].

(8) The appropriate Government or the appellate authority, as the case may be, may, after giving the parties to the appeal a reasonable opportunity of being heard, confirm, modify or reverse the decision of the controlling authority [Section 7 (8)].

In the Payment of Gratuity (Central) Rules, 1972 Rule 7 dealing with application for gratuity Rule 8 giving the information about notice for payment of gratuity Rule 9 making clear the mode of payment of gratuity Rule 10 dealing with the application to controlling authority for direction, Rule 11 making clear the procedure for dealing with application for direction are incorporated. These rules and various forms relating to these rules are given below.

Rule 7: Application for gratuity:

(1) An employee who is eligible for payment of gratuity under the Act, or any person authorised in writing, to act on his behalf, shall apply, ordinarily within thirty days from the date of the gratuity became payable, in Form 'I' to the employer.

Provided that where the date of superannuation or retirement of an employee is known, the employee may apply to the employer before thirty days of the date of superannuation or retirement.

(2) A nominee of an employee who is eligible for payment of gratuity under the second proviso to sub-section (I) of Section 4 shall apply, ordinarily within thirty days from the date the gratuity became payable to him, in Form 'J' to the employer.

Provided that an application on plain paper with relevant particulars shall also be accepted. The employer may obtain such other particulars as may be deemed necessary by him.

(3) A legal heir of an employee who is eligible for payment of gratuity under the second proviso to sub-section (1) of Section 4 shall apply, ordinarily within one year from the date the gratuity became payable to him in Form 'K' to the employer.

(4) Where gratuity becomes payable under the Act before the commencement of these rules, the periods of limitation specified in sub-rules (1), (2) and (3) shall be deemed to be operative from the date of such commencements.

(5) An application for payment of gratuity filed after the expiry of the periods specified in this rule shall also be entertained by the employer, if the applicant adduces sufficient cause for the delay in preferring his claim, and no claim for gratuity under the Act shall be invalid merely because the claimant failed to present his application within the specified period. Any dispute in this regard shall be referred to the controlling authority for his decision.

(6) An application under this rule shall be presented to the employer either by personal service or by registered post acknowledgement due.

Various forms required to be submitted under Rule 7:

(1) Application for Gratuity by an Employee:

FORM 'I'

[*See* sub-rule (1) of Rule 7]

Application for Gratuity by an Employee

To,

(Give here name or description of the establishment with full address)

Sir/Gentlemen,

I beg to apply for payment of gratuity to which I am entitled under sub-section (1) of Section 4 of the Payment of Gratuity Act, 1972 on account of my superannuation / retirement / resignation after completion of not less than five years of continuous service / total disablement due to accident / total disablement due to disease with effect from the .... Necessary particulars relating to my appointment are given in the statement below.

Statement

(1) Name in full
(2) Address in full
(3) Department / Branch / Section where last employed
(4) Post held with Ticket No., or Serial No., if any

(5) Date of appointment
(6) Date and cause of termination of service
(7) Total period of service
(8) Amount of wages last drawn
(9) Amount of gratuity claimed
    2. I was rendered totally disabled as a result of –
       (Here give the details of the nature of disease or accident)
The evidences/witnesses in support of my total disablement are as follows:
       (Here give details)
    3. Payment may please be made in cash/open or crossed bank cheque.
    4. As the amount of gratuity payable is less than Rupees one thousand, I shall request you to arrange for payment of the sum due to me by Postal Money Order at the address mentioned above after deducting postal money order commission therefrom.

Yours faithfully,
Signature/Thumb-impression of the applicant employee

Place ....
Date ....

Notes: (1) Strike out the words not applicable
       (2) Strike out paragraph or paragraphs not applicable.

(2) Application for Gratuity by a nominee:

FORM 'J'
[*See* sub-rule (2) of Rule 7]

    1. ***Application for Gratuity by a Nominee***

To,
    (Give here name or description of the establishment with full address)
Sir/Gentlemen,

I beg to apply for payment of gratuity to which I am entitled under sub-section (1) of Section 4 of the Payment of Gratuity Act, 1972 as a nominee of late ....
....(Name of the employee) who was an employee of your .... establishment and died on the .... The gratuity is payable on account of the death of the aforesaid employee while in service / superannuation of the aforesaid employee on .... / retirement or resignation of the aforesaid employee on .... after completion of .... years of service / total disablement of the aforesaid employee due to accident or disease while in service with effect from the .... Necessary particulars relating to my claim are given in the statement below:

Statement

(1) Name of the applicant nominee
(2) Address in full of the applicant nominee
(3) Marital status of the applicant nominee (unmarried / married / widow / widower)
(4) Name in full of the employee
(5) Marital status of the employee
(6) Relationship of the nominee with the employee
(7) Total period of service of the employee
(8) Date of appointment of the employee
(9) Date and cause of termination of service of the employee
(10) Department / Branch / Section where the employee last worked
(11) Post last held by the employee with Ticket or Serial No., if any
(12) Total wages last drawn by the employee.
(13) Date of death and evidence / witness as proof of death of the employee.
(14) Reference No. of recorded nomination if available
(15) Total gratuity payable to employee
(16) Share of gratuity claimed

    2. I declare that the particulars mentioned in the above statement are true and correct to the best of my knowledge and belief.

    3. Payment may please be made in cash / crossed or open bank cheque.

    4. As the amount payable is less than rupees one thousand, I shall request you to arrange for payment of the sum due to me by postal money order at the address mentioned above after deducting postal money order commission therefrom.

Yours faithfully,

Signature/Thumb-impression of

the applicant nominee

Place ....

Date ....

Notes: (1) Strike out the words not applicable

           (2) Strike out the paragraph or paragraphs not applicable.

(3) Application for Gratuity by a Legal Heir:

FORM 'K'

[*See* sub-rule (3) of Rule 7]

1. ***Application for Gratuity by Legal Heir***

To,

(Give here the name or description of the establishment with full address)

Sir/Gentlemen,

I beg to apply for payment of gratuity to which I am entitled under sub-section (1) of Section 4 of the Payment of Gratuity Act, 1972 as a legal heir of late ....

(Name of the employee) who was an employee of your .... establishment and died on the .... without making any nomination. The gratuity is payable on account of the death of the aforesaid employee while in service / superannuation of the aforesaid employee on the .... retirement or resignation of the aforesaid employee on the .... after completion of .... years of service / total disablement of the aforesaid employee due to accident or disease while in service with effect from the .... Necessary particulars relating to my claim are given in the statement below:

Statement

(1) Name of the applicant legal heir
(2) Address in full of applicant legal heir
(3) Marital status of the applicant legal heir (unmarried / married / widow / widower)
(4) Name in full of the employee
(5) Relationship of the applicant with the employee
(6) Religion of both the applicants.
(7) Date of appointment and total period of service of the employee
(8) Department / Branch / Section where the employee worked last
(9) Post last held by the employee with Ticket or Serial No., if any
(10) Total wages last drawn by the employee
(11) Date and cause of termination of service of the employee (death or otherwise)
(12) Date of death of the employee and evidence / witness in support thereof
(13) Total gratuity payable to the employee
(14) Percentage of the gratuity claimed
(15) Basis of the claim and evidence / witness in support thereof

2. I declare that the particulars mentioned in the above statement are true and correct to the best of my knowledge and belief.
3. Payment may please be made in cash/open or crossed bank cheque.
4. As the amount payable is less than Rupees one thousand, I shall request you to arrange for payment of the sum due to me by postal money order at the address mentioned above, after deducting postal money order commission therefrom.

Yours faithfully,
Signature/Thumb-impression of
the applicant legal heir

Place ....
Date ....

Note: Strike out the words not applicable

Rule 8: Notice for payment of gratuity:

(1) Within fifteen days of the receipt of an application under Rule 7 for payment of gratuity, the employer shall –
- (i) if the claim is found admissible on verification, issue a notice in Form 'L' to the applicant employee, nominee or legal heir, as the case may be, specifying the amount of gratuity payable and fixing a date, not being later than the thirtieth day after the date of receipt of the application, for payment thereof, or
- (ii) if the claim for gratuity is not found admissible, issue a notice in Form 'M' to the applicant employee, nominee or legal heir, as the case may be, specifying the reasons why the claim for gratuity is not considered admissible.

In either case a copy of the notice shall be endorsed to the controlling authority.

(2) In case payment of gratuity is due to be made in the employer's office, the date fixed for the purpose in the notice in Form 'L' under clause (i) of sub-rule (1) shall be re-fixed by the employer, if a written application in this behalf is made by the payee explaining why it is not possible for him to be present in person on the date specified.

(3) If the claimant for gratuity is a nominee or a legal heir, the employer may ask for such witness or evidence as may be deemed relevant for establishing his identity or maintainability of his claim as the case may be. In that case the time-limit specified for issuance of notices under sub-rule (1) shall be operative with effect from the date, such witness or evidence, as the case may be, called for by the employer is furnished to the employer.

(4) A notice in Form 'L' or Form 'M' shall be served on the applicant either by personal service after taking receipt or by registered post with acknowledgement due.

(5) A notice under sub-section (2) of Section 7 shall be in Form 'L'.

(1) Form 'L' for notice for payment of Gratuity:

FORM 'L'
[*See* clause (i) of sub-rule (1) of Rule 8]
Notice for Payment of Gratuity

To,
   (Name and address of the applicant employee / nominee / legal heir)

1. You are hereby informed as required under clause (*i*) of sub-rule (1) of Rule 8 of the Payment of Gratuity (Central) Rules, 1972 that a sum of ₹ ……………….. (Rupees ………………….) is payable to you as gratuity / as your share of gratuity in terms of nomination made by ……………… on ……………… recorded in this …………… as a legal heir of ……………… an employee of this ……………… establishment.

2. Please call at …………… on ……………………… (Here specify place) (date) at ……………………… for collecting your payment in cash / open or crossed cheque.

3. Amount payable shall be sent to you by postal money order at the address given in your application after deducting the postal money order commission, as desired by you, by …………………….

Brief statement of calculation

(1) Total period of service of the employee concerned ………… years …………… months.
(2) Wages last drawn
(3) Proportion of the admissible gratuity payable in terms of nomination / as a legal heir
(4) Amount payable

Place …………
Date …………

Signature of the Employer/authorised officer.
Name or description of establishment or rubber stamp thereof

Copy to the Controlling Authority
Note: Strike out the words not applicable.

(2) Form 'M' for Notice rejecting Claim for Payment of Gratuity:

FORM 'M'

[*See* clause (ii) of sub-rule (1) of Rule 8]

Notice Rejecting Claim for Payment of Gratuity

To,

(Name and address of the applicant employee/nominee/legal heir)

You are hereby informed as required under clause (ii) of sub-rule (1) of Rule 8 of the Payment of Gratuity (Central) Rules, 1972 that your claim for payment of gratuity as indicated on your application in Form .... under the said rules is not admissible for the reasons stated below:

Reasons

(Here specify the reasons)

Place ....   Signature of the employee/authorised officer.

Date ....

Name or description of establishment or rubber stamp thereof.

Copy to Controlling Authority

Note: Strike out the words not applicable

Rule 9: Mode of payment of gratuity:

The gratuity payable under the Act shall be paid in cash or, if so desired by the payee, in Demand Draft or bank cheque to the eligible employee, nominee or legal heir, as the case may be.

Provided that in case the eligible employee, nominee or legal heir, as the case may be, so desires and the amount of gratuity payable is less than one thousand rupees, payment may be made by postal money order after deducting the postal money order commission thereof from the amount payable.

Provided further that intimation about the details of payment shall also be given by the employer to the controlling authority of the area.

Provided further that in the case of a nominee, or heir, who is a minor, the controlling authority shall invest the gratuity amount deposited with him for the benefit of such minor in term deposit with the State Bank of India or any of its subsidiaries or any Nationalised Bank.

Explanation: "Nationalised Bank" means a corresponding new bank specified in the First Schedule of the Banking Companies (Acquisition and Transfer of Undertakings) Act, 1950 (5 of 1970) or a corresponding new bank specified in the First Schedule of the Banking Companies (Acquisition and Transfer of Undertakings) Act 1980 (40 of 1980).

Rule 10: Application to controlling authority for direction:

(1) If an employer –
- (i) refuses to accept a nomination or to entertain an application sought to be filed under Rule 7, or
- (ii) issues a notice under sub-rule (1) of Rule 8 either specifying an amount of gratuity which is considered by the applicant less than what is payable or rejecting eligibility to payment of gratuity, or
- (iii) having received an application under Rule 7 fails to issue any notice as required under Rule 8 within the time specified therein,

the claimant employee, nominee or legal heir, as the case may be, may within ninety days of the occurrence of the cause for the application, apply, in Form 'N' to the controlling authority for issuing a direction under sub-section (4) of Section 7 with as many extra copies as are the opposite parties:

Provided that the controlling authority may accept any application under this sub-rule, on sufficient cause being shown by the applicant, after the expiry of the specified period.

(2) Application under sub-rule (1) and other documents relevant to such an application shall be presented in person to the controlling authority or shall be sent by registered post acknowledgement due.

Form 'N' for Application for Direction:

FORM 'N'

[See sub-rule of Rule 10]

Application for Direction

Before the Controlling Authority under the Payment of Gratuity Act, 1972

Application ....   Date ....

BETWEEN

(Name in full of the applicant with full address)

AND

(Name in full of the employer concerned with full address)

The applicant is an employee of the above mentioned employer/a nominee of late .... an employee of the above mentioned employer / a legal heir of late .... an employee of the above mentioned employer, and is entitled to payment of gratuity under Section 4 of the Payment of Gratuity Act, 1972 on account of his own/aforesaid employee's superannuation on .... /his own retirement/aforesaid employee's resignation .... on .... after completion of .... years of (date) continuous service / his own / aforesaid .... employees' total disablement with effect from .... due to accident / (date) disease / death of aforesaid employee on ....

2. The applicant submitted an application under Rule of the Payment of Gratuity Act, 1972 on the .... but the above mentioned employer refused to entertain it/issued a notice dated the .... under the clause .... of sub-rule of rule .... offering an amount of gratuity which is less than my due / issued a notice dated the .... under clause .... of sub-rule .... of rule .... rejecting my eligibility to payment of gratuity. The duplicate copy of the said notice is enclosed.

3. The applicant submits that there is a dispute on the matter (specify the dispute).

4. The applicant furnishes the necessary particulars in the annexure hereto and prays that the Controlling Authority may be pleased to determine the amount of gratuity payable to the petitioner and direct the above-mentioned employer to pay the same to the petitioner.

5. The applicant declares that the particulars furnished in the annexure hereto are true and correct to the best of his knowledge and belief.

Date:

Signature of the applicant/Thumb-impression
    of the applicant

ANNEXURE

1. Name in full of applicant with full address
2. Basis of claim:
   (Death/Superannuation/Retirement/Resignation/Disablement of employee)
3. Name and address of the employee in full
4. Marital status of the employee (unmarried/married/widow/widower)
5. Name and address in full of the employer
6. Department/Branch/Section where the employer was last employed (if known)
7. Post held by the employee with Ticket or Serial No. if any (if known)
8. Date of appointment of the employee (if known)
9. Date and cause of termination of service of the employee (superannuation/retirement/resignation/disablement/death)
10. Total period of service by the employee
11. Wages last drawn by the employee
12. If the employee is dead, date and cause thereof
13. Evidence/witness in support of death of the employee
14. If a nominee, No. and date of recording of nomination with the employer
15. Evidence/witness in support of being a legal heir if a legal heir
16. Total gratuity payable to employee (if known)
17. Percentage of gratuity payable to the applicant as nominee/legal heir
18. Amount of gratuity claimed by the applicant

Place ....   Signature/Thumb-impression of the applicant
Date ....

Note: Strike out the words not applicable.

11. Procedure for dealing with application for direction:

(1) On receipt of an application under Rule 10, the controlling authority shall, by issuing a notice in Form 'O', call upon the applicant as well as the employer to appear before him on a specified date, time and place, either by himself or through his authorised representative together with all relevant documents and witnesses, if any.

(2) Any person desiring to act on behalf of an employer or employee, nominee or legal heir, as the case may be, shall present to the controlling authority a letter of authority from the employer or the person concerned, as the case may be, on whose behalf he seeks to act together with a written statement explaining his interest in the matter and praying for permission so to act. The controlling authority shall record thereon an order either according to his approval or specifying, in the case of refusal to grant the permission prayed for, the reasons for the refusal.

(3) A party appearing by an authorised representative shall be bound by the acts of the representative.

(4) After completion of hearing on the date fixed under sub-rule (1), or after such further evidence, examination of documents, witnesses, hearing and enquiry, as may be deemed necessary, the controlling authority shall record his finding as to whether any amount is payable to the applicant under the Act. A copy of the finding shall be given to each of the parties.

(5) If the employer concerned fails to appear on the specified date of hearing after due service of notice without sufficient cause, the controlling authority may proceed to hear and determine the application *ex parte*. If the applicant fails to appear on the specified date of hearing without sufficient cause, the controlling authority may dismiss the application.

Provided that an order under this sub-rule may, on good cause being shown within thirty days of the said order, be reviewed and the application re-heard after giving not less than fourteen days' notice to the opposite party of the date fixed for re-hearing of the application.

Form 'O' for Notice for appearance before the Controlling Authority:

FORM 'O'
[*See* sub-rule (1) of Rule 11]

Notice for Appearance before the Controlling Authority

From: The Controlling Authority under the Payment of Gratuity Act, 1972.

To ....

(Name and address of the employer/applicant)

Whereas Shri .... an employee under you/a nominee(s)/legal heir(s) of Shri .... an employee under the above-mentioned employer, has /have filed an application under sub-rule (1) of Rule 10 of the Payment of Gratuity (Central) Rules, 1972 alleging that –

[A copy of the said application is enclosed]

Now, therefore, you are hereby called upon to appear before me at ....

(place)

either personally or through a person duly authorised in this behalf for the purpose of answering all material questions relating to the application on the .... day of 20 ..... at .... 'o' clock in the forenoon/afternoon in support of/to answer the allegation; and as the day fixed for your appearance is appointed for final disposal of the application you must be prepared to produce on that day all the witnesses upon whose evidence, and the documents upon which you intend to rely in support of your allegation/defence.

Take notice that in default of your appearance on the day before-mentioned the application will be dismissed/heard and determined in your absence.

Given under my hand and seal, this .... day of .... 20 ....

Controlling Authority

Note: Strike out the words and paragraphs not applicable.

5.13.1 Direction of Payment of Gratuity

Rule 17 provides for the direction of payment of gratuity. It states that, "if a finding is recorded under sub-rule (4) of Rule 11 that the applicant is entitled to payment of gratuity under the Act, the controlling authority shall issue a notice to the employer concerned in Form 'R' specifying the amount payable and directing payment thereof to the applicant under intimation to the controlling authority within thirty days from the date of receipt of the notice by the employer. A copy of the notice shall be endorsed to the applicant employee, nominee or legal heir, as the case may be".

Form 'R' for making clear the Contents of Notice for Payment of Gratuity:

FORM 'R'
[*See* Rule 17]
Notice for Payment of Gratuity

To,
    (Name and address of the employer)
    Whereas Shri/Smt./Kumari .... of .... an employee (address) .... under you/a nominee(s) legal heir(s) of late .... an employee under you, filed an application under Section 7 of the Payment of Gratuity Act, 1972, before me:

And whereas the application was heard in your presence on .... and after the hearing I have come to the finding that the said Shri/Smt./Kumari .... is entitled to a payment of ₹ .... as gratuity under the Payment of Gratuity Act, 1972;

Now, therefore, I hereby direct you to pay the said sum of ₹ .... to Shri/Smt/Kumari .... within thirty days of the receipt of this notice with an intimation thereof to me.

Given under my hand and seal, this .... day of .... 20 ....

Controlling Authority

Copy to
    (Applicant under rule)
He is advised to contact the employer for collecting payment.
Note: The portion not applicable to be deleted.

5.13.2 Maintenance of Records of Cases by the Controlling Authority

Rule 16 of the Payment of Gratuity (Central) Rules, 1972 provides for maintaining the records of cases by the controlling authority. Rule 16 is reproduced below.

(1) The controlling authority shall record the particulars of each case under Section 7, in Form 'Q' and at the time of passing the order shall, sign and date the particulars so recorded.

(2) The controlling authority shall, while passing orders in each case, also record the findings on the merits of the case and file it together with the memoranda of evidence with the order sheet.

(3) Any record, other than a record of any order or direction, which is required by these rules to be signed by the controlling authority, may be signed on behalf of and under the direction of the controlling authority by any subordinate officer appointed in writing for this purpose by the controlling authority.

Form 'Q' shows the particulars of application under Section 7 as follows:

FORM 'Q'
[*See* sub-rule (1) of Rule 16]
Particulars of Application under Section 7

1. Serial No.
2. Date of the application.
3. Name and address of the applicant.
4. Name and address of the employer.
5. Amount of gratuity claimed.
6. Dates of hearing.
7. Findings with date.
8. Amount awarded.
9. Cost, if any, awarded.
10. Date of notice issued for payment of gratuity.
11. Date of appeal, if any.
12. Decision of the appellate authority.
13. Date of issue of final notice for payment of gratuity.
14. Date of payment of gratuity by employer with mode of payment.
15. Date of receipt of application for recovery of gratuity.
16. Date of issue of Recovery Certificate.
17. Date of recovery.
18. Other remarks.
19. Signed.
20. Date.

5.14 Recovery of Gratuity

As gratuity is a compulsory payment according to the provisions of this Act, it must be paid to an employee on fulfilling the conditions laid down in the Act by his employer. If the amount of gratuity payable under this Act is not paid by the employer within the time limit prescribed for the payment, he must make an application to the controlling authority. On receiving the application by the aggrieved person, the controlling authority issues the certificate for that amount to the collector who recovers the same together with compound interest. The provisions relating to the recovery of the amount of gratuity are made in Section 8 which is as follows:

"If the amount of gratuity payable under this Act is not paid by the employer, within the prescribed time, to the person entitled thereto, the controlling authority shall, on an application made to it in this behalf by the aggrieved person, issue a certificate for that amount to the Collector, who shall recover the same, together with compound interest thereon at such rate as the Central Government may, by notification, specify from the date of expiry of the prescribed time, as arrears of land revenue and pay the same to the person entitled thereto" [Section 8].

It is also provided that the controlling authority shall, before issuing a certificate under this section, give the employer a reasonable opportunity of showing cause against the issue of such certificate [Proviso 1 to Section 8].

It is further provided that the amount payable under this section shall, in no case exceed the amount of gratuity payable under this Act [Proviso 2 to Section 8].

5.14.1 Application for Recovery of Gratuity

"Where an employer fails to pay the gratuity due under the Act in accordance with the notice by the controlling authority under Rule 17 or Rule 18, as the case may be, the employee concerned, his nominee or legal heir, as the case may be, to whom the gratuity is payable, may apply to the controlling authority in duplicate in Form 'T' for recovery thereof under Section 8 of the Act" [Rule 19 of the Payment of Gratuity (Central) Rules, 1972. Form 'T' is given below -

---

FORM 'T'

[*See* Rule 19]

Application for Recovery of Gratuity

1. Before the Controlling Authority under the Payment of Gratuity Act, 1972

Application No. ....   Date ....

BETWEEN

(Name in full of the applicant with address)

AND

(Name in full of the employer with full address)

The applicant is an employee of the above-mentioned employer/a nominee of late .... an employee of the above mentioned employer/a legal heir of late .... an employee of the above mentioned employer, and you were pleased to direct the said employer in your notice dated the .... under Rule .... of Payment of Gratuity (Central) Rules, 1972 for payment of a sum of ₹ .... as gratuity payable under the Payment of Gratuity Act, 1972.

> 2. The application submits that the said employer failed to pay the said amount of gratuity to me as directed by you although I approached him for payment.
> 3. The applicant therefore prays that a certificate may be issued under Section .... of the said Act for recovery of the said sum of ₹ .... due to me as gratuity in terms of your direction.
>
> Signature/Thumb-impression of the applicant
>
> Place ....
> Date ....
>
> **Note:** Strike out the words not applicable.

Rule 18 referred to in Rule 19 pertain to appeal. Rule 18 is reproduced below.

Rule 18: Appeal:

(1) The Memorandum of appeal under sub-section (7) of Section 7 of the Act be submitted to the appellate authority with a copy thereof to the opposite party and the controlling authority either through delivery in person or under registered post acknowledgement due.

(2) The Memorandum of appeal shall contain the facts of the case, the decision of the controlling authority, the grounds of appeal and the relief sought.

(3) There shall be appended to the Memorandum of appeal a certified copy of the finding of the controlling authority and direction for payment of gratuity.

(4) On receipt of the copy of Memorandum of appeal, the controlling authority shall forward records of the case to the appellate authority.

(5) Within 14 days of the receipt of the copy of the Memorandum of appeal, the opposite party shall submit his comments on each paragraph of the memorandum with additional plea, if any, to the appellate authority with a copy to the appellant.

(6) The appellate authority shall record its decision after giving the parties to the appeal a reasonable opportunity of being heard. A copy of the decision shall be given to the parties to the appeal and a copy thereof shall be sent to the controlling authority returning his records of the case.

(7) The controlling authority shall, on receipt of the decision of the appellate authority, make necessary entry in the records of the case maintained in Form 'Q' under sub-rule (1) of Rule 16.

(8) On receipt of the decision of the appellate authority, the controlling authority shall, if required under that decision, modify his direction for payment of gratuity and issue a notice to the employer concerned in Form 'S' specifying the modified amount payable and directing payment thereof to the applicant, under intimation to the controlling authority within fifteen days of the receipt of the notice by the employer. A copy of the notice shall be endorsed to the applicant employee, nominee or legal heir, as the case may be, and to the appellate authority.

Form 'S' makes clear the contents of notice for payment of gratuity as determined by the Appellate Authority.

FORM 'S'
[*See* sub-rule (5) of Rule 18]
Notice for Payment of Gratuity as Determined by Appellate Authority

To
          (Name and address of employer)

Whereas a notice was given to you on .... Form 'R' requiring you to make a payment of ₹ .... to Shri/Smt./Kumari .... as gratuity under the Payment of Gratuity Act, 1972.

Whereas you/the applicant went in appeal before the appellate authority, who has decided that an amount of ₹ .... is due to be paid to Shri/Smt./Kumari .... as Gratuity due under the Payment of Gratuity Act, 1972;

Now, therefore I hereby direct you to pay the said sum of ₹ .... to Shri/Smt./Kumari .... [within 15 days] of the receipt of this notice with an intimation thereof to me.

Given under my hand and seal, this .... day of .... 20.

Controlling Authority

Copy to:
  1. The applicant.
     He is advised to contact the employer for collecting payment.
  2. The Appellate Authority.

Note: The portion not applicable to be deleted.

5.15 Protection of Gratuity

Section 13 of this Act, expressly provides for the protection of gratuity. It states that, "no gratuity payable under this Act and no gratuity payable to an employee employed in any establishment, factory, mine, oilfield, plantation, port, railway company or shop exempted under Section 5 shall be liable to attachment in execution of any decree or order of any civil, revenue or criminal court".

However, gratuity payable to the heirs of an employee on his death is attachable.

5.16 Appointment and Powers of Inspectors

Section 7-A deals with the appointment of Inspectors while Section 7-B makes clear the powers of Inspectors appointed for the purposes of this Act.

5.16.1 Appointment of Inspectors

(1) The appropriate Government may, by notification, appoint as many Inspectors, as it deems fit, for the purposes of this Act [Section 7-A (1)].

(2) The appropriate Government may, by general or special order, define the area to which the authority of an Inspector so appointed shall extend and where two or more

Inspectors are appointed for the same area, also provide, by such order, for the distribution or allocation of work to be performed by them under this Act [Section 7-A (2)].

(3) Every Inspector shall be deemed to be a public servant within the meaning of Section 21 of the Indian Penal Code (45 of 1860) [Section 7-A (3)].

5.16.2 Powers of Inspectors

The powers of an Inspector appointed under this Act have been enumerated in Section 7-A. These powers are as under:

Subject to any rules made by the appropriate Government in this behalf, an Inspector may, for the purpose of ascertaining whether any of the provisions of this Act or the conditions, if any, of any exemption granted thereunder, have been complied with, exercise all or any of the following powers, namely

- (a) to require an employer to furnish such information as he may consider necessary;
- (b) to enter and inspect, at all reasonable hours, with such assistants (if any), being persons in the service of the Government or local or any public authority, as he thinks fit, any premises of or place in any factory, mine, oilfield, plantation, port, railway company, shop or other establishment to which this Act applies, for the purpose of examining any register, record or notice or other document required to be kept or exhibited under this Act or the rules made thereunder, or otherwise kept or exhibited in relation to the employment of any person or the payment of gratuity to the employees, and require the production thereof for inspection;
- (c) to examine with respect to any matter relevant to any of the purposes aforesaid, the employer or any person whom he finds in such premises or place and who, he has reasonable cause to believe, is an employee employed therein;
- (d) to make copies of, or take extracts from, any register, record or notice, or other document, as he may consider relevant, and where he has reason to believe that any offence under this Act has been committed by an employer, search and seize with such assistance as he may think fit, such register, record, notice or other document as he may consider relevant in respect of that offence;
- (e) to exercise such other powers as may be prescribed [Section 7-B (1)].

Any person required to produce any register, record, notice or other document or to give any information by an Inspector under sub-section (1) shall be deemed to be legally bound to do so within the meaning of Sections 175 and 176 of the Indian Penal Code (45 of 1860). Section 7-B (2)].

The provisions of the Code of Criminal Procedure, 1973 (2 of 1974) shall so far as may be, apply to any search or seizure under this section as they apply to any search or seizure made under the authority of a warrant issued under Section 94 of that Code. [Section 7-B (3)].

5.17 Penalties

Provisions have been made in Section 9 of this Act for imposing penalties for false statement or false representation and also for contravention of the Act. The penalties for these offences are mentioned below:

(a) Penalty for false representation or false statement:

Whoever, for the purpose of avoiding any payment to be made by himself under this Act or of enabling any other person to avoid such payment, knowingly makes or causes to make any false statement or false representation shall be punishable with imprisonment for a term which may extend to six months, or with fine which may extend to ten thousand rupees or with both [Section 9 (1)].

(b) Penalty for contravention of the Act:

An employer who contravenes, or makes default in complying with any of the provisions of this Act or any rule or order made thereunder shall be punishable with imprisonment for a term which shall not be less than three months but which may extend to one year, or with fine which shall not be less than ten thousand rupees but which may extend to twenty thousand rupees, or with both [Section 9 (2)].

It is provided that where the offence relates to non-payment of any gratuity payable under this Act, the employer shall be punishable with imprisonment for a term which shall not be less than six months but which may extend to two years unless the court trying the offence, for reasons to be recorded by it in writing, is of opinion that a lesser term of imprisonment or the imposition of a fine would meet the ends of justice. [Proviso to Section 9 (2)].

(c) Penalty for failure to pay insurance premium or contribution:

If an employer fails to pay insurance premium under Section 4-A (1) or any contribution to an approved gratuity fund under Section 4-A (2), such employer is held liable to pay the amount of gratuity due along with the interest for delayed payment forthwith to the controlling authority. Whoever contravenes this provision is punishable with fine which may extend to ₹ Ten thousand and in the case of continuing offence with a further fine which may extend to ₹ One thousand for each day during which the offence continues [Section 4-A (6)].

5.18 Exemption of the Employer from Liability in Certain Cases

According to the provisions of Section 10, when an employer is charged with the offence punishable under this Act, such employer is entitled to have any other person whom the employer charges as the actual offender brought before the Court at the time appointed for hearing the charge. However, the employer is entitled to do so only upon the complaint duly made by him and on giving to the complaint not less than three clear days' notice in writing of his intention to do so. If the employer can prove to the satisfaction of the Court that he has used due diligence to enforce the execution of this Act and the said other person committed the offence in question without that employer's knowledge, consent or connivance, then the other person shall be convicted of the offence and will be held liable to the like punishment as if he were the employer. The employer then is discharged from any liability under this Act in respect of such offence. Section 10 is reproduced below to know fully the provisions of this Act relating to exemption of employer from liability in certain cases.

"Where an employer is charged with an offence punishable under this Act, he shall be entitled upon complaint duly made by him and on giving to the complaint not less than three clear days' notice in writing of his intention to do so, to have any other person whom he charges as the actual offender brought before the court at the time appointed for hearing the charge; and if, after the commission of the offence has been proved, the employer proves to the satisfaction of the court –
- (a) that he has used due diligence to enforce the execution of this Act, and
- (b) that the said other person committed the offence in question without his knowledge, consent or connivance,

 that other person shall be convicted of the offence and shall be liable to the like punishment as if he were the employer and the employer shall be discharged from any liability under this Act in respect of such offence:

It is provided that in seeking to prove as afore said, the employer may be examined on oath and his evidence and that of any witness whom he calls in his support shall be subject to cross-examination on behalf of the person he charges as the actual offender and by the prosecutor [Proviso 1 to Section 10].

It is provided further that, if the person charged as the actual offender by the employer cannot be brought before the court at the time appointed for hearing the charge, the court shall adjourn the hearing from time to time for a period not exceeding three months and if by the end of the said period the person charged as the actual offender cannot still be brought before the court, the court shall proceed to hear the charge against the employer and shall, if the offence be proved, convict the employer [Proviso 2 to Section 10].

5.19 Cognisance of Offences [Section 11]

No court shall take cognisance of any offence punishable under this Act save on a complaint made by or under the authority of the appropriate Government. [Section 11 (1)].

It is provided that where the amount of gratuity has not been paid, or recovered, within six months from the expiry of the prescribed time, the appropriate Government shall authorise the controlling authority to make a complaint against the employer, whereupon the controlling authority shall, within fifteen days from the date of such authorisation, make such complaint to a Magistrate having jurisdiction to try the offence [Proviso to Section 11].

No court inferior to that of a Metropolitan Magistrate or a Judicial Magistrate of the first class shall try any offence punishable under this Act [Section 11 (2)].

5.20 Protection of Action Taken in Good Faith

No suit or other legal proceeding shall lie against the controlling authority or any other person in respect of anything which is in good faith done or intended to be done under this Act or any rule or order made thereunder [Section 12].

5.21 Act to Override other Enactments

The provisions of this Act or any rule made thereunder shall have effect notwithstanding anything inconsistent therewith contained in any enactment other than this Act or in any instrument or contract having effect by virtue of any enactment other than this Act [Section 14].

5.22 Power to Make Rules

(1) The appropriate Government may, by notification, make rules for the purpose of carrying out the provisions of this Act [Section 15 (1)].

(2) Every rule made by the Central Government under this Act shall be laid, as soon as may be after it is made, before each House of Parliament while it is in session, for a total period of thirty days which may be comprised in one session or in two or more successive sessions, and if, before the expiry of the session immediately following the session or the successive sessions aforesaid, both Houses agree in making any modification in the rule or both Houses agree that the rule should not be made, the rule shall, thereafter, have effect only in such modified form or be of no effect as the case may be, so, however, that any such modification or annulment shall be without prejudice to the validity of anything previously done under that rule [Section 15 (2)].

5.23 Display of Abstract of the Act and Rules

Rule 20 of the Payment of Gratuity (Central) Rules of 1972 states that, "the employer shall display an abstract of the Act and the rule made thereunder as given in Form 'U' in English and in the language understood by the majority of the employees at a conspicuous place at or near the main entrance of the establishment".

Form 'U' is given below:

FORM 'U'

Abstract of the Act and Rules

1. **Extent of the Act:** The Act extends to the whole of India:

Provided that in so far as it relates to plantations or ports, it shall not extend to the State of Jammu and Kashmir [Section 1(2)].

2. **To whom the Act Applies:** Act applies to (a) every factory, mine, oilfield, plantation, port and railway company; (b) every shop or establishment within the meaning of any law for the time being in force in relation to shops and establishments in a State, in which ten or more persons are employed, or were employed, on any day of the preceding twelve months; and (c) such other establishments or class of establishments in which, ten or more employees are employed, or were employed, on any day of the preceding twelve months, as the Central Government may, by notification, specify in this behalf. [Section 1(3)].

3. **Definitions:** (a) "Appropriate Government" means (i) in relation to an establishment –
   (a) belonging to, or under the control of, the Central Government,
   (b) having branches in more than one State,
   (c) of a factory belonging to, or under the control of, the Central Government.
   (d) of a major port, mine, oilfield or railway company, the Central Government,

   (ii) in any other case, the State Government [Section 2(a)].
   (a) "Completed year of service" means continuous service for one year [Section 2(b)].
   (b) "Continuous Service" means uninterrupted service and includes service which is interrupted by sickness, accident, leave, lay-off, strike or a lock-out or cessation of work not due to any fault of the employees concerned, whether such uninterrupted or interrupted service was rendered before or after the commencement of this Act.

Explanation I: In the case of an employee who is not in uninterrupted service for one year, he shall be deemed to be in continuous service if he has been actually employed by an employer during the twelve months immediately preceding the year for not less than –
   (i)   190 days, if employed below the ground in a mine, or
   (ii) 240 days, in any other case, except when he is employed in a seasonal establishment.

Explanation II: An employee of a seasonal establishment shall be deemed to be in continuous service if he has actually worked for not less than seventy-five per cent of the number of days on which the establishment was in operation during the year [Section 2(d)].

(d) "Controlling authority" means an authority appointed by an appropriate Government under Section 3 [Section 2(d)].

(e) "Family", in relation to an employee, shall be deemed to consist of –
   (i)   in the case of a male employee himself, his wife, his children, whether married or unmarried, his dependent parents and the widow and children, of his pre-deceased son, if any;
   (ii) in the case of a female employee, herself, her husband, her children, whether married or unmarried, her dependent parents and the dependent parents of her husband and the widow and children of her pre-deceased son, if any

Provided that if a female employee by a notice in writing to the Controlling Authority, expresses her desire to exclude her husband from her family, the husband and his dependent parents shall no longer be deemed, for the purposes of this act be included in the family of such female employee unless the said notice is subsequently withdrawn by such female employee.

Explanation III: Where the personal law of an employee permits the adoption by him of a child, any child lawfully adopted by him shall be deemed to be included in his family, and where a child of an employee has been adopted by another person and such adoption is under the personal law of the person making such adoption, lawful, such child shall be deemed to be excluded from the family of the employee [Section 2(h)].

4.   Nomination: (1) Each employee, who has completed one year of service, after the commencement of the Payment of Gratuity (Central) Rules, 1972 shall make within thirty days of completion of one year of service, a nomination [Section 6 (1)].

(2) If an employee has a family at the time of making a nomination, the nomination shall be made in favour of one or more members of his family and any nomination made by such employee in favour of a person who is not a member of his family shall be void [Section 6(3)].

(3) If at the time of making a nomination, the employee has no family, the nomination can be made in favour of any person or persons, but if the employee subsequently acquires a family, such nomination shall forthwith become invalid and the employee shall make within 90 days fresh nomination in favour of one or more members of his family [Section 6(4) read with Rule 6(3)].

(4) A nomination or a fresh nomination or a notice of modification of nomination shall be signed by the employee or, if illiterate, shall bear his thumb-impression in the presence of two witnesses, who shall also sign a declaration to that effect in the nomination, fresh nomination or notice of modification of nomination as the case may be [Rule 6(5)].

(5) A nomination may, subject to the provisions of sub-sections (3) and (4) of Section 6, be modified by an employee any time after giving to his employer a written notice of his intention to do so. [Section 6(5)].

(6) A nomination or fresh nomination or notice of modification of nomination shall take effect from the date of receipt of the same by the employer [Rule 6 (6)].

5. Application for gratuity: (1) An employee who is eligible for payment of gratuity under the Act, or any person authorised in writing, to act on his behalf, shall apply ordinarily within thirty days from the date gratuity becomes payable:

Provided that where the date of superannuation or retirement of an employee is known, the employee may apply to such employer before thirty days of the date of superannuation or retirement [Rule 7(1)].

(2) A nominee of an employee who is eligible for payment of gratuity shall apply, ordinarily within thirty days from the date the gratuity became payable to him, to the employer [Rule 7(2)].

(3) A legal heir of an employee who is eligible for payment of gratuity shall apply, ordinarily within one year from the date the gratuity became payable to him, to the employer [Rule 7(3)].

(4) An application for payment of gratuity filed after the expiry of the periods specified above shall also be entertained by the employer if the applicant adduces a sufficient cause for the delay. [Rule 7(5)].

6. Payment of gratuity: (1) Gratuity shall be payable to an employee on the termination of his employment after he has rendered continuous service for not less than five years –

    (a) on his superannuation, or
    (b) on his retirement or resignation, or
    (c) on his death or disablement due to accident or disease

Provided that the completion of continuous service of five years shall not be necessary where the termination of the employment of any employee is due to death or disablement.

Disablement means such disablement which incapacitates an employee for the work which he was capable of performing before the accident or disease resulting in such disablement [Section 4(1)].

(2) For every completed year of service or part thereof in excess of six months, the employer shall pay gratuity to an employee at the rate of fifteen days' wages based on the rate of wages last drawn by the employee concerned:

Provided that in the case of a piece-rated employee, daily wages shall be computed on the average of the total wages received by him for a period of three months immediately preceding the termination of his employment, and, for this purpose, the wages paid for any overtime work shall not be taken into account:

Provided further that in the case of an employee employed in a seasonal establishment, the employer shall pay the gratuity at the rate of seven days' wages for each season [Section 4(2)].

(3) The amount of gratuity payable to an employee shall not exceed ₹ 3,50,000.

7. Forfeiture of gratuity: (1) The gratuity of an employee, whose services have been terminated for any act of wilful omission or negligence causing any damage or loss to, or destruction of property belonging to the employer, shall be forfeited to the extent of the damage or loss so caused.

(2) The gratuity payable to an employee shall wholly be forfeited –
- (a) if the services of such employee have been terminated for his riotous or disorderly conduct or of any other act of violence on his part, or
- (b) if the services of such employee have been terminated for any act which constitutes an offence involving moral turpitude, provided that such offence is committed by him in the course of his employment [Section 4(6)]

8. Notice of opening, change or closure of the establishment: (1) A notice shall be submitted by the employer to the controlling authority of the area within thirty days of any change in the name, address, employer or nature of business [Rule 3(2)].

(2) Where an employer intends to close down the business he shall submit a notice to the controlling authority of the area at least sixty days, before the intended closure [Rule 3(3)].

9. Application to Controlling Authority for direction: If an employer –
- (i) refuses to accept a nomination or to entertain an application for payment of gratuity, or
- (ii) issues a notice either specifying an amount of gratuity which is considered by the applicant less than what is payable or rejecting eligibility to payment of gratuity, or
- (iii) having received an application for payment of gratuity, fails to issue notice within fifteen days; the claimant employee, nominee, or legal heir, as the case may be, may within ninety days of the occurrence of the cause for the application, apply to the controlling authority for issuing a direction under sub-section (4) of Section 7 with as many extra copies as are the opposite party:

Provided that the controlling authority may accept any application on sufficient cause being shown by the applicant, after the expiry of the period of ninety days [Rule 10].

10. Appeal: Any person aggrieved by an order of the controlling authority may, within sixty days from the date of the receipt of the order, prefer an appeal to the Regional Labour Commissioner (Central) of the area, who has been appointed as the appellate authority by the Central Government:

Provided that the appellate authority may, if it is satisfied that the appellant was prevented by sufficient cause from preferring the appeal within the said period of sixty days, extend the said period by a further period of sixty days [Section 7(7)].

11. Machinery for enforcement of the Act or Rules in Central sphere: All Assistant Labour Commissioners (Central) have been appointed as Controlling Authorities and all the Regional Labour Commissioners (Central) as Appellate Authorities.

12. Powers of the Controlling Authority: The Controlling Authority for the purpose of conducting an inquiry as to the amount of gratuity payable to an employee or as to the admissibility of any claim of, or in relation to, an employee for payment of gratuity, or as to the person entitled to receive the gratuity, shall have the same powers as are vested in a court, under the Code of Civil Procedure, 1908, in respect of the following matters, namely –
- (a) enforcing the attendance of any person or examining him on oath;
- (b) requiring the discovery and production of documents;
- (c) receiving evidence on affidavits; and
- (d) issuing commissions for the examination of witnesses [Section 7(5)].

13. Recovery of gratuity: If the amount of gratuity payable is not paid by the employer, within the prescribed period(?)to the person entitled thereto, the controlling authority shall, on an application made to it in this behalf by the aggrieved person, issue a certificate for that amount to the Collector, who shall recover the same, together with compound interest thereon at the rate of nine per cent per annum, from the date of expiry of the prescribed time, as arrears of land revenue and pay the same to the person entitled thereto [Section 8].

14. Protection of gratuity: No gratuity payable under the Payment of Gratuity Act and the rules made thereunder shall be liable to attachment in execution of any decree or order of any civil, revenue or criminal court [Section 13].

15. Penalties for offences: (1) Whoever, for the purpose of avoiding any payment to be made by himself or of enabling any other persons to avoid such payment, knowingly makes or causes to be made any false statement or false representation, shall be punishable with imprisonment for a term which may extend to six months, or with fine which may extend to one thousand rupees, or with both [Section 9(1)].

(2) An employer who contravenes, or makes default in complying with, any of the provisions of the Act or in any rule or order made thereunder shall be punishable with imprisonment for a term which may extend to one year, or with fine which may extend to one thousand rupees, or with both;

Provided that if the offence relates to non-payment of any gratuity payable under the Payment of Gratuity Act, the employer shall be punishable with imprisonment for a term which shall not be less than three months unless the court trying the offence for reasons to be recorded by it in writing, is of opinion that a lesser term of imprisonment or the imposition of a fine would meet the ends of justice   [Section 9(2)].

16. Display of Notice: The employer shall display conspicuously a notice at or near the entrance of the establishment in bold letters in English and in the language understood by the majority of the employees specifying the name of the officer with designation authorised by the employer to receive on his behalf notices under the Payment of Gratuity Act or the rules made thereunder [Rule 4]

17. Display of Abstract of the Act and Rules: The employer shall display an abstract of the Payment of Gratuity Act and the rules made thereunder in English and in the language understood by the majority of the employees at a conspicuous place at or near the main entrance of the establishment [Rule 20].

Questions for Discussion

1. Explain the nature of gratuity payment and state the objects of the payment of gratuity Act of 1972.
2. Explain the scope and extent of the Payment of Gratuity Act of 1972.
3. How is the concept of continuous service defined in the Payment of Gratuity Act of 1972?
4. Explain the meaning of the concept of Continuous Service as used in the Payment of Gratuity Act.
5. Define the following as used in the Payment of Gratuity Act of 1972.
   (a) Appropriate Government   (b) Employee and Employer
   (c) Controlling Authority   (d) Wages

6. Who are the persons included in the family of a male and female according to the provisions of the Payment of Gratuity Act of 1972?
7. When is a gratuity payable? Explain various points relating to the payment of gratuity incorporated in Section 4 of the Act.
8. What are the provisions of the Payment of Gratuity Act of 1972 relating to the rate of the gratuity to be paid to the employees?
9. What are the circumstances in which gratuity becomes payable to an employee under the payment of Gratuity Act of 1972?
10. (a) Explain the conditions for payment of gratuity.
    (b) Mr. A is the employee whose last drawn salary which included basic salary and D.A. is ₹ 5,200/- per month. He has completed Thirty years of service. Calculate the amount of gratuity payable to him.
11. When does an employee forfeit his right of gratuity?
12. Explain the provisions of the Payment of Gratuity Act, 1972 relating to compulsory insurance.
13. Describe the rules relating to nomination by an employee under the Payment of Gratuity, Act of 1972.
14. How is the amount of gratuity determined under the Payment of Gratuity Act, 1972?
15. Explain the mode of Payment of Gratuity under the Payment of Gratuity Act, 1972.
16. Explain the provisions of the Gratuity Act, 1972 relating to recovery of gratuity.
17. Describe the provisions as to the determination and recovery of the amount of gratuity under the Payment of Gratuity Act, 1972.
18. Who is the Controlling Authority under the Payment of Gratuity Act of 1972? Explain his powers and duties.
19. Can gratuity payable to an employee under the Payment of Gratuity Act of 1972 be attached in execution of any decree of a Court?
20. Explain the penalties for offences under the Payment of Gratuity Act, 1972.
21. Write short notes on the following:
    (a) Objects of the Payment of Gratuity Act, 1972.
    (b) Scope and extent of the Payment of Gratuity Act, 1972.
    (c) Maximum amount of gratuity.
    (d) Provisions relating to better terms of gratuity.
    (e) Forfeiture of gratuity.
    (f) Power of the appropriate Government to exempt an employee.
    (g) Compulsory insurance for payment of gratuity.
    (h) Provisions relating to nomination
    (i) Determination of the amount of gratuity.
    (j) Appointment and powers of Inspectors.
    (k) Nature of penalties for various offences.
    (l) Exemption of the employer from liability in certain cases.
    (m) Payment of gratuity even if prescribed period of employment is not completed.

-product-compliance